ISSUES IN PARTICIPANT OBSERVATION:

A TEXT AND READER

Edited by

GEORGE J. McCALL
University of Illinois at Chicago Circle

J. L. SIMMONS
University of California at Santa Barbara

ADDISON-WESLEY PUBLISHING COMPANY
Reading, Massachusetts
Menlo Park, California · London · Amsterdam · Don Mills, Ontario · Sydney

Addison-Wesley Series in
BEHAVIORAL SCIENCE: QUANTITATIVE METHODS

Frederick Mosteller, Consulting Editor

ISBN 0-201-07027-8
MNOPORST-AL-898765432

Much of the seminal work on the whole range of social organizations—preliterate societies, modern communities, hospitals, prisons, factories, bureaucracies, military units, cults, families, gangs, etc., as well as on cultures and subcultures—has been carried out by scientific observers who have in some sense actually abided in these organizations and cultures through the course of their studies, scrutinizing in depth virtually all aspects of the complex functioning of these units. The conceptual frameworks and empirical data of sociology, anthropology, criminology, industrial relations, administrative science, social work, political science, and small groups social psychology are heavily indebted to this sort of field study.

Yet, of all the research methods now employed in these various disciplines, direct fieldwork—or participant observation, as it is most commonly termed in sociology—is the least systematized and codified, with the result that it is least often and least adequately taught.

There are, of course, important reasons for this lack of codification of procedures. In the first place, participant observation is not a single method but rather a characteristic style of research which makes use of a number of methods and techniques—observation, informant interviewing, document analysis, respondent interviewing, and participation with self-analysis.

Second, participant observation is intentionally unstructured in its research design, so as to maximize discovery and description rather than systematic theory testing. That is, refusing preconceived hypotheses, participant observers do not employ a priori standardization of concepts, measures, samples, and data but rather seek to discover and revise these as they learn more about the organization being studied. Subsequent analysis and presentation of data therefore present quite complicated problems of reliability, validity, and comprehensiveness.

Third, these problems are exacerbated by the fact that the resulting data are typically qualitative rather than quantified scores readily amenable to standard statistical analysis. Rigorous procedures for qualitative analysis have not developed apace with those for quantitative analysis.

Fourth, participant observation is a relatively expensive procedure in that it demands months or years of active field involvement for the researcher. Survey, questionnaire, or laboratory work, on the other hand, typically requires little or no field work by the investigator himself.

Fifth, the practical problems met by the researcher having to substantially live among (though not necessarily to reside with) the very subjects of his study require considerable thought and human relations work if months of effort are not to be distorted, jeopardized, or invalidated.

This book does not in the least presume to have surmounted or circumvented these difficulties or to have made any substantial progress toward codification of participant observation procedures. However, such progress can hopefully be facilitated by bringing together in one volume the full range of problems and issues, along with the major statements and solutions presently available in the literature.

This indeed was the first of our two objectives in compiling this book. The second was to facilitate the teaching of participant observation by presenting an integrated coverage of the problems and partial solutions pertinent to all phases of the research process. This book cannot present pat "textbook" directives for the novice participant observer, and we feel that it is equally important for the student to be aware of *why* he is doing research in a particular fashion as it is for him to be told *how* to do it that way.

Thus, the present volume, while not quite a textbook, is rather more than a book of readings or an analytic review of the methodological issues. We hope, therefore, that this book will be of value in the classroom as a text, in the field as a manual, and on the professional's shelf as a convenient sourcebook.

Chicago, Illinois   G.J.M.
Santa Barbara, California   J.L.S.
January, 1969

CONTENTS

CHAPTER ONE

THE

NATURE

OF

PARTICIPANT
OBSERVATION

► Many people feel that a newspaper reporter is a far cry from a social scientist. Yet many of the data of social science today are gathered by interviewing and observation techniques that resemble those of a skilled newspaper man at work on the study of, say, a union strike or a political convention. It makes little sense for us to belittle these less rigorous methods as "unscientific." We will do better to study them and the techniques they involve so that we can make better use of them in producing scientific information.[1] ◄

Surely no social scientific method has given rise to more criticism and controversy in the past twenty years than has that broad approach known as participant observation.[2] Yet the numerous attempts to bring this classical tool of inquiry more nearly into line with methodological canons as these are currently understood in social science have by and large merely muddied the waters. Students and practitioners are, it seems to us, increasingly confused as to precisely what "participant observation" entails.

As a number of commentators have observed, it is probably misleading to regard participant observqtion as a single method. Rather, in common parlance, it refers to a characteristic blend or combination of methods and techniques that is employed in studying certain types of subject matter: primitive societies, deviant subcultures, complex organizations (such as hospitals, unions, and corporations), social movements, communities, and informal groups (such as gangs and factory worker groups). This characteristic blend of techniques, as exemplified by the work of the lone anthropologist living amongst an isolated people, involves some amount of genuinely social interaction in the field with the subjects of the study, some direct observation of relevant events, some formal and a great deal of informal interviewing, some systematic counting, some collection of documents and artifacts, and open-endedness in the directions the study takes.[3]

Reprinted from *American Journal of Sociology*, 1962, **67**, 566–576, by permission of the author and The University of Chicago Press.

[1] Dean, Eichhorn, and Dean (1967), p. 274.

[2] See, for example, the selected bibliography at the end of the book.

[3] Some writers would prefer to call this broad blend "field work," reserving the term "participant observation" for the techniques in which the scientist virtually performs the role of a genuine member and counts as very critical data his resulting subjective experiences, which provide leads to be pursued by interviewing his fellow participants. However, few studies have employed this technique exclusively or even primarily, so that it is not sufficiently representative of the studies which the social science public has come to include under the rubric of participant observation. As good field workers should, we feel that socially established categories afford good beginning points for eventual refinement; accordingly, we follow common usage here in our definition of participant observation.

Because of the rather omnibus quality of this blend we call participant observation, it has not lent itself to the standardization of procedure that social scientists have come to expect of their methods, as in testing, survey, laboratory, and ecological work. Profound questions of reliability, validity, and generality of results have thus been raised, injecting terms such as "observer bias," "personal equation," "going native," and "hearsay" into the literature of the social sciences. The techniques of participant observation are regarded as difficult to communicate or to teach. The nonquantitative nature of the results causes difficulties in presenting evidence and proof for propositions. Critics deride participant observation as a romantic attempt to "get close to the data," which attempt gives rise to a host of ethical problems concerning the human rights and interests of the subjects in relation to the study.

Proponents of participant observation, on the other hand, have sometimes championed it as being *less* likely than other methods to be biased, unreliable, or invalid because it provides more internal checks (of more direct nature) and is more responsive to the data than are the imposed systems of other methods. Moreover, according to such proponents, participant observation is not restricted to static cross-sectional data but allows real study of social processes and complex interdependencies in social systems. Therefore, they consider the data of participant observation richer and more direct.

The nature of these criticisms, claims, and counterclaims should provide the older sociologist with a clue to the underlying reason for the heat generated by the controversy over participant observation—namely, this controversy is the major residue of the two great methodological issues which sharply divided sociologists during the formative period of 1920–1930.[4] These issues, persisting today, were disputes over the merits of case studies versus statistics and over the concept of *Verstehen* (subjective interpretation). An uneasy truce was struck in these disputes, to the effect that case studies (not so much of individuals as of organizations or communities) could still be usefully done, *as studies,* but that as a method the case study was not as scientifically impressive and advantageous as the statistical method. Similarly, subjective data from the subjects, such as motives and intentions, were admitted to good standing in the field so long as they were classified and counted. Indeed, these could be made the basis for a theoretical *interpretation* of certain statistical relationships between other types of facts.

Though this summary does not do entire justice to the *de facto* "resolution" of these disputes, it remains true today that sociologists do not in general maintain that there is any special methodological advantage to studying the complicated inner dynamics of a particular case in all details or to seeking out the perspectives or interpretations actually held by subjects themselves. Virtually the only place in which these sorts of arguments *are* put forward (or attacked) today is in the literature on participant observation.

In this book we hope to assemble and discuss the major methodological articles on participant observation at a less heady level, largely eschewing issues of epistemology and focusing rather on concrete issues of method and technique. In the spirit of the quotation that opened this chapter, it makes little sense for us to belittle or champion participant observation; we will do better to study the methods and the techniques involved so that we can make better use of them in producing scientific information.

---

4.   Hinkle and Hinkle (1954).

In order to facilitate our study, we will sketch out in this first chapter a view of the nature of participant observation which we hope may be useful (1) in disposing of some matters as essentially mutual misunderstandings and (2) in squarely confronting certain others as genuine issues.[5]

To begin, let us recall our view that participant observation is most sensibly regarded, operationally, as the blend of methods and techniques that is characteristically employed in studies of social situations or complex social organizations of all sorts. These are studies that involve repeated, genuine social interaction on the scene with the subjects themselves as a part of the data-gathering process. That is, we shall view participant observation not as a single *method* but as a type of research enterprise, a style of combining several methods toward a particular end.

That end is an *analytic description* of a complex social organization (primitive band, criminal gang, occupational group, mental hospital, community, or the like). By an analytic description we mean something much more than a journalistic description: An analytic description (1) employs the concepts, propositions, and empirical generalizations of a body of scientific theory as the basic guides in analysis and reporting, (2) employs thorough and systematic collection, classification, and reporting of facts, and (3) generates new empirical generalizations (and perhaps concepts and propositions as well) based on these data.

Thus, an analytic description is primarily an empirical application and modification of scientific theory rather than an efficient and powerful test of such a theory, since only one case—however complex—is involved in the study. *This is not to say that participant observation studies cannot be used to test theory.* That test of theory comes in *comparing* such analytic descriptions of complex cases when these are available in sufficient number and variety. Anthropologists test theories by comparing analytic descriptions of societies, and community sociologists by comparing community studies.[6] Note that these tests cannot be made by comparing casual or journalistic accounts of societies or communities but only by comparing careful analytic descriptions of the type described above.

One important reason for the insistence on *analytic* descriptions is that social scientists conceive of these complex social organizations as being largely *latent* organizations—largely unintended and unrecognized by the members themselves—and therefore not apparent to or describable by laymen (including the actual members).[7] Because many of the features of organization are not recognized by the members, they cannot report them even when carefully questioned by a skilled social science interviewer. Consequently, in order to obtain an analytic description, the scientist himself must observe the organization directly. Even to the trained eye of the scientist many of these features are not readily apparent and emerge only through systematic classification, enumeration, and comparison of particular facts.

---

5.   The view to be presented here is not, of course, the consensus of all writers on participant observation. Apart from the terminological issue discussed in footnote 3, we may note two recent treatments of participant observation as particularly at variance with our own.   Bruyn (1966) regards participant observation as a means of obtaining disciplined but stylistically faithful descriptions of social meanings. Weiss (1966) depicts participant observation as a technique for discovering holistic, nonnomothetic characterizations of complex social situations.

6.   Eggan (1954); Lewis (1953); Reiss (1954, 1959); Bendix (1963).

7.   Merton (1957), pp. 19–84; McCall (1963).

Although direct observation is thus necessary, it alone is not sufficient to enable the scientist to obtain a thorough description. Among other reasons, three particularly stand out: (1) the organization is typically being manifested in several locales simultaneously, (2) the organization has typically been in existence for some time before the scientist undertook his study, and (3) many of its features or determinants (such as the motives, intentions, interests, and perceptions of its members) are only imperfectly inferable by direct observation.

From reasons (1) and (2) there follows the need to supplement the scientist's direct observations with *indirect observations,* which can only be obtained from perceptive persons who were on the scene in the scientist's absence. These persons, called *informants,* must be carefully questioned by the scientist in order to piece together the particular facts of the events from which the scientist himself was absent. In order to avoid a casual or misleading account, the informant must not be allowed to report mere impressions or his own subjective generalizations; he must be gotten to report hard, particular facts so that the scientist can form his own, often quite different generalizations.

One very important class of "informants" or "surrogate observers" are the various records and documents pertaining to the organization, such as budgetary records, rule books, minutes of meetings, personnel files, diaries, etc., which record certain facts and events that the scientist was unable to observe directly. There are, of course, many limitations on the usefulness of this kind of indirect observation, but historians and others have evolved certain scientific criteria to serve as guides.[8]

The third reason (mentioned above) for the insufficiency of direct observation alone—that some features of an organization are only imperfectly inferable from direct observation—emphasizes the need for yet another technique: interviewing the members or participants concerning their motives, their intentions, and their interpretations of the events in question. This provides, then, a critical check on the validity of *some,* but not all, types of inferences made by the scientist. Such interviewing casts the interviewee not in the role of a substitute scientist-observer but merely in the role of himself, reporting only his own personal behavior and thoughts. This is the role of *respondent,* as in ordinary survey interviewing, and is to be contrasted with the role of informant. (Note that any one person may at some time perform the role of respondent and at other times perform the role of informant.) In checking inferences concerning, say, the motives of a certain *category* of participants, it should be obvious that the scientist must not employ informant interviewing but must resort to respondent interviewing of a suitably drawn sample from the category involved.[9]

As another check on the feelings and thoughts of the members of the organization under study, the scientist himself may take active part in the relevant activities—taking drugs, receiving psychotherapy, taking classes, driving a truck, dancing in a tribal rite. By doing so, he receives the same socialization as ordinary members, acquires similar perspectives, and encounters similar experiences. In this way the scientist acquires some sense of the subjective side of events which he could less readily infer if he ob-

8.   Gottschalk, Kluckhohn, and Angell (1945); Allport (1942); Martel and McCall (1964); Webb, Campbell, Schwartz, and Sechrest (1966), pp. 53–111.
9.   Kish (1965).

served *without* taking part. (Indeed, for those commentators who restrict the term "participant observation" to this particular procedure, such direct entrance into the subjective elements constitutes the primary advantage of participant observation; others, who define it more broadly, treat actual participation in the events as a variable which can range from being a member of the audience to an event up to complete submergence in it.) Although the scientist can thus acquire directly some sense of the subjective states of the participants, this sense remains his own and cannot merely be assumed to correspond to that of the others. Respondent interviewing is, therefore, necessary for acquiring information about subjective states.

As we have seen, a number of techniques—direct observation, informant interviewing, document analysis, respondent interviewing, and direct participation—are typically and to some degree necessarily involved in a field study of any complex social organization.[10] We have also seen that each of these techniques is especially important for obtaining a particular type of information. In one of the most important papers on participant observation, Morris Zelditch, too, argues for the necessity of distinguishing the various techniques involved, and he also evaluates their utility in obtaining several types of information.

SOME METHODOLOGICAL
PROBLEMS OF FIELD STUDIES[1]

MORRIS ZELDITCH, JR.

The original occasion for this paper was a reflection on the use of sample survey methods in the field: that is, the use of structured interview schedules, probability samples, etc., in what is usually thought of as a participant-observation study. There has been a spirited controversy between, on the one hand, those who have sharply criticized field workers for slipshod sampling, for failing to document assertions quantitatively, and for apparently accepting impressionistic accounts—or accounts that the quantitatively minded could not distinguish from purely impressionistic accounts;[2] and, on the other hand, those who have, sometimes bitterly, been opposed to numbers, to samples, to

---

10. Other, supplementary techniques—such as sociometry, panel analysis, or mapping—may, of course, also be employed.

Reprinted from *American Journal of Sociology*, 1962, **67,** 566–576, by permission of the author and The University of Chicago Press.

1.   This paper reports part of a more extensive investigation of problems of field method in which Dr. Renée Fox is a collaborator. The author gratefully acknowledges the partial support given this investigation by funds from Columbia University's Documentation Project for Advanced Training in Social Research.

2.   See, e.g., Harry Alpert, "Some Observations on the Sociology of Sampling," *Social Forces*, XXXI (1952), 30–31; Robert C. Hanson, "Evidence and Procedure Characteristics of 'Reliable' Propositions in Social Science," *American Journal of Sociology*, LXIII (1958), 357–63.

questionnaires, often on the ground that they destroy the field workers' conception of a social system as an organic whole.[3]

Although there is a tendency among many younger field workers to accent criticisms made from the quantitative point of view,[4] there is reason to believe that the issue itself has been stated falsely. In most cases field methods are discussed as if they were "all of a piece."[5] There is, in fact, a tendency to be either *for* or *against* quantification, as if it were an either/or issue. To some extent the battle lines correlate with a relative concern for "hardness" versus "depth and reality" of data. Quantitative data are often thought of as "hard," and qualitative as "real and deep"; thus if you prefer "hard" data you are for quantification and if you prefer "real, deep" data you are for qualitative participant observation. What to do if you prefer data that are real, deep, *and* hard is not immediately apparent.

A more fruitful approach to the issue must certainly recognize that a field study is not a single method gathering a single kind of information. This approach suggests several crucial questions: *What* kinds of methods and *what*

---

3.   See W. L. Warner and P. Lunt, *Social Life of a Modern Community* (New Haven, Conn.: Yale University Press, 1941), p. 55; Conrad Arensberg, "The Community Study Method," *American Journal of Sociology,* LX (1952), 109–24; Howard Becker, "Field Work among Scottish Shepherds and German Peasants," *Social Forces,* XXXV (1956), 10–15; Howard S. Becker and Blanche Geer, "Participant Observation and Interviewing: A Comparison," *Human Organization,* XVI (1957), 28–34; Solon Kimball, "Problems of Studying American Culture," *American Anthropologist,* LVII (1955), 1131–42; and A. Viditch and J. Bensman, "The Validity of Field Data," *Human Organization,* XIII (1954), 20–27.

4.   See particularly Oscar Lewis, "Controls and Experiments in Field Work," in *Anthropology Today* (Chicago: University of Chicago Press, 1953), p. 455 n.; also cf. Howard S. Becker, "Problems of Inference and Proof in Participant Observation," *American Sociological Review,* XXIII (1958), 652–60; Elizabeth Colson, "The Intensive Study of Small Sample Communities," in R. F. Spencer (ed.), *Method and Perspective in Anthropology* (Minneapolis: University of Minnesota Press, 1954), pp. 43–59; Fred Eggan, "Social Anthropology and the Method of Controlled Comparison," *American Anthropologist,* LVI (1954), 743–60; Harold E. Driver, "Statistics in Anthropology," *American Anthropologist,* LV (1953), 42–59; Melville J. Herskovitz, "Some Problems of Method in Ethnography," in R. F. Spencer (ed.), *op. cit.,* pp. 3–24; George Spindler and Walter Goldschmidt, "Experimental Design in the Study of Culture Change," *Southwestern Journal of Anthropology,* VIII (1952), 68–83. And see the section "Field Methods and Techniques" in *Human Organization,* esp. in its early years and its early editorials. Some quantification has been characteristic of "field" monographs for a very long time; cf. Kroeber's *Zuni Kin and Clan* (1916). Such classics as *Middletown* and the *Yankee City* series are studded with tables.

5.   A significant exception is a comment by M. Trow directed at Becker and Geer. Becker and Geer, comparing interviewing to participant observation, find participant observation the superior method and seem to imply that it is superior for all purposes. Trow insists that the issue is not correctly formulated, and that one might better ask: "What kinds of problems are best studied through what kinds of methods; . . . how can the various methods at our disposal complement one another?" In their reply, Becker and Geer are more or less compelled to agree. See Becker and Geer, "Participant Observation and Interviewing: A Comparison," *op. cit.,* Trow's "Comment" (*Human Organization,* XVI [1957], 33–35), and Becker and Geer's "Rejoinder" (*Human Orgainzation,* XVII [1958], 39–40).

kinds of information are relevant? How can the "goodness" of different methods for different purposes be evaluated? Even incomplete and imperfect answers—which are all that we offer here—should be useful, at least in helping to restate the issue. They also pose, order, and to some extent resolve other issues of field method so that in pursuing their implications this paper encompasses a good deal more than its original problem.

THREE TYPES OF INFORMATION

The simplest events are customarily described in statements predicating a single property of a single object at a particular time and in a particular place. From these descriptions one may build up more complex events in at least two ways. The first is by forming a configuration of many properties of the same object at the same time in the same place. This may be called an "incident." A more complex configuration but of the same type would be a sequence of incidents, that is, a "history."

A second way to build up more complex events is by repeating observations of a property over a number of units. Units here can be defined formally, requiring only a way of identifying events as identical. They can be members of a social system or repetitions of the same type of incident at different times or in different places (e.g., descriptions of five funerals). The result is a frequency distribution of some property.

From such information it is possible to deduce certain underlying properties of the system observed, some of which may be summarized as consequences of the "culture" of S (S stands here for a social system under investigation). But at least some portion of this culture can be discovered not only by inference from what is observed but also from verbal reports by members of S—for example, accounts of its principal institutionalized norms and statuses. The rules reported, of course, are to some extent independent of the events actually observed; the norms actually followed may not be correctly reported, and deviance may be concealed. Nevertheless, information difficult to infer can be readily and accurately obtained from verbal reports. For example, it may take some time to infer that a member occupies a given status but this may readily be discovered by asking either him or other members of S.

We thus combine various types of information into three broad classes.

Type I: Incidents and Histories. A log of events during a given period, a record of conversations heard, descriptions of a wedding, a funeral, an election, etc. Not only the actions observed, but the "meanings," the explanations, etc., reported by the participants can be regarded as part of the "incident" insofar as they are thought of as data rather than actual explanations.

Type II: Distributions and Frequencies. Possessions of each member of S, number of members who have a given belief, number of times member m is observed talking to member n, etc.

Type III: Generally Known Rules and Statuses. Lists of statuses, lists of persons occupying them, informants' accounts of how rules of exogamy apply, how incest or descent are defined, how political leaders are supposed to be chosen, how political decisions are supposed to be made, etc.

This classification has nothing to do with what is *inferred* from data, despite the way the notion of reported rules and statuses was introduced. In particular, more complex configurations of norms, statuses, events which are "explained" by inferring underlying themes or structures involve a level of inference outside the scope of this paper: the classification covers only information *directly* obtained from reports and observations. Moreover, this classification cuts across the distinction between what is observed by the investigator and what is reported to him. Although Type III consists only of reports, Types I and II include both observations by the investigator himself *and* reports of members of S, insofar as they are treated as data. Later we talk of an event as seen through the eyes of an informant, where the investigator trusts the informant as an accurate observer and thinks of the report as if it were his own observation. Now, however, interest is focused not on the facts of the report but rather on what the report reveals of the perceptions, the motivations, the world of meaning of the informant himself. The report, in this case, does not transmit observational data; it is, itself, the datum and so long as it tells what the person reporting thinks, the factual correctness of what he thinks is irrelevant. (This is sometimes phrased as making a distinction between *informants* and *respondents,* in the survey research sense.) Thus Type I includes both observations (what we see going on) and the statements of members telling what they understand the observed events to mean, which is regarded as part of the event. In a somewhat different way, Type II also includes both reports (e.g., an opinion poll) and observations (e.g., systematically repeated observations with constant coding categories).

THREE TYPES OF METHOD

It is possible to make a pure, logically clear classification of methods of obtaining information in the field, but for the present purpose this would be less useful than one that is, though less precise, rather closer to what a field worker actually does.

Two methods are usually thought of as characteristic of the investigator in the field. He invariably keeps a daily log of events and of relatively casual, informal continuous interviews, both of which go into his field notes. Almost invariably he also develops informants, that is, selected members of S who are willing and able to give him information about practices and rules in S and events he does not directly observe. (They may also supply him with diaries, autobiographies, and their own personal feelings; i.e., they may also function as respondents.) Contrary to popular opinion, almost any well-trained field worker also keeps various forms of census materials, records of systematic observations, etc., including a basic listing of members of S, face-sheet data on them, and systematically repeated observations of certain recurrent events. Many field workers also collect documents; however, we will classify field methods into only three broad classes which we conceive of as primary. These are:

Type I. Participant-observation. The field worker directly observes and also participates in the sense that he has durable social relations in S. He may or may not play an active part in events, or he may interview participants in events which may be considered part of the process of observation.

Type II. Informant-interviewing. We prefer a more restricted definition of the informant than most field workers use, namely that he be called an "informant" only where he is reporting information presumed factually correct about others rather than about himself; and his information about events is about events in their absence. Inverviewing during the event itself is considered part of participant-observation.

Type III. Enumerations and samples. This includes both surveys and direct, repeated, countable observations. Observation in this sense may entail minimal participation as compared with that implied in Type I.

This classification excludes documents on the ground that they represent resultants or combinations of primary methods. Many documents, for example, are essentially informant's accounts and are treated exactly as an informant's account is treated: subjected to the same kinds of internal and external comparisons, created with the same suspicions, and often in the end, taken as evidence of what occurred at some time and place from which the investigator was absent. The fact that the account is written is hardly important. Many other documents are essentially enumerations; for example, personnel and cost-accounting records of a factory, membership rolls of a union, tax rolls of a community.

TWO CRITERIA OF "GOODNESS"

Criteria according to which the "goodness" of a procedure may be defined are:

1. *Informational adequacy,* meaning accuracy, precision, and completeness of data.
2. *Efficiency,* meaning cost per added input of information.

It may appear arbitrary to exclude validity and reliability. Validity is excluded because it is, in a technical sense, a relation between an indicator and a concept, and similar problems arise whether one obtains information from an informant, a sample, or from direct observation. Construed loosely, validity is often taken to mean "response validity," accuracy of report, and this is caught up in the definition of informational adequacy. Construed more loosely yet, validity is sometimes taken as equivalent to "real," "deep" data, but this seems merely to beg the question. Reliability is relevant only tangentially; it is a separate problem that cuts across the issues of this paper.

FUNDAMENTAL STRATEGIES

Certain combinations of method and type of information may be regarded as formal prototypes, in the sense that other combinations may be logically reduced to them. For example: Instead of a sample survey or enumeration, an informant is employed to list dwelling units, or to estimate incomes, or to tell who associates with whom or what each person believes with respect to some issue. The information is obtained from a single informant, but he is treated *as if he himself* had conducted a census or poll. More generally, in every case in which the information obtained is logically reducible to a distribution of the members of S with respect to the property a, the implied method of obtaining the information is also logically reducible to an enumeration. The enumeration may be either through direct observation (estimating the number of sheep each Navaho has by actually counting them; establishing the sociometric structure of the community by watching who interacts with whom), or through a questionnaire survey (determining household composition by questioning a member of each household, or administering a sociometric survey to a sample of the community). If an informant is used, it is presumed that he has himself performed the enumeration. We are not at the moment concerned with the validity of this assumption in specific instances but rather in observing that regardless of the actual way in which the information was obtained, the logical and formal character of the procedure is that of a census or survey.

Suppose an informant is asked to describe what went on at a community meeting which the observer is unable to attend; or a sample of respondents is asked to describe a sequence of events which occurred before the observer entered S. In either case his reports are used as substitutes for direct observation. Such evidence may, in fact, be examined critically to establish its accuracy —we begin by assuming the bias of the reports—but it is presumed that, having "passed" the statements they become an objective account of what has occurred in the same sense that the investigator's own reports are treated as objective, once his biases have been taken into account. The informant, one usually says in this case, is the observer's observer; he differs in no way from the investigator himself. It follows that the prototype is direct observation by the observer himself.

The prototype so far is not only a formal model; it is also a "best" method, efficiently yielding the most adequate information. In learning institutionalized rules and statuses it is doubtful that there is a formal prototype and all three methods yield adequate information. Here we may choose the *most efficient* method as defining our standard of procedure. To illustrate: We wish to study the political structure of the United States. We are told that the principal national figure is called a "president," and we wish to know who he is.

We do not ordinarily think of sampling the population of the United States to obtain the answer; we regard it as sufficient to ask one well-informed member. This question is typical of a large class of questions asked by a field worker in the course of his research.

A second example: Any monograph on the Navaho reports that they are matrilineal and matrilocal. This statement may mean either of two things:

1. All Navaho are socially identified as members of a descent group defined through the mother's line, and all Navaho males move to the camp of their wife's family at marriage.

2. There exists a set of established rules according to which all Navaho are supposed to become socially identified as members of a descent group defined through the mother's line, and to move to the camp of their wife's family at marriage.

The truth of the first interpretation can be established only by an enumeration of the Navaho, or a sample sufficiently representative and sufficiently precise. It is readily falsified by exceptions, and in fact there *are* exceptions to both principles. But suppose among thirty Navaho informants at least one says that the Navaho are patrilineal and patrilocal. If this is intended to describe institutionalized norms as in (2) above, we are more likely to stop using the informant than we are to state that there are "exceptions" in the sense of (1) above. We might sample a population to discover the motivation to conform to a rule, or the actual degree of conformity, but are less likely to do so to establish that the rule *exists,* if we confront institutionalized phenomena. This also constitutes a very large class of questions asked by the field worker.

ADEQUACY OF INFORMANTS FOR VARIOUS PROBLEMS IN THE FIELD

It does not follow from the definition of a prototype method that no other form of obtaining information can suffice; all we intend is that it *does* suffice, and any other method is logically reducible to it. Further, comparison with the prototype is a criterion by which other forms can be evaluated. In considering the adequacy in some given instance of the use of an informant as the field worker's surrogate census, for example, we are interested primarily in whether he is likely to know enough, to recall enough, and to report sufficiently precisely to yield the census that we ourselves would make. Comments below, incidentally, are to be taken as always prefixed with the phrase, "by and large." It is not possible to establish, at least yet, a firm rule which will cover every case.

The informant as a surrogate censustaker.   A distinction must again be made between *what* information is obtained and how it is obtained. It is one thing to criticize a field worker for not obtaining a frequency distribution where it is required—for instance, for not sampling mothers who are weaning children in order to determine age at weaning—and another to criticize him for not ob-taining it *directly* from the mothers. If the field worker reports that the average age at weaning is two years and the grounds for this is that he asked an in-formant, "About when do they wean children around here?" it is not the fact that he asked an informant but that he asked the wrong question that should be criticized. He should have asked, "How many mothers do you know who are now weaning children? How old are their children?"

The critical issue, therefore, is whether or not the informant can be assumed to have the information that the field worker requires, granting that he asks the proper questions. In many instances he does. In some cases he is an even better source than an enumerator; he either knows better or is less likely to falsify. Dean, for example, reports that workers who are ideologically pro-union, but also have mobility aspirations and are not well-integrated into their factory or local unions, are likely to report attending union meetings which they do not in fact attend.[6] She also shows that, when *respondent-reported* attendance is used as a measure of attendance, this tends spuriously to increase correla-tions of attendance at union meetings with attitudes toward unions in general, and to reduce correlations of attendance at union meetings with attitudes more specifically directed at the local union. The list of those actually attending was obtained by an observer, who, however, had sufficient rapport with officers of the local to obtain it from them.[7] Attendance, largely by "regulars," was stable from meeting to meeting so that the officers could have reproduced it quite accurately.[8]

On the other hand, there are many instances in which an informant is *prima facie* unlikely to be adequate, although no general rule seems to identify these clearly for the investigator. The nature of the information—private versus public, more or less objective, more or less approved—is obviously relevant, yet is often no guide at all. Some private information, for example, is better obtained from informants, some from respondents. The social structure of S, particularly its degree of differentiation and complexity, is also obviously relevant. An informant must be in a position to know the information desired, and if S is highly differentiated and the informant confined to one part of it, he can hardly enumerate it. Probably to discover attitudes and opinions that are relatively private and heterogeneous in a structure that is relatively differen-tiated, direct enumeration or sampling should be used.

The informant as a "representative respondent." An "average" of a distribu-tion is sometimes obtained not by asking for an enumeration by the informant, nor even by asking a general question concerning what people typically do; sometimes it is obtained by treating the informant as if he were a "representa-

---

6.   L. R. Dean, "Interaction, Reported and Observed: The Case of One Local Union," *Human Organization,* XVII (1958), 36–44.

7.   *Ibid.,* p. 37, n. 4.

8.   *Ibid.*

tive respondent." The informant's reports about himself—perhaps deeper, more detailed, "richer," but nevertheless like those of a respondent in a survey rather than an informant in the technical sense—stand in place of a sample. Where a multivariate distribution is thought of, this person is treated as a "quintessential" subject, "typical" in many dimensions. Some field workers speak favorably of using informants in this way, and it is likely that even more of them actually do so.

Since, as yet, we have no really hard and fast rules to follow, it is possible that in some cases this is legitimate; but, by and large, it is the most suspect of ways of using informants. It is simply a bad way of sampling. The legitimate cases are probably of three types: first, as suggestive of leads to follow up; second, as illustration of a point to be made in a report that is verifiable on other grounds. But in this second case the proviso ought to be thought of as rather strict: it is not sufficient to "have a feeling" that the point is true, to assume that it is verifiable on other grounds. The third case is perhaps the most legitimate, but is really a case of using informants to provide information about generally known rules: for example, using informants to collect "typical" gene-alogies or kinship terms, the assumption being that his kin terms are much like those of others (which is not always true, of course) and his genealogy suffi-ciently "rich"—this being the basis on which he was chosen—to exhibit a wide range of possibilities.

The informant as the observer's observer. The third common use of the infor-mant is to report events not directly observed by the field worker. Here the investigator substitutes the observations of a member for his own observation. It is not simply interviewing that is involved here, because participant-observa-tion was defined earlier as including interviewing on the spot, in conjunction with direct observation. Thus, some of the most important uses of the infor-mant—to provide the meaning and context of that which we are observing, to provide a running check on variability, etc.—are actually part of participant observation. It is the use of informants as if they were colleagues that we must now consider.

Such a procedure is not only legitimate but absolutely necessary to ade-quate investigation of any complex structure. In studying a social structure by participant observation there are two problems of bias that override all others, even the much belabored "personal equation." One results from the fact that a single observer cannot be everywhere at the same time, nor can he be "every-where" in time, for that matter—he has not been in S forever, and will not be there indefinitely—so that, inevitably, something happens that he has not seen, cannot see, or will not see. The second results from the fact that there exist parts of the social structure into which he has not penetrated and probably will not, by virtue of the way he has defined himself to its members, because of limita-tions on the movement of those who sponsor him, etc. There has never been a participant-observer study in which the observer acquired full knowledge of all roles and statuses through his own direct observation, and for that matter there never will be such a study by a single observer. To have a team of observers is one possible solution; to have informants who stand in the relation of team members to the investigator is another. The virtue of the informant used in this way, is to increase the accessibility of S to the investigator.

EFFICIENCY OF SAMPLING FOR VARIOUS PROBLEMS IN THE FIELD

Sampling to obtain information about institutionalized norms and statuses. It has already been argued that a properly obtained probability sample gives adequate information about institutionalized norms and statuses but is not very efficient. Two things are implied: that such information is *general* information so that any member of S has the same information as any other; and that the truth of such information does not depend solely on the opinions of the respondents—the information is in some sense objective.

The first of these implications is equivalent to assuming that S is homogeneous with respect to the property a, so that a sample of one suffices to classify S with respect to it. It then becomes inefficient to continue sampling. The principal defect in such an argument is a practical one: By what criterion can one decide S is homogeneous with respect to a without sampling S? There are two such criteria, neither of which is wholly satisfactory. The first is to use substantive knowledge. We would expect in general that certain norms are invariably institutionalized, such as incest and exogamy, descent, inheritance, marriage procedures, patterns of exchange of goods, formal structure of labor markets, etc. We may assume a priori, for example, that a sample of two hundred Navaho is not required to discover that marriage in one's own clan is incestuous. But the pitfall for the unwary investigator is that he may stray beyond his substantive knowledge or apply it at the wrong time in the wrong place.

A second is to employ a loose form of sequential sampling. Suppose, for example, that we ask an informed male in S whom he may marry, or whom any male may marry. He answers, "All who are A, but no one who is B." We ask a second informant and discover again that he may marry all who are A, but no one who is B. We ask a third, a fourth, a fifth, and each tells us the same rule. We do not need to presume that the rule is actually obeyed; that is quite a different question. But we may certainly begin to believe that we have found an institutionalized norm. Conversely, the more variability we encounter, the more we must investigate further. The pitfall here is that we may be deceived by a homogeneous "pocket" within which all members agree but which does not necessarily represent all structural parts of S. For this reason we try to choose representative informants, each from a different status group. This implies, however, that we are working outward from earlier applications of this dangerous principle; we have used some informants to tell us what statuses there are, thereafter choosing additional informants from the new statuses we have discovered.

The second implication—that in some sense the truth of the information obtained depends not on the opinions of respondents but on something else that is "objective" in nature—simply paraphrases Durkheim: institutions are "external" to given individuals, even though they exist only "in" individuals; they have a life of their own, are *sui generis*. Illustrating with an extreme case: a "belief" of S's religion can be described by an informant even where neither he nor any living member of S actually believes it, although if no member ever did believe it we might regard the information as trivial. In other words, this type of information does not refer to individuals living at a given time, but rather to culture as a distinct object of abstraction. It is this type of information that we mean by "institutionalized norms and statuses." It bears repeating at this point that if one Navaho informant told us the Navaho were patrilineal and patrilocal, we would be more likely to assume he was wrong than we would be to assume that the Navaho had, for the moment, changed their institutions.

Sampling to obtain information about incidents and histories. If we had the good fortune to have a report from every member of S about what happened in region R at time T, would it really be good fortune? Would we not distinguish between those in a position to observe the event and those not? Among those who had been in the region R itself, would we not also distinguish subregions which provided different vantage points from which to view the event? Among those viewing it from the same vantage point, would we not distinguish more and less credible witnesses? Enumeration or not, we would apply stringent internal and external comparisons to each report in order to establish what truly occurred. Formally, of course, this describes a complex technique of stratification which, if carried out properly, would withstand any quantitative criticism. But if all the elements of a decision as to what is "truth" in such a case are considered, it is a moot point how important enumeration or random sampling is in the process.[9]

Informants with special information. Some things happen that relatively few people know about. A random sample is not a sensible way in which to obtain information about these events, although it is technically possible to define a universe U containing only those who do know and sample from U. A parallel case is the repetitive event in inaccessible parts of a social structure. A social structure is an organized system of relationships, one property of which is that certain parts of it are not readily observed by members located in other parts. There is a considerable amount of relatively esoteric information about S. It may be satisfactory from a formal point of view to regard S as consisting in many universes U_i, each of which is to be sampled for a different piece of information, but again the usefulness of such a conception is questionable, particularly if most U_i contain very few members.

---

9.   None of this applies to *repeated* events. If we are interested in comparing several repetitions of the same event, generalizing as to the course that is typical, care must be taken in sampling the events.

EFFICIENCY AND ADEQUACY OF PARTICIPANT
OBSERVATION FOR VARIOUS PROBLEMS IN THE FIELD

Ex post facto quantitative documentation.   Because certain things are observed repeatedly, it sometimes occurs to the field worker to count these repetitions in his log as quantitative documentation of an assertion.   In such cases, the information obtained should be subjected to any of the canons by which other quantitative data are evaluated; the care with which the universe is defined and the sense in which the sample is representative are particularly critical.   With few exceptions, frequency statements made from field logs will *not* withstand such careful examination.

This sharp stricture applies only to ex post facto enumeration or sampling of field logs, and it is because it is ex post facto that the principal dangers arise.   Events and persons represented in field logs will generally be sampled according to convenience rather than rules of probability sampling.   The sample is unplanned, contains unknown biases.   It is not so much random as haphazard, a distinction which is critical.   When, after the fact, the observer attempts to correlate two classes of events in these notes very misleading results will be obtained.   If we wish to correlate *a* and *b* it is characteristic of such samples that *"a"* will be more frequently recorded than *"not-a,"* and *"a and b"* more frequently than *"not-a and b"* or *"a and not-b."*   As a general rule, only those data which the observer actually intended to enumerate should be treated as enumerable.

There are, of course, some valid enumerations contained in field notes.   For example, a verbatim account kept of all meetings of some organization is a valid enumeration; a record kept, in some small rural community, of all members of it who come to the crossroads hamlet during a year is a valid enumeration.   These will tend, however, to be intentional enumerations and not subject to the strictures applicable to ex post facto quantification.   A much rarer exception will occur when, looking back through one's notes, one discovers that, without particularly intending it, every member of the community studied has been enumerated with respect to the property *a,* or that almost all of them have.   This is likely to be rare because field notes tend not to record those who do *not* have the property *a,* and, of all those omitted in the notes, one does not know how many are *not-a* and how many simply were not observed.   If everyone, or almost everyone, can be accounted for as either *a* or *not-a,* then a frequency statement is validly made.[10]   But, if such information

---

10.   We may make a less stringent requirement of our notes, using what might be called "incomplete" indicator spaces.   Briefly, if we wish to classify all members of S with respect to the underlying property A, and behaviors *a, b, c, d . . . ,* all indicate A, then it is sufficient for our purpose to have information on *at least one* of these indicators for each member of S.   For some we might have only *a,* for some only *b,* etc., but we might have one among the indicators for all members, even though not the same one for all members; and thus be able to enumerate S adequately.

were desired in the first place, participant observation would clearly be a most inefficient means of obtaining it.

Readily verbalized norms and statuses. It is not efficient to use participant observation to obtain generally known norms and statuses so long as these can be readily stated. It may take a good deal of observation to infer that which an informant can quickly tell you. Participant observation would in such cases be primarily to check what informants say, to get clues to further questions, etc. It is, of course, true that the concurrent interviewing involved in participant observation will provide the information—it is necessary to make sense out of the observations—but it comes in bits and pieces and is less readily checked for accuracy, completeness, consistency, etc.

FIGURE 1

INFORMATION TYPES   METHODS OF OBTAINING INFORMATION

	ENUMERATIONS AND SAMPLES	PARTICIPANT OBSERVATION	INTERVIEWING INFORMANTS
Frequency distributions	Prototype and best form	Usually inadequate and inefficient	Often, but not always, inadequate; if adequate it is efficient
Incidents, histories	Not adequate by itself; not efficient	Prototype and best form	Adequate with precautions, and efficient
Institutionalized norms and statuses	Adequate but inefficient	Adequate, but inefficient, except for unverbalized norms	Most efficient and hence best form

Latent phenomena. Not all norms and statuses can be verbalized. Consequently, there remains a special province to which participant observation lays well-justified claims. But certain misleading implications should be avoided in admitting them. Because such phenomena may be described as "latent"—as known to the observer but not to the members of S—it may be concluded that *all* latent phenomena are the province of participant observation. This does not follow. The term "latent" is ambiguous; it has several distinct usages, some of which do not even share the core meaning of "known to the observer, unknown to members." Lazarsfeld, for example, refers to a dimension underlying a series of manifest items as a "latent" attribute; it cannot be observed by anyone, and is inferred by the investigator from intercorrelations of observables. But the members of S may also make these inferences. (They infer that a series of statements classify the speaker as "liberal," for example.) The most advanced techniques for searching out such latent phenomena are found in survey research and psychometrics, not in participant observation.

These are matters of inference, not of how data are directly obtained. The same is true of the discovery of "latent functions." Often the observer is aware of connections between events when the members of S are not, even though they are aware of the events themselves. But again, relations among events are not the special province of any one method; we look for such connections in *all* our data. In fact, owing to the paucity and non-comparability of units that often plague the analysis of field notes, it might be argued that participant observation is often incapable of detecting such connections. The great value of participant observation in detecting latent phenomena, then, is in those cases in which members of S are unaware of actually observable events, of some of the things they do, or some of the things that happen around them, which can be directly apprehended by the observer. Any other case requires inference and such inference should be made from *all* available data.

SUMMARY AND CONCLUSION

Figure 1 offers a general summary.

With respect to the problem with which this paper originated the following conclusion may be drawn: Because we often treat different methods as concretely different types of study rather than as analytically different aspects of the same study, it is possible to attack a field study on the ground that it ought to be an enumeration and fails if it is not; and to defend it on the ground that it ought to be something *else* and succeeds only if it is. But, however we classify types of information in the future—and the classification suggested here is only tentative—they are not all of one type. True, a field report is unreliable if it gives us, after consulting a haphazard selection of informants or even a carefully planned "representative" selection, a statement such as, "All members of S believe that . . ." or "The average member of S believes that . . ." *and* (1) there is variance in the characteristic reported, (2) this variance is relevant to the problem reported, *and* (3) the informants cannot be seriously thought of as equivalent to a team of pollsters, *or* (4) the investigator has reported what is, essentially, the "average" beliefs of his *informants,* as if *they* were a representative, probability sample of respondents. But to demand that every piece of information be obtained by a probability sample is to commit the researcher to grossly inefficient procedure and to ignore fundamental differences among various kinds of information. The result is that we create false methodological issues, often suggest quite inappropriate research strategies to novices, and sometimes conceal real methodological issues which deserve more discussion in the literature—such as how to establish institutionalized norms given only questionnaire data. It should be no more satisfactorily rigorous to hear that everything is in some way a sample, and hence must be sampled, than to hear that everything is in some sense "whole" and hence cannot be sampled.

We have seen, thus far, the manner in which the objective of participant observation studies—to obtain analytic descriptions of complex social organizations—dictates the use of several techniques, each of which is especially suited to obtain particular types of information.

We have now to examine how the above objective dictates the rather unusual style in which these various techniques are actually combined and used. The primacy of the goal of description calls for an intellectual responsiveness on the part of the scientist toward the organization, a willingness to *see* what is there, and a reluctance to hastily superimpose a preconceived framework of the observer. This attitude, espoused by scientists in every connection, is particularly important in studying complex organizations because of the intricate and manifold interdependencies among its parts. The observer must give the facts every opportunity to penetrate his consciousness and to revise his thinking about the organization. At the same time, of course, facts never speak for themselves; the scientist must avoid allowing the conceptions held by the members to unduly influence his own interpretations of the organization under study.

This aim of *description* rather than mere *classification* (though the description itself is ultimately framed in terms of theoretical categories) gives participant observation two of its chief characteristics: (1) an unusual quality of open-endedness and constant revision of the study design, and (2) an unusual degree of receptiveness within the study to the subjects' conceptions. J. P. Dean, R. L. Eichhorn, and L. R. Dean analyze the limitations and advantages of these characteristics as compared to those of the more conventional studies.

LIMITATIONS AND
ADVANTAGES OF UNSTRUCTURED METHODS

JOHN P. DEAN, ROBERT L. EICHHORN, AND LOIS R. DEAN

Many sociologists feel that a newspaper reporter is greatly removed from a social scientist. Yet much of the data of social science today are gathered by interviewing and observation techniques that resemble those of a skilled newspaper man covering, for instance, a rent strike or a political convention. It makes little sense for us to belittle these less rigorous methods by claiming them unscientific. We will do better to study them and the techniques they involve so that we can make better use of them in producing valid, scientific information.

As scientists we naturally want to be as rigorous as possible. Whenever a crucial experiment or a survey will provide data of testing relevance for our theories, we will want to use them. But there are many areas of social science where this cannot be done. Sometimes quantitative data is difficult, almost impossible, to obtain; sometimes the relationships we want to examine are not explicit; often the problem is in the exploratory stages of research; or perhaps we want to obtain elaborate qualitative data on an individual case history. For these or other reasons the more structured methods are often not in order. Among the most frequent uses of observation and interviewing are the following: testing of hypotheses where structured methods cannot be employed; reconstruction of an event or series of events; case histories of an individual, an organization, or even a community; and pilot inquiries into new problem areas where the purpose is the production of hypotheses rather than the verification of them.

One hesitates to characterize unstructured field inquiry as a *single* method. Research workers make use of observation and interviewing, as we have seen, in different ways depending on the specific purposes at hand. The hallmark of the survey method is standardized data gathering. *A major characteristic of observation and interviewing in the field is its non-standardization.* In fact, it aims to make a virtue of non-standardization by frequently redirecting the inquiry on the basis of data coming in from the field to ever more fruitful areas of investigation. Changes in the research direction are made in order to chase down more critical data for the emerging hypotheses. Informants are not treated uniformly but are interviewed about the things they can illuminate most. Each field situation is exploited to yield the most helpful data without unduly worrying about their comparability for statistical purposes. The aim is usually a flexible and skillful guiding of field work to make the most of the individual peculiarities of the situation in which you find yourself.

A second characteristic of observation and interviewing is that it makes effective use of the relationships the researcher establishes with informants in the field for eliciting data. He aims to establish himself as a friend who can be trusted: he often wants to ask questions that touch confidential and personal subjects; he often wants to participate in informal situations where informants are relaxed and spontaneous; he may want to be admitted to conferences or meetings that are off the record. To do these things he must have the confidence of persons around him. For some kinds of inquiries this trusted relationship is more important than for others. Studying an underworld gang would be almost impossible without a confidential relationship; it would be less necessary for studying a community chest campaign.

The major limitations of observation and interviewing in the field are directly related to the characteristics noted above. *Because of the non-standardized way the data are collected, they are not generally useful for statistical treatment.* This means that quantitative relationships usually cannot be established and the researcher has to depend on a more impressionistic interpretation of the data for arriving at generalizations. In the long run, social science will have to rest on rigorously established generalizations, and methods that yield quantifiable data are probably best suited for establishing them. Field inquiries, using unstructured methods, will often suggest hypotheses to be tested, but seldom provide the data for testing them.[1]

Because of the obvious difficulties of generalizing from field notes collected under disparate conditions, observation and interviewing frequently end with masses of undigested data, the meaning of which are not clear. Because of the elaborate detail that can be apprehended by a good field worker, each situation or person is likely to be perceived as unique as indeed they actually are. This very uniqueness inhibits attempts to define variables and to specify relations among them. If a researcher becomes genuinely familiar with a local political party committeeman, for example, he can judge to his own satisfaction from the various activities of the committeeman how motivated, active, and energetic the party worker is in promoting the interests of the organization. He can see the ways that one committeeman differs from another in his activities. He may never actually force himself to formulate what he means by "very active," "fairly active," and "not active." He may find himself reluctant to classify committeemen into types in accordance with certain common patterns that apply to their activities, and to relate these types to race or class origins. This lack of formulation is not an inherent shortcoming of the method, but it is a frequent concomitant. The more structured methods require an operational definition of variables and a statement of relations among them. Unstructured observation and interviewing do not necessarily do this.

A second major limitation flows from the researcher's use of the relationships he establishes in the field, that is, *the likelihood of bias.* Since the direction the investigation takes frequently changes on the basis of the emerging data, there is great danger that the research worker will guide the inquiry in accord with wrong impressions he has gotten from the first informants contacted. Or his own personal characteristics or personality needs may attract him into stronger relationships with certain kinds of informants than with others, and thus prepare the way for his receiving an undue amount of information from persons who are biased toward one point of view. Perhaps, too, the first hunches or hypotheses that emerge attract the field worker to instances that confirm these notions and blind him to data that point the other way. It is difficult for the researcher to tell how representative a picture he is getting. Some biases are almost certain to be present when the field situations the researcher can participate in, or the relationships he can establish, are limited by his role and status. A man may be able to join a precinct captain he wants to know for a drink in a tavern, but not interview the politician's wife at home

---

1. The validity of one's conclusions is a relative thing, and unstructured observation and interviewing are sometimes the only means for data collection suitable for testing hypotheses. Yet, the refinements of the experiment still serve as the model toward which we strive.

during the day. A woman researcher might find the circumstances reversed. The great flexibility of unstructured observation and interviewing, besides being a major advantage, is also a clear invitation to bias that must be guarded against.

In compensation, unstructured observation and interviewing have a number of advantages over the survey. The field worker is not as bound by prejudgment: *he can reformulate the problem as he goes along.* The Erie County Voting Study, a panel survey undertaken in 1940, based much of its data gathering upon the hypothesis that the mass media strongly influenced how people made up their minds about candidates.[2] It paid only scant attention to interpersonal influences. When the analysis began to suggest that personal contacts were extremely important, the data for establishing this fact were quite scanty.

Because of his closer contact with the field situation, *the researcher is better able to avoid misleading or meaningless questions.* Respondents in one cross-sectional sample of a middle-sized city were asked if they belonged to the AFL or the CIO. The largest union in town was an independent union formerly affiliated with the AFL. As a consequence, many union members said, "AFL," while many more fell into the "other" category, having rejected both the AFL and the CIO as appropriate to their situation.

The impressions of a field worker are often more reliable for classifying respondents than a rigid index drawing upon one or two questions in a questionnaire. The field worker can classify party members as "more active" or "less active" on the basis of considerable information about them. A survey, using the number of hours spent working for the party on election day, might lump together the tireless worker who hauled voters all day long in his car and the idler who stayed around party headquarters.

Unstructured observation and interviewing usually uses the highest paid talent in direct contact with the data in the field. The survey director is typically several steps removed from the data-gathering process. This remoteness frequently impairs the researcher's understanding of the difficulties of communication that his questions evoke when asked by a semi-skilled interviewer.

Using unstructured methods, *the researcher can ease himself into the field at an appropriate pace* and thereby avoid rebuff by blundering into delicate situations or subject matter. The survey researcher may find to his surprise that some aspects of his questionnaire are explosive in certain localities.

The field worker can constantly modify his categories, making them more suitable for the analysis of the problem he is studying. The survey researcher is often stuck with the categories or variables he originally used in conceiving the problem.

---

2.   P. F. Lazarsfeld *et al., The People's Choice,* New York, Columbia University Press, 1948.

Imputing motives is always hazardous in social science, even though often essential. *The field worker can generally impute motives more validly by* contrasting stated ideals with actual behavior, supplemented by the informant's reactions to "feed-back." Here, the researcher describes the informant's motives as they appear to him for corroboration or modification.

The field worker can select later informants in such a way as to throw addi-tional light on emerging hypotheses. Suppose several young party workers insist that the older leaders are afraid the younger men will take away their party posts. The researcher can then approach some of the older party leaders who are in close contact with energetic, younger workers to find out what their reactions are. The survey researcher is likely to find such a diversion limited by his sample and questionnaire. This problem of redirection may be solved by *repeated* surveys, if time and budget permit.

The field worker can generally get at depth material more satisfactorily than the survey researcher. He can postpone immediate data gathering to cultivate the relationship and draw out depth material only when the informant is ready for it. In one instance, preparatory to designing a questionnaire on the problems of elderly persons, a field worker using unstructured interviewing found half of his informants moved to tears at some time in the interview. When the questionnaire was used by trained interviewers, weeping was rare.

The field worker absorbs a lot of information that at the time seems ir-relevant. *Later, when his perspective on the situation has changed, this informa-tion may turn out to be extremely valuable.* The survey researcher limits him-self to what he considers important at the offset even though he has some serious misconceptions about the problem.

It is much easier for the field worker to make use of selected informants' skills and insights by giving these informants free rein to describe the situation as they see it. The field worker frequently wants his informants to talk about what they want to talk about; the survey researcher has to get them to talk about what he wants.

The field worker can usually move more easily back and forth from data gather-ing in the field to analysis at his desk. He has less of an investment to junk, if he started out on the wrong track, than the survey researcher does.

Difficult-to-quantify variables are probably less distorted by unstructured observation and interviewing than by an abortive effort to operationalize them for quantification by a survey. There is no magic in numbers; improperly used they confuse rather than clarify.

The field worker has a big advantage over the survey researcher in delicate situations where covert research is essential, that is, where he wants to make observations while ostensibly just participating. For example, if the researcher wanted to establish the existence of police protection for underworld opera-tions, he might try to place a bet with the bookies in a poolroom while an officer was present: he would have trouble in direct questioning.

Finally, there is the ever-present dollar sign. Because the survey involves expenses such as recruiting and training interviewers, administering and supervising the field work, coding and punching the questionnaires, and running the hundreds of tables for analysis, *surveys are generally more expensive than field observation and interviewing.*

It may be helpful to compare more explicitly participant observation with conventionally structured program research. While such program research follows the textbook sequence of (1) exploratory studies (to generate concepts and propositions about an area), (2) descriptive studies (to validate measuring instruments and to estimate the relevant parameters and the relationships among these), and (3) explanatory studies (to test, empirically, certain theoretical propositions arising out of the earlier studies), participant observation research typically coalesces this sequence of studies into a single multiplex process described below by Anselm Strauss and his collaborators.

THE PROCESS OF FIELD WORK

ANSELM STRAUSS *et al.*

Two general characteristics of fieldwork must be pointed out before its associated logic and techniques are considered. First, the propositions dealt with are rarely of the "A causes B" type, the usual causal interrelationships between two or more variables dealt with in experimental research. If the fieldworker offers such propositions, they tend to be only part of a total propositional set. This characteristic is attributable to the preoccupation of most fieldworkers either with problems of social structure or with specific phenomena as they relate to an ongoing social situation. The outcome of such research is not one, two, or a few carefully tested hypotheses but a set of many interrelated propositions. For example, in our study, propositions about how psychiatrists handle patients in a hospital setting are related to propositions about the psychiatrists' professional affiliations and careers, as well as to propositions about the organization of the hospital's wards. Similarly, propositions about the perspectives of nurses toward their work mesh with propositions about their professional identities, the behavior of psychiatrists, the structural necessities of ward organization, and lines of hospital authority. Fieldwork is well advanced when many apparently scattered observations are related to one or more propositional sets and these sets in turn are demonstrably and logically related to one another.

This feature of fieldwork suggests corollaries: Evidence mustered for sets of propositions is of various kinds and is interrelated. For our propositions

Reprinted from Anselm Strauss, Leonard Schatzman, Rue Bucher, Danuta Ehrlich, and Melvin Sabshin, *Psychiatric Ideologies and Institutions,* New York: Free Press, 1964, pp. 19–21, by permission of the authors and publisher.

about how psychiatrists use the hospital, there is evidence from intensive interviews in which the psychiatrists express their points of view and report upon recent cases; from observations in the nurses' station (where the doctor discusses his cases with nurses and residents and leaves orders); from observed crises that occur around the doctor's patients; from the nurses' testimony, both observed and elicited in interviews, concerning the doctors' usual behavior. Of this evidence, some may prove relevant to further hypotheses about, for example, the kinds of interaction through which work is accomplished. Indeed, once it is well established, a proposition may become evidence for further propositions.

A second general characteristic of fieldwork is its temporally developing character. The fieldworker usually does not enter the field with specific hypotheses and a predetermined research design. To be sure, he does have general problems in mind, as well as a theoretical framework that directs him to certain events in the field. The trained sociologist or anthropologist is equipped to make discriminations rather quickly between what may be theoretically important or unimportant. The initial phase of fieldwork is a period of general observation: Specific problems and foci have not yet been determined. The fieldworker is guided mainly by sensitivities to data derived both from his professional background and from his general notions about the nature of his research problem. As he surveys the field initially, he is continually "testing"—either implicitly or explicitly—the relevance of a large number of hypotheses, hunches, and guesses. Many preconceptions fall by the wayside during this initial period, as the observer struggles to ascertain the meaning of events and to place them in some initial order.

During the second phase of fieldwork, the investigator has begun to make sense of the massive flow of events. Significant classes of persons and events have begun to emerge, certain aspects of the field have become important, and genuine propositions have been formulated. His initial general problems may have undergone considerable revision and are now coming into clear focus. This second phase then is marked by greater attention to particular aspects of the field and by an emerging set of propositions.

A final phase consists of systematic effort to pinpoint various hypotheses. By this time, the number of propositions with which the researcher is concerned has dwindled considerably. Some hypotheses are short-lived, proving patently incorrect; others are simply lost sight of as new propositions and hypotheses emerge. Those hypotheses that survive the informal tests of daily observation are then subjected to more deliberate, controlled inquiry. The fieldworker concentrates upon obtaining evidence relevant to those propositions; he searches for negative or qualifying, as well as for supporting, instances. It has been said that science turns upon negative evidence, for such evidence not only helps to refute certain propositions but also helps to develop new classifications along with more tenable propositions about these classifications. The pinpointing phase then involves a hard look at one's understanding of the reality under investigation—understanding that is most critical to the emerging propositional set.

In one instance, for example, we suspected that lower-class nurses' aides did not participate in the psychiatric universe of discourse, despite their work within the psychiatric province. Our conversations and interviews with aides assured us that we were correct. We found an even more critical test in a class on "The Doctor's Words" conducted for the aides by a sophisticated nursing supervisor. We attended these classes, listening to psychiatric concepts concretely explained and reiterated. Then we interviewed the aides again. We found that they still did not understand the concepts.

Pinpointing tactics tested another hypothesis: that *milieu* therapists on certain treatment wards of the state hospital did not concern themselves with, or even recognize, the problem of chronicity. We had noted, from many of their actions, that they made no apparent distinction between "acute" and "chronic" patients. Furthermore, the treatment ideology was explicitly equalitarian, although not equally optimistic, for all patients. We had, therefore, to search beyond ideology and practices closely dictated by ideology for evidence bearing upon long-term patients. That evidence was associated with how the personnel handled their census and bed space and used their time.

In much field research, critical hypotheses sometimes do not reach full maturity until after the worker has left the field. Then he will comb his field notes for evidence *pro* and *con*. But it is perfectly possible to combine analytic and data-gathering operations so that one has the opportunity deliberately to pinpoint the hypotheses before leaving the field. Our view of fieldwork emphasizes a process of data-gathering that involves continual analytic activity, and leads the fieldworker to control his operations increasingly as he goes along, in terms of an emerging propositional set.

To be sure, the discrimination of stages in fieldwork, as set forth above, is highly abstract. In actuality, the investigator may be working within two stages during a single period of time. A given problem area may be ready for pinpointing while propositions are still being developed in another area. There are, however, two points about fieldwork directly associated with its chronological process. First, because the researcher is in the field for an extended period of time, unexpected hypotheses will most certainly emerge, with ample opportunity to qualify and refine hypotheses. Second, the fieldworker's activity varies according to the stage of research. As he goes along, he increasingly must make deliberate choices about what data to gather and how to gather them, adapting his techniques to the situation.

In summary, we have viewed participant observation as a style of research characteristically used for seeking analytic descriptions of complex social organizations. This style emphasizes direct observation, informant interviewing, document analysis, respondent interviewing, and direct participation and is made possible in large part by repeated, genuinely social interaction with the members of the organization under study. The use of these techniques is organized by an unusual research design in which hypothesis generation, data gathering, and hypothesis testing are carried on simultaneously at every step of the research process.

Already a number of methodological and ethical issues pertaining to participant observation have been touched on simply in defining the approach. In the remainder of the book we shall delineate these issues more precisely and present the major views on each.

In Chapter 2 we shall examine a number of questions that have been raised in the social science literature concerning the nature of the social relationships established between the participant observer and the various types of members in the organization under analysis. What sorts of relationships are most advantageous— simply from the technical point of view—for optimal attainment of information? What sorts of relationships are desirable on the basis of ethical and humane considerations? What are the psychological implications for the observer in each of the various sorts of observer-subject relationships? And what are the tensions and conflicts between these various criteria?

Chapter 3 deals with more technical matters of data collection, recording, and retrieval. How should the five major techniques be combined in a particular study? How is information best recorded? How are the resulting enormous masses of data to be catalogued and effectively summarized?

Chapter 4 discusses certain determinants of the quality of data, emphasizing characteristics of the observer, the subjects, and the various sorts of relationships among them. Here we are confronted with the various issues of bias, distortion, and error, and we are provided with certain criteria for detecting and correcting these.

Various techniques for generating useful concepts and hypotheses comprise the subject matter of Chapter 5, such as the use of insightful informants, the use of analytic induction, and the technique of constant comparison.

In Chapter 6, important issues dealt with are the nature of evidence for and the proof of propositions in participant observation.

Chapter 7 treats various problems encountered in publishing the results of participant observation studies. These problems center around the bulkiness of evidence and the ethical responsibilities of the investigator to avoid harming the interests of the subjects and/or those of social science.

In the eighth and concluding chapter, participant observation is compared with other methods and research approaches current in the various social sciences.

CHAPTER TWO

FIELD
RELATIONS

An inspection of the literature on participant observation would reveal that the bulk of it consists of lore on establishing and maintaining good working relations with subjects in the field. This lore details recurrent problems encountered by observers, proffers analyses of the sources of these problems, recounts expedients that have succeeded in certain situations, and underlines certain mistakes to be avoided. As with the literature on interviewing, this emphasis on the difficulties that may be encountered tends to discourage neophyte or would-be participant observers. Such readers become convinced that extraordinary insight, social skill, and even outright courage and pluck are necessary to execute such a study successfully.

It is our hope that we can avoid conveying such an impression, for it is our conviction that virtually any mature social scientist can, with good sense and close attention to his methodology, carry out participant observation of, at least, the less demanding varieties. Partly for this reason, but also because this kind of literature is so extensive and is reasonably well collected elsewhere,[1] we have included only a few selections on field relations. Our concern here is to delineate the issues, choices, and criteria that confront the participant observer in field relations.

The primary reason that the observer finds his field relations so problematical is that his subjects, accustomed to life in a more or less ordinary social world, do not know how to be studied. That is, first of all, they do not know what kind of a creature a participant observer is—what runs in his veins and his mind, how much he should count for on the scales of human goodness and worth, or how he may be evaluating them. After all, what motives, what alien causes, would lead a man to turn on his brethren with analytic eye?

Moreover, once the subjects have reconciled themselves to such a person being somewhat human, perhaps even remotely worthwhile and legitimate, they do not know what he expects of them or offers to them. Does he know all? What does he want to know, and what does he deserve to know? For what ulterior purpose or group does he seek this knowledge? Beyond these considerations, many subjects are simply ill-equipped to understand and communicate the information the observer seeks. They must be taught the skills requisite to the role of subject, once they have learned what an observer and subjects are.

If the participant observer is to succeed in his research, it is therefore incumbent on him to structure for the subjects the respective roles of subject and observer. This is not as deliberate and rational a process as it sounds, for the subjects on their own initiative will be shaping among themselves a collective definition of the observer as he relates to their own interests. The observer thus can inject certain inputs into this ongoing definitional process, and he can correct or modify some of the feedback, but he can only hope that the final outcome will be a workable set of relationships.

1.   Adams and Preiss (1960); Junker (1960); Paul (1953); Hammond (1964); Vidich, Bensman, and Stein (1964).

In attempting to shape these relationships, the participant observer can be aided considerably by some careful backgrounding on the organization he is to study. From reading, from conversations with others who are somewhat acquainted with the type of organization, and from judicious preliminary scouting of it before making his presence known, the observer can gain a rough idea of the sorts of relationships that exist among subjects and of the existing roles that are likely to be reference points in classifying the observer when he does arrive among them. Lacking any conception of the observer role, the subjects can only assimilate him toward some existing role or roles, such as writer, investigator, reporter, missionary, etc. Or, it may turn out that they have been studied before, in which case it is most helpful to know what role the previous researcher claimed and what residue of expectations and sentiments remains among the subjects.[2]

In any case, it is extremely useful for the observer to acquire some advance knowledge of the role structure among the subjects and to determine where he is most likely to fit within that structure. The role which he claims—or to which he is assigned by the subjects—is perhaps the single most important determinant of what he will be able to learn. Every role is an avenue to certain types of information but is also an automatic barrier to certain other types. The role assumed by the observer largely determines where he can go, what he can do, whom he can interact with, what he can inquire about, what he can see, and what he can be told. If he cannot freely define his own role, the observer must be careful to assume that role which is most strategic for obtaining information that is central to his scientific concerns.

Unfortunately, however, strategic considerations are seldom the only factors influencing the observer's choice of role. Certain personal attributes are typically prerequisite to or associated with occupancy of a particular role—attributes such as age, sex, social class, ethnic group, technical skills, experience, certification, and physique. Thus, the observer may be unsuited for the role that he judges to be strategically optimal. Even if he should wangle his way into the role he wishes, he may come to find it too demanding to be personally comfortable, taxing his limited ability to get by in that role.

Acceptance into the desired role often hinges upon offering appropriate *auspices* or invoking appropriate *sponsors*. Auspices for a research role may include the claim to be (1) writing a book on the history of the organization, (2) analyzing a locally felt problem so that it may be alleviated by proper authorities, (3) making the organization's honorable story known to the world, (4) simply trying to understand its way of life on its own merits, (5) analyzing local ways so that they may be applied to help similar organizations elsewhere, etc. Auspices for *existing* roles typically center around the ordinary desires for a job or position of that sort, the desire to locate there, and so on.[3]

Appropriate sponsorship likewise varies according to the role sought. In the research role, valuable sponsors may include the boss or formal leader of the organization, a powerful informal leader, the local government, a well-known newspaper or magazine, a federal or state agency, a national association, an acquaintance within the group, and so on. For more ordinary, previously existing roles, sponsorship may come in the form of letters of recommendation from previous employers, a

2.   Paul (1953); Gallaher (1964).

3.   Leznoff (1956); Paul (1953); Whyte (1955); Richardson, Dohrenwend, and Klein (1965), Chapter 4.

local official or recruiting agent, a respected friend who is already a member, etc. Effective sponsorship serves to vouch for the observer's character, worth, and ability as ratified by a respected insider and thus simplifies the subjects' definitional task. However, the observer must be careful not to jeopardize his sponsor's standing by misbehavior or poor performance, since subjects tend to hold the sponsor responsible in some degree for the observer's subsequent conduct.[4]

One of the most critical decisions the participant observer must make concerning his role is the degree to which it will be openly defined as a research role or will be concealed beneath a performance of some existing role in the organization.[5] The available choices, and the consequences thereof, have been rewardingly analyzed by Raymond L. Gold in the following selection.

ROLES IN
SOCIOLOGICAL FIELD OBSERVATIONS

RAYMOND L. GOLD

Buford Junker has suggested four theoretically possible roles for sociologists conducting field work.[1] These range from the complete participant at one extreme to the complete observer at the other. Between these, but nearer the former, is the participant-as-observer; nearer the latter is the observer-as-participant. As a member of Junker's research team, I shared in the thinking which led to conceptualization of these research roles. After the work of the team was completed, I continued the search for insight regarding processes of interaction learning in field observation in a special study of my own.[2] A considerable portion of this study was devoted to exploration of the dimensions of Junker's role-conceptions and their controlling effects on the product of field study.

My aim in this paper is to present extensions of Junker's thinking growing out of systematic interviews with field workers whose experience had been cast in one or more of these patterns of researcher-subject relationship. All of these field workers had gathered data in natural or nonexperimental settings. I would like in this paper to analyze generic characteristics of Junker's four field observer roles and to call attention to the demands each one places on an observer, as a person and as a sociologist plying his trade.

---

4.   *Ibid.*

5.   R. Gold (1958); Junker (1960).

Reprinted from *Social Forces* (1958), **36,** 217–223, by permission of the author and publisher.

1.   Buford Junker, "Some Suggestions for the Design and Field Work Learning Experiences," in Everett C. Hughes, *et al.,* Cases on Field Work (hectographed by The University of Chicago, 1952), Part III-A.

2.   Raymond L. Gold, Toward a Social Interaction Methodology for Sociological Field Observation, unpublished Ph. D. dissertation, University of Chicago, 1954.

Every field work role is at once a social interaction device for securing information for scientific purposes and a set of behaviors in which an observer's self is involved.[3] While playing a field work role and attempting to take the role of an informant, the field observer often attempts to master hitherto strange or only generally understood universes of discourse relating to many attitudes and behaviors. He continually introspects, raising endless questions about the informant and the developing field relationship, with a view to playing the field work role as successfully as possible. A sociological assumption here is that the more successful the field worker is in playing his role, the more successful he must be in taking the informant's role. Success in both role-taking and role-playing requires success in blending the demands of self-expression and self-integrity with the demands of the role.

It is axiomatic that a person who finds a role natural and congenial, and who acts convincingly in it, has in fact found how to balance role-demands with those of self. If need be he can subordinate self-demands in the interest of the role and role-demands in the interest of self whenever he perceives that either self or role is in any way threatened. If, while playing the role, someone with whom he is interacting attacks anything in which he has self-involvement, he can point out to himself that the best way to protect self at the moment is to subordinate (or defer) self-expression to allow successful performance in the role. In other words, he uses role to protect self. Also, when he perceives that he is performing inadequately in the role he can indicate to himself that he can do better by changing tactics. Here he uses self as a source of new behaviors to protect role. The case of using role to protect self from perceived threat is one of acute self-consciousness, a matter of diminishing over-sensitivity to self-demands by introspectively noting corresponding demands of role. The case of using self to protect role from perceived threat is one of acute role-consciousness, a matter of diminishing over-sensitivity to role-demands by introspectively indicating that they are disproportionately larger than those of self. Both cases represent situations in which role-demands and self-demands are out of balance with each other as a result of perceived threat, and are then restored to balance by appropriate introspection.

Yet, no matter how congenial the two sets of demands seem to be, a person who plays a role in greatly varied situations (and this is especially true of a sociologist field observer) sometimes experiences threats which markedly impair his effectiveness as an interactor in the situation. When attempting to assess informational products of field work, it is instructive to examine the field worker's role-taking and role-playing in situations of perceived, but

---

3.   To simplify this presentation, I am assuming that the field worker is an experienced observer who has incorporated the role into his self-conceptions. Through this incorporation, he is self-involved in the role and feels that self is at stake in it. However, being experienced in the role, he can balance role-demands and self-demands in virtually all field situations, that is, all except those to be discussed shortly.

unresolved, threat. Because he defines success in the role partly in terms of doing everything he can to remain in even threatening situations to secure desired information, he may find that persevering is sometimes more heroic than fruitful.

The situation may be one in which he finds the informant an almost intolerable bigot. The field worker decides to stick it out by attempting to subordinate self-demands to those of role. He succeeds to the extent of refraining from "telling off" the informant, but fails in that he is too self-conscious to play his role effectively. He may think of countless things he would like to say and do to the informant, all of which are dysfunctional to role-demands, since his role requires taking the role of the other as an informant, not as a bigot. At the extreme of nearly overwhelming self-consciousness, the field worker may still protect his role by getting out of the situation while the getting is good. Once out and in the company of understanding colleagues, he will finally be able to achieve self-expression (i.e., finally air his views of the informant) without damaging the field role.[4]

Should the situation be such that the field worker finds the informant practically inscrutable (i.e., a "bad" informant), he may decide to persevere despite inability to meet role-taking and role-playing demands. In this situation he becomes acutely role-conscious, since he is hypersensitive to role-demands, hyposensitive to self. This partial breakdown of his self-process thwarts his drawing upon past experiences and current observations to pose meaningful questions and perceive meaningful answers. At the extreme, a role-conscious field worker may play his role so mechanically and unconvincingly that the informant, too, develops role-and-self problems.

The following discussion utilizes these conceptions of role and self to aid in analyzing field work roles as "master roles" for developing lesser role-relationships with informants.[5] While a field worker cannot be all things to all men, he routinely tries to fit himself into as many roles as he can, as long as playing them helps him to develop relationships with informants in his master role (i.e., participant-as-observer, etc.).

---

4.   An inexperienced field worker might "explode" on the spot, feeling that role and self are not congenial in *this or any other* situation. But an experienced field worker would leave such a situation as gracefully as possible to protect the role, feeling that role and self are not congenial in *this* situation only.

5.   Lesser role-relationships include all achieved and ascribed roles which the field worker plays in the act of developing a field relationship with an informant. For example, he may become the "nice man that old ladies can't resist" as part of his over-all role-repertoire in a community study. Whether he deliberately sets out to achieve such relationships with old ladies or discovers that old ladies ascribe him "irresistible" characteristics, he is still a participant-as-observer who interacts with local old ladies as a "nice man." Were he not there to study the community, he might choose *not* to engage in this role-relationship, especially if being irresistible to old ladies is not helpful in whatever master role(s) brought him to town. (Cf. any experienced community researcher.)

COMPLETE PARTICIPANT

The true identity and purpose of the complete participant in field research are not known to those whom he observes. He interacts with them as naturally as possible in whatever areas of their living interest him and are accessible to him as situations in which he can play, or learn to play, requisite day-to-day roles successfully. He may, for example, work in a factory to learn about inner-workings of informal groups. After gaining acceptance at least as a novice, he may be permitted to share not only in work activities and attitudes but also in the intimate life of the workers outside the factory.

Role-pretense is a basic theme in these activities. It matters little whether the complete participant in a factory situation has an upper-lower class background and perhaps some factory experience, or whether he has an upper-middle class background quite divorced from factory work and the norms of such workers. What really matters is that he knows that he is pretending to be a colleague. I mean to suggest by this that the crucial value as far as research yield is concerned lies more in the self-orientation of the complete participant than in his surface role-behaviors as he initiates his study. The complete participant realizes that he, and he alone, knows that he is in reality other than the person he pretends to be. He must pretend that his real self is represented by the role, or roles, he plays in and out of the factory situation in relationships with people who, to him, are but informants, and this implies an interactive construction that has deep ramifications. He must bind the mask of pretense to himself or stand the risk of exposure and research failure.

In effect, the complete participant operates continually under an additional set of situational demands. Situational role-and-self demands ordinarily tend to correspond closely. For this reason, even when a person is in the act of learning to play a role, he is likely to believe that pretending to have achieved this correspondence (i.e., fourflushing) will be unnecessary when he can actually "be himself" in the role. But the complete observer simply cannot "be himself"; to do so would almost invariably preclude successful pretense. At the very least, attempting to "be himself"—that is, to achieve self-realization in pretended roles—would arouse suspicion of the kind that would lead others to remain aloof in interacting with him. He must be sensitive to demands of self, of the observer role, and of the momentarily pretended role. Being sensitive to the set of demands accompanying role-pretense is a matter of being sensitive to a large variety of overt and covert mannerisms and other social cues representing the observer's pretended self. Instead of being himself in the pretended role, all he can be is a "not self," in the sense of perceiving that his actions are meaningful in a contrived role.

The following illustration of the pretense of a complete participant comes from an interview with a field worker who drove a cab for many months to study big-city cab drivers. Here a field worker reveals how a pretended role fosters a heightened sense of self-awareness, an introspective attitude, because of the sheer necessity of indicating continually to himself that certain experiences are merely part of playing a pretended role. These indications serve as self-assurance that customers are not really treating *him* as they seem to do, since he is actually someone else, namely, a field worker.

▶ Well, I've noticed that the cab driver who *is* a cab driver acts differently than the part-time cab drivers, who don't think of themselves as real cab drivers. When somebody throws a slam at men who drive only part of the year, such as, "Well, you're just a goddamn cab driver!," they do one of two things. They may make it known to the guy that they are not a cab driver; they are something else. But as a rule, that doesn't work out, because the customer comes back with, "Well, if you're not a cab driver what the hell are you driving this cab for?" So, as a rule, they mostly just rationalize it to themselves by thinking, "Well, this is not my role or the real me. He just doesn't understand. Just consider the source and drop it." But a cab driver who *is* a cab driver, if you make a crack at him, such as, "You're just a goddamn cab driver!" he's going to take you out of the back seat and whip you. ◀

Other complete participant roles may pose more or less of a challenge to the field worker than those mentioned above. Playing the role of potential convert to study a religious sect almost inevitably leads the field worker to feel not only that he has "taken" the people who belong to the sect, but that he has done it in ways which are difficult to justify. In short, he may suffer severe qualms about his mandate to get information in a role where he pretends to be a colleague in moral, as well as in other social, respects.

All complete participant roles have in common two potential problems; continuation in a pretended role ultimately leads the observer to reckon with one or the other. One, he may become so self-conscious about revealing his true self that he is handicapped when attempting to perform convincingly in the pretended role. Or two, he may "go native," incorporate the role into his self-conceptions and achieve self-expression in the role, but find he has so violated his observer role that it is almost impossible to report his findings. Consequently, the field worker needs cooling-off periods during and after complete participation, at which times he can "be himself" and look back on his field behavior dispassionately and sociologically.

While the complete participant role offers possibilities of learning about aspects of behavior that might otherwise escape a field observer, it places him in pretended roles which call for delicate balances between demands of role and self. A complete participant must continually remind himself that, above all, he is there as an observer: this is his primary role. If he succumbs to demands of the pretended role (or roles), or to demands of self-expression and self-integrity, he can no longer function as an observer. When he can defer self-expression no longer, he steps out of the pretended role to find opportunities for congenial interaction with those who are, in fact, colleagues.

PARTICIPANT-AS-OBSERVER

Although basically similar to the complete observer role, the participant-as-observer role differs significantly in that both field worker and informant are aware that theirs is a field relationship. This mutual awareness tends to minimize problems of role-pretending; yet, the role carries with it numerous opportunities for compartmentalizing mistakes and dilemmas which typically bedevil the complete participant.

Probably the most frequent use of this role is in community studies, where an observer develops relationships with informants through time, and where he is apt to spend more time and energy participating than observing. At times he observes formally, as in scheduled interview situations; and at other times he observes informally—when attending parties, for example. During early stages of his stay in the community, informants may be somewhat uneasy about him in both formal and informal situations, but their uneasiness is likely to disappear when they learn to trust him and he them.

But just when the research atmosphere seems ripe for gathering information, problems of role and self are apt to arise. Should field worker and informant begin to interact in much the same way as ordinary friends, they tend to jeopardize their field roles in at least two important ways. First, the informant may become too identified with the field worker to continue functioning as merely an informant. In this event the informant becomes too much of an observer. Second, the field worker may over-identify with the informant and start to lose his research perspective by "going native." Should this occur the field worker may still continue going through the motions of observing, but he is only pretending.

Although the field worker in the participant-as-observer role strives to bring his relationship with the informant to the point of friendship, to the point of intimate form, it behooves him to retain sufficient elements of "the stranger" to avoid actually reaching intimate form. Simmel's distinction between intimate content and intimate form contains an implicit warning that the latter is inimical to field observation.[6] When content of interaction is intimate, secrets may be shared without either of the interactors feeling compelled to maintain the relationship for more than a short time. This is the interaction

---

6. "In other words, intimacy is not based on the *content* of the relationship.... Inversely, certain external situations or moods may move us to make very personal statements and confessions, usually reserved for our closest friends only, to relatively strange people. But in such cases we nevertheless feel that this 'intimate' *content* does not yet make the relation an intimate one. For in its basic significance, the whole relation to these people is based only on its general, unindividual ingredients. That 'intimate' content, although we have perhaps never revealed it before and thus limit it entirely to this particular relationship, does nevertheless not become the basis of its form, and thus leaves it outside the sphere of intimacy." K. H. Wolff (ed.), *The Sociology of Georg Simmel* (Glencoe, Illinois: The Free Press, 1950), p. 127.

of sociological strangers. On the other hand, when form of interaction is intimate, continuation of the relationship (which is no longer merely a field relationship) may become more important to one or both of the interactors than continuation of the roles through which they initiated the relationship.

In general, the demands of pretense in this role, as in that of the complete participant, are continuing and great; for here the field worker is often defined by informants as more of a colleague than he feels capable of being. He tries to pretend that he is as much of a colleague as they seem to think he is, while searching to discover how to make the pretense appear natural and convincing. Whenever pretense becomes too challenging, the participant-as-observer leaves the field to re-clarify his self-conceptions and his role-relationships.

OBSERVER-AS-PARTICIPANT

The observer-as-participant role is used in studies involving one-visit interviews. It calls for relatively more formal observation than either informal observation or participation of any kind. It also entails less risk of "going native" than either the complete participant role or the participant-as-observer role. However, because the observer-as-participant's contact with an informant is so brief, and perhaps superficial, he is more likely than the other two to misunderstand the informant, and to be misunderstood by him.

These misunderstandings contribute to a problem of self-expression that is almost unique to this role. To a field worker (as to other human beings), self-expression becomes a problem at any time he perceives he is threatened. Since he meets more varieties of people for shorter periods of time than either the complete participant or the participant-as-observer, the observer-as-participant inclines more to feel threatened. Brief relationships with numerous informants expose an observer-as-participant to many inadequately understood universes of discourse that he cannot take time to master. These frustratingly brief encounters with informants also contribute to mistaken perceptions which set up communication barriers the field worker may not even be aware of until too late. Continuing relationships with apparently threatening informants offer an opportunity to redefine them as more congenial partners in interaction, but such is not the fortune of a field worker in this role. Consequently, using his prerogative to break off relationships with threatening informants, an observer-as-participant, more easily than the other two, can leave the field almost at will to regain the kind of role-and-self balance that he, being who he is, must regain.

COMPLETE OBSERVER

The complete observer role entirely removes a field worker from social interaction with informants. Here a field worker attempts to observe people in ways which make it unnecessary for them to take him into account, for they do not know he is observing them or that, in some sense, they are serving as his informants. Of the four field work roles, this alone is almost never the dominant one. It is sometimes used as one of the subordinate roles employed to implement the dominant ones.

It is generally true that with increasingly more observation than participation, the chances of "going native" become smaller, although the possibility of ethnocentrism becomes greater. With respect to achieving rapport in a field relationship, ethnocentrism may be considered a logical opposite of "going native." Ethnocentrism occurs whenever a field worker cannot or will not interact meaningfully with an informant. He then seemingly or actually rejects the informant's views without ever getting to the point of understanding them. At the other extreme, a field worker who "goes native" passes the point of field rapport by literally accepting his informant's views as his own. Both are cases of pretending to be an observer, but for obviously opposite reasons. Because a complete observer remains entirely outside the observed interaction, he faces the greatest danger of misunderstanding the observed. For the same reason, his role carries the least chance of "going native."

The complete observer role is illustrated by systematic eavesdropping, or by reconnaissance of any kind of social setting as preparation for more intensive study in another field role. While watching the rest of the world roll by, a complete observer may feel comfortably detached, for he takes no self-risks, participates not one whit. Yet, there are many times when he wishes he could ask representatives of the observed world to qualify what they have said, or to answer other questions his observations of them have brought to mind. For some purposes, however, these very questions are important starting points for subsequent observations and interactions in appropriate roles. It is not surprising that reconnaissance is almost always a prelude to using the participant-as-observer role in community study. The field worker, feeling comfortably detached, can first "case" the town before committing himself to casing *by* the town.

CONCLUSIONS

Those of us who teach field work courses or supervise graduate students and others doing field observations have long been concerned with the kinds of interactional problems and processes discussed above. We find such common "mistakes" as that of the beginner who over-identifies with an informant simply because the person treats him compassionately after others have refused to grant him an interview. This limited, although very real, case of "going native" becomes much more understandable to the beginner when we have analyzed it for him sociologically. When he can begin utilizing theory of role and self to reflect on his own assets and shortcomings in the field, he will be well on the way to dealing meaningfully with problems of controlling *his* interactions with informants.

Beyond this level of control, sophistication in field observation requires manipulating informants to help them play their role effectively. Once a field worker learns that a field relationship in process of being structured creates role-and-self problems for informants that are remarkably similar to those he has experienced, he is in a position to offer informants whatever kinds of "reassurances" they need to fit into their role. Certainly a field worker has mastered his role only to the extent that he can help informants to master theirs. Learning this fact (and doing something about it!) will eliminate nearly all excuses about "bad" or "inept" informants, since, willy-nilly, an informant is likely to play his role only as fruitfully or as fruitlessly as a field worker plays his.[7]

Experienced field workers recognize limitations in their ability to develop relationships in various roles and situations. They have also discovered that they can maximize their take of information by selecting a field role which permits them to adjust their own role-repertoires to research objectives. Objectively, a selected role is simply an expedient device for securing a given level of information. For instance, a complete participant obviously develops relationships and frames of reference which yield a somewhat different perspective of the subject matter than that which any of the other field work roles would yield. These subjective and objective factors come together in the fact that degree of success in securing the level of information which a field role makes available to a field worker is largely a matter of his skill in playing and taking roles.

Each of the four field work roles has been shown to offer advantages and disadvantages with respect to both demands of role and self and level of information. No attempt has been made in this report to show how a sociological conception of field work roles can do more than provide lines of thought and action for dealing with problems and processes of field interaction. Obviously, however, a theory of role and self growing out of study of field interaction is in no sense limited to that area of human activity. Learning to take and play roles, although dramatized in the field, is essentially the same kind of social learning people engage in throughout life.

In any case, the foregoing discussion has suggested that a field worker selects and plays a role so that he, being who he is, can best study those aspects of society in which he is interested.

---

7. In a recent article on interviewing, Theodore Caplow also recognizes the key role played by the field worker in structuring the field relationship. He concludes, "The quality and quantity of the information secured probably depend far more upon the competence of the interviewer than upon the respondent." "The Dynamics of Information Interviewing," *American Journal of Sociology,* LXII (September 1956), 169. Cf. also the studies by Junker and Gold, *op. cit.*

Of the roles discussed by Gold, that of complete participant (or covert observer "in disguise") has been most criticized in the literature on participant observation, not only for its ethical implications,[6] but for its rather severe technical limitations in data collection.[7]

THE UNIDENTIFIED INTERVIEWER

HENRY W. RIECKEN

During a participant-observation study of an apocalyptic group,[1] the interviewers faced a number of difficulties in developing a suitable role for themselves. They sought to collect essential data but yet to remain ostensibly just ordinary members of the group of believers being studied. Furthermore, the observers tried to behave in such a way as to minimize the effect they might have on the members' beliefs and actions.

The group had gathered around a middle-aged housewife in a suburb of an American city. She believed that, through "automatic writing," she had received a number of messages from beings dwelling in outer space, forecasting the destruction of the earth by flood on a certain date. She made known this prediction among her acquaintances, and a number of people began calling on her regularly to be instructed in the "lessons" from outer space and to discuss the possibilities of salvation. Most "members" were adult men and women, of between about twenty to about fifty-five years of age, of middle socioeconomic status and well educated, all but two having at least attended college. About twenty-five people at one time or another showed interest in the prophet's messages. During the last month before the flood was expected the most convinced believers (about a dozen people) often met in the living room of the prophet's home in what resembled social gatherings. No formal organization was ever established.

The study of the group was undertaken in order to test a hypothesis derived from the theory of dissonance.[2] The hypothesis can be stated as follows: Under certain specified conditions, when a belief or prediction is demonstrated

---

6.   M. Sullivan, Queen, and Patrick (1958); Coser, Roth, Sullivan, and Queen (1959); Erikson (1967).

7.   Caudill (1958); Festinger, Riecken, and Schachter (1956); Riecken (1956).

Reprinted from *American Journal of Sociology* (1956), **62,** 210–212, by permission of the author and The University of Chicago Press.

1.   A complete account of the study will appear very shortly in a book by Leon Festinger, H. W. Riecken, and Stanley Schachter, *When Prophecy Fails* (Minneapolis: University of Minnesota Press, 1956). The present article draws upon the "Methodological Appendix" of the forthcoming book.

2.   *Ibid.,* chap. i. A full presentation of the theory and a number of derivations will appear in a forthcoming book by Festinger.

to have been wrong, those who have held the belief not only will fail to relinquish it but will try even harder than before to convince others of its validity. Among the specified conditions are that the believers, before the predicted event, were sincerely *convinced* of the validity of their belief, and they must have taken some action, consistent with the belief, that is hard or impossible to revoke or undo (i.e., they must be *committed*). The major problem for the participant-observers in this study was to determine, for each believer, the degree of his *conviction,* the amount and kind of his *commitment,* and, of course, the extent of his *proselyting.* It was essential, of course, that the participant-observers obtain data on all three variables both before and after the crucial date.

Furthermore, it was important that the observers avoid exerting influence on the beliefs and actions of the members. We wished especially to avoid doing or saying anything that would affect the extent of proselyting; but we also wanted to avoid increasing or decreasing the conviction and the commitment of the members.

From our very first contact with the chief figures it was apparent that a study could not be conducted openly. The leaders had not yet adopted a policy of secrecy and exclusion, but they were at that time neither seeking publicity nor recruiting converts. Rather, their attitude can be best described as one of passive acceptance of individuals who came to call and seemed to be interested in the messages from outer space. Our observers were welcomed politely, and their questions were answered, for the most part, fully, but they were not proselyted vigorously or enlisted to spread the word. To obtain entree and maintain contact with the group, our observers posed as ordinary inquirers and, later, as ordinary members who believed in the tenets of the group as the others did.

Because they took the part of ordinary members, the observers obviously could not play the usual role of interviewers. They were effectively prevented from using any kind of formal schedule of questions, and even attempts to cover a systematic list of topics by ordinary questions were not feasible. The only interviewing possible was necessarily conversational in style and carefully casual. In gathering the data on conviction, commitment, and proselyting, the observers tried to be non-directive, sympathetic listeners—passive participants who were inquisitive and eager to learn whatever others might want to tell them. But such a role was not without its difficulties.

In the first place, the passive-member role greatly hampered inquiry. Unable to take command of the situation as an interviewer ordinarily does, the observers were forced to maintain constant alertness for relevant data that members of the group spontaneously brought forth and had to be extremely tactful and skillful in following up leads so as not to appear too inquisitive. Second, while the attitude we strove for was easy enough for an observer to take during his first few contacts, it became increasingly difficult to maintain as he began to be seen as a "regular." Non-directive inquiry about others, while revealing little about one's own feelings or actions, is appropriate enough behavior for a newcomer, but, if prolonged, it tends to cast doubt on either the intelligence or the motives of interrogator. In ordinary social intercourse it is reasonably expected that the members of a group will give as well as receive information about beliefs, opinions, and actions relevant to their common purpose. But in the role we defined privately for ourselves such expectations did not fit.

Nearly every conversation he had with a member about his conviction, commitment, or proselyting presented the observer with an unsought opportunity to influence the other; for it is difficult, outside the interviewer's role, to inquire of an individual how he feels about a matter without having him return the question. Such reciprocal questioning was especially common in this group, because their beliefs concerned the future and the non-material world. Since the beliefs could not be validated (at least not until the cataclysm) by physical reality, the only confirmation available was from social reality— the beliefs and actions of fellows. The pressure on observers to take part in the process of mutual support and confirmation was ever present and often strong.

The alternatives for dealing with such pressures were all unattractive. Had the observers been completely truthful about their convictions, they would unquestionably have weakened the convictions of other members and would, in addition, have been in the absurd position of trying to maintain membership in a group whose beliefs they flatly denied. On the other hand, had they simulated the sincerity and depth of conviction of the regular members, they would have strongly reinforced conviction. A third choice, non-committal responses and evasive replies, soon became embarrassing and awkward, besides jeopardizing the observer's status in the group. The observers were forced, therefore, to present the appearance of agreement with the major beliefs of the group. While they avoided taking strong stands on these issues and never voluntarily or spontaneously spoke up to reinforce conviction, their general air of acceptance as well as their mere presence and interest in the affairs of the group undoubtedly had some strengthening effect on the conviction of the others. The goal of avoiding influence completely, proved unrealistic, for, in order to remain members and yet gather the necessary data, the observers had to offer some support to the members' convictions. And this, while indeed minimal, must have had some effect.

In the matter of commitment the effect of the observers is difficult to assess. Many members of the group committed themselves by spending appreciable amounts of money to attend meetings, by making public declarations of belief, at least among acquaintances and neighbors, by giving up friendship with skeptics, by giving away possessions, or by quitting their jobs. Until the week or two before the date of the expected flood, there was little or no pressure on observers to make or to report commitments, and, when the pressure to quit jobs grew, the observers were able to invent various reasons why they could not or should not quit their jobs. But even though they did not quit jobs, give away possessions, or make public declarations of faith, the observers must have appeared to the regular members to have committed themselves by spending both time and money to attend meetings. One observer may have seemed heavily committed, since he made a number of trips by air from a distant city to attend meetings; two others, who resided in the city where the group was located, devoted a great deal of time to its activities, not only attending all meetings but paying numerous additional calls at the home of the prophet. All the observers spent virtually full time at the prophet's home during the four days immediately preceding the date when the flood was expected.

It is hard to estimate the effect of this apparent commitment by the observers. On the one hand, it probably reinforced members' convictions and confidence that they had been right in making whatever commitments they had made; on the other hand, the observers' commitments may have made those of other members seem either more or less important. The perceived amount of the observers' commitment probably ranged from moderate to slight: there were at least two members whose commitment was less than that of any observer and at least four or five who exceeded that of any observer. For the latter, the lesser commitment of the observers probably made their own seem greater and more binding, whereas the former probably perceived their commitment to be even slighter in contrast to the observers'. In short, for most of the group the observers' investment in group activity was supportive, but the amount of support varied.

Only in proselyting were we able to avoid exercising any influence. During the greater part of the period of our observation, the attitude of the leaders and most of the members toward proselyting was ambivalent, and there had been at least one pronouncement by the prophet that proselyting was forbidden. Although this policy was not strictly adhered to, the observers were able to fall back on it as a convenient justification for their inactivity. During the brief time when potential converts were appearing at the prophet's home and asking for information and instruction, the observers managed to stay largely in the background and to observe rather than take part. On the one or two occasions when the observers were specifically asked to talk to an inquirer, they managed either to turn the occasion into an interview with the visitor or else to repeat only information that was already public knowledge and otherwise act in so uninformed a fashion that the inquirer quickly became bored and left the house.

In summary, then, the role that was forced on us as observers prevented us from achieving the unrealistic goal of avoiding *any* influence on conviction and commitment. That we were able to avoid any observer effect on the major dependent variable—proselyting—is of the utmost importance in judging the scientific value of the research, however, and our success here should not be overlooked. But, from our experience, it seems likely that observers cannot avoid exercising *some* influence on behavior and beliefs. The conflict in roles and its attendant consequences seem to be inherent in the process of doing a

study such as this, although it may be possible to devise better ways of handling the conflict and of further reducing observer effect. Such inventions would
indeed be welcome.

The conclusion, then, of most commentators on the role of complete participant,
i.e., covert observer, is that for the vast majority of studies the observer is well-advised
to structure his role in such a way as to include explicitly the concept of researcher.
As mentioned previously, however, the subjects of a study are often totally unfamiliar
with the research role, even if they have been led to accept the observer *qua* observer
through his adoption of more ordinary ancillary roles, through presentation of legitimate auspices, and through strategic choice of sponsorship. Therefore, the observer
must teach the subjects what the role of "researcher" is.

The observer must acquaint them with (1) the sorts of activities that this role involves (e.g., asking questions, reading old documents, looking over shoulders), with
(2) the sorts of information that fall within the legitimate purview of his study, with
(3) the uses to which this information will be put, and with (4) the manner in which he
would like the subjects to aid him in his pursuits (e.g., to relate *specific* facts to him
rather than vague generalizations and impressions, to guide him to pertinent sources,
and to correct him when his assumptions and conclusions seem to be in error). In
short, he must teach the subjects the norms governing the ideal role relationships between observer and subjects.[8]

As sociologists have become increasingly aware in recent years, one of the most
important bonds in any sort of social relationship is the rewards that each party receives from it; if a relationship is not profitable to the participants in some sense, it will
tend to be terminated.[9] It is quite clear what the observer will gain from such relationships, but the implicit problem is what the research subjects will get out of their relationship with the observer—typically it is a quite critical strain which must be effectively
dealt with in the observer's structuring of his role. Some subjects will expect to be
paid for their time and efforts, some will expect the observer to take their part in a local
controversy, or find jobs for them, or get their poems published. Some will expect to
obtain information about their rivals and associates from the observer or to have him
transmit certain information to others. To comply with such expectations in any degree, of course, will ordinarily prejudice and jeopardize the observer's relations with
other subjects. It is critical for the researcher to anticipate and dispel such erroneous
expectations in the very earliest phases of his study so that resentment does not arise
when he necessarily fails to comply with them.[10]

Nevertheless, the participant observer cannot, and should not, exploit his subjects
by unilaterally benefiting from their cooperation with him. He will do well to consider
the sorts of rewards he can afford to provide his subjects—rewards which can be fairly

---

8.   R. Wax (1957); Paul (1953).
9.   Homans (1961); Blau (1964); Thibaut and Kelley (1959); McCall and Simmons (1966).
10.   Dalton (1964); Vidich and Bensman (1954); Paul (1953).

distributed, yet are of sufficient value to compensate them in some sense for their time and trouble.[11]

Rosalie Wax (1952) suggests that a researcher who knows he is giving something in return finds it easier to maintain his own respect for himself and for his scientific endeavors. For example, subjects may divulge information out of loneliness, situational boredom, curiosity about the researcher, aggression toward third parties, or desire to play the ego-enhancing role of an authority or teacher. Leaders or aspiring leaders are often quite cooperative because they are vain, need converts or sympathizers, or cannot resist the opportunity to have their public-spirited activities recorded by a sympath   ¬bserver. Gusfield (1955) extends the latter motive to ordinary members of organizations. They are anxious to communicate a favorable image of the organization to the researcher who is, to them, an important member of the organization's public. Gusfield also points to the status-conferring function of being singled out for study and to the rewarding experience of conversing with an informed, understanding outsider.

(On the other hand, if the researcher fails to respond favorably to the public relations interests of leaders or organization members, he may jeopardize the basis for cooperation of these subjects. In any case, an awareness of what rewards the subject is receiving from the researcher will improve the latter's evaluation of his data. Even the subject who cooperates out of loneliness is somewhat suspect, as his loneliness indicates that he probably has few friends in his own social context and may therefore be atypical or poorly informed.)

Nonetheless, close attention to the problem of rewards (especially of the social psychological variety)[12] and of justice in their distribution greatly facilitates the establishment of that trust and rapport typically to be desired between the researcher and his subjects.[13]

This cultivation of a viable and fruitful relationship with a subject does not typically develop in a smooth and deliberate fashion, however. In most participant observation studies, the establishment of field relations is complicated by the complex network of communication among the subjects. Most subjects will have gleaned some information and opinions about the study and the observer before they actually come in contact with him. It is this fact that makes the initial approach to the social organization— the announcement of auspices and sponsorship, the choice of role, and the selection of the initial subjects—so critical to the eventual establishment of workable field relations.

If this initial approach is propitious, the communications among subjects may actually *ease* the researcher's task in setting up relations with them, as they are already aware of the study and are favorably disposed toward it. If, on the other hand, the initial approach is bungled or ill-chosen, the researcher may encounter resistance

---

11. R. Wax (1952); Gusfield (1955); Cannell and Axelrod (1956); Caplow (1956); Blum (1952); Richardson, Dohrenwend, and Klein (1965).

12. McCall and Simmons (1966).

13. At times, however, such trust and rapport have been overemphasized in the literature and may constitute something of a hazard to meaningful research. The observer must always somewhat mistrust the statements of the subjects, holding them up for careful scrutiny as to motives, credibility, etc. The necessity for this, as well as certain relevant tactics, will be taken up in Chapters 4 and 6. See also Miller (1952); Becker (1954, 1956); Rose (1945); J. P. Dean (1954).

and prejudice from the majority of subjects when he attempts to initiate relations with them.[14]

Perhaps the most pernicious feature which may characterize such a communication network is its malfunctioning—discontinuities in the network imposed by the existence of sharply defined factions or strata.[15] In such cases early contact with or favorable reception by one of the factions may cause the others to identify the observer with the interests and viewpoint of that faction. The same phenomenon may result from failure to obtain some kind of sponsorship from both the formal and the informal leaders of the social organization; if gatekeepers are circumvented they will ordinarily strive to undercut the study, at the very least until they have forced the researcher to approach them and seek their approval.

DEVELOPING RESEARCH PARTNERSHIPS

ROBERT KAHN AND FLOYD MANN

The academic stereotype places the professor in the library for research purposes, or if his field of endeavor requires it, in a laboratory populated either by white mice or sophomores. In recent years a good deal has been done to change this stereotype. Increasing numbers of social scientists have come to see the importance of studying functioning organizations. Many of the more complex problems which social scientists are presently tackling yield themselves only imperfectly to laboratory treatment. As a result, it is sometimes safer to generalize from studies of real life situations than from the laboratory, other things being equal.

If we grant the importance of doing social research in functioning organizations, we immediately face the problem of how such studies are to be conducted. How can the scientist get access to functioning organizations in the first place, and how can he so conduct himself that it is possible for him to maintain access to these organizational laboratories, acquiring the information that he needs? Problems of this kind clearly have put new demands on social scientists. They have made it necessary for social scientists to modify their usual methods and to begin developing new methodologies. Social researchers can get into organizations and stay in organizations only to the extent to which they can learn how to integrate and coordinate the needs of the research group and the needs of the collaborating organization.

Relatively little has been written on this complicated problem of establishing collaborative relationships with subjects in the field research sites which

---

14. Richardson, Dohrenwend, and Klein (1965), pp. 74–82.

15. Kahn and Mann (1952); Merton (1947); Gullahorn and Strauss (1954); Dalton (1964).

Reprinted from *Journal of Social Issues* (1952), **8,** No. 3, 4–10, by permission of the authors and publisher.

the social scientist wishes to study.[1] Anthropologists have had the longest experience of this kind but their experiences for the most part are based on societies greatly different from our own, infinitely less complex, and typically characterized by a single authority structure. For these reasons it is usually possible for the anthropologist to rely heavily upon the sponsorship of the tribal chief, head of the kinship system, or some "key person." Some insights into the problem have also been provided by the experiences of participant observers. But for the most part the description of these experiences serves to convince us only that the technique of participant observation is more an art than a systematic, codified methodology. Even the most successful participant observers have seldom tried to reduce their techniques to a specific set of methodological practices.

There is a real need, therefore, for the development of a specific methodology of doing social science research in functioning organizations of various kinds. This means the development of new concepts, the evaluation and measurement of various practices in present use, and the development of some theory or at least theoretical rationale which will permit scientists to understand and build upon their own best practices. A beginning can best be made by spelling out some of the important requirements which the researcher must meet when working in organizations, and then relating such requirements to some of the basic characteristics of large scale organizations. In this article we will attempt to describe four concepts which in our own experience have assumed increasing importance as part of our research methodology. These are: (1) dual or multiple entry, (2) contingent acceptance at successive organizational levels, (3) double liaison, and (4) double access.

DUAL OR MULTIPLE ENTRY

The term dual or multiple entry emphasizes the necessity for the researcher to gain access to a research site by two or more paths simultaneously. The need for this procedure reflects the complexities of formal organizations. Such organizations frequently have within them several overlapping hierarchies of authority, or are characterized by cliques or factions. In extreme cases an organization may be completely polarized into conflict groups. In all these situations, the researcher faces the same problem in varying degree: how to obtain the cooperation of all groups, not to by-pass or slight the leadership of any group, or become identified with any one group. The researcher can gain access to the organization only if he is successful in getting internal sponsor-

---

1.   For a discussion of the ways in which the interaction of research requirements and client demands determines the relationship between a research group and various ongoing organizations, see: Jacobson, E., Kahn, R. L., Mann, F. C., and Morse, N. C., "Research in Functioning Organizations," *Journal of Social Issues*, 1951, **7** (No. 3), 64–71. Also see Bakke, E. Wight, *Bonds of Organization.* New York: Harper and Brothers, 1950.

ship; that is, if he is introduced into the organization with the cooperation of people who have membership status in it. At the same time, if a factional or conflict situation exists in the organization, the researcher faces the problem that exclusive sponsorship by one group will handicap him severely in dealing with the others.

The extreme case, of course, is one in which two groups within an organization are in such conflict that sponsorship by one automatically means condemnation by the other and consequent veto of the research project even before it gets a hearing. The solution to this sort of problem is for the researcher to take the time and trouble, and considerable of both may be required, to get himself introduced into the organization simultaneously by representatives of both authority structures or factions. It is essential that this not be carried out as a piece of subterfuge. The researcher must be introduced into the organization by a key person in Faction A and Faction B at about the same time. All of the cards must be laid on the table; Faction A must be aware of the fact that the researcher is talking with members of Faction B, and *vice versa*. Proposed research emphases, financial bases of support, and other relevant matters are discussed openly.

The procedure we are describing here is quite general; it holds in every circumstance where cliques, factions, or multiple authority structures characterize the organizations to be studied, or where the organization to be studied has a close interdependent relationship with some other organizational structure. Merton first called attention to this problem and suggested the term "dual entry" in his study of a planned community having two hierarchies of authority.[2] Festinger and his colleagues encountered similar problems in a study where they attempted to change the level of citizen participation in a housing project.[3] Other situations in which the technique of dual entry or multiple entry has been found essential are as follows:

1. The study of business or industrial organizations in which a labor union has the status of recognized bargaining agent, or the power which usually is associated with that status. In such situations it is absolutely essential, almost regardless of the subject matter of the study, for the researcher to come into the situation with union sponsorship as well as management sponsorship. In our own experience this is sufficiently important for us to make it a precondition for any industrial research.

2. The study of political parties or voluntary organizations in which there is rivalry between a well-defined new leadership and an older group of leaders.

3. The study of an individual plant which is a part of a large "decentralized" corporation.

2.   Merton, R. K., "Selected Problems of Field Work in the Planned Community." *American Sociological Review*, 1947, **12**, 304–312.

3.   Festinger, L., et al. "A Study of Rumor: Its Origin and Spread," *Human Relations*, 1948, **1**, 464–486.

CONTINGENT ACCEPTANCE AT SUCCESSIVE ORGANIZATIONAL LEVELS

Multiple entry is a way of taking into account certain organizational complexities—particularly the overlapping vertical authority structures of some organizations. Another characteristic of large scale organizations is that they are hierarchically organized. The researcher thus must be concerned not only with the relationship between two such vertical structures as a business organization and its complementing labor union, but must take account of the successive hierarchical levels and their interrelations. The procedure we will present here recognizes the "multiple-layeredness" of organizations and the demands which this characteristic makes on the researcher.

In many hierarchical organizations each echelon typically attempts to please the higher echelons, especially the one immediately superior. At the same time each is often in conflict with these higher orders of authority in that it attempts to maintain as much independent authority as possible. The traditional procedure for the introduction of any innovation is one in which the higher echelons order the new item or procedure for those in the lower parts of the organization. Any communication from the top of the authority structure has overtones of command for those at lower levels, and is responded to accordingly. Since the researcher requires spontaneity and cooperation rather than docility and obedience, it is not enough for him to use the ready-made authority structure, and to try to gain acceptance with those at lower levels by having those at the top of the organization communicate the purpose of the study to the rest of the structure. Even when supervisors only "suggest" that subordinates might be interested in a particular research project, the suggestions tend to be responded to as orders, whether obeyed or resisted. If the researcher is hopeful of getting real acceptance of his project, and eventually obtaining information on how people within the organization actually feel and think, it is necessary for him to be very careful how he relates to the authority structure. This does not mean that he will slight the authority structure to gain acceptance of those at lower levels. While it is seldom possible to do research in an organization without gaining acceptance of the top levels of the authority, status, and prestige structures, it is seldom possible to gain real acceptance on the part of subordinates by having the research team ordered in by the top control figures.

It would be difficult, however, to enter into discussions about the study simultaneously with representatives of all echelons. Moreover, such a procedure would probably be perceived as an affront to those in upper authority levels. The procedure which we have found most workable is one in which a series of contingent acceptance decisions are arrived at by the researcher and the several echelons within the organization. The researcher asks the head of the organization only that he himself agree to the project and that he agree to have the question put before the next level in the organization. When the researcher has gained acceptance from the people at that level, he asks only that they allow him to talk with their subordinates, and so on. It is implicit in this method that a higher level within the authority structure will not veto the study if the researcher can gain the acceptance of those at successively lower levels. Under this procedure the researcher refuses to take any of the power of the hierarchical structure down which he is moving to gain acceptance at successively lower levels. The procedure demonstrates concretely, for those with whom the researcher hopes to do research, that his relationship with them will differ from that which exists between themselves and higher authority figures.

What are the disadvantages of this procedure? First, the research project may be rejected by any single level or group in the organization. Secondly, while agreement within any echelon is a necessary condition, it is not a sufficient condition for the researcher to go ahead. The prize that the researcher is attempting to gain through this tedious procedure is independent acceptance by all relevant groups, and the initiation of relationships without intimidation or prejudice. The gains from the procedure include: (1) more valid and extensive information from respondents, and (2) a greater likelihood that research findings may be used subsequently for change within the organization. The researcher who is seen as being wholly dependent upon the authority structure of the organization for the initiation of a study is in a very poor position to attempt experimental research. His dependence on and utilization of the authority structure will have cost him the "neutrality" which he requires.

An example of the procedure of contingent acceptance is provided by the following case, in which a field experimental design was set up to evaluate the effectiveness of a training program for foremen. A research committee was established first to develop the major dimensions of the project and to facilitate the collection of the necessary information. The members of this committee included staff men from the training division of the personnel department, a consulting psychologist who was in charge of the training, and members of the Survey Research Center. The superintendent of one of the departments in which the study might be made was also asked to meet with the group to consider the feasibility of evaluating the training program which he already had experienced and which his first-line foremen were soon to take.

The superintendent showed great interest in the study designs and the different types of measurements under consideration, but was extremely cautious about participating in any experiment which might upset the equilibrium of his department. He finally agreed to participate if his division heads were informed of the study, and given an opportunity to decide whether or not to participate in it. The proposed study was then discussed thoroughly with the business manager of the union whose members might be involved, and a tentative agreement to proceed was reached with him.

The project and its experimental design were next presented to the division heads and their general foremen by the superintendent, members of the central personnel department of the company, the psychologist who was conducting the training program, and representatives of the Survey Research Center. The line officials agreed to participate but only under the same conditions that their superintendent had set forth earlier. They wanted the foremen in their respective divisions to be given the same information concerning the project that they had received and also be given the same freedom to refuse to participate. In a subsequent series of meetings the proposed study was presented to all the first-line foremen. Again the voluntary nature of the program was stressed. The study was accepted after thorough discussions of the relative advantages and disadvantages of participating in the experiment.

DOUBLE LIAISON

The concept of double liaison suggests that in order to develop a maximally effective research relationship, it is necessary for both the subject organization and the research group to find and to develop specialized liaison personnel. It is not the function of the representatives of the subject organization to provide all the translating facilities to make the researcher and his work understandable to the organization in which the research is being done. Nor is it the responsibility of the research group to make the entire adjustment that is required to render research findings intelligible to the most "hard-headed" member of the line organization.

What in fact seems to have come about in the most successful research relationships is that a kind of double liaison has formed. This bridge is composed of some members of the research organization who are particularly good in thinking through and searching out the implementation value of the research, and stating the research findings in terms intelligible to "operating" personnel. It is also composed of a similar group which develops out of the members of the subject organization who are particularly interested in research and who have experience or education which permits them to play this role.

One of the implications of this arrangement is that the people playing the liaison role are to some extent deviant in their home organizations. They might be thought of as marginal to both structures. It is this very deviancy, of course, which enables them to get into such successful communication with each other. What is required for maximum efficiency on their part is that they maintain that nice balance which makes them sufficiently deviant to play the liaison role while remaining acceptable members of their own organizations.

DOUBLE ACCESS

This term refers to the procedure of getting access to the top of the subject organization both through internal and external channels. External access to the top is achieved directly by the researcher. Internal access to the top comes indirectly via the internal structure of the subject organization. Our present thinking suggests that it is necessary for the researcher to have access to the top of the organization by means of both routes. It is occasionally essential for the researcher to be able to go directly to the top in order to communicate certain kinds of information or to achieve action on particular kinds of decisions. It is not, however, sufficient for the researcher's access to the top of the organization to depend upon this direct means. The individual who occupies the top position in an organization usually will be unable to devote a large part of his time and effort to the research and related activities. Moreover, the researcher seldom can live in the organization on a day-to-day basis or be constantly available for communication with the top individuals in the subject organization. The researcher therefore needs to have a direct working relationship with one or more individuals who are not at the top of the organization but who may be several echelons down in any one of a variety of specialized positions. Individuals in this situation then become the "maintainers" of the research relationship. They are in frequent communication with the researcher and have continuing access to the top of the organization via some internal channel of communication. An additional advantage of such an arrangement is that the person at the top of the organization receives communications and information regarding the research from two sources: directly from the researcher, and indirectly through the line organization on which he regularly depends for a large part of his intelligence.

There is, of course, a good deal of variation possible in any given situation in the extent to which the researcher depends upon his own direct access to the top of the organization and the extent to which he depends upon major liaison through some lower point in the organizational structure.

The four concepts described in this article do not constitute anything like a complete codification of this phase of research methodology. These ideas may, however, serve to accelerate the process of working out systematically the important elements in the procedures which social scientists use in developing research partnerships with off-campus organizations. Moreover, they suggest the kinds of skills in which social researchers will need to be trained, and something of the specialization of roles needed within research teams.

This problem of factionalism is a continuing one that must be reckoned with throughout a study. Factions and leaders who initially support or at least go along with a study may, without warning or explanation, turn sour on it when it fails to provide the benefits or take the directions they may have anticipated, when the researcher begins to associate with other persons or to probe new areas, or when changed conditions in the larger context make their own position less secure.[16]

Field relations, then, are not something one simply establishes at the beginning of a study and relies on thereafter. Human relationships are always in flux and must be modified to be maintained. The subjects' impressions of and feelings toward the researcher change as they come to know him more fully, as their own external situations change, as he engages in more and different activities with more and different people,

16. Dalton (1964); Vidich and Bensman (1954); R. Wax (1957); Gullahorn and Strauss (1954).

and as his own views of them (often expressed subconsciously) change. Rumors and impressions arise and circulate through the communication network, leading the subjects to alter the sorts of information and cooperation they are ready to tender the observer. Obviously, the observer must continually deal with these rumors and impressions, modifying the role which he presents and the relationships which he has established with the subjects.[17] Fortunately, the course of these changing role relationships seems to exhibit some order, as, for example, that observed by Robert Janes in the context of community studies.

A NOTE ON PHASES OF THE
COMMUNITY ROLE OF THE PARTICIPANT-OBSERVER

ROBERT W. JANES

A persistent question in community field research is: how does the community role of the investigator affect statements made by local respondents? This issue is of particular interest to field-workers who use participant-observation, since formalization of this research technique has not been pursued to the level of refinement achieved for the interview.[1] Participant-observation differs from the interview in that the subject observed is not aware that the investigator is using his behavior as a source of information. In the interview the respondent consciously adjusts to the stimuli offered by the interviewer as a

---

17. *Ibid.*

Reprinted from *American Sociological Review* (1961), **26,** 446–450, by permission of the author and publisher. The research for this report was supported in part by a grant from the University Research Board of the University of Illinois. The writer is indebted to his colleague, Edward H. Winter, for critical suggestions and comments on the manuscript.

1.   *Cf.* Benjamin Paul, "Interview Techniques and Field Relationships," A. L. Kroeber *et al.*, editors, *Anthropology Today: An Encyclopedic Inventory,* Chicago: University of Chicago Press, 1953, pp. 430–451; Florence Kluckhohn, "The Participant-Observer Technique in Small Communities," *American Journal of Sociology,* 46 (November, 1940), pp. 331–343; Arthur J. Vidich, "Participant Observation and the Collection and Interpretation of Data," *American Journal of Sociology,* 60 (January, 1955), pp. 354–360; Morris S. Schwartz and C. G. Schwartz, "Problems in Participant Observation," *American Journal of Sociology,* 60 (January, 1955), pp. 343–353; J. Gullahorn and G. Strauss, "The Field Worker in Union Research," *Human Organization,* 13 (Fall, 1954), pp. 28–34; S. Richardson, "A Framework for Reporting Field Relations Experiences," *Human Organization,* 12 (Fall, 1953), pp. 31–37; S. M. Miller, "The Participant Observer and 'Over-Rapport'," *American Sociological Review,* 17 (February, 1952), pp. 97–99; Howard S. Becker, "Inference and Proof in Participant Observation," *American Sociological Review,* 23 (December, 1958), pp. 652–660; M. A. Sullivan, Jr., S. A. Queen, and R. C. Patrick, Jr., "Participant Observation in a Military Program," *American Sociological Review,* 23 (December, 1958), pp. 660–667; Robert L. Kahn and C. F. Cannell, *The Dynamics of Interviewing,* New York: John Wiley and Sons, 1957; Herbert H. Hyman *et al., Interviewing in Social Research,* Chicago: University of Chicago Press, 1954; David Riesman and M. Benney, "The Interview in Social Research," *American Journal of Sociology,* 62 (September, 1956), pp. 137–217; Neal Gross and W. S. Mason, "Some Methodological Problems of Eight-Hour Interviews," *American Journal of Sociology,* 59 (November, 1953), pp. 197–204; Robert K. Merton and P. L. Kendall, "The Focused Interview," *American Journal of Sociology,* 51 (May, 1946), pp. 541–557.

person known to be seeking information in his occupational role. In participant-observation respondents adjust to the community role of the investigator
unaware of the fact that their behavior is being treated as information.

From the viewpoint of the would-be practitioner of participant-observation,
it would be useful to be able to predict stages in the investigator's community
role and the kind of unsolicited information which is acquired by participant-
observation in each phase. This approach to community investigation postu-
lates that the aim of the community participant-observer is planned social
mobility directed toward achieving *rapport* with his respondents. *Rapport*
can be seen as a level of social interaction where an investigator is securing a
maximum of useful information with a minimum of effort on his part. Understanding of the conditions which enter into achievement of *rapport* offers a
reference point for formalizing or standardizing the technique of participant-
observation. The present note is based on one case describing changes in the
community role of a field-worker that conditioned information gained through
participant-observation in a small American community.

THE FIELD SITUATION

The field situation for this case is a small mid-Western town located in the
lower Ohio Valley. The community is a farm-service center, approximately
two thousand people in size, and it is one of the oldest settlements in the region. The author, his wife, and year-old son lived in Riverville (a pseudonym)
for a period of eight months. The research interests were description and analysis of the increase in urbanization of small town life and study of the community capacity to meet the challenge of a declining regional economy. The
principal research techniques were interview, participant-observation, and
documentary analysis.

The author had made a series of visits to Riverville and the adjacent
counties about fifteen years earlier to observe the impact of a disastrous flood
on community activity. Most of the informants from that time, however, had
either moved away or were deceased. The community as a whole treated him
and his wife as a newcomer family as they went about the tasks of new arrivals
—renting a house, opening a charge account at a grocery, renting a post-office
box, etc. Presence as newcomers was formally recognized when three Protes-
tant ministers called separately to welcome the family and to invite its attendance at church.

Field work was begun by visiting town, county and school officials, and the
newspaper editor to explain the purpose of the study and to ask their cooperation. Courthouse and school records and newspaper files were checked and
interviews begun with officials and leading citizens. In time social interaction
was initiated by attending church, joining a veterans' organization, returning
visits of neighbors, and, later, spending social evenings with the families of
several of the younger business men of the community. The pattern of initial
interaction of other newcomers with the community was later checked through

informal conversations, and it appeared that the author's family underwent the typical experience of families whose class background was defined by local standards as upper middle class. This record of reaction by the community to the author and his family provided the data for establishing the phases of the community role accorded to the investigator.

The assumption under which the author began his study of Riverville was that his class position as it was defined by local people would constitute the role which would influence respondent behavior in participant-observation situations. This assumption was based on the findings of Schatzman and Strauss relative to the influence of class on interaction in interviewing.[2] River-ville possessed a four-class system, three grades of whites and the Negro population. It was assumed then that information gathered by participant-observation would show differences in content reflecting the disparity between the author's imputed class position and the class level of respondents. It was also assumed that the length of time required to achieve *rapport* with individuals would vary directly with the disparity in class position of the author and re-spondent.

After the field work was completed and an analysis of the field notes was begun the original assumptions appeared questionable. There was evidence of having achieved *rapport* with individuals and families, but the results did not confirm the assumption that the disparity in class position between the author and respondent was the major variable that affected the content of data secured by participant-observation. Rather, it appeared that it was the stage of the com-munity role of the investigator that determined the behavior of townspeople in participant-observer situations and not simply his imputed class position.

To test this new assumption the whole field record was reviewed and the following conclusions developed. The community role of the author and his family apparently underwent a progressive redefinition in the course of their residence. The steps in this redefinition consisted of five phases: (1) newcomer (2) provisional member (3) categorical member (4) personalized member (*rapport*) and (5) imminent migrant. In each phase participant-observation tended to yield data which were specific to that phase. There were a number of cases in which the content of such observation was not of the same nature as other data secured during the same phase. An explanation of these exceptions will be suggested later in the discussion of "social circles" as the local units that actually defined community roles.

INFORMATION SECURED IN DIFFERENT PHASES OF COMMUNITY ROLE

Typical participant-observer situations in Riverville included any gathering of one or more local persons and the author or his wife where his or her pres-ence was given some recognition. Examples were: waiting for the mail at the

---

2.   Leonard Schatzman and A. Strauss, "Social Class and Modes of Communication," *American Journal of Sociology,* 60 (January, 1955), pp. 329–338.

post office, conversation between the halves of a basketball game, standing around in a store on Saturday night, sitting at a bar, attending an American Legion dance, visiting a home for an evening, waiting in a barber-shop, etc. Such events were repeated in their essential form throughout the eight months. Since the actual conditions of the gatherings did not change materially, it appeared reasonable to assume that differences in the information-content of behavior occurring or statements made in the presence of the field-workers at the gatherings reflected their changing community role.

The newcomer phase was relatively short, and in public situations consisted of townspeople questioning the author about what he did and where he was from or confirming through conversation what they had already heard about him. There was much spontaneous offering of general orienting information about Riverville; several well-known popular stories about the history of the town were related repeatedly and comments were made on the weather, the stage of the river and vagaries of the local seasons. This phase was a period of looking over the newcomers to see how they would respond to the community, and ended when they began to participate in the local social structure by going to church and by practicing "neighboring."

The provisional phase was a testing out, in the eyes of the community, of how the author's family met the requirements for being accepted somewhere in the community structure. In participant-observer situations queries addressed to the investigators took new forms. They were asked if they belonged to organizations such as the Masons and Eastern Star. The author was asked if he were a member of a veterans' group and was invited to join the American Legion. Questioning about his occupational interest in the community became more specific: "Just exactly what do you do?" There were a number of questions on recreational interest. There was a constant thread of sensitivity to any reaction to Riverville itself. "How do you like it here?" was reiterated. Information about the community that was volunteered without any probes by the field-workers included characterization of local persons, descriptions of issues which faced the community but without any of the invidious intimations of later statements. The activity of the field-workers that appeared important in evaluation by local people was joining the Legion, going to church regularly, attending the meetings of the men's and women's groups associated with the church, going to service club dinners and appearing at public events like basketball games, community bingo, and Legion dances. This associational interest apparently satisfied the demands for being accepted for fuller membership into the local structure, and the end of this phase was signalized when the author's wife was invited as the weekly guest of the women's bridge club.

The next phase, called categorical acceptance, was a period of several months during which Rivervillers came to the conclusion that the occupational interest of the author, the study of the local community and region, was both legitimate and perhaps potentially useful within the community division of labor. During this period unsolicited comments in participant-observer situations presented "the inside story" on local issues and conflicts, suggestions about the community power structure, and showed curiosity about what other persons had told the investigator. There were a number of strong probes interrogating the author on what he was "really finding out."

The field data indicate that for a number of weeks the author was being "sized up" as to his "job." Local people had observed that his occupational behavior consisted of interviewing, discussion, consulting courthouse records, searching for historical sources, and the like. Yet, they did not seem sure how this occupational activity fitted into their conception of the proper work role of an adult male residing in the community. This suspicion was shown in a prevalent local attitude which might be termed "the FBI complex." This view of the author was revealed only in later phases, and its basis was a local sense that a man who lived by asking questions of Rivervillers and studying official records was an agent of investigation for some government agency.

This attitude was supported by another local belief complex that Riverville was so unimportant within the perspective of the larger national society that any kind of investigative interest in the community could be only directed toward unfolding evidence of wrong-doing by local persons. What is more, it also appeared that there was an actual desire by some people that evidence of illegal behavior by local leaders somehow be uncovered. This wish developed from factional tensions within the community that were expressed in a belief, or local myth, that the town was "controlled by insiders" for their own quasi-legal interest. It was against this background that the occupational behavior of the investigator was evaluated.

The particular event that appeared finally to "trigger" the author's acceptance was an after-dinner address he gave before a local service club. The topic was social and economic trends of the region, and his remarks seemed to make evident to Rivervillers, for the first time, that his job in their community was a genuine investigation that might conceivably be of value to them. The talk was reported in the newspaper and a repeat performance before a larger audience was given several weeks later.

Within a few weeks after the second address, the author and family had moved into the fourth phase of personalized acceptance. Only then was there a continuing sense of *rapport* with respondents in participant-observation situations. The rate of informal social interaction with Rivervillers increased as the author and his wife were invited more frequently for dinners, parties, drives, and card-playing. The content of conversation at these events changed from volunteered remarks which oriented the field-workers to the community and turned toward expressions of personal experiences and problems. There were few references to or queries about what the author was learning about the community, and often he was treated as if he were fully knowledgeable about local issues and persons. Only in this phase were there any expressions of animus toward the author. The degree of acceptance was signalized by the vigorous personal campaign of the wife of a local minister to convert the author's wife to a different religious persuasion.

The final phase, imminent migrant, was initiated by an allusion to an expected date of departure from Riverville. Very quickly, literally overnight, townspeople began a new line of interaction. References to and questions about the research findings were made. These remarks occasionally contained a tone of anxiety about what kind of an impression the author held about the town, and a number of persons appeared hopeful of keeping contact with him and his wife after he had left town. Several parties and dinners in honor of the couple were held, but there was not a strong valedictory emphasis to these occasions. Rather, their conduct and tone were apparently intended to encourage the author to think well of the hosts. During this period no new information was informally volunteered. Instead, conversations accentuated a review of the experiences of the author during his residence.

"SOCIAL CIRCLES" AS PHASE–DEFINING AGENTS

The local social unit that was the actual agent of the redefinition of the various phases noted above was defined as "the social circle." This term, following Znaniecki's usage,[3] appears meaningful in describing social interaction in a small community. The social circles of Riverville were informal communication networks made up of cliques, households, and individuals who exchanged information on matters involving the community. Their membership cut across associational ties such as church or political affiliation, but tended to fall within the limits of "class" as the community itself defined it. Circles contained from a dozen to two-dozen families, households, and individuals linked by a variety of bonds including residential propinquity, kinship, long acquaintance, and a record of common participation in conflict issues in the community. Redefinition of the phases of community role of newcomers proceeded at a differential pace between social circles, since it was dependent upon personal contact of some member or members of the circle with the newcomer. Information about the newcomer was then transmitted to the rest of the circle. The circle appeared in Riverville to be the social unit that evaluated the behavior and attributes of the field-worker against local standards and expectation, and in this fashion served to redefine the phases of his community role.

Since the rate and timing of contact by the field-worker varied with social circles, there would be a "lead" and "lag" in the definition of his role in the total community. Certain information about him, for example, newspaper reports of his arrival and certain of his activities, might have general community dissemination and become part of the information fund of the social circles, but apparently it was verbal exchange and comment within circle membership, stimulated by personal contact, that was conclusive in phase

3.   Florian Znaniecki, *Social Role of the Man of Knowledge,* New York: Columbia University Press, 1940.

redefinition. The ultimate implication of this observation is that the meaning of data collected by participant-observation reflects the phase definition of the field-worker current in the social circle of which the respondent is a part.

THE ETHICAL ISSUE

If the strategy of participant-observation calls for achieving access to and acceptance by "social circles" for the purpose of encouraging unwitting revelation of information by their members, does this practice constitute a violation of prevailing ethical principles of our society? Anthropologists, according to Paul, are generally willing in their study of other cultures to regard participant-observation as ethically legitimate.[4] In investigations in our own society the matter is still controversial, as indicated by the recent exchange between Coser and Roth and Queen and Mortimer regarding the purposes to which this technique can properly be put.[5] The present note suggests certain criteria for judging when the practice of participant-observation is ethically acceptable. If a social group under observation has a newcomer's role which permits the practice of participant-observation, and if the long-run functioning of the group is not disrupted by the unsuspected observation made by the investigator and his subsequent departure from the group, then there would appear no violation of prevailing ethical norms. This statement assumes, of course, that the investigator's report does not "damage" any respondent or subject, nor does it make it impossible for another investigator to enter this group as a participant-observer at a later date. If all these conditions hold, standards of both the local group and the larger society would appear to be met.

CONCLUSIONS

The evidence from this single case of the use of participant-observation in the study of a small American community suggests tentative conclusions regarding how the community role of the investigator affects the content of information communicated to him by local persons. During his period of residence his community role undergoes a successive redefinition. This redefinition includes five phases: newcomer, provisional acceptance, categorical acceptance, personal acceptance, and imminent migrant. In each phase the content of interpersonal communication to the investigator in participant-observer situations is specific for that phase. *Rapport* with respondents is characteristic of the fourth phase, personal acceptance. The agents of phase redefinition are social circles, loosely structured informal communication networks. From these findings it is concluded that much of the meaning of

4.   Paul, *op. cit.,* p. 434.
5.   "Communications," *American Sociological Review,* 24 (June, 1959), pp. 397–400.

items of information secured by participant-observation rests in the community role phase between the field-worker and local persons with whom he is interacting.

As the above selection suggests, not all problems of field relations are caused by the subjects. The observer may find participant observation, with its lack of structure, the many uncertainties intrinsic to its design, and the strains of maintaining complex and multitudinous relations with subjects, a quite stressful experience, particularly if he must live among his subjects around the clock.[18]

Physical and mental fatigue are frequent problems. The observer often must gather data for a full day and then spend several hours of the night making notes and taking stock. The sheer paperwork involved in keeping track of and sorting through huge volumes of data can be considerable. The observer is constantly on the go, traveling widely, interacting with a great many people of many varieties. If the role he has chosen is not altogether suited to his personal characteristics, the strain of keeping up a good performance may sap his energies.

Frustrations may accumulate rapidly. The magnitude of the task—attempting to assimilate large quantities of unfamiliar data and attempting to penetrate these to discover meaningful descriptions and propositions—bars the observer from making rapid (or sometimes even perceptible) progress. Moreover, to maintain good field relations he may have to suppress his own habits, his feelings toward subjects, and his own feelings about events he witnesses. Typically, the crowning frustration is the refractory and undependable character of his field relations.

Often, when the observer has been in the field too long and has been swamped by data, he may feel either that he no longer understands what is going on or that nothing significant is happening. He has become so immersed in the data that he has lost his direction and must get away for a time to recover his perspective on the problem.

These are all problems of the weary, veteran observer. The beginner may also experience certain personal difficulties unique to the early stages of his career in participant observation.[19] Some beginners feel guilty about inquiring into others' affairs; some feel forward and embarrassed to ask strangers about somewhat personal matters; some feel they lack the social skills necessary to enter into the life of a social organization for which they are not particularly qualified.

Certainly the problems of establishing and maintaining good field relations in participant observation are manifold and complex. A convenient checklist and some useful tactics are provided by Richardson (1953, 1960). He lists the major problems to be solved in field relations as the determination of the following:

1) The types of knowledge about the organization that should be obtained before entering the field;

2) The sources from which information about the organization may be obtained;

3) The preparation for and entry into the field;

---

18. Whyte (1955); Junker (1960); Bain (1950); Paul (1953).

19. Junker (1960), pp. 105–157.

4) The initial field research activities;

5) The structuring of the field worker's role;

6) The sequence and timing of field activities;

7) The incentives to be offered to the subjects;

8) The process of selecting sponsors and subjects;

9) Ways of dealing with rumors encountered while in the field concerning the field workers and the research project;

10) How to report research progress and findings to persons in the organization being studied;

11) The ethical problems involved in field research;

12) The human relations within the research team and the emotional costs of

CHAPTER THREE

DATA
COLLECTION,
RECORDING,
AND
RETRIEVAL

In participant observation studies, it will be recalled, data collection is not a distinct *phase* in the research process but rather is one analytically distinguishable *aspect* of a multiplex process. Design, analysis, and write-ups are also being carried out simultaneously with data collection, and all four aspects continually influence and impinge upon one another. In each of the next four chapters, however, we shall look closely at one of these aspects at a time, always bearing in mind that isolation of these four aspects is an artificial simplification.

In the present chapter we will be considering the techniques and tactics by which data are selected and obtained; how such complicated qualitative data are recorded in the field; and how pertinent data are subsequently retrieved from the accumulated masses of field notes.

Once an organization or situation has been selected as the subject of a participant observation study and initial steps have been taken toward gaining *entree* to it, the researcher will find himself developing a suitable and comfortable blend of the research techniques at his disposal. One study may emphasize direct observation, another may stress informant interviewing, while yet another leans most heavily upon respondent interviewing, and so on. But in virtually every case all five of the techniques enumerated in Chapter 1 will be employed in some varying proportion. The relative role which each plays in a given study depends not only on the personal preferences and differential abilities of the researcher but also on the relative prevalence and importance of the types of data for which each is best suited. This topic has been touched on in Chapter 1 (pp. 3–10) but bears elaboration here.

Uses and Limitations of Methods

Direct observation is, of course, the archtypical technique of scientific inquiry in virtually every field.[1] If one seeks to know and understand what exists or what is happening, the commonsense impulse is to go and look at it, closely and repeatedly. Some topics of investigation, however, do not lend themselves to this sort of direct observation by the scientist. Many events, such as lynchings and earthquake disasters, occur so infrequently and unpredictably that waiting for them to happen within the range of the observer is simply not productive. Other events, like love-making and

---

1. For discussions of direct observation in social research, see Whyte (1951); Selltiz, Jahoda, Deutsch, and Cook (1959), pp. 199–234; Heyns and Lippitt (1954); Barker (1963); Goode and Hatt (1952), pp. 119–131, among others.

strategic military decisions, take place in settings from which the observer is pro-hibited.[2]   Still others have taken place in the past, before the observer began his study, or will only occur in the somewhat distant future.   Certain objects and events prove to be so ambiguous, complicated, tentative, or opaque that the observer cannot be certain of the meaning of what he has himself observed.   Under all these circum-stances, other techniques are more profitably employed.[3]

Observation, however, is virtually indispensable in obtaining certain types of data. For example, there are many actions and relationships of which the actors them-selves are simply unaware, particularly in complex social organizations, where each category of persons is typically uninformed about what goes on in other sectors or in the organization as a whole.   Other facts may be vaguely perceived by the actors but they lack the concepts and vocabulary necessary to communicate these facts.[4] Observation is also especially valuable when the actors will not, rather than cannot, communicate facts; deviant acts, for example, are often more readily observed than discussed.[5]   Similarly, where the actors are strongly motivated to distort information (e.g., to justify their own behaviors or to elevate their own status), direct observation may be more useful than interviewing.[6]   Finally, where it is the *absence* of some phe-nomenon that is critical, such an absence should not be inferred from the failure of interviewees to mention the phenomenon, since they may not have observed or re-ported it even though it was indeed present.   Here again direct observation is pref-erable.

Informant interviewing is often the technique chosen to seek information on events that occur infrequently or are not open to direct observation by the scientist for whatever reason.[7]   It is also an economical means of learning the details and meaning of highly institutionalized practices and norms with which the informant is familiar by dint of considerable experience.   In this case, where institutionalization is sufficiently firm that all knowledgable informants contacted by the researcher are in almost complete agreement among themselves, he need interview only a few well-chosen cases rather than the whole population relevant to that pattern.[8]

If one is not seeking information on external events by treating the interviewee as an indirect or "deputized" observer, the interview process takes the form of *respon-dent interviewing,* especially where the information sought concerns the personal feelings, perceptions, motives, habits, or intentions of the interviewee.[9]   Here it is the person rather than the event that is of interest to the researcher.   When persons are thus the focus, it is usually because of *variability* in phenomena rather than institu-tionalized sameness; therefore, one cannot safely interview just a few persons but

2.   Selltiz, Jahoda, Deutsch, and Cook (1959), pp. 199–234.

3.   Richardson, Dohrenwend, and Klein (1965), pp. 7–31.

4.   Strauss and Schatzman (1955).

5.   Richardson, Dohrenwend, and Klein (1965), pp. 11–12.

6.   *Ibid.,* p. 12.

7.   For discussions of informant interviewing, see Richardson, Dohrenwend, and Klein (1965); Mead and Metraux (1953); Osgood (1940).

8.   Zelditch (1962).

9.   For discussions of respondent interviewing, see Kahn and Cannell (1957); Richardson, Dohrenwend, and Klein (1965); Hyman, Cobb, Feldman, Hart, and Stember (1954).

must interview all of them in the particular category or a sample of them from which one can justifiably describe the entire category.[10]

In general, interviewing, of whichever kind, is more flexible than observation, allowing the researcher to circumvent the barriers of time, space, and closed doors. Moreover, interviewing is usually more economical in that any number of topics can be covered in a short span of time, whereas the observer can only wait and watch through many irrelevant events in hopes that those pertinent to his interests will soon transpire.[11] Thus, the observer typically lacks that degree of control over the sequence and timing of his information gathering that the interviewer enjoys. As noted, however, under some circumstances the observer's patience, like that of the tortoise, enables him to attain certain objectives denied the interviewer, with his hare-like pace.

Document analysis is often employed in a fashion similar to interviewing, both the informant and respondent varieties.[12] Certain documents such as journalistic accounts, archives, and official statistics and reports may be used much like informants to establish facts about events which the researcher was unable to observe directly.[13] Often such documents are superior to informants in that official reports and statistics cover sectors of the organization beyond the sphere of a particular informant, are based on regularized procedures often under external audit, are more precise than the informant's memory, and may extend farther into the past than any living informant. Typically, of course, the views conveyed by such documents are partisan or merely official views, but these are often important data in themselves, and in any case, those imparted by informants may be no less partisan or official.

Other documents, such as diaries, letters, and life histories, are sometimes employed to obtain data much like those of respondent interviewing, such as personal characteristics and states.[14]

The chief difficulty with such documentary surrogates for informants and respondents is that they are usually incomplete, unsystematic, and tantalizing but tangential.[15] Unlike live informants and respondents, documents cannot be probed and cajoled in an attempt to overcome these deficiencies. Once again, the degree of control that is possible in the interview is a strong plus factor.

Direct participation, for its own sake, in the events under study can be a very heuristic technique. A number of investigators have thus discovered, through introspection, important phenomena that they would not have turned up through observation or interview but that were subsequently demonstrated by means of these other techniques.[16] It is critical, however, that data obtained from participation be verified by observing or interviewing other relevant actors and not merely be assumed to hold for them. Furthermore, prolonged direct participation entails the risk that the

---

10. Zelditch (1962).

11. Whyte (1953, 1960).

12. Gottschalk, Kluckhohn, and Angell (1945); Allport (1942).

13. Angell and Freedman (1953); Martel and McCall (1964).

14. Thomas and Znaniecki (1927); Dollard (1935).

15. Webb, Campbell, Schwartz, and Sechrest (1966), pp. 53–111; Blumer (1939).

16. Roy (1953); Baldamus (1951); Malinowski (1932); Oeser (1939).

researcher will lose his detached wonder ("go native") and fail to discover certain phenomena that the relatively uninvolved researcher would observe.[17] Also, as discussed in Chapter 2, the degree of participation elected by the researcher has great implications for establishing various sorts of relations with gatekeepers, factions, informants, and respondents.

Given the relative importance of each of the various types of information to a particular study, then, the use of the relevant techniques should ideally be about proportional to their utility in obtaining such information (e.g., if cultural norms are the major type of information desired, then informant interviewing should be the predominant technique, etc.). More realistically, the bounds of the study and of the data are perhaps more often modified in such a way that those techniques at which the researcher is most adept become paramount in the data collection process. From one perspective, it makes little difference whether the data dictate the techniques to be used or whether the choice of techniques dictates the selection of phenomena to be studied. Whichever comes first, it is important that they be well-matched and that the techniques be well-employed.

Whatever the techniques, they must be applied to something concrete if data are to be generated; i.e., phenomena, persons, objects, events, times, and locales must be selected to observe, inquire about, and so on. What are the possible selections and how are they made in participant observation studies?

Sampling

Unlike the procedures in many other types of research, sampling in participant observation studies is not designed and executed in advance of data collection but is continually carried on throughout the study. For example, a sample is drawn, of variables, indicators, informants, respondents, or whatever. The study of these typically gives rise to further ideas or hypotheses on the part of the observer, and these then lead him to draw still further samples of different sorts in order to pursue the emerging ideas. As a consequence, participant observers can seldom *prescribe* their samples in advance but can only *describe* and justify them after the fact.

Nonetheless, there are at least three general types of sampling procedure which the observer can indicate in advance that he may employ. The first of these is some sort of *quota sample,* in which, for example, the observer is aware of certain formal categories of organization members and he determines beforehand that he will interview and observe at least a few persons from each of these categories.[18] Having done so, he will often modify and add to these categories of persons so that he now has a new set of categories from which to sample. This new sample will typically give rise to still further categories of persons and events, and this may occur several more times.

A second type of sampling procedure often employed in participant observation is the *snowball sample,* in which, for example, choosing one informant may generate information about other persons which leads the observer to contact one of these

---

17. Paul (1953).

18. Chein (1959).

others as a second informant, who in turn directs him to a third informant, etc., in an extensive chain of contacts.[19]

A third type, employed when empirical relationships have been hypothesized between categories of persons, events, or variables, is the *search for exceptions* to such relationships.[20] If, for example, advanced medical students are thought to be cynical concerning medical training while first-year students are idealistic, the observer might probe for any remaining idealistic attitudes or persons among the older students and for cynicism among the younger in order to try more strenuously the validity of the hypothesis.

These procedures are not restricted to any particular type of content, nor are they the only sampling procedures that may be employed. Random sampling techniques, for instance, with all their attendant advantages, may sometimes be applicable, particularly in sampling respondents.[21] Generally speaking, however, vagaries of an observer's access to information, field relations, and the reportorial abilities of subjects make it impossible that every element in the sampled population have the same likelihood of contributing to the study. Therefore, the less rational and less defensible sampling procedures, such as those mentioned above, are generally the best available.

Let us now consider *what* is being sampled. The two most important decisions in a participant observation study are determining the specific *organization* or situation to be investigated and the substantive *topic* of research. It appears to us that the organization (the United Nations or the Hooterville Chamber of Commerce) may be chosen before the topic (socialization or power dynamics) about as frequently as the other way around. In these cases, the organization is typically chosen either because one is offered an exceptional opportunity of access to it or because one is fascinated by the organization and is willing to study almost any aspect of it. The reverse sequence—choosing first a topic and then an organization in which to study it—appears more rational on the face of things, but the history of the sciences reveals that each sequence in comparable degree has generated useful theory and data.

These sequences do present somewhat differing problems of selection, however. If one is primarily committed to a topic, such as the influence of stratification on decision-making, then the selection of the specific organization to be studied should be made ideally in terms of systematically augmenting and rounding out the types of organization that have already been studied with respect to that topic. For example, if all the previous studies have dealt with one-industry cities and rural trading communities, one might well choose to study a small two-industry city. Of course, the further choice of a specific city from this category will ordinarily turn on less abstract criteria of accessibility, convenience, etc.

If, on the other hand, one is primarily committed to studying the specific organization, then the choice of topic is typically made in terms of the investigator's frame of reference and of the sorts of topics studied by others in similar contexts. For example, a researcher who becomes involved in studying a particular delinquent gang

---

19. Coleman (1958).

20. Robinson (1951); Turner (1953).

21. Kish (1965).

will normally have strong dispositions toward a handful of topics pertinent to such an organization.

In general, however, choosing the organization in terms of the topic tends to be associated with theory testing, whereas choosing the topic in terms of the organization favors description and discovery of theory.

The next sampling choice, logically speaking, is that of the *theoretical variables* thought pertinent to the topic in the context of the particular social organization. One investigator may feel that unrealistic application of middle-class norms to scholastically unsuccessful boys is the most pertinent factor in the emergence of delinquent gangs. Another may feel that differential identification with rebellious characters is the principal determinant. Thus, depending on one's theoretical frame of reference, the same topic—such as the emergence of delinquent gangs among high school boys—may suggest quite different variables or influences to be investigated systematically. Very often this selection of variables does not involve conscious choice at all but is so conditioned by the researcher's frame of reference that he finds himself quite "naturally" thinking in terms of the particular variables indicated by that framework.

Somewhat less frequently, perhaps, this selection of the variables of interest follows, rather than precedes, initiation of actual fieldwork. By tentatively scouting around the organization, the researcher may notice or come to suspect that a certain variable, related to his own topic of interest, is important in the workings of this organization. While it is seldom the case that the scientist approaches a field situation wholly without preconceptions of what things may be important, it is also infrequent that his fieldwork fails to suggest at least a few variables that he had not anticipated.

Regardless of which variables may be selected for investigation, the means of measuring these variables must be chosen from a number of alternative means. Any empirical concept or measure, if it is to be useful scientifically, must suggest certain events or properties that serve as *indicators* of the presence, or measures of the magnitude, of that concept or variable.[22] Supposing that middle-class norms had been defined, the application of these middle-class norms to scholastically unsuccessful boys could be detected, among many other ways, by looking up any school regulations concerning dress and hair styles, by asking the boys what is expected of them by their teachers, or by asking the teachers what they are hoping for in these boys' performances. Any or all of these indicators might be employed, but all too often participant observers neglect to specify what indicators they actually employed or, still worse, they fail to employ them in systematically uniform fashion. For example, in one case the researcher might use one of the indicators, but in another case within the same study he might employ a different indicator of the same variable. The comparability of the two cases on the same variable thus becomes problematic.

We should not convey the impression that consistency of use is the only important criterion in the selection of indicators or measures. Among other important criteria are the comparative validity, reliability, precision, and economy of the possible means of assessing the presence or magnitude of the given variable.[23] It is not

---

22. Lazarsfeld (1959), pp. 108–113.

23. Selltiz, Jahoda, Deutsch, and Cook (1959), pp. 146–149; Richardson, Dohrenwend, and Klein (1965), pp. 21–30.

necessary that these criteria be fulfilled to the maximum degree. Every study represents a tissue of compromises with regard to these criteria: measures are ordinarily made no more valid, reliable, or precise (beyond some adequate minimum) than is consonant with the overall economy of the study. To do otherwise would be as wasteful of scientific effort as hunting houseflies with a howitzer.

The most common referent for sampling is the actual *units* being studied—i.e., persons, acts, or events, rather than topics, organizations, variables, or indicators. Systematic sampling theory, as it is known to experimental statisticians, implicitly takes these units as the relevant ones to be selected and presents a codified corpus of techniques for this purpose.[24] As noted earlier, however, such highly rational prescriptive procedures are seldom truly applicable in sampling informants or events for participant observation studies. (For these purposes, the three general procedures described on pp. 64–65 are more often employed. Beyond these, certain criteria for sampling time-units are given by Arrington and by Brookover and Back,[25] and for sampling informants by Back and by Mead and Metraux.[26]) Systematic sampling theory in participant observation is almost entirely confined to the selection of respondents; even here, the results obtained from such a systematically drawn sample are likely to give rise, indirectly, to a new set of categories which in turn may or may not be amenable to systematic sampling procedures.

It is not our intention in this chapter to present a defensible rationale for confronting the hoary problems of sampling in participant observation studies. Rather, it is our wish to direct the attention of our readers to the problems and actual practices of contemporary workers in the hope that such attention may in time result in the discovery of more rational sampling procedures.[27] In the meanwhile, lacking the ability to prescribe their samples, participant observers should take pains to *describe* and justify their selection of samples on all levels—topics, organizations, variables, indicators, events or time-samples, informants, documents, and respondents. In this way their readers can more reasonably evaluate and perhaps replicate their procedures and results. The importance of this problem will be touched on again when we turn to questions of providing evidence for conclusions in Chapter 6.

Tactics in Data Collection

Having selected one's theoretical and empirical armament and the concrete particulars to which it will be applied in the study, one has yet to assemble this material in order to execute the study. If relevant data are to be generated, one technique has to be applied to one category of people with respect to a particular variable, and another technique to other people with regard to a different variable. What are the *tactics* of data collection in participant observation? What does one do, when and where?

We have already seen (pp. 24–26), that there is no clean-cut progression from exploratory work to description to hypothesis testing. All of these take place more

24. Kish (1965).

25. Arrington (1943); Brookover and Back (1966).

26. Mead and Metraux (1953); Back (1956).

27. One promising possibility is the method of sequential analysis, as broached by Wald (1947).

or less simultaneously and recurrently. Nonetheless, certain gross regularities in the execution of participant observation studies are detectable.

There is slowly emerging a body of case descriptions of the actual procedures used in important participant observation studies, which will eventually give rise to a codification of such tactics.[28] While we cannot yet undertake such a codification here, we do note that the general pace of such studies and the sequence of use for various techniques tends to be determined by the stages of (1) the developing field relations and of (2) the progressive sampling procedures.

ESTABLISHING FIELD RELATIONS

JOHN P. DEAN, ROBERT L. EICHHORN, AND LOIS R. DEAN

Because the relationship between the research worker and the persons in the field is the key to effective observation and interviewing, much depends on the initial field contacts. They often determine whether the door to research will be open or shut. Although each field setting has its own peculiar characteristics to be taken into account, a few rough principles guiding entry into the field are worth noting.

1. *Generally field contacts should move from persons in the highest status and authority positions down to the actual participants in the field situation one wants to study.* Where there are two lines of authority (in a plant with both union and management organizations present or in a local political campaign with two contending parties, for example), early contacts with leaders of both groups may be essential to prevent either from identifying the researcher as a partisan. Top leaders are often in the best position to have the vision and perspective to understand what the research is trying to accomplish. Once they have offered cooperation, persons farther down the hierarchy will generally go along with the research if they are properly approached.

2. *The field worker needs to have a plausible explanation of the research, that makes sense to the people whose cooperation he seeks.* While this sounds obvious, it is not an easy thing to provide. If informants get the impression that they are going to be carefully scrutinized in all they do and perhaps compared to others, resistance may develop. Compare the following explanations.

We want to study what makes for good and bad union leadership.	We want to learn how a union carries on its day-to-day work.

---

28. Hammond (1964); Vidich, Bensman, and Stein (1964); Whyte (1955), pp. 279–358.

Reprinted from *An Introduction to Social Research,* 2nd ed., edited by John T. Doby, pp. 281–283. Copyright © 1967 by Meredith Publishing Company. Reprinted by permission of the authors and Appleton-Century-Crofts.

We want to learn what the roots of effective political organizations are—how much patronage, hired help, volunteer help, figure in local party campaigns.	We want to understand how a local political party goes about a campaign.
We are interested in racial tension, discrimination, and prejudice and how they are related to each other in a community.	We are interested in the different groups that make up a city like this—the Jewish community, the Negro community, the foreign-extraction groups—how they are organized and participate in the total life of the community.

This principle underlies the better examples above: *the researcher should indicate interest in understanding the legitimate activities of a person or group, rather than evaluating them.* Field workers who do not give careful thought to the explanation of their research in advance, even to the selection of specific phrases they will use, often find themselves turned down.

3. *The field worker should try to represent himself, his sponsors, and his study, as honestly as possible.* Bluffing, pretending naiveté, misrepresenting oneself or one's sponsors, or pretending that the study is more or less important than is the case are all dangerous tactics. Subsequent events or other sources of information may bring to light the real situation and seriously damage field relations. Further research may become impossible.

4. As the first research step *the field worker should have in mind some rather routine fact-gathering that makes sense to those in the field.* This will provide him with an acceptable reason for contacting people where he wants to work. Gathering these facts will give others an opportunity to become accustomed to his presence and will generate contacts for further inquiry. Acceptance of the field worker depends more upon the kind of person he is than the perceived value of his research. Informants want to be reassured that the researcher is a "good guy" and can be trusted with what he uncovers. They are not usually interested in the complete rationale for the study. The researcher should not, of course, appear to be reticent in talking about his study; a willingness to tell people more about the study than they want to know allays fears and suspicions.

The field worker's aim is to participate *naturally* within the group he is studying (he would probably retain his identity as a researcher, although this would not be the case if his mission was covert). He hopes this will give him greater understanding of its members and of their social circumstances. At first the presence of an outsider may seriously inhibit behavior. But as he becomes fully accepted, others will behave quite spontaneously in his presence. Acceptance depends in part on the field worker having an appropriate role in the eyes of the informants. But even though he may appear novel, a pleasant, sincere researcher can become accepted.

5. Acceptance depends upon time spent in the field, a legitimate role in the eyes of the informants, and the expression of a genuine interest in the people being studied. Therefore, *the researcher should sacrifice initial data in order to speed acceptance.* He should not be overly eager to collect crucial data; instead, he should let circumstances carry him along. He should not give the impression that his only reason for being there is to collect data, but that he genuinely enjoys the informants' company and is interested in the activities of the group. He should avoid constant probing with questions—he is better advised to inject his comments or questions when the conversation naturally turns to his area of concern. Once he is accepted, he will have time to ask more direct questions, and while he waits he can win the informants' confidence, identify those having the most insight, and judge which questions will be threatening.

In general, field work progresses from passive observation, to participation in group activities, to interviewing and, finally, to experimental intervention. Trying to move too quickly from one phase to the next can destroy good working relations and delay data collection.

The manner in which this sequence of data-collection techniques is paced by the stages of developing field relations is elaborated in the selection by Anselm Strauss *et al.*

FIELD TACTICS

ANSELM STRAUSS *et al.*

Let us briefly note only that the fieldworker's identity shifts when he spends an extended period of time interacting with the same people. Initially we presented ourselves as sociologists doing a study on "how a hospital works," and this identification was maintained throughout the research. The qualities encompassed in this identification altered, however, with familiarity. In particular, when we approached participants during early stages of the research, we assumed a high degree of naïveté. We played learners (often genuinely), inducing participants to instruct us in the ways of the hospital.

Reprinted from Anselm Strauss, Leonard Schatzman, Rue Bucher, Danuta Ehrlich, and Melvin Sabshin, *Psychiatric Ideologies and Institutions,* New York: Free Press, 1964, pp. 26–27, by permission of the authors and publisher.

This role could not be maintained indefinitely. Also, as propositions developed and we began to pin down propositions, other kinds of interactional tactic became more valuable: argumentation, for example. Furthermore, as personnel became accustomed to our presence, the usual kinds of friendship and camaraderie arose between fieldworkers and hospital workers.

When first we appeared at each work setting, we came prepared with statements about our "identity and purpose." For days—sometimes for weeks—we found it necessary to restate our identities and purposes. For example, our explanation to a nurse calmly charting might not suffice when, some days later, we observed her outburst of anger at a resident: She had changed, and we too appeared different to her. Eventually, as we had to abandon the naïve role, so the observed ceased making direct queries about our presence. Still, suspicion occasionally reappeared in more subtle guises, particularly in unusually delicate or explosive situations.

As we became increasingly active in the field, we used more interview tactics with participants. We never, at any point, interviewed with a preset schedule of questions. When we did formal interviewing, we worked from an interview guide. But most of our information was gathered through more informal interviewing, when we approached respondents on the wards or at coffee or hailed them—particularly the doctors—as they passed our strategically placed offices.

In due time, the respondents would themselves hail the fieldworker with, "You should have been here last night" or "How come you didn't ask *me* about the ——— incident?" When this kind of thing began to happen with increasing frequency, the fieldworker had become part of the natural flow of events, without necessarily determining its course. Yet, much of our informal questioning consisted of the *reportorial* type of question—the who, what, where, how, and why of events. In the later stages of research, we increasingly adopted a *posing* type of question, which involved putting a case to the respondent. We can list the following types of posing question.

The challenge or devil's-advocate question. The fieldworker deliberately confronts the respondent with the arguments of opponents. The idea is to elicit rhetorical assertion and thus to round out the respondent's position by forcing him to respond to challenge.

The hypothetical question. This kind of question is another technique for rounding out the respondent's thought structure but without accompanying rhetorical heat. The fieldworker poses a number of possible occurrences—for example, "What if a patient did this or that? What if the physician told you to . . . ? What would happen to that patient on the ward next door?"

Posing the ideal. There are two variations on this technique. First, the respondent can be asked to describe the ideal situation, the ideal doctor, the ideal nurse, the ideal conditions for work. Second, while the fieldworker can still pretend to be somewhat naïve, he can assert an ideal to see what response is elicited. Happily, what usually happens is that, when the investigator poses an ideal, respondents not only counter with other ideals but, in the process, tend to point out the shortcomings of reality.

Offering interpretations or testing propositions on respondents. It is sometimes very useful to tell respondents about the propositions that one is beginning to pull together about events interesting to them. If they disagree, they will usually volunteer information to counter a proposition, which may lead the fieldworker into further unanticipated search. If they agree, the tendency is to qualify the proposition: It does not quite meet the case. Again, the fieldworker comes away with additional valuable information.

Often such artificial devices for eliciting verbal data are quite unnecessary. The observed feel that their perspectives, statuses, or personal interpretations of observed events are underrepresented or misunderstood. Then it is difficult for the fieldworker to avoid becoming a captive audience. As frequently, the fieldworker may be given a lecture on the dangers of misinterpreting or failing to see events. Here, the observed becomes a self-styled investigator, especially when the fieldworker is known to have listened to such "questionable sources" as patients—or literally anyone. ("Let me tell you what really happened.") Sociologically, the "reality" referent may be important or irrelevant. In either case, one comes away with selective data on both the event and the representation of it, as voiced by a person of particular status, ideology, and so forth. In addition, the fieldworker sometimes discovers that his very presence at staff meetings or at small congregations of personnel—especially his first visits—acts as catalyst of public argumentation. His interested face and willing ear spur some proponents into articulate restatements of their positions.

The specific interviewing tactics mentioned here by Strauss *et al.* exemplify a second, and very important, level of research tactics—rules of thumb on *how* data-collection techniques are to be applied in the concrete situations encountered in participant observation. Despite the obvious usefulness of knowledge of such tactics, these are beyond the possible scope of the present chapter, for interviewing tactics alone are the subject of virtually countless books and articles. For tactics in informant interviewing,[29] respondent interviewing,[30] observation,[31] and document analysis,[32] we must reluctantly return the reader to the relevant methodological literature.

---

29. Richardson, Dohrenwend, and Klein (1965); Metraux and Mead (1953); Caplow (1956); J. P. Dean (1954); Leznoff (1956); J. P. Dean and Whyte (1958).

30. Becker (1954, 1956); Richardson, Dohrenwend, and Klein (1965); Dexter (1956); Payne (1951); Riesman and Benney (1956); Rose (1945); M. Wax and Shapiro (1956).

31. Whyte (1951); Barker (1963).

32. Angell and Freedman (1953).

Data Recording

Once in the field, the participant observer is typically somewhat overwhelmed by data, the meaning of which is not always immediately apparent and therefore must be mulled over. The observer cannot always be sure what is relevant or important, and he wants to record every fact so that he will have it if it should later turn out to be important. The problem of excessive data is especially pertinent to interviewing, where data impinge at a particularly high rate.

Of course it is quite impossible to literally record everything, but it is a good principle to record more detail than the researcher thinks he will really need. Given the frequent redirection of participant observation studies, it is not possible to determine until quite late in the research what is or is not an irrelevant detail. If not recorded, that detail will not be available to guide or support any subsequent redirection.

Fullness of recording can be maximized through use of mechanical means (filming an event, tape recording an interview, or photocopying a document). On the other hand, the cost is also thereby maximized. Not only is there a large investment in machinery, film, tape, etc., but expensive data reduction procedures (e.g., coding of filmed events or transcription of interview tapes) are subsequently required in order to extract relevant information in verbalized form. Consequently, mechanical recording is probably best reserved for the more important, complicated, or information-packed situations.

Moreover, the use of such mechanical means often makes subjects uncomfortable, resulting in stilted or unnatural behavior. As an extreme, some subjects who would otherwise be cooperative may seriously resist any attempts at such direct recording. These reactive effects can, of course, be circumvented by concealing the machinery, although there are both ethical objections and practical liabilities to such concealment. Ethically, concealed recording is questionable practice in that the right to privacy is violated without waiver by the subject.[33] Practically, the risk of subjects discovering or even suspecting such invasions—and angrily withholding any further cooperation—is always substantial.

In the majority of contexts, therefore, the most practical recording procedure is note-taking by the researcher. Taking notes while actually involved in observation or interviewing is, however, generally incompatible with good data collection, as it entails a shift in attention from the behavior to the researcher's notebook.[34] Actions, gestures, and expressions will be missed while he is jotting down a note, particularly if he should fall behind the pace of the action. Furthermore, in interviewing, the researcher cannot be a passive recorder. He must constantly reflect on what is being said, asking himself what each statement means and how he can best encourage the interviewee to clarify or expand on a certain point. A good observation or interview recorded with less than perfect accuracy is generally preferable to a mediocre interview with very high quality recording.

Furthermore, overt and continual note-taking during an observation or interview frequently gives rise to reactive effects similar to those created by mechanical recording. (On the other hand, some subjects may be affronted by failure to take notes, feeling that this implies a lack of interest in what they are doing or saying.)

---

33. Burchard (1958); Erikson (1967).
34. Whyte (1960).

In light of these considerations, most experienced participant observers generally prefer to make only mental notes during observation or interviewing, committing these notes to paper immediately after leaving the situation. This is certainly a difficult feat to perform with a high degree of accuracy, but experience indicates that even a small amount of practice allows the researcher to recall in quite literal detail an astounding proportion of what he has witnessed. Periodic comparisons with tape recordings of the same interviews are desirable to check and sharpen this ability, particularly early in the research. Such checks typically reveal that the main outlines of the event or interview are correctly recalled, together with the detail of most segments, albeit with some reordering and total omission of some segments. Flaws of this sort are not ordinarily very serious; the errors to be feared, and therefore checked against, are distortions of the important meaning of statements and the misattribution of statements.

(Demands of the field situation are often such that it is impossible to undertake a full transcription of mental notes immediately afterward. In such cases, every attempt should be made to write down at least a few key phrases that will go far toward calling up full recollection as soon as circumstances permit a more comprehensive transcription. The full recording should always be carried out as soon as possible, and it is a good rule to complete such recording at least before retiring for the night.)

Because of the possibilities of distortion or misrepresentation, Strauss *et al.* suggest the use of certain notational conventions to minimize these dangers.

► Verbal material recorded within quotations signified exact recall; verbal material within apostrophes indicated a lesser degree of certainty or paraphrasing; and verbal material with no markings meant reasonable recall but not quotation. Finally, the interviewer's impressions or inferences could be separated from actual observations by the use of single or double parentheses.[35] ◄

Such distinctions, we shall note in Chapter 4, can be of considerable aid in evaluating the quality of the recorded data.

The recording of interviews and observations is undertaken primarily to preserve empirical data for later systematic analysis, but it serves additional purposes as well, particularly if the researcher is not working alone in the study.[36] Such records allow the study supervisor, if any, to monitor and constructively evaluate the interviewing or observational tactics of his workers and to suggest more fruitful approaches. Moreover, such recorded notes help to orient one's fellow workers (or even oneself at a later date) as to what the field situation was at the time certain data were obtained. As we shall see in Chapter 5, the review of such full recordings, particularly of the context and the researcher's impressions, is a critical source of hypotheses for the redirection of the study.

In the light of these additional functions of recorded notes, many researchers advocate recording them in the form of a field diary or log of events.[37] The diary form, of course, facilitates the notation of the sequence and context of events, undertakings, data, hunches, and changing field relations. Some writers would add that this form of

---

35. Strauss, Schatzman, Bucher, Ehrlich, and Sabshin (1964), p. 29, by permission of the authors and publisher.

36. Whyte (1960).

37. E.g., Geer (1964).

recording further facilitates study of social change and of the changing biases of the researcher.[38]

Regardless of the form in which the data may actually be recorded, most participant observers find that the range of material which seems important enough to warrant recording begins to diminish once they are far enough along in their studies to have more or less settled on a set of major hypotheses. At such a point, facts not pertinent to the guiding hypotheses can more safely be ignored.

Data Retrieval

At the conclusion of a participant observation study, a process which typically requires months or even years of daily note-taking, enormous masses of qualitative data have been accumulated. If these are to be analyzed in systematic fashion, some reasonably efficient means of information retrieval must be made available.

Modern high-speed computers have opened vast horizons in technological aids to information retrieval, ranging from sophisticated microfilm-punch card-Xerox linkups to the relatively crude General Inquirer mode of content analysis.[39] As yet, however, the application of such technology to automated retrieval of participant observation data is still an uncharted possibility.

Contemporary participant observers must still rely on laborious hand-indexing processes for locating relevant data within field diaries. Such indexing is well explicated by William F. Whyte (1960).

Whyte's system involves a page in three columns containing for each interview or observation report (1) its number, pages, and date of collection, (2) the person(s) interviewed or observed (together with, in parentheses, the names of people referred to in the interview or observation), and (3) the pertinent topics and social relationships (e.g., a discussion of industrial incentives might be indexed with several headings: piece rates, foreman-worker, worker-steward, steward-foreman). For one ordinary folder of field notes, such an index would cover from three to eight pages.

Whyte recommends that construction of the indexing categories be deferred until eight or ten observations and interviews have been accumulated and some sense of the situation has been obtained. At that point the researcher can reread the notes, pencilling in appropriate categories on the margins of each page. These marginal notes are then typed into the third column of the index. This procedure is repeated periodically as further quantities of field notes are accumulated.

When ready to write a research report, the researcher can gain a reasonably systematic idea of the available material by simply rereading the whole index. Then, for each topic in the outline of the report, he can note the numbers of the interviews and of the relevant pages therein. These pages can then be pulled from the file, reread, and the contents incorporated into the report.

Whyte notes that the index should not merely be a clerical device but should evolve in line with the type of analysis the researcher eventually intends to make. In that way, the process of indexing the field notes constitutes a preliminary analysis of the data as well as helping to locate materials.

---

38. Vidich (1955b).
39. Lipetz (1966); Stone, Bales, Namenwirth, and Ogilivie (1962).

The senior author (McCall) is experimenting with a somewhat different indexing system which is predicated upon the fact that indexing and the continuous process of data analysis facilitate one another, as noted by Whyte and by many others. In this system, each day's field notes are typed directly upon mimeograph stencils and multiple copies are run off and filed in labeled folders, each of which pertains to a single topic, category, variable, or hypothesis. The verbal material pertinent to the subject matter of a given folder is circled in red and only those pages which contain circled material are inserted in that folder. A complete copy of the day's field notes are placed in chronological order in a cumulative file folder which then serves the purposes of an ordinary field diary. The stencils and a few extra copies are labeled and filed separately in chronological order so that, should further categories emerge later in the study, pertinent pages of field notes from the past can be added to the new files.

Periodically the contents of each substantive folder are reviewed, distilled, and interpreted in a position paper, making explicit date and page references to the documenting notes, after which the reviewed materials can be removed to a more or less dead file until such time as they may need to be returned to in order to clarify some point.

In this way, one has virtually instantaneous access to all data bearing on a given subject, eliminating the need to thumb through a chronologically ordered field diary according to a separate index volume. Moreover, the position papers facilitate the continuous analysis of incoming data and help point the way to further categories and hypotheses which can be indexed in a similar manner.

CHAPTER FOUR

THE
QUALITY
OF
DATA

Participant observation, as it has been described in the preceding chapter, is a very complex tactical blend of a number of data-collection techniques. The overall structure of a participant observation study is almost undefinable, with research design, data collection, data analysis, and write-up activities all proceeding more or less simultaneously. As a consequence of this lack of standardized procedure, many scientists remain unconvinced of the quality of the data and of the empirical conclusions arrived at.

If measurement and sampling procedures, for example, are unsystematized, can we have any real confidence in the resulting data? Would any two investigators come up with equivalent results? Are data obtained early in such a study comparable with those obtained later, or has the researcher so altered his framework over time that early and late data are quite different entities? Are the data valid indicators of the underlying phenomena?[1]

Such questions deserve most serious consideration, of course, and the answers are quite difficult to establish, for the standard means of ascertaining the validity and reliability of data-collection operations are largely inapplicable to such a study design.[2]

Given the end of obtaining an accurate and reasonably complete analytic description of some social organization or situation, how can we be confident that the data of participant observation are adequate to the task? Most social scientists already accept the utility of the fundamental techniques—observation, interviewing, and document analysis. What remains to be established in a given study, then, is that these techniques were adequately employed—i.e., employed systematically, comprehensively, and rigorously. We shall take up only the last of these criteria here, deferring the remaining two to Chapter 6.

When we speak here of employing data-collection techniques rigorously, we mean employing them with adequate safeguards against the many potentially invalidating or contaminating factors which threaten to diminish the interpretability of the resulting data.

Fortunately, a good deal of the literature on participant observation is concerned precisely with the enumeration and analysis of the many threats to the interpretability of observation and interview data.[3]

---

1. Such traditional questions of reliability and validity are not the only criteria of data quality, of course, but because they stand prior to other considerations—such as precision, relevance, and economy—we shall be emphasizing them here.

2. A sound, conventional presentation of such means is provided, for example, in Selltiz, Jahoda, Deutsch, and Cook (1959), pp. 146–198.

3. In this chapter we will be concerned only with direct observation, informant interviewing, and respondent interviewing. The actual data of participation are usually handled more reasonably by pooling them with the data of observation or respondent interviewing. Threats to document analysis are cogently treated in Angell and Freedman (1953) and in Webb, Campbell, Schwartz, and Sechrest (1966), pp. 53–111.

Threats to Observational Data

With respect to observational data, the three, broad, primary categories of threats to interpretability, which have received wide discussion, are: (1) reactive effects of the observer's presence or activities on the phenomena being observed; (2) distorting effects of selective perception and interpretation on the observer's part; and (3) limitations on the observer's ability to witness all relevant aspects of the phenomena in question.

Within these categories many specific problems have been encountered. In the following selection by Arthur Vidich, the socially defined role of the observer is seen as giving rise to potential problems in all the above categories.

PARTICIPANT OBSERVATION AND THE COLLECTION AND INTERPRETATION OF DATA

ARTHUR J. VIDICH

The practical and technical problems as well as many of the advantages and disadvantages of participant observation as a data-gathering technique have been well stated.[1] We propose to discuss some of the effects on data of the social position of the participant observer. The role of the participant observer and the images which respondents hold of him are central to the definition of his social position; together these two factors shape the circumstances under which he works and the type of data he will be able to collect.

In a broad sense the social position of the observer determines *what* he is likely to see. The way in which he sees and interprets his data will be largely conditioned by his theoretical preconceptions, but this is a separate problem with which we will not be concerned.[2]

What an observer will see will depend largely on his particular position in a network of relationships. To the extent that this is the case, this discussion of relatively well-known but frequently unstated observations is not purely aca-

Reprinted from *American Journal of Sociology* (1955) **60**, 354–360, by permission of the author and The University of Chicago Press.

1.   See especially the following: Florence R. Kluckhohn, "The Participant Observer Technique in Small Communities," *American Journal of Sociology*, XLVI (November, 1940), 331–43; William F. Whyte, *Street Corner Society* (Chicago: University of Chicago Press, 1943), Preface, pp. v–x, and also his "Observational Field-Work Methods" in Marie Jahoda, Morton Deutsch, and Stuart W. Cook (eds.), *Research Methods in the Social Sciences* (New York: Dryden Press, 1951), II, 393–514; Marie Jahoda *et al.*, "Data Collection: Observational Methods," *ibid.*, Vol. I, chap. v; Benjamin D. Paul, "Interview Techniques and Field Relations," in A. L. Kroeber *et al.* (eds.), *Anthropology Today: An Encyclopedic Inventory* (Chicago: University of Chicago Press, 1953), pp. 430–51; and Edward C. Devereux, "Functions, Advantages and Limitations of Semi-controlled Observation" (Ithaca, N. Y.: Staff Files, "Cornell Studies in Social Growth," Department of Child Development and Family Relationships, Cornell University, 1953).

2.   Oscar Lewis has devoted considerable attention to this problem. See especially his *Life in a Mexican Village: Tepoztlan Restudied* (Springfield: University of Illinois Press, 1951) and "Controls and Experiments in Field Work," in Kroeber *et al.* (eds.), *Anthropology Today*, pp. 452–75.

demic. The task assumes the necessity of less concern with methodological refinements for handling data after they are collected and more concern with establishing canons of validity and the need, too, for a better balance between the standardization of field techniques and the establishment of standards for the evaluation of field data according to their source and the collector.

BROADER RELEVANCE OF PARTICIPANT OBSERVATION

As a technique, participant observation is central to all the social sciences. It has been singled out and treated as a rather specialized field approach with peculiar problems of its own, but this has obscured the extent to which the various social sciences depend upon it. Participant observation enables the research worker to secure his data within the mediums, symbols, and experiential worlds which have meaning to his respondents. Its intent is to prevent imposing alien meanings upon the actions of the subjects. Anthropologists dealing with cultures other than their own have consciously recognized and utilized the technique as a matter of necessity. Experimental psychologists who try their own instruments out on themselves as well as psychiatrists who undergo analysis are practicing a form of participant observation for much the same purpose as the anthropologist.

The sociologist who limits his work to his own society is constantly exploiting his personal background of experience as a basis of knowledge. In making up structured interviews, he draws on his knowledge of meanings gained from participation in the social order he is studying. He can be assured of a modicum of successful communication only because he is dealing in the same language and symbolic system as his respondents. Those who have worked with structured techniques in non-Western societies and languages will attest to the difficulty encountered in adjusting their meanings to the common meanings of the society investigated, a fact which highlights the extent to which the sociologist is a participant observer in almost all his work.[3]

In view of this widespread dependence upon participant observation as a source of data and as a basis for giving them meaning, a discussion of the factors which condition data obtained by this method is warranted.

Our source of immediate experience is the Springdale community of Upstate New York.[4] Experience as a participant observer in one's own culture sets

---

3. F. C. Bartlett's "Psychological Methods and Anthropological Problems," *Africa*, X (October, 1937), 401–19, illustrates this problem.

4. This work was conducted under the sponsorship of the Department of Child Development and Family Relationships in the New York State College of Home Economics at Cornell University. It is part of a larger project entitled "Cornell Studies in Social Growth" and represents an outgrowth of a study in the determinants of constructive social behavior in the person, the family, and the community. The research program is supported in part by grants from the National Institute of Mental Health, United States Public Health Service, and the Committee on the Early Identification of Talent of the Social Science Research Council with the aid of funds granted to the Council by the John and Mary R. Markle Foundation.

the major problems of this technique into clearer focus. The objectification and self-analysis of the role of the participant observer in one's own society has the advantage that communication is in the same language and symbolic system.

FORMATION OF RESPONDENT
IMAGES OF THE PARTICIPANT OBSERVER

Whether the field worker is totally, partially, or not at all disguised, the respondent forms an image of him and uses that image as a basis of response. Without such an image the relationship between the field worker and the respondent, by definition, does not exist.

The essential thing in any field situation is the assumption of some position in a structure of relationships. The position is assumed not only by various types of participant observers but by all interviewers. The undisguised interviewer establishes his personal identity or the identity of the organization he works for and, hence, makes himself and the questions he asks plausible to his respondent. In disguised interviewing, including that of the totally disguised participant observer, a plausible role is no less important even though it may be more complex and more vaguely defined; but the first concern remains the assumption of a credible role. Likewise the totally disguised social scientist, even as genuine participant, is always located in a given network of relationships.

Every research project is in a position partly to influence image formation by the way it identifies itself. However, these self-definitions are always dependent on verbalizations, and, at best, the influence they have is minimal unless supported overtly by the research worker. Field workers are well aware that the public is likely not to accept their statements at face value; gossip and talk between potential respondents when a research program first enters the field attests to this fact. This talk places the research worker in the context of the values, standards, and expectations of the population being studied, and its effect is to establish the identity of the field worker in the eyes of the public.

There is tremendous variation from field situation to field situation in the assignment of identity to the field worker. In the usual anthropological field situation he is identified as a trader, missionary, district officer, or foreign spy —any role with which the native population has had previous contact and experience. In time these ascriptions can and do change so that the anthropologist, for example, may even gain an identity within a kinship structure:

▶ He was assigned on the basis of residence to an appropriate Kwoma lineage and, by equation with a given generation, was called "younger brother" or "father" or "elder uncle," depending on the particular "kinsman" who addressed him. Having found a place for Whiting in the kinship, the Kwoma could orient their social behavior accordingly.[5] ◀

---

5. Benjamin D. Paul in Kroeber *et al.* (eds.), *Anthropology Today*, p. 434.

In every case the field worker is fitted into a plausible role by the population he is studying and within a context meaningful to them. There seem to be no cases where field workers have not found a basis upon which subjects could react toward them. This is true even in the face of tremendous language barriers. Moreover, the necessary images and the basis for reaction which they provide are not only always found, but they are demanded by the mere fact of the research worker's intrusion into the life of his subjects. Even when a field worker is ejected, the image and meaningful context exists.

SOCIAL ROLE OF THE PARTICIPANT OBSERVER

Once he is placed in a meaningful context, the social position of the researcher is assured. His approach to the social structure is subsequently conditioned by his position.

Obviously the ascription and the assumption of a plausible role are not the equivalent of placing the participant observer in the experiential world of his subjects. Indeed, this impossibility is not his objective. For to achieve the experience of the subject, along with the baggage of perceptions that goes along with it, is to deny a chance for objectivity. Instead, an observer usually prefers to keep his identity vague; he avoids committing his allegiance—in short, his personality—to segments of the society. This is true even when he studies specialized segments of mass societies and organizations. In this case the observer may deliberately antagonize management, for example, in order to gain the confidence of the union or segments of it. However, within the union he has further to choose between competing factions, competing leaders, or leadership-membership cleavages. The anthropologist integrated into a kinship system or class faces the same problem. Eventually, no matter the size of the group he is studying, the observer is forced to face the problem of divided interests. He is "asked" to answer the question, "Who do you speak for?" and it is an answer to this question which, in the interests of research, he avoids.

Consequently, the observer remains marginal to the society or organization or segments of them which he studies. By his conscious action he stands between the major social divisions, not necessarily above them, but surely apart from them. Occupationally concerned with the objectification of action and events, he attempts to transcend all the local cleavages and discords. In avoiding commitments to political issues, he plays the role of political eunuch. He is socially marginal to the extent that he measures his society as a noninvolved outsider and avoids committing his loyalties and allegiances to segments of it. This is not hypocrisy but rather, as Howe has noted of Stendhal, it is living a ruse.[6] Being both a participant and an observer is "the strategy of having one's cake and eating it too": "Deceiving the society to study it and wooing the so-

---

6. Irving Howe, "Stendhal: The Politics of Survival," in William Phillips and Philip Rahv (eds.), *The Avon Book of Modern Writing* (New York: Avon Publishing Co., 1953), pp. 60–61.

ciety to live in it." His position is always ambivalent, and this ambivalence shapes the character of the data he secures and the manner of securing them.

THE PARTICIPANT OBSERVER'S DATA

All the information which the participant observer secures is conditioned by the meaningful context into which he is placed and by his own perspective as shaped by his being socially marginal. Together these circumstances greatly affect the kind of data he can get and the kind of experience he can have. The meaningful context into which he is placed by the public provides the latter with their basis for response, and his marginality specifies the order of experience possible for him.

To the extent that the observer's data are conditioned by the basis upon which subjects respond to him, the anthropologist studying another culture has one important advantage. He can justifiably maintain an attitude of naïveté and on this basis exploit his situation as a stranger to the fullest possible extent. Indeed, it is relatively easy to breach local customs and standards and still maintain a tenable research position in the society. This naïve attitude cannot be assumed in working in his own culture, for the simple reason that the respondent cannot accept it as plausible. In fact, the difficulty of securing data may be increased by the "ethnocentrism" of some respondents who assume that their own experiences are similar to those of others. Yet with the increased complexity, specialization and pluralization of roles in American society, the social science observer is likely to have had no direct contact at all with whole ranges of experience. With the exception of his professional world (and partly because of his professionalization), he is something of a stranger in his own society without being in a position to exploit his innocence. He has the disadvantage of living in a society in which his experience is limited, while, at the same time, he is regarded as a knowledgeable member of all segments of it.

If the participant observer seeks genuine experiences, unqualifiedly immersing and committing himself in the group he is studying, it may become impossible for him to objectify his own experiences for research purposes; in committing his loyalties he develops vested interests which will inevitably enter into his observations. Anthropologists who have "gone native" are cases in point; some of them stop publishing material entirely.[7] And all anthropologists have learned to make appropriate compensation in data interpreted by missionaries, traders, and government officials, no matter how excellent the material may be.

In practice, the solution to the dilemma of genuine versus spurious experiences is to make use of individuals who are socially marginal in the society being studied. In almost any society in this postcolonial and specialized age,

---

7.   Paul, in *Anthropology Today*, p. 435, names Frank Cushing as one.

the observer is likely to find persons with a penchant for seeing themselves objectively in relation to their society, such as the traveled Pacific Islander and the small-town "intellectual." But they differ from the social scientist in one important respect: a portion of their experience, no matter how much it is subsequently objectified, has been gained within the society under study. When the social scientist studies a society, he characteristically makes his first contacts with these marginal persons, and they will vary according to his interests and the identity he claims for himself. Even when the observer tries to avoid the marginal individuals, he is nevertheless sought out by them. This is not unfortunate, for these types are a bridge, perhaps the most important one, to the meanings of the society. It is they who provide him with his first insights into the workings of the society. The sociologist studying his own society is, to varying degrees according to the relation between his background of experience and his object of study, his own bridge. Without such a bridge, without at least an interpreter or one lone native who can utter a word or two in another language, the observer would have no basis for approaching his data. The social marginality of the participant observer's role with all the limitations it imposes provides a basis for communication and, hence, ultimately, for understanding.

FIELD TACTICS AND DATA EVALUATION

When the participant observer sets out to collect his data, he is faced with two types of problems: the tactical problem of maneuver in the field and the evaluation of the data. The two problems are related in that the data to be evaluated are conditioned by the field tactics. The discussion of them will be limited to selected problems central to the technique of participant observation: the tactical problem of conformity or nonconformity, the observer's experience as related to the imputation of meaning and the formulation of categories, and the significance of participant observation to the study of social change.

Conformity or nonconformity to local standards and styles of living when engaging in field research is a relevant issue only in so far as the choice affects the research. Conformity is always conformity to specified standards and implies nonconformity to other possible standards. Almost all societies or groups in the contemporary world present alternative forms of behavior based on differing internal standards. Consequently it is hardly possible to conform to the standards of an entire society, and, hence, to follow a general policy of conformity is to follow no policy at all. Any policy which is designed to guide the field worker's actions must be based on a deliberate judgment as to which sources of information must be used to secure data. In the adopting of standards necessary to keep these sources open, other sources are likely to be alienated and closed off, or data from them may be distorted.

Moreover, conscious conformity to any standards, at best, is "artificial," for the participant observer does not commit himself to the point of genuine partisan action. In the interests of objectivity this is necessarily the case. In failing to make genuine commitments, he reveals his socially marginal position and the outside standards upon which he acts. In these terms the old argument posed by Radin, who said, "For any anthropologist to imagine that anything can be gained by 'going native' is a delusion and a snare," and by Goldenweiser, who said of sharing the lives of the natives and participating in their culture, "The more successful an anthropologist is in doing this, the better foundation he has laid for his future work,"[8] is no argument at all. The decision to assume standards and values or the degree to which participation is required is best made on the basis of the data to be collected and not on the basis of *standard* field practice.

The related tactical problem of conscious identification with groups, causes, or issues can be treated similarly. Complete and total neutrality is extremely difficult, if not impossible, to assume even where research considerations seem to demand it. By virtue of his research, no matter how transitory and irrespective of the exact dimensions of his marginal position, the investigator must react to the actions of his respondents. Neutrality even to the point of total silence is a form of reaction and not only will be considered as such by all parties to the conflict but also implies a specific attitude toward the issue—being above it, outside it, more important than it, not interested in it. Whatever meanings respondents attach to neutrality will, henceforth, be used as a further basis for response. This is true even when respondents demand an opinion or approval in structured interview situations. Failure to make a commitment can create resentment, hostility, and antagonism just as easily as taking a stand. In both cases, but each in its own way, relationships will be altered and, hence, data will be affected.

The data secured by the participant observer, except in so far as he reports personal experiences, cannot be independent of his subjects' ability and willingness to report. He is obliged to impute meaning to both their verbal and their nonverbal actions. His own experiences, though genuine, are at best vicarious approximations of those of his respondents; he never completely enters their world, and, by definition, if he did, he would assume the values, premises, and standards of his subjects and thereby lose his usefulness to research except as another subject. If the action observed is purely physical— the daily, routine physical movements of an individual, for example—the observer-interpreter cannot understand its meaning unless he communicates with the person involved in the action and gains insight into its meaning for the actor. Of course, studying within the meanings of his own society gives the observer a background of standardized meanings on which to draw. One knows that a man walking down the street at a certain time every morning is probably going to work. But the action of Raymond in *One Boy's Day*[9] was ob-

---

8. Both quoted in Paul, *ibid.,* p. 438.
9. Roger G. Barker and Herbert F. Wright, *One Boy's Day* (New York: Harper & Bros., 1951).

served precisely because it was not known. In more complicated action in a segment of society in which the observer does not have experience, he gains it vicariously by talking with others and in that way secures almost all his data.

The respondent, on the other hand, is not necessarily able to verbalize his experiences, and, as attested to by psychoanalysis, it is quite probable that he will not understand their meaning. The greater the social distance between the observer and the observed, the less adequate the communication between them. Hence, as stated above, the observer's data are determined by the subjects' ability and willingness to report. Since he cannot duplicate their experience, he cannot draw his conclusions from his own marginal experiences. He always operates in the borderland of their experience and, hence is still faced with the problem of *imputing* meaning to their actions. Whereas his subjects base their own interpretations and evaluations on folklore, religion, myth, illusion, special and vested interests or even on the basis of local standards of social analysis, the social science observer-analyst uses the independent and extraneous standards of science.

The participant-observation technique has been offered as one of the best techniques on which to base prearranged observational and structured interview categories. The assumption is that, with his greater familiarity with the respondents' experiences and their meanings, the participant observer is in the best position to draw up meaningful categories. However, with the passage of time and the assumption and ascription of new roles and statuses, his perspective on the society is constantly changing. His marginal position allows him more social movement by virtue of which his perceptions will change with time, particularly as he gains greater and greater familiarity. Categories which initially seemed meaningful later on may appear superficial or even meaningless. Moreover, as long as he remains a participant observer, his social marginality undergoes continuous redefinition.   As a result any categories he formulates in advance or at any given time will seem inadequate later when his social perspective has changed.[10] Attempts to establish categories into which directly observed action can be classified threaten to reduce the action to static entities which influence later observations, a condition which the technique of participant observation is designed to avoid. Indeed, it is this last condition which makes participant observation most suitable to the study of social change.

The technique of participant observation more than any other technique places the observer closer to social change as it takes place in a passing present. Change, as measured by the succession of days and hours rather than by years or arbitrary measures, takes place slowly. The desire of, and necessity for, individuals is to act in terms of what is possible in specific immediate situations. The immediacy of social change to those who are involved in the moving present tends to obscure their perspective on it: a continuous altering of his mem-

---

10. These changes in circumstances refer not only to his position in the society he studies but also to the professional society with which he works and changes in research focus.

ories and definitions of reality makes the individual involved unaware of change. The participant observer is also involved in these changes, but, by his marginal position and his conscious effort to objectify himself, he achieves a measure of noninvolvement. Hence, his perspective is conditioned by considerations other than involvement. If the participant observer changed his perspective in phase with continuous changes in reality, he too could not see the change. For as long as changes in perspective accompany changes in reality, the change is likely not to be recognized. The participant who studies change as an observer must therefore maintain a perspective outside and independent of change. Noninvolvement helps to prevent the alteration of memory structures and permits the observer to see cumulative changes.

To refresh his memory, the participant observer can turn to his records. But, if his perspective has changed with time, he may disregard or discount early notes and impressions in favor of those taken later. Field notes from two different periods in a project may, indeed, be one of the more important means of studying change. Instead, what probably happens is that the field worker obscures change by treating his data as though everything happened at the same time. This results in a description from a single perspective, usually that held just before leaving the field, but redefined by the rereading of his notes.

CONCLUSIONS

Data collection does not take place in a vacuum. Perspectives and perceptions of social reality are shaped by the social position and interests of both the observed and the observer as they live through a passing present. The participant observer who is committed to relatively long periods of residence in the field experiences a continuous redefinition of his position. In this context the respondent's basis of response, as conditioned by his image of the observer, changes in accordance with new images based on the changing definitions of the observer's position. These forces influence the data.

A valid evaluation of data must necessarily include a reasonably thorough comprehension of the major social dimensions of the situation in which data were collected. The social positions of the observer and the observed and the relationship between them at the time must be taken into account when the data are interpreted. To fail to take account of these conditions is to assume an equivalence of situations which does not exist and leads to distortion.

To the extent that a participant observer can participate and still retain a measure of noninvolvement, his technique provides a basis for an approach to the problem of validity. The background of information which he acquires in time makes him familiar with the psychology of his respondents and their social milieu. With this knowledge he is able to impose a broader perspective on his data and, hence, to evaluate their validity on the basis of standards extraneous to the immediate situation. To accomplish this, it is necessary that the participant observer be skeptical of himself in all data-gathering situations;

he must objectify himself in relation to his respondents and the passing present. This process of self-objectification leads to his further alienation from the society he studies. Between this alienation and attempts at objective evaluation lies an approach to the problem of validity.

In the preceding selection by Vidich, the social marginality of the observer's role was seen as offering certain advantages as well as limitations in the process of data collection. This idea is expanded upon by S. M. Miller in the selection below.

THE PARTICIPANT OBSERVER AND "OVER-RAPPORT"

S. M. MILLER

In making a field study involving a participant observer relationship, the writer made mistakes which could have been avoided if earlier researchers had pointed out these possible pitfalls.[1] The error in question is that of "over-rapport." This neologism has been adopted because no existing word expresses the idea that the researcher may be so closely related to the observed that his investigations are impeded. Studies of the participant observer method concentrate on such problems as how to gain entry and achieve rapport. The usual difficulties pointed to are those of insufficient rapport or under-rapport, for in such cases it is difficult to continue the study. But is it not possible to gain too much rapport?

In my study of local union leadership, I grew very close to the leaders. I was accepted by them, even liked by them, despite my academic background. Many personal things were told to me in a friend-to-friend relationship; undoubtedly I gained information because of this relationship which would not have been available to me in any other way.

On the other hand, once I had developed a close relationship to the union leaders I was committed to continuing it, and some penetrating lines of inquiry had to be dropped. They had given me very significant and delicate information about the internal operation of the local; to question closely their basic attitudes would open up severe conflict areas. To continue close rapport and to pursue avenues of investigation which appeared antagonistic to the union leaders was impossible. To shift to a lower level of rapport would be difficult because such a change would induce considerable distance and distrust. It would reveal that the attitude of the participant observer to the leaders was not

Reprinted from *American Sociological Review* (1952), **17**, 97–99, by permission of the author and publisher.

1.   The field study referred to in this note is my doctoral dissertation, *Union Structure and Industrial Relations: A Case Study of a Local Labor Union*, Princeton University, 1951 (microfilm).

the same as the leaders' feelings of friendship for the observer. They accepted the observer as an individual, a friend, not as one playing a delimited social role. Friendship connotes an all-accepting attitude; to probe beneath the surface of long-believed values would break the friend-to-friend relationship. It may also be that development of a friend-to-friend relationship between the leaders and the participant observer was a means used by the former to limit the observer's investigations and criticisms. In a sense, the observer may be co-opted into friendship, a situation which may have prevailed in some studies of management-worker interaction.

Over-rapport had a second limiting effect of greater subtlety. We have been told of situations in which rapport with leaders may mean lack of rapport with rank and file individuals.[2] This situation does not merely mean that rank and file members may be diffident in articulating their grievances to "administration men," which is how the observer, who is friendly to the leaders, may appear to them. The neglected element is what happens to the observer: he first hears about things from the leaders with whom he has rapport; he develops their "set" toward problems; when he talks to rank and filers he readily accepts those of their statements which conform to articulated leadership attitudes, even when these statements are not deeply meaningful to the rank and file members. In short, the observer has become so attuned to the sentiments of the leaders that he is ill-attuned to the less clearly articulated feelings of the rank and file.

The researcher should not become a mere machine, but in situations involving overt and covert controversy, he should be wary of identifying himself symbolically and emotionally with a particular group.[3]

In other words, the participant observer relationship requires rapport combined with objectivity.[4] The achievement of such a relationship is difficult and complex. The researcher has to gauge how much rapport is necessary to get the cooperation required to continue the study.[5] In most situations, it should not be too difficult to develop this basic level of rapport. The second problem of preventing the rapport from growing to such an extent that it hinders the

---

2.   Marvin K. Opler, review of Dorothy S. Thomas and Richard S. Nishimoto, *The Spoilage,* in *American Anthropologist,* No. 50 (April-June, 1948), pp. 307–10.

3.   The amount of covert controversy is frequently underestimated by investigators, because they tend to accept the leading group's analysis of the situation. Industrial sociology studies, in particular, should avoid this error of perception and feeling.

4.   This statement of the problem bears many similarities to that of "over-identification" of social workers with clients.

5.   Researchers probably overestimate rather than underestimate the amount necessary for the continuation of the study. The desire to get along extremely well with his observed subjects may be in part a function of the insecurity of the researcher, particularly in relation to non-academic people. The anxiety of the researcher in his work is similar to the counter-transference of the therapist in a psychotherapeutic situation. This latter problem, interestingly enough, is becoming increasingly discussed in the psychoanalytical literature.

study is more difficult. When rapport does move beyond what is necessary for the study is difficult to decide, for rapport is more than a technique of acceptance. It involves a sensitive understanding of individuals so that one is able to make insightful analyses of behavior. To protect himself from developing impeding over-rapport, the researcher should ask himself: At what point does closeness to the subjects limit the research role? He should try to make clear that he is interested in a number of people in the particular situation, and that his research activities are his prime reasons for being present. In some cases, he must resolutely decide to prevent relationships from becoming more personal than is desirable for the development of insight and the maintenance of rapport. For the participant observer, the problem is not merely that of developing rapport; the question rather is what kind and quality of rapport are desirable?

Perhaps the most important paper on potential threats to the interpretability of observational data is the following selection by Morris and Charlotte Schwartz. This paper closely analyzes some of the many nonrational determinants of the observer's perceptions and interpretations and pays particular attention to the effects of the observer's interactive relations with the observed persons.

PROBLEMS IN PARTICIPANT OBSERVATION[1]

MORRIS S. SCHWARTZ AND CHARLOTTE GREEN SCHWARTZ

In the analysis of the process of participant observation as experienced in a sociological study of a mental hospital ward, we shall be concerned with three interrelated themes: (1) an operational statement of the process as it is experienced from the observer's point of view; (2) a description of the component parts of the process in terms of the observer's transactions in the social field he is observing; and (3) an evaluation of the human instrument and the consequences of its use in gathering data. Our frame of reference is common to the sociology of knowledge,[2] social psychological studies of perception,[3] communi-

Reprinted from *American Journal of Sociology* (1955), **60**, 343–354, by permission of the author and The University of Chicago Press.

1.   The studies on which this paper is based were supported (in part) by two research grants (MH51 and M493) made to the Washington School of Psychiatry by the National Institute of Mental Health of the National Institutes of Health, Public Health Service.

2.   Karl Mannheim, *Ideology and Utopia* (London: Kegan Paul, Trench, Trubner & Co., Ltd., 1936).

3.   R. R. Blake and G. V. Ramsey, *Perception: An Approach to Personality* (New York: Ronald Press Co., 1951); Hadley Cantril, *The "Why" of Man's Experience* (New York: Macmillan Co., 1950); Gustav Ichheiser, "Misunderstandings in Human Relations," *American Journal of Sociology*, LX, Part II (September, 1949), 1–70.

cation theory,[4] and interpersonal theory.[5] These systems of analysis maintain that man's perceptions, especially as they relate to his interactions with other people, are shaped and modified by his social and psychological assumptions and value judgments. Since, in any social research, the observer is the instrument through which and by which the phenomena of the investigation are selected and filtered as well as interpreted and evaluated, the way in which he operates is crucial in transposing "reality" into data and in producing a close correspondence between the actual and the recorded event.

THE RESEARCH SITUATION

We shall discuss the process of participant observation as we have engaged in it within the setting of a small mental hospital ward.[6] In the formal role of participant observers we studied the interactions of patients and staff (as well as our own interactions with patients and staff) in an attempt to delineate the interpersonal processes and the prevailing social structure as well as to evaluate the effects of such processes on the patients.[7]

The ward ordinarily has fourteen to fifteen patients, and from two to seven personnel on a shift. During the day shift (8:00 A.M.–4:00P.M.), when most of our observations were made, there were four to seven personnel ordinarily present. In this article the examples we shall cite and the conclusions we shall draw are derived from our experiences in this small and circumscribed social system.

Because of its unique characteristics, the situation afforded both advantages and disadvantages for participant observation. On the one hand, since this

---

4.   J. Ruesch and G. Bateson, *Communication: The Social Matrix of Psychiatry* (New York: W. W. Norton & Co., 1951), and J. Ruesch, "Synopsis of the Theory of Human Communication," *Psychiatry*, XVI (August, 1953), 215–43.

5.   H. S. Sullivan, *The Interpersonal Theory of Psychiatry* (New York: W. W. Norton & Co., 1953).

6.   For other discussions of the process of participant observation see, for example J. D. Lohman, "The Participant Observer in Community Studies," *American Sociological Review*, II (December, 1937), 890–97; F. R. Kluckhohn, "The Participant-Observer Technique in Small Communities," *American Journal of Sociology*, XLVI (November, 1940), 331–43; S. M. Miller, "The Participant Observer and 'Over-Rapport,'" *American Sociological Review*, XVII (February, 1952), 97–99.

7.   The following publications have resulted from two projects: A. H. Stanton and M. S. Schwartz, "The Management of a Type of Institutional Participation in Mental Illness," *Psychiatry*, XII (February, 1949), 13–26; "Medical Opinion and the Social Context in the Mental Hospital," *ibid.*, August, 1949, pp. 243–49; "Observations on Dissociation as Social Participation," *ibid.*, November, 1949, pp. 339–354; M. S. Schwartz and A. H. Stanton, "A Social Psychological Study of Incontinence," *Psychiatry*, XIII (November, 1950), 399–416; C. G. Schwartz, M. S. Schwartz, and A. H. Stanton, "A Study of Need-Fulfillment on a Mental Hospital Ward," *Psychiatry*, XIV (May, 1951), 223–42; and M. S. Schwartz and G. T. Will, "Low Morale and Mutual Withdrawal on a Mental Hospital Ward," *Psychiatry*, XVI (November, 1953), 337–53.

milieu permitted their expression, certain covert emotional processes which are ordinarily concealed were more readily open to view and appeared in an accentuated form. On the other hand, the overt tension prevailing on the ward and the lack of clarity in the communication of some of the patients made it difficult at times for the observer to understand the nature of the interaction, especially from the patient's point of view. We believe, however, that our findings are at least partially applicable to the participant-observer situation in other social systems—the state mental hospital, the general hospital, the factory, the school, or the community.

DEFINITION OF PARTICIPANT OBSERVATION

For our purposes we define participant observation as a process in which the observer's presence in a social situation is maintained for the purpose of scientific investigation. The observer is in a face-to-face relationship with the observed, and, by participating with them in their natural life setting, he gathers data. Thus, the observer is part of the context being observed, and he both modifies and is influenced by this context. The role of participant observer may be either formal or informal, concealed or revealed; the observer may spend a great deal or very little time in the research situation; the participant-observer role may be an integral part of the social structure or largely peripheral to it.

COVERT TRANSACTIONS IN THE
PROCESS OF PARTICIPANT OBSERVATION

There is a tendency to assume that there is a simple correspondence between the occurrence of an event and the recording of the event by the observer.[8] Upon inquiry into this process we have discovered that there is a significant time gap between the occurrence of an event and the recording of this event as data. We have seen the process of observation as a succession of steps in which the time gap between the event and its recording increases from one step to the next. These are (1) the split second subsequent to the event, during which it is registered; (2) an interpretation of its significance in the context within which it occurred, resulting in a more expanded awareness of the event; and (3) the transcription of the event into data in the form of mental or written notes. From this point of view, participant observation becomes, in part, a *process of registering, interpreting, and recording.* Since not all aspects of an

---

8.   We are using the term "event" to refer to more than a single occurrence. We intend it to mean a constellation of acts bound together in a pattern, the boundaries of which are not easily located, because they can be expanded or narrowed depending upon the observer's ability to encompass them and upon his purposes in the investigation. The term is similar to Mead's concept of the "social act" (see George H. Mead, *Mind, Self, and Society* [Chicago: University of Chicago Press, 1934]).

event are observed simultaneously, the "filling-out" or bringing into awareness of the components of the event, as well as the field within which it took place, becomes unavoidably a retrospective process. An example from our study of incontinence[9] illustrates this. In observing a patient performing an act of incontinence, a variety of factors were selected, evaluated, organized, and finally recorded as data. Some determination and selection was made as to (1) the significant events preceding the incontinence and contributory to it, especially the kinds of transactions the patient was carrying on with others immediately preceding the incontinence; (2) the nature of the social context in which it occurred; (3) the patient's perception of the social situation in which she found herself and the meaning she gave to the incontinent act; (4) the meaning of the act to the audience and their reaction to it; (5) the patient's reaction to the audience's reaction; (6) the nature of the patient's transactions during and immediately following the incontinent act; (7) the observer's response to this event as a whole and to each of the constituent parts; (8) the effect of his response upon his observations; and (9) the effect of his response upon the act itself. It is obvious that any segment of the event moved so rapidly that its meaning and its relation to other segments was obscured, and the organization of the total pattern was difficult to identify.

What happens in the time interval between the event and its final recording is of utmost importance. In retrospective observation the investigator re-creates, or attempts to re-create, the social field in his imagination, in all its dimensions, on a perceptual and feeling level. He takes the role of all the other people in the situation and tries to evoke in himself the feelings and thoughts and actions they experienced at the time the event occurred. He assesses the accuracy of this role-taking and then takes his own role, as he was reacting during the event, and examines the effect of his reaction on his perceptions of the situation. Finally, he tries to integrate his own perceptions of the situation with those of the participants and arrives at one or more pictures of the event which are recorded as data. What occurs is a type of reworking of the representation of the phenomenon as initially registered. A continuous shuttle process occurs in which the observer moves back and forth in his imagination (either wittingly or unwittingly) from his recall of the event as it was initially registered to his evaluation of the event at the time of retrospection. What are finally recorded are the end product of evaluation during this retrospective period and the further evaluation made at the time of the physical recording of the data. In effect, observation is a continuous process of evaluation. During this reworking the observer's evaluations proceed at a more leisurely pace than was possible in the urgency of the immediate situation. At this pace he can explore the event in its fuller ramifications. In this exploration some covert transactions occur which need to be specified more fully.

---

9.   "A Social Psychological Study of Incontinence," *op. cit.*

A certain amount of this retrospective reworking (and it is difficult to estimate how much) goes on without the observer being aware of it. Rather than finding a simple and direct connection between the occurrence of the event and its representation as data, we discovered that our observation began to expand the longer we thought about it. This expansion occurs by bringing into focal awareness those aspects of the event that were on the fringe of consciousness— certain segments of the event that are registered on the periphery of the observer's awareness. These may be brought to central awareness by permitting one's self to be open to their emergence through recollection, rumination, and free association around the event. In this self-conscious attempt to bring the fringe material into focal awareness, a dual process may occur. The observer may follow the clues that come into awareness during the retrospective evaluation, or he may try to take his own role at the time the event occurred and evoke in himself or recall what was on the periphery of his awareness at that time. In either case, aspects of the event will emerge which are clearly recognized as having been registered by the observer but previously were not seen clearly or were grasped only momentarily and then put out of awareness. Thus, the data represent a coalescence between the recalled fringe material (which originally was noted around the time of event-occurrence) and the evoked peripheral material (which came into awareness during the retrospective reworking). This coalescence in turn merges with the other segments of the event that have already been registered and interpreted in clear awareness. In this reworking the previous data may be maintained unaltered; they may be added to or changed; significant aspects of the event may appear which were previously omitted; and connections between the segments of the event and between this event and others may appear which were previously unrecognized.

The retrospective analysis may be of value in partially rectifying restrictions in observation brought about by the observer's partial lack of readiness to observe. For any particular event his preparedness for observation may be inadequate; there may be distractions which make it difficult to observe, or his psychological constellation may be such that his ability to focus on and encompass the field may be reduced. Despite these restrictions of preparedness, segments of the event register on the observer's peripheral awareness and may be brought into focal awareness retrospectively.

We have indicated previously that it is difficult to estimate how much of this retrospective reworking goes on unconsciously. Despite the difficulties, the significant area of potential distortion and misinterpretation must be explored, even if only partially, if we are to increase the validity of our observations. We must try to get answers to questions such as the following: What is the unconscious significance of the event to the investigator, and what is the relation of this to the unconscious significance the event has for the participants? How does the investigator's unconscious motivation influence the way he initially registers the event and symbolically modifies it in the retrospective reworking?

THE RECIPROCITY BETWEEN THE OBSERVER AND THE OBSERVED

The participant observer is an integral part of the situation he is observing. He is linked with the observed in a reciprocal process of mutual modification. Together the observer and the observed constitute a context which would be different if either participant were different or were eliminated. In the course of an investigation the observer and observed become important to each other, and it is the background of their past experiences together, merging with and reflecting itself in a present situation, which determines the nature of the reciprocity. Continuing observed-observer transactions influence in many ways both the kinds of data that emerge (for the observer creates them to some degree) and the registering, interpreting, and recording of them.

THE OBSERVER'S EFFECT ON THE OBSERVED

The mere presence of the observer means that movements are made and orientations are developed toward him which would not otherwise have occurred. The "typicality" of these movements, their difference from or similarity to other activities undertaken by the observed before the observer role had been established, must be evaluated. Also, the fact that the role of observer has been established may alter the course of events, even when the observer is temporarily absent. Conspicuous during the early stages of our research was the great amount of feeling aroused in both patients and staff by the investigator's presence. The patients were curious and, at times, hostile to the investigator; they watched him closely and sometimes attacked him verbally, insisting they did not want to be guinea pigs. The ward staff was covertly, and sometimes overtly, suspicious of his intentions and role; sometimes they used him as a scapegoat; in general, they were interested but wary. However, these feelings gradually diminished, and at the end of six months the observed no longer reacted to the observer with strong negative feelings, and responded to him much as they would to a regular ward staff member.

In our research situation a process of mutual habituation gradually took place between the observer and the observed. As a result of this process we were able to delineate some factors that facilitated the process of participant observation. It is important that the investigator does not maintain situations in which he is in conflict with the observed, provokes excessive anxiety in them, or demonstrates disrespectful attitudes toward them. In addition, it is essential that he recognize the importance of participating with the observed on a "simply human" level—relating with them not only in his specific formal role, but also in terms of the sentiments Cooley described as constituting the core of human nature.[10] He must share these sentiments and feelings with the

---

10. See C. H. Cooley, *Social Organization* (New York: Charles Scribner's Sons, 1913), and *Human Nature and the Social Order* (New York: Charles Scribner's Sons, 1902).

observed on a sympathetic and empathic level. Thus the observer and observed are bound together through sharing the common role of human being. When the observed become convinced that the observer's attitude toward them is one of respect and interest in them as human beings as well as research subjects, they will feel less need for concealing, withholding, or distorting data. Through this type of simply human interaction, the psychological distance between observer and subject may be diminished and restraint in communication reduced, and the alteration of the situation which ensues from the impact of the observer may be minimized. However, in interacting on the simply human level, the observer must be careful not to abandon or restrict his role.

Instead of attempting to withhold or conceal data, the observed may "produce" data for the investigator, but it is difficult to determine the significance of such productions for the problem under study. We found that some patients put on a "performance" and started "acting up" (or acting out) for him. One of the patients said, "Since we're supposed to be crazy, let's act like it for him." Another patient, when she discovered the investigator was interested in the problem of incontinence, said to a nurse, "Tell him that I've just done it on the floor, and he can come and find out about it," a statement we interpreted as at once an attempt to help the investigator and a sarcastic response to his interest in this problem. The observed, as the result of his orientation toward the investigator, may behave in accordance with or contrary to the latter's expectations, desires, or interests. If the investigator attempts to study the meaning or motivation of these productions, he may find himself abandoning the problem originally selected for study; in our investigation we would have become interested in the reasons for the patient's relating to the investigator as she did rather than in the context of the incontinent act. But it is also true that interest in these meanings and motivations may reveal connections with the original problem that were not immediately apparent. For example, the patient's performance of the incontinent act for the investigator may be related to the nature of her integration with him. This integration may be similar to other integrations in which she becomes incontinent.

MODES OF PARTICIPANT OBSERVATION

The kinds of data the investigator gathers will depend in part upon how he participates as an observer. Two interrelated modes of participation proceed concurrently but should be distinguished for the purpose of analysis. These are: (1) participation as role activity in the research situation and (2) affective participation in which the investigator's emotional responses are evoked in the situation. While role participation is controllable to some degree, the observer cannot prevent himself from being affected by the emotional interplay between the subjects or between himself and the observed.

Each of these modes can be seen as a continuum. The variable on the continuum of role activity is the degree to which the observer participates in the research situation, the scale extending from "passive" participation to "active" participation. We have stated previously that the observer cannot remain emotionally untouched. Thus, on the continuum of affective participation, the variables are the nature of the investigator's emotional involvement in the interaction he is observing as well as the degree to which he becomes involved.

PARTICIPANT OBSERVATION AS A ROLE

In discussing participant observation as a role, we assume that the function of the observer is to observe as fully, intensively, and extensively as possible and thus are concerned with the way in which different forms of participation facilitate or deter effective, valid, and meaningful observation.

The "passive" participant observer. As an ideal type the "passive" participant observer interacts with the observed as little as possible. He conceives his sole function to be observation and attempts to carry it on in the same mode as an observer behind a one-way viewing screen. Maintaining contact with the observed outside the role of observer is viewed as an interference rather than as an opportunity for gathering additional data. The investigator assumes that the more passive he is the less will he affect the situation and the greater will be his opportunity to observe events as they develop. The "passive" role is used as a way of detaching himself emotionally from what is transpiring and of minimizing the interferences that might be occasioned by his affective reactions and evaluations. The observer remains an outsider and relatively anonymous to the observed, while they, in turn, look upon him as having a special role that is not integrated with the other roles in their situation.

In our research it appeared that certain problems could best be studied by "passive" participant observation; for example, the study of need fulfillment on the ward. Here the investigator recorded the requests of patients and the staff's responses to them and obtained a quantitative record. It became clear, however, that in addition to playing the role of observer, it was also necessary to interact with the observed on the simply human level. We found it desirable for the investigator to engage in these two modes at different times, attempting to exclude interaction on the simply human level while playing the role of observer. Paying some attention to the necessity of relating himself to the observed in a human way resulted in the acceptance of the observer in his passive role; moreover, it made it possible for him to withdraw at times of intense anxiety, such as collective upsets; and then, being less involved than the participants, he could observe more easily. But, because they regarded the observer as an outsider, the observed tended to refrain from bringing certain problems to his attention. In general, this role had both advantages and disadvantages. On the one hand, the observer was freer to study the problem which was the focus of his attention; on the other hand, not being in the confidence of the observed, he was unaware of some events that related directly to his problems of study. Because the observer tended to remain somewhat outside the stream of events, it became more difficult to evaluate his effect on the situation.

In playing the role of passive observer, certain problems have to be recognized and handled. Often, the passive participant observer will experience impulses, sometimes weak and sometimes strong, to abandon the role of observer, the restraint of which may evoke strong feeling in him. For example, he may feel anger, discomfort, or frustration because his usual naturalness and spontaneity has to be checked. Under these circumstances, some restriction in observation may occur. He may become preoccupied with his feelings and cease observing, or become evaluative of others. In this role, as contrasted with the active role, there is less opportunity to share in the life of the observed and to experience the meaning of events which are emotionally significant to them. When the observer attempts to keep himself outside the stream of events, he may come to believe that he is not experiencing *any* affect. He then tends not to recognize his affective reactions or their effect on his observations. Finally, in this role the investigator must deal with the resistance and hostility directed toward the outsider.

The "active" participant observer. As an ideal type, the "active" participant observer maximizes his participation with the observed in order to gather data and attempts to integrate his role with other roles in the social situation. His activity is accepted, both by himself and by the observed, as part of his role. His intention is to experience the life of the observed so that he can better observe and understand it. In some situations his behavior is similar to that of the observed; in other situations he plays complementary roles. He attempts to share the life of the observed on a simply human level as well as on a planned role level and uses both these modes of participation for research purposes. That is, while participating and identifying with the observed, he looks upon his relations with them as data and also as clues for uncovering further data. As this continues, he becomes more a part of, and more comfortable in, the social field. He attempts to strike that balance between active participation in the lives of the subjects and observation of their behavior which will be most productive of valid data.

In our first type of active participant observation the investigator played the formal role of observer on the ward and was free, within broad limits, to participate with the observed as he wished. He talked with patients and staff individually, conversed informally with groups of patients, participated in games, etc., on the assumption that if he lessened the difference between himself and others, he could reduce the effect of his role on the observed and at the same time more fully understand the meaning of the patients' behavior and the nature of the integration between staff and patients. We found this role valuable in discovering covert and obscure social processes and integrations as well as in understanding the affective meaning of ward events for the staff.

In our second type of active participant observation, the observer, in the formal role of investigator, planned interventions in the social structure with

the ward staff for the purpose of developing a more therapeutic "milieu."
He attempted to develop an empirical basis for introducing social change into
the social structure. Although he had no formal authority on the ward and no
responsibility, the investigator, nevertheless, was an integral part of ward
activities, participating in ways similar to those described in the first type of
active participant observation. He transmitted his initial findings to the ward
staff as information that might be used in furthering accepted therapeutic
values. We found this role facilitated the study of social change as it proceeded
on the mental hospital ward.

In active participant observation a shuttle process occurs in which the
observer, participating actively at one moment, shifts imaginatively the next
moment to observing what he and others have been doing and then shifts
back to the interaction, thereby continuing the participation uninterruptedly.
This back-and-forth shift in imagination has the character of immediate retrospective analysis and is later combined with subsequent retrospective analysis
(the constituents of which have been described earlier).

The observer must be able to derive satisfaction from and see the value of
active participation; otherwise, his discomfort or resentment stemming from
his active role may distort his observation. In this role there is increased
possibility of affective involvement with the observed so that the observer
loses his perspective—especially the perspective of the outsider. As a result,
the assumptions and values which characterize the observational situation
may be unwittingly accepted and thus remain unnoticed and unrecorded.

Comparing the passive and active roles, we found that in the latter the
observer increased his identification with the observed and was better able
to become aware of the subtleties of communication and interaction. Active
participant observation appears to be more conducive to self-observation.
By experiencing the effects of the subjects on himself, he may be able to perceive more clearly their effects on those with whom they ordinarily are in
interaction. It also may afford the investigator greater opportunity to discover
the operation of his own distortions in perception.

Whether a relatively passive or relatively active participant observer role
is selected in any research project depends upon the kinds of data desired,
what is prohibited and what is permitted in the observational situation, the
nature of the subjects being studied, and the observer's capabilities and
preferences. We have found, however, that if the observer continues his work
for long in the same situation, he develops a tendency to participate more
actively.

AFFECTIVE PARTICIPATION

The ways in which the observer and the observed are joined to each other,
constitute part of each other's field of influence and operation, and form a
social field are strikingly demonstrated in their affective relationship. If the

observer works continuously in a situation, whether as passive or as active participant, he will inevitably become involved in and with the observed's emotional life. Much of this involvement may go on outside of awareness; between observer and observed there will be a continuous process of moving away from and moving toward, sympathy and disgust, anger and affection, fear and trust based on conscious and unconscious motives, emotions, thoughts, feelings, and imagery. These affective relations are maintained in many complex ways, possess significance both in intensity and duration, and link observer and observed in mutually important integrations despite their individual wishes. For example, we found that without being aware of it at the time the observer tended to withdraw when a patient was withdrawn. Similarly, when low morale was a dominant aspect of the ward context, the investigator discovered that he, too, was functioning less effectively.

The two ends of the continuum represent types of affective involvement that will influence the nature and validity of the data. At one end of the continuum the investigator is affectively involved in such a way and to such a degree that he loses his perspective, and his feelings obliterate his ability to observe. The distortions of reality and the misinterpretations that stem from the observer's interpersonal difficulties in living virtually eliminate his ability to record valid data. At the other end of this continuum the observer's empathic relationship with the observed facilitates his understanding of their inner life and their social world and increases the validity and meaningfulness of his observations.

We have noted that it is inevitable that in observing other human beings in interaction, especially in emotionally significant areas of living, the observer's own emotional life will be stimulated. The issue is not whether he will become emotionally involved, but rather, the nature of the involvement. The involvement, whether it is closer to one end of the continuum (sympathetic identification) or to the other end (projective distortion), is very little a function of the observer's role. Rather, it is primarily a function of his experience, awareness, and personality constellation and the way these are integrated with a particular social situation. Since the investigator has control over neither his affective responses nor their effects on his observations, he must contend with his feelings as part of his data. Only by increasing his own awareness of them, their bases, and their effects on him will he be able to counteract their distorting influences.

We noted some indexes of the distorting of data as a result of affective involvement. These included strong moral or valuational reactions, such as judging staff's or patient's behavior as "good" or "bad." We found that such reactions as anger, resentment, disgust, condemnation, pity, and excessive worry or concern about a patient or her therapeutic progress were signs that the investigator was not functioning as an objective observer. In addition, whether overt or not, taking sides (e.g., siding with staff against patients or vice versa or with one staff subgroup against another) made it difficult to see the interaction clearly. Sometimes the observer may overtly or covertly, consciously or unconsciously, use the research situation to prove he is superior to the observed or that he can be kinder, more sympathetic, or more understanding to patients than others. All such affective responses indicate that the observer's involvement with his own emotional responses is taking precedence over his performance as scientific observer.

In certain types of situations the observer's personal problems, blind spots, and recurrent inappropriate responses toward certain kinds of people may be evoked. Then his unconscious motivations and attitudinal sets—his personally significant images, symbols, and meanings from the past—obscure his vision and act as a filter between his perception and what "actually is." Another problem is the possibility that his morale will vary with that of the persons with whom he is identified. Under these circumstances he may have less enthusiasm for the investigation and have less devotion to the task of observation, and the investigation thus becomes dependent upon the vicissitudes of the situation.

However, the distorting type of involvement need not have only negative effects. If the observer can view the involvement as a signal that something significant is happening in the interactional field—as a communication that important data are emerging—he can convert the involvement into a partial asset. Through the reorientation of his attitude toward the involvement, he can exercise a tour de force in developing some detachment from the situation and in reducing the distorting impact of the involvement as well as sensitizing himself to new aspects of the phenomena under study.

In the same way that it is more difficult to describe mental health than to identify the processes that interfere with it, it is more difficult to describe that type of affective participation—sympathetic identification—which results in more meaningful and valid data than to describe projective distortion. Sympathetic identification includes empathic communication and imaginative participation in the life of the observed through identification and role-taking. In this type of involvement the observer is, at the same time, both detached and affectively participating; he feels no need to moralize or judge the interaction; his attitude is one of interested curiosity and matter-of-fact inquiry directed toward understanding the observed. His reactions are "appropriate," and his appraisals are realistic. In sum, the observer's emotional involvement, observation, and awareness of both himself and the observational field come together in optimum balance.

ANXIETY AS A SOURCE OF DISTORTION

The potentiality for the emergence of anxiety "in" the observer during the course of his investigation exists in two interrelated areas: those aspects of the observer's personality that are especially sensitive to anxiety and those situations that evoke anxiety easily in every observer. Whatever the source, anxiety may influence both the way in which data are obtained and the kinds of data gathered.

Anxiety which stems primarily from the observer's sensitivities may be aroused in such ways as the following: The observer may become anxious because he is an outsider and as such is not accepted by the observed. The degree of such anxiety, his capacity to sustain it, and the defenses he uses against it are important in influencing his observational ability. He may be anxious about a particular research problem because it touches on some interpersonal difficulty. For example, if he is studying the authority and power relations in a social structure, his own difficulties in accepting authority or wielding power may prevent him from seeing the situation realistically. In addition, if he cannot accept withholding by the subjects or sustain frustration, but reacts instead with anxiety, the observer is apt to impair or limit his data.

The anxieties inherent in our research were conspicuous and atypical. There were instances of extreme upset on the part of a particular patient as well as situations of collective disturbance in which the ward as a whole was upset. In collective disturbances where ward tension was sharp and intense, the effects of anxiety on the investigator's ability to observe were especially conspicuous: here he saw only a blur when he tried to encompass the total field, and even very narrow and restricted segments of the field were indistinct. It was difficult to focus on the interaction and to maintain the focus consistently. Gross movements of the participants were observed and not the subtleties of their interaction. A defense frequently used by the investigator was his preoccupation with handling his own anxiety. The observer thus focused his attention away from the events and toward himself. This refocusing was not useful in providing data about the event under observation, nor was the observer able to learn much about the nature of his interaction with the observed.

However anxiety is aroused and whatever its source, it seriously affects the ability of the observer to play his role. In some instances his defenses against anxiety may take the form of psychological or physical withdrawal. In others his anxiety may lead him to falsify a particular situation. For example, in trying to assess kinds and degrees of stresses, strains, and tensions, he may project his own anxiety and see the situation as more disorganized and fraught with anxiety than it actually is. Restrictions in focus that anxiety occasions may lead him to select certain aspects of the situation as important and to minimize, overlook, or be completely unaware of other aspects. The impairment in observational ability brought about by anxiety permeates all phases of the observational process, registering, interpreting, and recording.

Anxiety can sometimes be converted into a partial asset as an observational tool. If it can be handled, its bases and sources understood, and its effects evaluated, its emergence can then become a significant indicator of important interpersonal activity transpiring in the social field that needs to be observed and analyzed.

BIAS AS A SOURCE OF DISTORTION

The most general bias to which all observers are subject and to which the sociologist has given much attention is the sociocultural bias—the bias of sharing the perspective and values of one's historical time and cultural milieu and of occupying various statuses and playing the attendant roles.[11] In addition, one's frame of reference, in part a product of one's professional training, influences the selections one makes from the phenomenon (e.g., whether it is viewed philosophically, biologically, institutionally, situationally, or in terms of individual psychodynamics) and determines how and what is observed. Since much work has been done in the sociology of knowledge to point out the importance of these biases and to evaluate their effects, we will not deal with them here beyond indicating that they form part of the observer's personality constellation.

The particular patterns of interpersonal dynamisms with which the observer operates will shape *what* he sees and will influence *how* he sees human interaction.[12] The observer may have some long-standing emotional blocks which prevent him from seeing certain aspects of reality clearly. To evaluate the way in which certain personality dimensions of the observer distort the data he is observing, such questions as the following, for example, must be asked: In general, what kinds of defenses does he use against anxiety? Is he usually cautious or incautious, pessimistic or optimistic, trusting or suspicious? What is his attitude toward persons in authority?

The emotional needs of the investigator with reference to the investigation itself play an important role. Such questions as the following need to be considered: How much does the investigator need to be right, especially with reference to proving his hypothesis? Will he tend to see what he wants or expects to see in his data? How much failure can the investigator sustain without becoming discouraged or unconsciously moving in the direction of forcing success by distorting the data?

Other important considerations are the observer's assumptions about human behavior in general. What does he believe people are "basically," and what does he feel they "ought to be"; what perspectives does he have on human activity: long or short range, broad or narrow, subtle or gross?

Some of the questions we posed for ourselves were the following: What cultural stereotypes of mental patients does the investigator bring to the study? What are his feelings about mental illness, and what are his emotional reactions toward patients? To what extent is he repelled or attracted, sympathetic or antipathetic? Are his feelings relatively stable, or do they vary with different circumstances and with different kinds of patients? What are the inves-

---

11. See, e.g., Mannheim, *op. cit.*

12. For a similar discussion of bias see John Dollard, *Caste and Class in a Southern Town* (New York: Harper & Bros., 1937), pp. 33–41.

tigator's attitudes toward various levels of staff, and what is the direction of his sympathy when staff and patients are in interaction? In studying inconti- nence, the following were some of the questions we asked: How much does the investigator share the cultural attitude of disgust? Is there a tendency on his part to avoid the situation?

Our approach to the problem of bias has been an attempt to expand as well as make more precise by formulating in concrete process terms. Myrdal's suggestion for excluding bias from social research: "There is no other device for excluding biases in social sciences than to face the valuations and to intro- duce them as explicitly stated, specific and sufficiently concretized value premises."[13] Implicit here is the assumption that bias is a universal phe- nomenon; that the observer can and does know what his biases are; and that, knowing what they are, he can, by specifying them, prevent distortion of his observations. There are at least three conditions that need to be fulfilled before this suggestion can be put into effect. The observer must (1) be moti- vated to look for his biases; (2) look for them actively and, having come upon a bias, explore its meaning and ramifications; and (3) look upon the uncovering of his biases as a continuous process of discovery—as an ongoing process to which there is no end.

From this point of view, facing one valuation, or one bias, is the beginning of pursuing other related valuations and biases. Thus, discovering one's biases becomes a continuous process of active seeking out and grappling with one's limitations and blocks. Satisfaction then derives not only from uncovering a bias but equally from seeking further. This view requires a certain attitude and habit of inquiry toward one's distortions. It means that old distortions might still influence one's observations despite their previous discovery and must be focused on again and again before their effects upon one's observa- tions will diminish. Any particular bias may appear in various disguises and take different forms in different contexts. Thus, the more perspectives from which we see the bias, the greater the possibility of minimizing its effect. Finally, no matter how arduous and seemingly successful one has been in dis- covering his biases, another look may still uncover something that up until then has not been seen.

CONCLUSION

We have attempted to examine some of the problems which appear to be inherent in using the human instrument for gathering and evaluating inter- personal data. Though we have limited our analysis to participant observation on a mental hospital ward, we believe that it has broader application. The operation of unconscious factors in observation, the influence of anxiety on

13. Gunnar Myrdal, *An American Dilemma* (New York: Harper & Bros., 1944), p. 1043.

how and what is seen, and the effect of the observer's personal interests, values, and orientation are problems which are present in any research in which interaction of human beings is being studied. One of the tasks of the social scientist is to continue to refine and sensitize the human instrument to insure greater validity of the data gathered. Some advance may be made by a more intensive and extensive study of the problems we have raised.

In this section of the chapter we have seen spelled out a good many sources and manifestations of the three primary threats to the interpretability of observational data, i.e., reactive effects of the observer, distortions in observation, and limitations on what the observer can witness. The previous selections all caution the participant observer to be hypersensitive to the various manifestations of these threats, so that if they seem to be operating in a particular case, steps can be taken to minimize their contaminating effects. By and large, the authors envision these steps as being primarily modifications of the observer's role *vis-à-vis* his subjects and the phenomena under study. For example, if the observer should find himself becoming too closely identified with one faction in the organization he is studying, and find that he is thus distorting his perspective on the whole organization, he should correct for this and perhaps seek a more balanced set of relations with all factions.

Yet another means of correcting for such observational problems is to compensate for them by supplementing observational data with interview data, i.e., the observer's interpretations of events he has witnessed directly should always be checked against those of various categories of his subjects. In this fashion, if systematic bias is creeping into the observational data, the observer is more likely to become alerted to its existence and its probable directions and is able to temper or revise his previous interpretations of the observed events. Similarly, strategically garnered interview data can aid the observer in discovering aspects of the phenomena which, for various reasons, he has not directly observed. If he cannot then modify his activities so as to be able to observe these neglected aspects, he may rely on informant interviewing to obtain information on these. Possible reactive effects of the observer can likewise be averted in many cases by reliance on informant interviewing.

But interviewing is itself subject to various contaminating effects, and it is to these that we now turn.

Threats to Interview Data

The primary threats to the interpretability of interview data can be broadly categorized as (1) the reactive effects of the interview situation upon the received testimony; (2) distortions in testimony; and (3) reportorial inabilities of the interviewee. Again, each of these categories encompasses many specific sorts of problems which must be taken up in some detail.

Most of the considerations in evaluating interview data seem to have focused on informant interviewing, asking how we can know whether the informant has given us an accurate account of some particular event. But, as J. P. Dean and W. F. Whyte point out, this is a somewhat oversimplified criterion for informant interviewing, and for respondent interviewing (in which the researcher may be more interested in the interviewee's subjective dispositions and reactions than in some objective "truth"[4]) it can be well nigh useless. The following selection by Dean and Whyte examines some of the specific threats to each type of interview data and reassesses the criteria pertinent to obtaining adequate data. (Note that in this selection the authors do not systematically distinguish informants from respondents.)

"HOW DO YOU KNOW IF THE INFORMANT IS TELLING THE TRUTH?"

JOHN P. DEAN AND WILLIAM FOOTE WHYTE

Research workers who deal with interview data frequently are asked the question: "How do you know if the informant is telling the truth?" If they are experienced research workers, they frequently push aside the question as one asked only by those unsophisticated in the ways of research. But the persistence with which it comes up suggests that we take it seriously and try to formulate it in respectable terms.

Those who ask the question seem bothered by the insight that people sometimes say things for public consumption that they would not say in private. And sometimes they behave in ways that seem to contradict or cast serious doubt on what they profess in open conversation. So the problem arises: Can you tell what a person *really* believes on the basis of a few questions put to him in an interview? Is this not a legitimate question?

The answer is, "No"—not as stated. It assumes that there is invariably some basic underlying attitude or opinion that a person is firmly committed to, i.e., his *real* belief. And it implies that if we can just develop shrewd enough interviewing techniques, we can make him "spill the beans" and reveal what this basic attitude really is.

To begin with, we must constantly bear in mind that the statements an informant makes to an interviewer can vary from purely *subjective* statements ("I feel terribly depressed after the accident") to almost completely *objective* statements ("The Buick swerved across the road into the other lane and hit the Ford head on"). Many statements, of course, fall somewhere in between: "The driver of the Ford was driving badly because he had been drinking"; or "It was the Ford driver's fault because he was drunk."

In evaluating informants' statements we do try to distinguish the subjective and objective components. But no matter how objective an informant seems to be, the research point of view is: *The informant's statement represents merely the perception of the informant, filtered and modified by his cognitive and*

---

4.   See also the discussion of the usefulness of interviewee "lies" in Passin (1942).

Reprinted from *Human Organization*, 1958, **17**, No. 2, 34–38, by permission of the authors and publisher.

emotional reactions and reported through his personal verbal usages. Thus we acknowledge initially that we are getting merely the informant's picture of the world as he sees it. And we are getting it only as he is willing to pass it on to us in *this particular interview situation.* Under other circumstances the moves he reveals to us may be much different.

Granted this, there are two questions that the research worker wants answered: A) What light does the statement throw on the subjective sentiments of the informant? and B) How much does the informant's report correspond in fact to "objective reality?"

I. THE INFORMANT'S REPORT OF "SUBJECTIVE DATA" (A)

The problem here is how to evaluate the informant's subjective report of what he feels or thinks about some subject under investigation. At the outset we must recognize that there are different kinds of subjective data that we may want the informant to report: (a) A *current emotional state* of the informant, such as anger, fear, anxiety or depression. Many informants have great difficulty in putting feelings of this sort into words. Even for the most articulate, the verbal expression of complex emotional states is a difficult thing; (b) *The informant's opinions,* that is, the cognitive formulation of his ideas on a subject; (c) *The informant's attitudes,* that is, his emotional reactions to the subjects under discussion; (d) *The informant's values,* that is, the organizing principles that underlie his opinions, attitudes, and behavior; (e) *The informant's hypothetical reactions,* that is, his projection of what he would do, think or feel *if* certain circumstances prevailed; and (f) *The actual tendencies of the informant to behave or feel* when confronted with certain stimulus situations. Generally, of course, verbal reports are only part of the data on the basis of which we infer persons' tendencies to act. Equally important in making these inferences are past behavior and a variety of non-verbal cues that we may detect.

Each of these various kinds of subjective data are elicited by different kinds of questions put in different ways to the informant. The assumption that any one of these represents his "real" feelings in the matter is, of course, unwarranted. For one thing, the informant may have conflicting opinions, values, attitudes, or tendencies to act. In fact, the conflict among these various subjective data may be the most important subjective information we obtain. This approach puts in quite a different light the problem of using behavior as a way of validating attitudes. Take, for example, a young housewife who in an interview expresses herself as much in favor of careful budgeting of household finances. She indicates that she and her husband have carefully worked out how much they feel they can afford to spend on various categories and have even gone so far as to make out envelopes in which they put the money allocated to these various purposes. Subsequent to the interview, however, she goes shopping with one of her close friends with whom she feels a good deal of social competition. Under the pressures of this situation she buys a dress which is out of line with her financial plan. It is not very meaningful to say that her behavior in buying the dress "invalidates" her opinions in favor of budgeting. Nor does it make sense to ask what her "real" attitudes toward budgeting are. But because we often expect reasonable behavior in the management of personal affairs and daily activities, we frequently try to get informants to give a rational and consistent picture of their sentiments and behavior when confronted with them in an interview situation. If this young housewife had been asked by the interviewer what she would do if she ran across an unusually attractive dress which was not within her budgetary planning, she might have said that she would refuse to buy it and would incorporate some budgeting plan for the future by which she might be able to purchase such a dress. But the sophisticated researcher does not expect informants to have consistent well-thought-out-attitudes and values on the subjects he is inquiring about.

The difficulties in interpreting informants' reports of subjective data are seriously increased when the informant is reporting not his present feelings or attitudes but those he recollects from the past. This is because of the widespread tendency we all have to modify a recollection of past feelings in a selective way that fits them more comfortably into our current point of view.

But perhaps the major consideration that makes the evaluation of reports of subjective data difficult is the fact that they are so *highly situational.* If, for example, a Democrat is among some Republican friends whose opinions he values highly, he will hesitate to express sentiments that might antagonize or disconcert these friends. If, however, he is among his own intimate friends who think pretty much as he does, he will not hesitate to express a Democratic point of view and, if he is at a Democratic party meeting where there is considerable enthusiasm in support of party causes and he is swept up in this enthusiasm, he may express Democratic sentiments even more strongly than among his own friends. *The interview situation must be seen as just ONE of many situations in which an informant may reveal subjective data in different ways.*

The key question is this: *What factors can we expect to influence this informant's reporting of this situation under these interview circumstances?* The following factors are likely to be important:

(1) Are there any ulterior *motives* which the informant has that might modify his reporting of the situation? While making a study among the foremen of a South American company, the researcher was approached one day by a foreman who expressed great interest in being interviewed. In the conversation which followed, he expressed himself with enthusiasm about every aspect of the company under discussion. When the interview closed, he said, "I hope you will give me a good recommendation to the management." His ulterior motives undoubtedly influenced his reporting.

(2) Are there any *bars to spontaneity* which might inhibit free expression by the informant? For example, where an informant feels that the affairs of his organization or his own personal life should be put forward in a good light for public consumption, he will hesitate to bring up spontaneously the more negative aspects of the situation.

(3) Does the informant have *desires to please* the interviewer so that his opinions will be well thought of? An interviewer known to be identified with better race relations might well find informants expressing opinions more favorable to minority groups than they would express among their own friends.

(4) Are there any *idiosyncratic factors* that may cause the informant to express only one facet of his reactions to a subject? For example, in a follow-up interview, an informant was told that she had changed her attitude toward Jews. She then recalled that just before the initial interview a dealer had sent her a wrong couch and she implied that he had tried to cheat her. She recalled that he was Jewish and that she was still mad about this incident and reacted in terms of it to the questions about Jews in the interview. A few days earlier or a few days later she would probably have expressed herself quite differently. Idiosyncratic factors such as mood, wording of the question, individual peculiarities in the connotations of specific words, and extraneous factors such as the baby crying, the telephone ringing, etc., all may influence the way an informant articulates his reactions.

Unless they are taken into account, these various factors that influence the interview situation may cause serious problems and misinterpretation of the informant's statements. To minimize the problems of interpretation, the interview situation should be carefully structured and the interview itself should be carefully handled in the light of these influences. Outside influences should be avoided by arranging an appropriate time and place for interviewing that will eliminate them as much as possible.

The influence of ulterior motives can sometimes be quashed by pointing out that the researcher is in no position to influence the situation in any way. Bars to spontaneity can usually be reduced by assurances to the informant that his remarks are confidential and will be reported to no one else. The confidence that develops in a relationship over a period of time is perhaps the best guarantee of spontaneity, and informants who are important should be developed *over time* with care and understanding. Naturally the interviewer should not express or, indicate in any way, his disapproval of statements made by the informant or indicate any of his own values that might intrude in the situation. Idiosyncratic factors of connotation and meaning are difficult to account for, but it is certainly a good precaution to ask questions in many different ways so that the complex configuration that a person's sentiments represents can be more accurately understood.

While we never assume a one-to-one relationship between sentiments and overt behavior, the researcher is constantly relating the sentiments expressed to the behavior he observes—or would expect to observe—in the situation under discussion.

In one field situation, the informant was a restaurant supervisor. It was already known that the restaurant owner was a graduate dietician who placed a great deal of stress upon maintaining high professional standards. Midway in the course of the interview, the supervisor remarked in a casual manner—perhaps too casual—that she herself was the only supervisor in the restaurant who was not a college graduate. The supervisor did not elaborate on the point, nor did the interviewer probe at this time. In a lull in the conversation a few minutes later, the interviewer, using the opportunity to return to a topic previously mentioned, said: "I was interested in something you said earlier: that you are the only supervisor here who is not a college graduate—" Before another word was uttered, the supervisor burst into tears. Clearly, the effect attached to the statement made earlier was repressed or concealed and became evident only as revealed in subsequent behavior when she cried.

In some cases the informant may be trying to tell himself—as well as the interviewer—that he does not have a certain sentiment, and may even have convinced himself. In the case of Joe Sloan, a gasoline plant operator, (see the article on "Engineers and Workers," *Human Organization,* Volume 14, No. 4, Winter, 1956) the interview took place shortly after Sloan, a highly ambitious worker, had been demoted to a lower classification. He followed up this rebuff by talking with the plant manager and personnel manager, and he reported calmly that they had not been able to give him any encouragement about his future with the company. Since, even before this setback, Sloan had expressed strong negative sentiments toward management—with apparent relish—one might have expected him to be even more explosive, now that he had this new provocation. The researcher was surprised and puzzled when he said, "I'm nonchalant now. Those things don't bother me anymore." Neither his gestures nor facial expression revealed any emotion.

A week later, Sloan suddenly walked off the job in response to a condition that had recurred often in the past, with only mild expressions of dissatisfaction from Sloan and the other workers. Reflecting on the incident later, we can see that we should have recognized Sloan's "nonchalant" statement as a danger signal. In the light of the recent events that must have intensified his negative sentiments toward management, he must have been making an effort to repress these sentiments. Probably, being unable or unwilling to "blow his top" as before, he no longer had a safety valve and might have been expected to take some rash and erratic action.

These cases suggest the importance of regarding any marked discrepancies between expressed sentiments and observed (or expected) behavior as an open invitation to the researcher to focus his interviewing *and* observation in this problem area.

II. THE INFORMANT'S REPORTING OF "OBJECTIVE" DATA (B)

Frequently the research worker wants to determine from an interview what actually happened on some occasion pertinent to the research. Can we take what the informant reports at face value? In many instances the answer, of course, is "No."

Suppose an informant reports that a number of people are plotting against him. He may be revealing merely his own paranoid tendencies, in which case his statement must be seen as casting light primarily on his distorted perception of the world. But even though plots of this kind are rare in the world, it may just happen that, in this instance, people actually *are* trying to undermine the informant. It is therefore important for the researcher to know in what respects an informant's statement must be taken as a reflection of his own personality and perception and in which respects as a reasonably accurate record of actual events.

How much help any given report of an informant will be in reconstructive "object reality" depends on how much distortion has been introduced into the report and how much we can correct for this distortion. The major sources of distortion in firsthand reports of informants are these:

1) The respondent just did not observe the details of what happened or cannot recollect what he *did* observe, and reports instead what he supposed happened. Data below the informant's observation or memory threshold cannot of course be reported.

2) The respondent reports as accurately as he can, but because his mental set has selectively perceived the situation, the data reported give a distorted impression of what occurred.

3) The informant unconsciously modifies his report of a situation because of his emotional needs to shape the situation to fit his own perspective. Awareness of the "true" facts might be so uncomfortable that the informant wants to protect himself against this awareness.

4) The informant quite consciously modifies the facts as he perceives them in order to convey a distorted impression of what occurred.

Naturally, trained research workers are alert to detect distortion wherever it occurs. How can they do this? First of all, there is an important negative check: *implausibility*. If an account strongly strains our credulity and just does not seem at all plausible, then we are justified in suspecting distortion. For example, an informant, who lived a few miles away from the campus of a coeducational college, reported that one of the college girls had been raped in a classroom during hours of instruction by some of the men college students. She was quite vague as to the precise circumstances—for example, as to what the professor was doing at the time. (Did he, perhaps, rap the blackboard and say, "May I have your attention, please?") This account was obviously lacking in plausibility. Things just do not happen that way. The account may, however, throw light on the informant's personal world. Through other reports we learned that a college girl had indeed been raped, but the offense had taken place at night, the girl was not on the college campus, and the men were not college students. The woman who told this story was a devout member of a fundamentalist sect that was highly suspicious of the "Godless university." In this context, the story makes sense as a distortion the informant might unconsciously introduce in order to make the story conform to her perception of the university. The test of implausibility must be used with caution, of course, because sometimes the implausible *does* happen.

A second aid in detecting distortion is any knowledge we have of the *unreliability of the informant as* an accurate reporter. In the courtroom, the story of a witness is seriously undermined by any evidence that he has been inaccurate in reporting some important point. In first interviews we will generally have little evidence for judging an informant's reliability unless he happens to be reporting on some situation about which we have prior knowledge. But in repeated interviews, after what the informant has told us has been checked or corroborated by other reports, we can form some idea of how much we can rely on his account. Thus we learn to distinguish reliable from unreliable informants, although we must always be careful not to assume that, just because an informant has proven reliable in the past, we can continue to believe his accounts without further checking.

A third aid in detecting distortion is our *knowledge of an informant's mental set* and an understanding of how it might influence his perception and interpretation of events. Thus we would be on guard for distortion in a labor union leader's report of how management welched upon a promise it made in a closed meeting.

But the major way in which we detect distortion, and correct for it, is by *comparing an informant's account with the accounts given by other informants.* And here the situation resembles the courtroom setting, since we must weigh and balance the testimony of different witnesses, evaluate the validity of eyewitness data, compare the reliability of witnesses, take circumstantial evidence into account, appraise the motives of key persons, and consider the admissability of hearsay information. We may have little opportunity in field research for anything that resembles direct cross-examination, but we can certainly *cross-check* the accounts given us by different informants for discrepancies and try to clear these up by asking for further clarification.

Since we generally assure informants that what they say is confidential, we are not free to tell one informant what the other has told us. Even if the informant says, "I don't care who knows it; tell anybody you want to," we find it wise to treat the interview as confidential. A researcher who goes around telling some informants what other informants have told him is likely to stir up anxiety and suspicion. Of course the researcher may be able to tell an informant what he has heard without revealing the source of his information.

This may be perfectly appropriate where a story has wide currency so that an informant cannot infer the source of the information. But if an event is not widely known, the mere mention of it may reveal to one informant what another informant has said about the situation. How can the data be cross-checked in these circumstances?

III.

An example from a field study of work teams at the Corning Glass Works illustrates this problem. Jack Carter, a gaffer (top man of the glass making team), described a serious argument that had arisen between Al Lucido, the gaffer and his servitor (his #2 man) on another work team. Lucido and his servitor had been known as close friends. Since the relationship of the interpersonal relations on the team to morale and productivity were central to the study, it was important (1) to check this situation for distortion and (2) to develop the details.

First, the account Carter gave of the situation did not in any way seem implausible. Second, on the credibility of the witness, our experience indicated that Jack Carter was a reliable informant. Third, we had no reason to believe that Carter's mental set toward this other work team was so emotionally involved or biased as to give him an especially jaundiced view of the situation. Furthermore, some of the events he described he had actually witnessed and others he had heard about directly from men on the particular work team. Nevertheless, to check the story and to fill in the details regarding the development of the conflict, we wished to get an account from one of the men directly involved. So an appointment was scheduled with Lucido one day after work. Because it might be disturbing to Lucido and to the others if the research worker came right out and said, "I hear you recently had an argument with Sammy, would you tell me about it?" the researcher sought to reach this point in the interview without revealing this purpose. Lucido was encouraged to talk about the nature of his work and about the problems that arose on his job, with the focus gradually moving toward problems of cooperation within the work team. After Lucido had discussed at length the importance of maintaining harmonious relationships within the work team, the research worker said, "Yes, that certainly is important. You know I've been impressed with the harmonious relationships you have on your team. Since you and the servitor have to work closely together, I guess it's important that you and Sammy are such close friends. Still, I suppose that even the closest of friends can have disagreements. Has there ever been a time when there was any friction between you and Sammy?" Lucido remarked that indeed this had happened just recently. When the researcher expressed interest, he went on to give a detailed account of how the friction arose and how the problem between the two men had finally worked out. It was then possible to compare Lucido's account with that of Carter and to amplify the data on a number of points that Carter had not covered. The informant in this case probably never realized that the research worker had any prior knowledge of the argument he had with his servitor or that this matter was of any greater interest to the researcher than other things discussed in the interview. The main point is this: by the thoughtful use of the information revealed in the account of one informant, the researcher can guide other interviews toward data which will reveal any distortions incorporated in the initial account and usually will provide details which give a more complete understanding of what actually happened.

The problems of distortion are heavily compounded if the researcher is dealing with informants who are giving him secondhand reports. Here, the researcher has to deal, not only with the original distortion that the witness incorporated in the story he told to the informant, but also with any subsequent distortions that the informant introduced in passing it along to the researcher. Of course, an informant who has a shrewd understanding of the situations about which he is reporting secondhand may be able to take into account any distortions or bias in the reports he receives from those who talked to him. It *may* even be that the informant's lines of communication are more direct and intimate than the research worker can establish. In this case, the picture the informant gives may have validity beyond the picture the researcher might get directly from the eyewitnesses themselves.

This kind of situation is illustrated by the case of Doc, a street corner gang leader discussed in *Street Corner Society*. Doc was an extraordinarily valuable informant. Whenever the information he gave could be checked, his account seemed highly reliable. But he had an additional strength: he was also well-informed regarding what was happening in his own group and in other groups and organizations in his district. This was due to the position he occupied in the social structure of the community. Since he was the leader of his own group, the leaders of other groups naturally came to him first to tell him what they were doing and to consult him as to what they should do. His informal leadership position within his own group made him a connecting link between that group and other groups and organizations. Hence developments in the "foreign relations" of the group were known by him before they reached the followers, and usually in more direct and accurate form.

Because of the wide variation in quality of informants, the researcher is always on the lookout for informants such as Doc who can give a reasonably accurate and perceptive account of events the research is interested in. These special informants are frequently found at key positions in the communication structure, often as formal or informal leaders in the organization. They have ability to weigh and balance the evidence themselves and correct for the distortions that may be incorporated from their sources of information. But it is important that they have no needs to withhold or distort the information they report to the researcher. Even so, wherever the researcher has to rest on secondhand reports he must be particularly cautious in his interpretation.

CONCLUSION

In conclusion, we should emphasize that the interviewer is not looking for *the true attitude or sentiment*. He should recognize that informants can and do hold conflicting sentiments at one time and they hold varying sentiments according to the situations in which they find themselves. As Roethlisberger and Dickson (*Management and the Worker*) long ago pointed out, the interview itself is a social situation, so the researcher must also consider how this situation may influence the expression of sentiments and the reporting of events.

With such considerations in mind, the researcher will not ask himself, "How do I know if the informant is telling the truth?" Instead, the researcher will ask, "What do the informant's statements reveal about his feelings and perceptions and what inferences can be made from them about the actual environment or events he has experienced?"

Vidich and Bensman (1954) amplify the preceding inventory of sources underlying misleading statements by interviewees:

1. Purposeful intent. Interviewees may slant information in an attempt to influence the results of the research. Information may be dramatized to make the interviewee or his organization seem less prosaic. Excessive information may be given by reformers who want to use the research to expose and reform their organizations. Myths and rationalizations may be offered in order to cover up unpleasant truths. Information may be distorted to serve personal ambitions, self-aggrandizement, or self-protection, or even to serve in carrying on personal feuds. Stereotyped responses may be offered, based on rumors about the research heard in advance of the interview.

2. The temporary role of "interviewee." All interviewees attempt to form an image of the interviewer and of the organization he represents. On the basis of this image, they often concentrate on providing that information which they believe will help the researcher to solve his particular problem, as they have defined it.

3. The psychology of the interviewee. Information communicated by the interviewee is influenced by the whole panoply of psychological processes—memory, attitudinal set, level of motivation, anxiety, fears, etc. Important among such factors are language style and vocabulary size, for if they are different from those of the researcher there can be considerable misunderstanding by both participants.

Research on the characteristics of good informants[5] tends to support the above analyses of the sources of misleading interview statements. Ability to collect and retain information is found to be positively related to: length (but not recency) of exposure to the situation; level (but not type) of interest; and generalized perceptual ability. Ability to communicate information is found to be positively related to level of education. These key abilities are themselves highly correlated, for the informant who has the data well organized, well remembered, and well verbalized can more

---

5.   Back (1956).

readily transmit the information to the researcher. Beyond ability, the informant's level and type of motivation affect performance in the interview. Genuine interest in the aims of the research is found to be the most efficacious motive, followed by interest in the interview as conversation, with extrinsic or ulterior motives being least effective in yielding good interview data.

Withholding of information may be as troublesome to the researcher as are misleading statements and may stem from the same general sources. The following selection by Chris Argyris examines in close detail many additional sources and signs of evasiveness in the interview situation, categorizing these roughly into those that are located in the individual interviewee and those located in the social organization itself.

DIAGNOSING DEFENSES AGAINST THE OUTSIDER

CHRIS ARGYRIS[1]

In the previous articles, the authors have been concerned with problems of establishing and maintaining research relationships from the point of view of the research worker. It is the purpose of this paper to switch the discussion to the point of view of the subjects of the research. How do they react to being interviewed, observed, and in general, "researched upon"? What are some of the common defenses they seem to employ? Why do they employ these defenses?

The material presented below is drawn primarily from one researcher's experience. As such it will be limited. We will further limit our examples to defenses that are commonly met during "in-plant" research in industrial organizations. Many possible examples related to unions, hospitals, and governmental agencies are not included. Furthermore, we will not discuss the defenses related to research conducted in the employee's homes. In spite of these limitations, we believe that the examples we present will include many of the basic types of defenses that researchers experience in social organizations.

TWO SOURCES OF DEFENSE MECHANISMS

Defense mechanisms may be related to the personality of the subject *vis à vis* the researcher. They may also be related to the social organization as it is expressed through the individual. For example, it is possible for a subject to delay or refuse an interview because he fears all new psychological situations.

Reprinted from *Journal of Social Issues* (1952), **8**, No. 3, 24–34, by permission of the author and publisher.

1.   The writer expresses his debt to Robert Guest, Yale University, for his constructive suggestions and examples.

On the other hand, experience suggests that it is equally possible for the same individual to refuse to be interviewed because he realizes there are important organizational pressures against the research (e.g., the boss doesn't like it).

Admittedly this distinction is not a sharp one in real life. But the researcher must study his subject closely in order to understand the meanings implicit in particular mechanisms. Knowledge of the various origins of the defense mechanisms is not only of research interest but is crucial in handling the underlying resistance and preparing for any changes that might be attempted in the organization later.

INDIVIDUALLY BASED MECHANISMS

To be interviewed by a research worker is not an easy experience for most subjects. Subjects are known to react to the interview by "being a little nervous" or "uneasy"; or by refusing to speak; or by a complete breakdown into tears; or by talking so much and being so aggressive that the research worker does not have much opportunity to carry out the interview.

Listed below are some of the general factors that operate to make subjects feel anxious about being "researched upon":

1. Interviews are new psychological situations. As such they tend to place a subject in a situation where the purposes are unclear or unknown; the perceptual structure is unstable; the "proper" behavior is unknown. Clearly, such situations tend to produce tension, anxiety, and conflict within individuals.

2. Some subjects know what an interview is like but dislike such a situation because it represents to them an authoritarian relationship where they are submitting to a researcher. This also arouses defenses.

3. Still other subjects are closely attached to and identified with their leader or their work group. They view a research interview as an attempt to make them talk about their very personal relationships with their leader or group, and therefore resist.

4. Research people introduced as being somehow connected with a University often tend to be perceived as "highly educated and rather sophisticated individuals." This connection with the "sacred halls of learning" tends to place some employees (especially top executives with no college education) in a situation which calls for defense of their self.

SOME EXAMPLES OF DEFENSE
MECHANISMS USED BY INDIVIDUALS

Manifestations of Fear. Some subjects simply couldn't control their feelings. They arrived for an interview in an obviously disturbed state. Some were jittery, others nervous, or uneasy. Some "held back their uneasiness" by wringing a handkerchief in their hand, while others arrived with a "death grip" on their clipboard or notebook. Such behavior usually had the effect of making the interviewer more cautious in his questioning, thereby protecting the subject.

Other subjects defended themselves from the researcher by stuttering, by behaving as if they had difficulty in hearing, or by behaving as if they constantly misunderstood the research worker. Still others said, "I'm not sure I understand you," "Would you repeat that please," or "I'm really not clear on your point." All these phrases served to help the subject defend himself from having to answer too many questions. Subsequent interviews with some of these subjects suggested that the blocking at times was rather unconscious.

Surface Collaboration. Subjects were known to insist, with politeness and diplomatic certainty, that they "really didn't know much about that problem," or "To be very honest with you, I've never heard of that problem." Others attempted to defend themselves by trying to get the researcher to tell them whether someone already suggested to him that this problem existed in the plant. The subjects then guided their comments according to the researcher's answers. For example, they were cautious in their answers if they were told this was a problem of interest to the management.

It was also not uncommon to find some subjects (usually supervisors) who defended themselves by simply giving the "correct" or "book" answer to every question. They tended to quote the "principles of supervision" listed in their organization's manual for supervisors. Or they answered questions with such general phrases as "You have to be good to people," "A supervisor must be a man among men," "A good supervisor hits hard, but is fair," etc.

Problem Denial. Still other subjects made no bones about their defensive position, and with a rather gruff manner or perhaps with a note of annoyance or surprise, quickly responded to the researcher, "No, definitely not, we never had any of these problems in our place. I'm dead sure of that."

Silent Treatment. Some subjects used the "silent treatment" to defend themselves from the researcher. This seemed to be especially successful with the researcher who was new and was out to set a new high in "nondirective" research interviewing. Quite naturally, the degree of silence varied. Some subjects answered all "projective" questions with a direct "yes" or "no." Other subjects took their cue and remained silent by noticing when the interviewer began to write in his notebook.

By-Path Seduction. Subjects have been known to "latch on" to the introductory comments the researcher has made and use them as a basis for a series of questions. For example, the subjects expressed an unlimited interest in the university that the researcher was from. Or some subjects asked many questions concerning the nature of the research and the use to be made of the material. Still other subjects wanted to obtain all sorts of details on who was to be interviewed, when and why. In a few instances, subjects defended themselves from the researcher by coercing him to discuss, in general terms, what other people had already said in their interviews.

Subjects came to the interview armed with interesting material concerning their specialty. Thus, in a study of the effect of cost budgets upon people, many of the accountants interviewed attempted to spend hours discussing the many multi-colored, complicated accounting instruments they use. "And of course", they would say, "You *do* want to know about our new cost budget . . ." Before the researcher could even wonder how he might offer a proper negative reply, the lecture began.

Stalling. Other top level accountants responded to an inquiry concerning the human factors of budgets in a questioning tone. "Mm . . . hmm . . . yes, of course, human factors in budgets . . . yes, that is important, isn't it." Some would simply deny the existence of the problem. For example, one controller said, "No, I don't think it is a problem in my company. It might be in others but I don't see it here," or "Well, I don't know if I could be of much help. My problems are technical ones."

The interesting aspect of these semi-denials and this hedging was that the same accountants terminated the interview with a sentence like, "And as I said before, the human factors in budgets are the most important factors. If only people would realize that . . . etc." This would be uttered in such a convincing manner that one would hardly suspect the same person, an hour before, doubted the existence of the problem. The accountants could have been "stalling for time" to think about the problem while wanting to conceal this from the researcher. In other words, some of them could have incorporated in their role as executives such values as "I will always be certain," "I will never procrastinate," "I will have the answers on the tip of my tongue," so that they could not comfortably lean back in their chairs and think for a few minutes concerning the problem.

Other Procedures. These include the use of such devices as the following: (1) *Protective forgetting.* Some subjects defend themselves by "accidentally" forgetting about their interview appointment. (2) *The rush act.* Other subjects did not forget their appointment, but "just had to schedule an important meeting which will, I'm afraid, cut the research interview in half." (3) *Handy hurdles.* Still other subjects have asked to be interviewed after their working hours and away from the plant. When the researcher remarked that he lived thirty miles away and might therefore have to delay the interview, it was interesting to note the smile and "Oh, that's perfectly all right. I understand. I don't mind waiting." (4) *Rumors.* One subject started a rumor which suggested that she spent a terrible night after the research interview and just couldn't see how she could go through it again. The rumor eventually reached the researcher as intended. Fearing he might jeopardize his position in the plant, the researcher cancelled the second and subsequent interviews with that employee.   (5) *Advance preparation.*   Finally, numerous subjects have attempted to defend themselves by trying to find out who had already been interviewed and then asking these people as many questions as possible concerning the nature of the interview, the researcher, etc.

ORGANIZATIONALLY BASED MECHANISMS

We now turn to the defense mechanisms that may be largely attributable to the organization. These defense mechanisms serve to protect the organization against the outsider until the role, objective, and methods of the researcher are clarified and accepted. The researcher may find that organizational mechanisms may be due to reasons similar to those listed below.

1. The agents of the organization may decide to resist the research program because they perceive it as a possible attempt to destroy something already existing in the organization. For example, some research projects are resisted because they are perceived as being designed to weaken a union. Others are resisted because they are perceived as being designed to "soften up" the workers for impending technological or administrative changes.

2. The agents of the organization may accept the program but find themselves in a conflict situation if they attempt to participate honestly and freely. On the one hand, they may like to cooperate with and speak freely to the researcher. On the other hand, they may fear that detrimental information might reach the boss who happens to be very "cool" toward the program. A more frequent example of this phenomenon is the foreman who may find himself torn between management and employee groups and therefore may feel very insecure about taking part in research that may be viewed by the employees as management sponsored.

3. The workers and their immediate supervisors might accept the research program, but the upper management officials may define certain overall policies which prevent the employees from speaking freely. These policies will tend to crystalize resistance on the part of the workers and lower level supervisors.

4. Resistance to research may occur because the research involves two departments which are fighting for power within the organization. The research is delayed until the "power struggle" is finished.

5. There are two cases on record where the complete cooperation of management and the unions was gained, but the research was considerably delayed because the local Chamber of Commerce was not in favor of the research. In both cases, we might add, the organizations to be studied were in small towns where they provided a primary source of revenue for the town people.

6. A rather frequent reason for resistance to research is the fear on the part of the management of the organization (union, industrial, or otherwise), that the research may uncover material which might not be favorable to the organization. Closely allied with this reason is fear that some important secret technical information may be required.

7. One research group reports that their research is being continually blocked because the organization they are studying seems to gain prestige from the research group. The organization therefore wants to delay the researchers in their work to keep them at the plant.

8. The day-by-day experiences of subjects may be filled with crises. For example, production is going bad; bonus pay is down; a lay-off is rumored; one of the men is annoying the other; the foreman is hopping on the boys; it is a terribly hot day; the tools are bad, etc. If the respondent is thrust into an interview suddenly, one of these factors may be in his mind. If the interview "hits" the respondent at such a time, there may be a tendency to look upon the researcher as a "big nuisance."

9. On the other hand, in highly repetitive types of operations workers may develop a work routine which is identical day in and day out, year in and year out. The research interview may seriously interrupt this routine.

10. Management people may dislike to be interviewed because they dislike anything that takes them away from their job and leaves them "out of touch" with organizational matters, over which they are personally responsible.

11. Many organizations create an authoritarian climate in which the subject is dependent upon a leader who tends to require complete loyalty to the organization. Working under such conditions for many years may make the subjects cautious in answering questions that might "place the boss in an unfavorable light."

Perhaps these examples may suffice to suggest the variety of possible reasons for organizational resistance to research.

EXAMPLES OF DEFENSE MECHANISMS RELATED TO ORGANIZATION

Creating Damaging Rumors. Recently, a researcher initiated his investigation after top management had participated in establishing the study objectives and had accepted the overall program for research. The second day of interviewing started with a phone call from the vice-president. He requested the researcher to come to his office immediately. Upon entering the office, the vice-president insisted the research be temporarily halted since the supervisors were "up-in-arms." They had heard a rumor that the researcher "is here to figure who is neurotic and who isn't, and to report to top management." The arrangements had proceeded so smoothly the first day that no resistance was expected. The researcher attempted to cover up his own astonishment with a statement that "Indeed, it would be difficult for the plant to permit research under these conditions and it would probably destroy much of the validity of the data."

The vice-president was ready to agree to an immediate postponement when the research worker pointed out that (a) top management, by postponing the research, would imply that the rumor might have validity, and (b) rumors in organizations, like fever in a human body, may be symptomatic of underlying problems and should not necessarily be "snuffed out." Rather, it would be vital that the rumor be understood clearly and its real purpose be uncovered.

Top management agreed and an investigation followed. During the investigation, the following significant facts were uncovered: The vice-president had personally telephoned all the middle management supervisors on the list that were to be interviewed. (This step was contrary to the plan originally defined whereby the personnel manager of the local plant was to make the contact). The vice-president began the telephone conversation with the usual remark, "How are things," and then informed the supervisors that a certain "Dr." was coming down to their department tomorrow to interview them. He informed the supervisors that the research worker would make no report to the vice-president, and encouraged them to speak freely. The supervisors, who were led by a stern, rather autocratic, plant manager, thereupon became quite anxious for at least three reasons. In the first place, the vice-president had never called them personally before. Secondly, the company had recently hired a psychiatrist who had just completed some personal interviews with some of the supervisors reputed to have ulcers. The supervisors felt that some of the results were reported to top management. Thirdly, the plant manager was on vacation. The supervisors, being very loyal to their plant manager, did not want to participate until they knew how he felt about the entire project. Since they could not reach him, they began to perceive the researcher as a personal "hatchet man" of the division office sent down to "wield the axe" while the plant manager was on his vacation. Once these feelings were brought out into the open and responded to appropriately, the rumor died down.

Not all research workers would recommend that action be taken during a rumor. In another plant, the writer worked jointly with a psychiatrist. A similar rumor was circulated concerning the psychiatrist. The rumor began, it was thought, because the psychiatrist had been badly introduced by the management to the employees. The psychiatrist chose to ignore the rumor. He simply continued his interviewing and answering questions concerning himself whenever requested. As far as the writer could ascertain, the psychiatrist maintained satisfactory relationships with the employees. The rumor faded away in about a week.

Giving the Researcher the Run-Around. There are numerous examples of research groups being delayed by being continually referred "to the appropriate authorities" for permission to release certain desired information.

One research group reported the following incident. They had received enthusiastic approval by the home office of a large corporation to study one of the smaller plants many miles away. Although the research group obtained blanket permission in writing, they found upon arrival at the local plant that they were being blocked at every turn. The local authorities insisted that they did not have authority to give out the information requested. When reminded of the blanket authority given by the home office, the local authorities replied that the authority granted was general rather than specific, and therefore, they were not certain that the specific information requested by the research group could be given to them. The research team soon found itself spending most of its time travelling to the home office acquiring specific permission for various data.

It was discovered, after a few months of patient investigation, that the plant personnel manager had made some private deals with the local union officials in order to keep the plant in operation. As it was, the union and the employees were being given services in excess of the home office policy. The personnel manager, fearing that this information would eventually get back to the home office, attempted to stop the research by placing obstacles in the path of the research workers.

Overwhelming the Researcher with Irrelevant Information. One research team reported that in the initial stages of their research they were guided through long tours of the many departments of a large manufacturing organization and were carefully limited to observing and asking questions related to the technical problems involved. The supervisors who acted as guides, curiously enough, refused to answer questions concerning other than technical problems. Some typical excuses were that they "didn't know much about the other problems," that "the departments have few if any human relations problems," and that "people are that way anyway, my real problems are helping to keep the production moving." After some months of research the supervisors admitted that they had deliberately refused to discuss the other subjects raised by the researchers. It seemed that they did not particularly trust top management or the research group who were observed to have periodic meetings with the top management. Much of the resistance began to break down after the research team began to become "part of the lay-out" (as one man said) and had noticed many human relations incidents that were apparently not reported to top management.

Stereotyping the Research Worker: "Long Hair." A top executive rationalized his resistance to the researcher by projecting upon him such dubious titles as "long hair," "a man up in the clouds," "an idealist," and "a philosopher spinning day dreams." The researcher could not institute any action research as long as he was perceived by the top executive in this light. Through this defense mechanism the top executive was able to ignore the changes that he was beginning to realize he should make in himself. "After all," he could say to himself, "why the devil should I listen to a long hair who is up in the clouds and does not realize my problems."

Another executive discussed the time factor associated with human relations changes as follows: "We just can't wait in business. We can't wait for years. It's today that is important. You can't think of tomorrow. It's today. Time is valuable in business. It costs money. What have you got that can change today? You know, that's the trouble with you fellows. You don't see the realistic practical side of life." Neither of the executives, be it noted, requested that the researcher leave the organization. In fact, both kept calling for meetings ostensibly to see how the research was coming along. Interestingly enough, the majority of the time was taken up discussing their problems in instituting some of the change.

Stereotyping the Research Worker: Communist. Stephen Richardson[2] reported an incident in which the subjects defended themselves from the research team and at the same time used it to further their own ends. A research was focused on two factions in a local union. The focus of the research became known in the local. The researcher had great difficulty in obtaining an interview with the chairman of the shop committee. However, he was able to interview a man, Mr. X, who had just been eased out of the shop committee and was very willing to talk about the factions. This man told the researcher that the chairman of the shop committee was spreading the rumor that the researcher was a communist and was discouraging the shop stewards from cooperating in the research. Mr. X also said that the chairman would shortly lose office (this happened as predicted) and advised the researcher to continue her work and make no comment.

Richardson diagnosed the rumor as follows. "The chairman of the shop was insecure and felt that with the present focus of the research a good deal of data damaging to himself would be obtained by the researcher. Therefore, he used the rumor as a way of attacking the researcher before she could attack him."

Trying to Make the Researcher a Detective. Top management executives have attempted to defend themselves from being examined by attempting to coerce the researcher into the role of a personal secret agent for top management. For example, a controller asked the researcher to "please pay special attention to Mr. Y when you interview him. You know, in my job I have a lot of headaches. I don't think these men are maturing properly for top level assignments. They don't seem to have the spark and the ability to be go-getters. I would be very much interested in hearing what you have to say about

---

2. S. A. Richardson, "Progress Report on Field Research Training Program," Feb. 1952, Cornell University, Ithaca, New York.

them." In another instance, a plant manager kept asking the research worker, "Tell me, what the hell have you fellows been learning around here? . . . I know, we've confidences to observe and I want them to be observed. I'm not trying to breach them. But, well, . . . for example, what's going on during the supervisory meetings . . . what do you think of my supervisors?"

In both cases, the executives attempted to use the researcher as a channel of communication. The formal channel, for some reason or other, was blocked for the type of information desired. If the researcher were to accept this role, he would not only be violating professional ethics but he would be preventing the executives from experiencing a need to examine why they were unable to obtain this information by themselves. Also, if the researcher were to provide the information, he would be likely to reinforce a probably mistaken self-perception on the part of the executives, namely that it was the others who were "immature and not developing adequately."

Still another example, with a different outcome: An engineer in a middle size plant approached the researcher and asked for a private interview. The interview was granted. During the discussion, the engineer unfolded a "hard luck story" concerning his relationship with his boss. After painting a dark picture of his future, the engineer pleaded with the researcher to "please tell me . . . just give me an idea of what the boss thinks of me." The researcher sympathized with the engineer and agreed that he was experiencing quite a lot of difficulty, but naturally, he refused to give the information. The engineer became quite upset over the "cold-bloodedness" of the researcher, became very aggressive, and left the room hurriedly. After some months, the researcher learned that the engineer had spoken to many of the supervisors in the plant. He described the research worker as a "selfish s.o.b., who wouldn't help a guy out when the going was rough." The interesting point was that according to the other supervisors the researcher's "stock" with them increased substantially. The supervisors commented that although they understood the engineer's problem, they were glad to hear that the confidence originally promised was maintained.

Changing Human Relations Problems into Administrative Problems. In the limited experience the writer has had in conducting research, he is increasingly being impressed by how many subjects hide their human relations problems from others and from themselves by consciously and unconsciously redefining them into technical problems. Once the switch is made, then it follows for the subject that the need for research into human relations problems is not important. The important problems become "to add a new machine," or "retrain the sales personnel," or "to have more accurate cost accounting records," etc. In this connection perhaps, one of the most often heard rationalizations is something to the effect that "our business, unlike others, is very complicated. One of the most complicated in the entire industry. Why we have hundreds of small little parts that go to make up our product. One slight error on anybody's part throws everything off . . . etc." If the researcher accepts this as being the actual fact without further information, then the subjects are spared from having to discuss any personal problems that they might have with other members of the organization.

Assigning the Researcher to Impotent Personnel. Another defense mechanism not so frequently experienced is to assign the researcher to an employee whose status and rank is low enough to make him rather impotent and unimportant as far as the research is concerned. As long as the researcher is tied to this impotent person, he will not tend to be much of a threat to the organization.

We would like to emphasize that one has to differentiate status and official rank in this problem. Thus, it is possible that a personnel manager or an old time supervisor ready to retire, or an executive vice-president may be highly impotent and helpless as far as the conduct of the research work is concerned. On the other hand, a janitor, a drill press operator, or a plant guard may be highly important and influential persons. It seems therefore advisable, to keep in mind that importance is not necessarily correlated with official rank.

Keeping the Researcher "Tied up." Finally, it is possible for an organization to defend itself by scheduling the researcher with many interviews with people who want to see him. If the researcher is to have all these interviews, he is not left much time to examine the problems he feels are more crucial. This defense mechanism does not in the writer's experience last long. First, the plant personnel probably do not have enough free time to continue such activity over a protracted period of time. Second, the primary purpose of this defense mechanism is usually to protect the subjects from the researcher until they understand him better and the purposes, goals, and methods of his research are clarified.

CONCLUDING STATEMENT

In closing, it seems worthwhile to mention briefly the following points concerning defense mechanisms. First, we suggest that defense mechanisms be viewed as attempts by the subject to adapt to the researcher. Thus the researcher need not worry or become unduly alarmed if subjects are defensive. In fact, it may not be unfair to suggest that he should worry when the subjects are not defensive. The researcher's task, it seems to us, is to learn to understand the defenses in the same manner a clinician understands the feelings of his patient. Viewing defense mechanisms in this light helps the researcher learn to use them in a constructive manner. It seems to us that defense mechanisms are important indicators of the psychological world of the subject, the "social climate" of the organization, the quality and strength of the relationship between the researcher and the subject.

Finally, we suggest that the researcher should study the defense mechanisms and the conditions under which they occur in order that he may better understand himself, his role as a researcher, and the effects that these two mutually dependent factors have upon the subject and the organization.

As was the case with threats to the interpretability of observational data, the prerequisite for coping with threats to the interpretability of interview data is constant monitoring of one's field operations, hoping to detect early any symptoms of problems that might affect the quality of data. (Such symptoms have been enumerated in the preceding selections.) If any symptoms are noted, the researcher must attempt to modify his interviewing operations in order to nullify or minimize the particular problems noted. For example, if interviewing subjects at their place of work seems to be producing many evasive and pat responses, the researcher might do well to attempt to replicate these interviews in a more relaxing setting, such as the subjects' homes. Similar adjustments are conceivable for the other major difficulties. For example, in order to deal with reportorial inability, the interviewer might first teach the informant the requisite skills,[6] or in order to deal with distortions due to a subject's emotional state, the interviewer might "work through" the subject's feelings or replicate the interview at a later date.

Parallel once more to the case with observational data, many threats to obtaining valid interview data can be offset by the considered use of direct observation. Distorted testimony, in particular, is amenable to this tactic. If one suspects that an informant is not giving an accurate report for some reason, this can often be checked by making it a point to observe the phenomenon once or a few times directly. In many cases, reportorial inabilities can also be circumvented in this fashion. And to some extent, even the reactive effects of interviewing can be countered, if one can observe the subjects spontaneously uttering to one another, or to other outsiders, the same contents that had been elicited in the interview situation.

Observational checks are not restricted to informant interviewing, of course, but are almost equally applicable to respondent interviewing, as Dean and Whyte pointed out before (pp. 106–109). If a respondent depicts his habits, dispositions, or feelings in some connection, this report can be checked by comparing it with observations of his actual behavior in relevant situations.

Assessment of Data Quality

The experienced participant observer is, of course, aware to some variable degree of the existence, sources, and manifestations of the manifold threats to the quality of observational and interview data. To the extent to which he is conscious of these threats, he will certainly attempt to avoid them beforehand, thus preventing the contamination of his data. The experienced researcher will not, for example, except for special purposes, interview an employee on his views toward management practices in the presence of that employee's supervisor, because he risks bars to spontaneity. However, simply because he is not yet well acquainted with all the dynamics of the social organization under study, the researcher will not be able to anticipate all the relevant sources of threat to his data and, consequently, will not be able to entirely avoid them.

Therefore, the researcher must constantly scrutinize his field experiences and his data for possible signs of contaminating factors and, having discovered such signs, must take action to counter these threats. This necessity is not confined to participant observation, of course, but is encountered equally in all social research.

---

6. R. Wax (1957).

In more highly structured studies, pretests or pilot studies are made in order to locate potential threats to obtaining valid data, and remedial adjustments are then made in the procedures of the actual study to minimize the effects of these threats. In this sort of approach, the pretest data—being possibly contaminated—are discarded and analysis is restricted to the more assured data of the actual, final study.

In participant observation studies, however, the focus is ordinarily on the peculiar dynamics of some particular social organization. Accordingly, it is not really possible to "pretest" one's operations on some similar organization and expect the particular sources of threat discovered to transfer very directly to the target organization. Discovery of such problems can only be made during the actual study. Some of the data, then,—particularly in the early phases of the study—are highly likely to be contaminated in some fashion. These data cannot simply be discarded, as pretest data can, because many of them are unique and irreplaceable, particularly those which reflect initial responses of personnel to the research inquiry itself. Because of this limitation, participant observation studies almost perforce will have to make use of some possibly contaminated data.

On the other hand, we know this situation is not at all peculiar to participant observation. No data, no matter how they are obtained, are entirely free of contamination, as the various studies of survey interviewer bias, of demand characteristics of an experiment, and of the effects of testing situations indicate.[7]

In this respect, in fact, the peculiar design features of participant observation studies afford a potential advantage over the more highly structured types of inquiry. That is, the flexible design of participant observation—the perpetual reflexive cycle of conceptualization, sampling, data collection, data analysis, and write-up—allows the researcher to assess the nature and magnitude of possible contamination at every point in the study and to compensate for it immediately. If, in this new cycle of data collection, the data obtained under the new set of safeguards substantially confirms the picture indicated by the earlier and presumably contaminated data, the onus of presumed contamination is effectively removed from these earlier data and they can safely be maintained within the accumulated corpus. In this way, the participant observation design allows one to essentially "salvage" important data that in other designs would have to be discarded.

In this light, then, assessment of the nature and magnitude of possible contamination in participant observation data takes on special importance. The following selection by George McCall provides one technique for such assessment.

---

7.   E.g., Kahn and Cannell (1957), pp. 186–202; Rosenthal (1966); Friedman (1967); Orne (1962); Masling (1960); Wohl (1963).

DATA QUALITY CONTROL IN PARTICIPANT OBSERVATION

GEORGE J. MCCALL

Many methodological commentators have expressed a certain skepticism concerning participant observation techniques on the grounds that these are particularly vulnerable to certain invalidating or contaminating effects.[1] Observational data in particular are singled out for suspicion although data obtained from the participant observer's interviews with subjects also receive criticism.

By and large, the principal concerns regarding the observational data of the participant observer can be summarized under three headings: (1) reactive effects of the observer's presence or behavior on the phenomenon under observation, with the result that the observer does not have the opportunity to observe the very thing that he may have hoped to observe and that he may in fact believe he is observing; (2) distorting effects of selective perception and interpretation on the observer's part; and (3) limitations on the observer's ability to witness all the relevant aspects of the phenomenon in question.

In the literature on participant observation, three general sources of such deleterious effects have been widely discussed. These sources are: the structural features of the observer's role-relations with subjects; personal characteristics of the observer, particularly his psychological functioning; and characteristics of the observer's intellectual frame of reference.[2]

Reactive effects, for example, may stem from the observer's role-relations to the subjects. The observer may be perceived as a critical outsider, a management spy, or a close friend, and the subjects' conduct may be modified accordingly. Similar effects may result from various personal characteristics of the observer, such as sex, race, education level, or snobbishness. Or, further, reactive effects may stem from the observer's frame of reference through the interpretations he places upon events, as these interpretations become manifested to the subjects by word or deed.

Prepared especially for this volume. The author gratefully acknowledges the valuable criticisms of preliminary versions of this paper on the part of Albert J. Reiss, Jr., and Paul F. Lazarsfeld.

1.   Bertha K. Stavrianos, "Research Methods in Cultural Anthropology in Relation to Scientific Criteria," *Psychological Review* (1950), **57**, 334–344; Martha W. Riley, *Sociological Research: I. A Case Approach,* New York: Harcourt, Brace, & World (1963), pp. 71–72; Eugene J. Webb, Donald T. Campbell, Richard D. Schwartz, and Lee Sechrest, *Unobtrusive Measures: Nonreactive Research in the Social Sciences,* Chicago: Rand McNally (1966), pp. 114–115.

2.   Frederica de Laguna, "Some Problems of Objectivity in Ethnology," *Man* (1957), **57,** 179–182; Eugene V. Schneider, "Limitations on Observation in Industrial Sociology," *Social Forces* (1950), **28**, 279–284; Morris S. Schwartz and Charlotte G. Schwartz, "Problems in Participant Observation," *American Journal of Sociology* (1955), **60**, 343–354; S. M. Miller, "The Participant Observer and 'Over-Rapport,'" *American Sociological Review* (1952), **17**, 97–99; Arthur J. Vidich, "Participant Observation and the Collection and Interpretation of Data," *American Journal of Sociology* (1955), **60, 354–360.

Distortions in the observer's perceptions may likewise be a result of his role-standpoint, such as overidentification with the management point of view or with the intellectual community. Such distortions may also arise from the observer's personal characteristics, such as mood, prejudices, or blind spots. And, of course, the observer's intellectual frame of reference may adversely condition his perceptions by leading him to pay selective attention to certain aspects of the phenomenon rather than to others.

Limitations on what is witnessed by the observer are often closely linked to the differential prerogatives and proscriptions of the role he has assumed in the field. If he has taken on the role of a factory worker, for example, he will find it difficult to gain access to management's closed-door meetings on labor policies. Similarly, the observer's personal characteristics may lead to a one-sided or even mutual avoidance between him and certain persons and events. And, once again, his intellectual frame of reference may not indicate certain events or categories of personnel as being of interest to his study of the overall phenomenon.

Many of these contaminating effects, as well as their sources, apply as fully to the interviewer as to the observer. Owing to his role-relations, his personal characteristics, or his frame of reference, the interviewer may fail to inquire after significant aspects of the phenomenon in question or may fail to accurately interpret the testimony he receives. Moreover, these same sources of contaminating effects on data may lead the interviewee to distort his own testimony.

With interview data, in fact, contaminating effects are not located exclusively in the researcher but may also be manifest in the interviewee.[3] The extent of the interviewee's knowledge of what he is reporting on must always be held somewhat in question. Furthermore, the researcher must always wonder whether the interviewee is giving an accurate account of what he does know. Potential reasons for an interviewee to slant or somewhat distort his account are numerous. They can be roughly grouped into a few broad categories: ulterior motives (e.g., to convey an unfavorable impression of an adversary in hopes of gaining the researcher's support in the conflict); bars to spontaneity in the interview situation (e.g., the presence of a superior or a close friend to whom an accurate account might prove embarrassing); idiosyncratic factors (e.g., the interviewee's mood or emotional state); and reportorial inabilities (e.g., a low level of verbal skill).

---

3.   John P. Dean and William F. Whyte, "How Do You Know If the Informant Is Telling the Truth?," *Human Organization* (1958), **17** (2), 34–38; Raymond L. Gorden, "Dimensions of the Depth Interview," *American Journal of Sociology* (1956), **62**, 158–164; Kurt W. Back, "The Well-Informed Informant," *Human Organization* (1956), **14** (4), 30–33; Chris Argyris, "Diagnosing Defenses Against the Outsider," *Journal of Social Issues* (1952), **8** (3), 24–34; Arthur Vidich and Joseph Bensman, "The Validity of Field Data," *Human Organization* (1954), **13** (1), 20–27.

Such inventories of potential contaminants of participant observation data are indeed quite sobering. How, under the circumstances, can one be confident that his data are any good?

The traditional first check in the evaluation of any datum in participant observation studies is to inquire whether the account seems plausible. Does it hold up internally and make any sense in light of one's broad understanding of human behavior? If an account does not seem plausible in itself, it is not taken seriously as a datum, although it may be taken quite seriously as an event to be probed and pursued as a possibly symptomatic distortion.

An important second check is to assess the stability of the account to determine whether it is consistent with other accounts from the same source. If it departs considerably from these other accounts, it may not be taken seriously as a direct datum but must be pursued in an attempt to resolve the inconsistency.

The two checks above should be applied as a continuous, intrinsic procedure in participant observation. Every item of information, whether derived from direct observation or from interviewing, should be continuously evaluated for its internal and external consistency. If a new item is inconsistent with others (i.e. its comparability is in question), both the new and the old accounts come under suspicion and are examined for some possible source of contamination that might explain the discovered discrepancy. If a particular source of contamination then seems likely to have caused the discrepancy, still further accounts—obtained under circumstances calculated to minimize that source of contamination—are sought as evidence bearing on the proposed explanation of the discrepancy.

The key to data quality control in participant observation is, thus, the thorough use of multiple indicants of any particular fact and an insistence on a very high degree of consonance among these indicants, tracking down and accounting for any contrary indicants.

In this sense, data quality is a statistical consideration, as some writers have explicitly recognized. Naroll, for example, has described certain statistical indices and tests of data quality that are applicable to anthropological field studies.[4] In his scheme of data quality control, Naroll assigns differential scores to field reports based on whether or not data were obtained under each of a series of observational conditions that promote validity. Examples of such conditions are the ability to speak the native language, duration and depth of study, etc. In his monograph, Naroll demonstrates that for a number of substantive issues, field reports with higher data quality indices yielded conclusions significantly different, by direct statistical test, from those of reports with lower indices.

Naroll's scheme, however, applies only to the overall quality of total studies and not to the quality of evidence on particular points. For the latter purpose,

---

4. Raoul Naroll, *Data Quality Control,* New York: Free Press (1962).

techniques described by Becker and Geer are more useful.[5]   These authors are especially concerned with controlling the quality of data to avoid three possibly contaminating effects: (1) that items reflecting content of interest are never provided spontaneously but only on elicitation by the researcher; (2) that such items are never provided in the company of other subjects but only when alone with the researcher; and (3) that such items are manifest only in interview testimony or only in observed behaviors but not in both. Becker and Geer suggest a convenient tabular form for evaluating the relative proportions of data possibly contaminated by these problems and further suggest certain numerical standards for such tabular evaluations.

Although the contaminating effects dealt with by Becker and Geer are important ones, they do not begin to exhaust the range of possibilities enumerated in the literature and briefly summarized in earlier sections of this paper. In consequence, I should like to propose an alternative scheme addressed to the wider range of contaminating effects, a scheme which, like Becker and Geer's, can apply to data on any particular substantive point and can evaluate the relative proportions of data possibly contaminated by each effect. Again as in Becker and Geer's procedure, the items to be classified are single, intact indicants or, as they call them, complete incidents. The exact delimitation of what shall be coded as an indicant or incident is not so important as the consistency of the coding itself.

The procedure takes the form of an "accounting scheme" or checklist of possible contaminating influences which may have shaped the contents of each item of data.[6] This accounting scheme is applied to items at the same time that they are evaluated for plausibility, stability, and comparability (as discussed above). For each item, the researcher must searchingly consider, not whether it was obtained under some favorable condition of data collection as in Naroll's procedure, but whether it was collected under the *possible* effect of some *contaminating* influence. If, upon such searching consideration, it is judged that there remains some reasonable possibility that the item may have been contaminated by a particular factor, the item is so classified. Thus, the researcher is stacking the cards against himself, so to speak, in order that he may be relatively certain that his "clean" items are indeed uncontaminated by a particular factor.

Every item must be evaluated repeatedly in terms of each category of the accounting scheme, since these categories are not mutually exclusive. In fact, it will rarely be the case that any given item is clearly free from all of the

---

5.   Howard S. Becker and Blanche Geer, "Participant Observation: The Analysis of Qualitative Field Data," in Richard N. Adams and Jack J. Preiss, editors, *Human Organization Research,* Homewood, Ill.: Dorsey Press (1960), pp. 267–289.

6.   For similar uses of the concept of accounting scheme, see Daniel Bell, "Twelve Modes of Prediction," in Julius Gold, editor, *Penguin Survey of the Social Sciences 1965,* Baltimore: Penguin Books (1965), pp. 96–127, and Barney G. Glaser and Anselm L. Strauss, *The Discovery of Grounded Theory,* Chicago: Aldine (1967), chapter 6.

potential contaminating influences, and many items will be classified as possibly contaminated by two or more such influences.

OBSERVATIONAL DATA

The following factors constitute the set of categories for classifying observational items:

A. Reactive Effects. Of each observational item, the researcher ought to ask himself whether his actions or presence might have affected the observed phenomenon itself. The best check, where available, is comparison with informant interview accounts of similar events at which the observer was not present. A similar check, but one which also may exert some reactive effect, is to directly ask informants in what ways, if any, the presence or actions of the observer seem to affect the phenomenon in question. In all cases, the researcher should seriously reflect on any possible consequences to the observed item, of his role-relations with the relevant subjects, of his personal characteristics (transient and enduring), and of his intellectual frame of reference. If such reflection should lead to suspicion of some particular influence on the phenomenon, the researcher may be able to experiment with that aspect of his behavior, modifying it during the next similar observational situation to see whether different behavior leads to different observations.

Should any of these checks reveal a reasonable possibility that reactive effects may have influenced the observed item, that item should be classified in Category *A*.

B. Ethnocentrism. Any observational item may reflect the researcher's imposition of a foreign, uncongenial perspective on the observed phenomenon. The meaning or significance of any human action or artifact may be manifold, and substantial aspects of its significance may easily be missed or misinterpreted by an observer unacquainted with that phenomenon. Comparison with pertinent respondent and informant interviews may suggest the observer's incomplete or inaccurate interpretation. Further, his interpretations should be discussed (at some point) with top informants within each of the major groupings or factions relevant to the phenomenon. Again, the observer ought always to ponder the likely perceptual consequences of the inflexibilities and peculiarities of his role-relations, personal characteristics, and frame of reference.

If such checks suggest that the observer may overly have imposed his own interpretations on the phenomenon, the observational item should be classified in Category *B*.

C. Going Native. Instead of failing to take into account the meaning attributed by participants to their own actions, the observer may sometimes fail to see anything else in these actions, overidentifying with the participants' viewpoint or, more likely, with the viewpoint of some particular faction among these participants. A useful check on this possibility of having "gone native" is for the observer to compare an observational item with comparable observations from his own earlier field notes, to determine how his viewpoint may have been changing. Again, at some point, it is important to discuss the observer's interpretations with top informants in each of the relevant groupings or factions and, if possible, with knowledgeable outsiders who are in frequent contact with the organization (e.g., missionaries, tradespeople, newsmen, labor mediators, or the like). The observer should also reflect on the direction and degree of his sympathies and antipathies toward the subjects, looking for the sources of these in his own role-relations, personal characteristics, and intellectual frame of reference. A particularly useful reflective exercise is to imagine, as vividly as possible, just how the phenomenon in question would have been seen and interpreted by a few particular colleagues with differing scientific viewpoints.

If such checks seem to indicate the possibility of overidentification with the viewpoint of some participants, the observational item should be classified in Category C.

INTERVIEW DATA

Data obtained from interviews, whether of the informant or the respondent type, represent a two-step flow of information, with dangers of contamination intrinsic to each of the steps. That is, an interviewee is first an observer, whether of external events or of his own feelings, dispositions, or habits. As such, he is subject to all the fallibilities of observation. Subsequent to being an observer, he is a reporter, who must relay his impressions to the researcher. As a reporter, he may, for many reasons, fail to convey an accurate account of these impressions. Therefore, it is important for the researcher to examine interview data for possible contamination at each step of this information flow.

D. *Knowledgeability.* Since the interviewee is being regarded as an indirect observer, the researcher will do well to examine his credentials. Is the interviewee in a position to have valid knowledge of what he is reporting? Is his knowledge direct and firsthand? At the time of the event, was he in a relatively collected and alert state? Is he generally an objective and reliable person? As an informant, does he seem to be a reasonably sensitive person, interpersonally? As a respondent, does he seem to be reasonably introspective?

If the researcher is not altogether confident of the interviewee in these respects, the item of information in question should be classified in Category D.

E. *Reportorial Ability.* Even if the interviewee is sufficiently knowledgeable, he may prove of little use if he is unable, under favorable conditions, to report adequately what he knows. Is his memory generally reliable and specific? Does he express himself well? Is he sufficiently patient to recount his impressions in detail and to explain features which may seem obvious to him? Is he sufficiently self-confident to respond to frequent probes without feeling that his honesty, knowledge, or judgment is being questioned?

If the interviewee may be deficient in these respects, the item in question should be classified in Category E.

F. Reactive Effects of the Interview Situation. Some interviewees want so much to be helpful that they strain to give the researcher the kind of answers they think he wants, while others will attempt to fly in the face of what the researcher seems to want. In any case, the comments, expressions, reactions, and status of the researcher will tend to condition the testimony received, and these effects must be examined. Did he seem combative? Was the interviewee trying to find out where the researcher stood on some issue? Was he trying to convert the researcher to some viewpoint? Was he hesitant and especially attentive to the researcher's reactions? Did he seem continually conscious of the researcher's status? Was he afraid of hurting the researcher's feelings or disrupting the relationship? Did the researcher say anything which seemed to shut him off or alter the tone or style of his testimony?

If any of these effects seem likely to have been operative, the item should be classified in Category F.

G. Ulterior Motives. Apart from his motive for participating at all in the interview, the interviewee's motives for uttering a particular account may cast doubt on the accuracy of that account. Was he trying to slant the results of the research in some direction? Was he trying to make things seem less prosaic to the outsider? Was he trying to expose someone? Was he trying to steer the researcher away from something? Was he trying to rationalize a fact he finds distasteful? Was he using the researcher as a go-between? Was he reverting to "public definitions" in addressing an outsider?

If any of these motives seem possibly applicable, the item should be classified in Category G.

H. Bars to Spontaneity. Often the social context of an interview—apart from the context of the relationship between researcher and interviewee—constrains the interviewee to modify the testimony he might otherwise give. Were there other persons present whose relationships with the interviewee might have been embarrassed or strained by the lines his testimony could conceivably have taken? Did he seem anxious about the possibility of someone overhearing or coming on the scene?

If either of these might have been relevant to the interview situation, the resulting item should be classified in Category H.

I. Idiosyncratic Factors. More or less transient features of the interviewee's life history immediately prior to the interview may sometimes color his testimony to considerable degree by inducing an uncharacteristic mood or set. Was the interviewee in some sort of mood (depressed, elated, sour, bitter, angry, cold, warm)? Had he been drinking? Was he fatigued? Did he seem animated by or obsessively focused on some recent or upcoming event? Did there seem to be a notable discontinuity from previously expressed attitudes? Did he seem to be "whistling in the dark"?

If any of these may have been the case, the item should be classified in Category *I*.

NULL DATA

Not all distortions of observational and interview data lend themselves to analysis in terms of the accounting scheme developed above, for in addition to such sins of commission there are important sins of omission. That is, an observer may fail to notice important aspects of some phenomenon, or an interviewee may fail to report such.

Sins of omission do not lend themselves so readily to discovery or analysis, for they constitute *null items* which are manifest only by thorough comparison of a given observational record or interview account with those which have already been obtained. A null item becomes apparent when previous data would lead the researcher to expect a given observation or interview to manifest a given content but this content is simply absent from the record.

In observational data, null items are typically discovered by comparison of observations with data from interviews, where informants or respondents make mention of some meaning, dimension, or event which simply has not appeared in the corresponding observational record. The common sources of such observational omissions—the researcher's role-relations, personal characteristics, and intellectual frame of reference—have been discussed in early sections of this paper. By and large, discrepancies between observational data and coordinate interview data have been treated as indicators of reactive effects of observation, ethnocentrism, and going native, Categories *A, B,* and *C,* above.

In interview data, however, null items lend themselves quite readily to more differentiated analysis, because null items are discovered principally through comparison of one interviewee's account with those of others. This is, of course, a more direct and precise procedure, with more degrees of freedom, than that discussed for observational data. Furthermore, null items in interviewing are frequently manifest, motivated acts of the interviewee— evasive *withholdings of testimony*. Being motivated, the sources of such distortions of data are more readily analyzed than are those of observation.

As one might reasonably expect, distortions by omission stem from the same factors as distortions by commission—knowledgeability, reportorial ability, reactive effects of the interview situation, ulterior motives, bars to spontaneity, and idiosyncratic factors. As we did with null observational items, we shall classify the null items of interviews in terms of our existing categories —in this case, Categories *D* through *I*. In this context, however, three of the categories are important enough to warrant amplification of their earmarks.

Reactive effects of the interview situation, Category *F*, often take the form of the interviewee's deep reluctance to discuss at any level certain topics which seem inappropriate, with relative strangers or with persons in particular statuses. It is well for the researcher to ask himself: "Was I too new to the interviewee?" "Was I still perceived as a possible risk?" "Were sex differences involved here (age, race, ethnic, religious, class, occupational, educational)?" "Was he embarrassed to admit he didn't know?"

Bars to spontaneity, Category *H*, frequently lead the interviewee to skirt certain topics altogether. Was someone else listening or otherwise likely to learn of the interviewee's testimony? Was the situation too formal and imposing for him to feel comfortable discussing this topic? Was it too intimate? Too foreboding?

Idiosyncratic factors, Category *I*, are often manifested in a general "choking up" on the part of the interviewee. Was he under great pressure? Was he strongly cross-pressured? Was he too emotionally involved in the topic? Was the topic inconsonant with his current mood?

QUALITY PROFILES AND EVALUATION OF DATA

Basic, then, to the use of such an accounting scheme is the continual comparison and recomparison of all items of observational and interview data bearing on a given substantive point. Any instabilities or inconsistencies, in particular, call for an investigation to determine whether these reflect true changes or true social differentiations, or whether they reflect contaminating influences on the data. Since one cannot tell *a priori* whether a new and inconsistent item is invalid and the earlier items accurate or vice versa, all items must be reexamined, with the possible result that the new item may lead the researcher to see that his previously accepted items may all have been contaminated in a fashion he had not suspected before.

To some degree, then, the classification of items in terms of this accounting scheme of possible contaminating influences is not a permanent one but is relative to the entire corpus of items on one point at one particular time. In practice, however, the classification of a given item is quite seldom altered by the acquisition of further items. Nonetheless, the recurrent analysis of data on a given point should include an evaluation of those data in terms of the proposed accounting scheme. Since the number of items applicable to a particular point is typically quite small, this practice is not prohibitive.

What form does such an evaluative analysis assume? The most useful form, no doubt, is a simple profile indicating for each category of potential contamination the proportion of items *not* considered contaminated. Table 1 is a sample working table for such evaluative analysis. All items (including null items) bearing on a single substantive point are classified in terms of the accounting scheme, placing tally marks in either the second or third column of the table as

TABLE 1 Sample Work Table for Determining Data Quality Profile and Data Quality Index on a Single Substantive Point

1 CATEGORY OF POTENTIAL CONTAMINATION	2 INFLUENCE PRESENT (NO. OF ITEMS)	3 INFLUENCE ABSENT (NO. OF ITEMS)	4 DATA QUALITY VALUE
A	4	9	.69
B	3	10	.77
C	4	9	.69
Observational quality index			.72
D	7	18	.72
E	10	15	.60
F	15	10	.40
G	12	13	.52
H	14	11	.44
I	4	21	.84
Interview quality index			.59
Overall data quality index			.63

appropriate. Next, for each category of potential contamination, the items judged free from such contaminating influence (Column 3) are expressed in proportion to the total number of observational or interview items and this proportion is recorded in Column 4 as the data quality value for that contaminating influence. The resulting profile of data quality values will hereafter be discussed as the data quality profile.

A rough summary index of data quality can be obtained by computing the mean of all the data quality values, as in Table 1. The usefulness of this index is supplemented by computing separate means for the observational and the interview data quality values, respectively.

The interpretation of such profiles and indices of data quality varies importantly with the use to which they are put. The major purposes are twofold: (1) to serve as a running check on the particular types of contaminating influence which the researcher must seek to minimize in succeeding collections of data, and (2) to communicate to the reader of the completed research a reasonably definite assessment of the degree to which the data have escaped the major contaminating influences to which participant observation may be liable.

The evaluation techniques put forward in this paper are surely more adequate for the first of these purposes than for the second. The techniques are most useful during the early and middle stages of data collection when the number of items bearing on a substantive point is fairly small and, as yet, not comprehensively sampled. When the first, preliminary running analyses of data are being made, data quality analysis can provide important direction to the ensuing rounds of data collection. It will very frequently happen that all or most of the early items on a given point will be classified as quite possibly contaminated by the same invalidating influence or influences. At that moment, the researcher will be unable to determine whether the contents of his items are accurate reflections of the phenomenon or are merely distortions induced by the particular contaminating influence(s), for the items are completely confounded with the potential effects of the influence(s). Having discovered this confounding, the researcher can then redesign his data collection tactics with the deliberate aim of obtaining comparable, additional items which are fairly clearly free of the particular influence(s).[7]

The use of data quality profiles to indicate the overall quality of the final body of data on a given point is not as clearly established. Apart from the extremes, very near 0 or 1, the significance of any data quality value is difficult to ascertain. First of all, the classification of items is rather subjective and certainly reflects the character of the researcher. For example, some analysts are hypersensitive to the possible contamination of their data and will classify many marginal cases as being contaminated, thus lowering the data quality values. Other researchers take a more relaxed view and would fail to adversely classify the very same cases and would thus inflate the data quality values. Second, high data quality values may not be necessary to validly establish a point, given the "balancing out" logic of participant observation. That is, if most of the items classified as possibly contaminated in a particular category yield the same contents as the few items regarded as free of that contamination, the researcher is reasonably justified in assuming that that particular influence did not actually distort his data. Therefore, he may not *bother* to seek further items, even though the formal data quality value is relatively low. Indeed, under extremely adverse field conditions, it may not be *possible* to obtain high data quality values, in which case the "balancing out" logic is the only recourse.

It must be concluded, then, that the absolute values of data quality scores remain difficult to evaluate. One cannot be certain that one researcher's data quality index of .55 means poorer data than another researcher's .70. Nor can one clearly establish limits of minimal acceptability, such as .50 and up.

Nonetheless, data quality profiles *can* help the reader evaluate the quality of data in a participant observation study. The profiles have primarily three applications. The first of these is in evaluating the quality of data on a single substantive point, by examining the *relative* data quality values for each of the nine categories of possible contaminating influences. Inspecting Table 1, for example, we may notice a considerably lower index value for interviewing than for observation. Further, relative to other values in the table, we may note special depression of the quality values for reactive effects of interviewing, ulterior motives of interviewees, and bars to spontaneity in the interview situation (*F*, *G*, and *H*). Reportorial ability (*E*) is noticeably lower than the knowledgeability of interviewees (*D*). This overall pattern of relative values suggests that,

---

7. Of course, these new items may be suspect in terms of still other categories of potential contamination.

TABLE 2   Summary Table of Data Quality Values over All Substantive Points, by Categories of Contamination

CATEGORY OF POTENTIAL CONTAMINATION	MEAN OF DATA QUALITY VALUES	RANGE OF DATA QUALITY VALUES
A		
B		
C		
D		
E		
F		
G		
H		
I		
Observational quality index		
Interview quality index		
Overall data quality index		

TABLE 3   Summary Table of Data Quality Indices, by Substantive Points

SUBSTANTIVE POINT	RANGE OF DATA QUALITY VALUES	OBSERVATIONAL QUALITY INDEX	INTERVIEW QUALITY INDEX	OVERALL DATA QUALITY INDEX
1				
2				
3				
4				
5				
·				
·				
·				
n				

with respect to the substantive point in question, the researcher was very likely dealing with a sensitive topic which subjects found difficult to verbalize to this particular interviewer, given his relation to vested interests among these subjects. Such an inference, though tenuous, may be quite important if the researcher has failed to consider this difficulty in field relations. We may decide that his interview data on the point are relatively shaky and therefore we may give comparatively greater weight to his direct observational data.

A second application of data quality profiles to communicating adequacy of data is very similar to the first, but differs in that it does not deal with with a single substantive point but with the relative importance of the contaminating factors in the study as a whole. If the researcher presents a summary table, such as Table 2, we are able to assess the relative strengths and weaknesses of his overall data collection procedures with respect to potential invalidating influences.

A third application of data quality profiles is demonstrated by the use of another type of summary table, as in Table 3. Such a table allows the reader to evaluate the relative soundness of data on one substantive point as compared to another, so that confidence can be placed in the researcher's various conclusions according to the values of the quality indices.

LIMITATIONS OF DATA QUALITY CONTROL TECHNIQUES

The techniques put forth in this paper, though more extensive and systematic than their predecessors, are beset by numerous limitations, many of which have already been touched upon.

The list of categories does not exhaust the possible sources of data contamination in participant observation, and the criteria for inclusion of an item in any category of this scheme are largely matters of subjective judgment of the researcher. These criteria may be interpreted severely or quite indifferently, depending on the disposition of the analyst—the results reflect the conscientiousness of the researcher. Moreover, the criteria for inclusion are often manifold, diverse, and sometimes rather broad. The scope of the categories is also somewhat variable, some covering narrowly conceived sources of contamination and others spanning important, sprawling sources.

The data quality profiles discussed here are essentially zero-order tables and do not take into account the fact that an item classifiable under one combination of categories may be much more dubious than another which falls into some other combination of categories.

The interpretability of absolute values of the data quality profiles and indices is greatly limited, as discussed in the previous section; however, the significance of relative values can be quite meaningfully evaluated, as is also discussed above. The utility of these profiles, it seems to me, lies primarily in their function as a data quality *control* through feedback during data collection, and in this primary function, the interpretation of data quality values presents a minimum of difficulties. The profiles function only secondarily in *post hoc* data quality *evaluation*.

The procedures described in this paper are tedious and time-consuming. However, many of the steps are also required in ordinary procedures of analytic review and cross-checking in participant observation, so that the extra labor is considerably less than it might at first appear.

The publication of data quality profiles for each major substantive point adds to the already considerable problem of bulkiness in reporting participant observation studies. This additional burden could be circumvented by reporting only the summary tables for the entire study (Tables 2 and 3), although important information is necessarily lost through such compression.

In summary judgment, then, the techniques advocated in this paper are crude, fallible, tedious, and yield somewhat ambiguous results. On the other hand, they make possible systematic quality control in data collection and provide a modest advance toward the more systematic, standardized presentation of the relative soundness of the data on which a researcher has based his conclusions. It is to be hoped that these advantages of the techniques will more than offset the limitations, and that the presentation of these techniques will stimulate other researchers to invent superior alternatives.

In this chapter we have addressed important questions concerning the quality of participant observation data from the standpoint of possible contaminating effects. Important as these questions are, the minimization of such contaminating effects in a particular study does not completely satisfy the criteria of validity and reliability of data as these are ordinarily conceptualized. That is, we have been treating the adequacy of data *qua* information, and *not* the adequacy of data *qua* measures of underlying theoretical constructs. Approaches to the latter consideration will be discussed in Chapters 5 and 6.

CHAPTER FIVE

GENERATION
OF
HYPOTHESES

It is a commonplace among methodological commentators that systematic procedures for evaluating scientific hypotheses far outstrip any procedures for generating such hypotheses. Indeed, this is the major thesis of the book, *The Discovery of Grounded Theory*,[1] which should be of considerable interest to participant observers. Yet, the generation of hypotheses is quite obviously a necessary prior condition for the employment of the many powerful research designs and techniques of verification now available to social scientists.

One of the outstanding strengths of participant observation studies, a strength acknowledged even by many severe critics, is the historic importance of these studies in generating many of the seminal ideas in the social sciences. This relative advantage is often attributed to the participant observer's "closeness to his data" or to his submersion in the data. This attribution is certainly erroneous, for no one is closer to the data than the participants themselves, and although an ordinary participant may exhibit unusual insight into his organization, these insights never resemble the systematically patterned insights of theoretical understanding. In addition, simple submersion in data is insufficient; a student or poorly trained observer may closely examine an organization for long periods of time yet see nothing of interest.

Rather, it would appear that the hypothesis-generating ability of participant observation stems from the researcher's ability to apply a theoretical perspective to his observations and to respond to both uniformities and irregularities in what he sees. These uniformities and departures, which provide theoretical richness, are seldom manifest in the data themselves but are obtained only through carefully designed theoretical sampling and analysis based upon the researcher's frame of reference. That is to say, data are not rich in and of themselves but may be *enriched* by proper use of discovery techniques.

The first major category of techniques—theoretical sampling—has already been discussed somewhat in Chapter 3, but one further selection on this topic is pertinent here. This selection is J. P. Dean, Eichhorn, and L. R. Dean's typology of insight-stimulating interviewees to be singled out in the early phases of fieldwork.

FRUITFUL INFORMANTS FOR INTENSIVE INTERVIEWING

JOHN P. DEAN, ROBERT L. EICHHORN, AND LOIS R. DEAN

The experienced field worker is well aware of the unevenness of interviews in providing new insights, hypotheses, and interpretations. One informant

---

1.   Glaser and Strauss (1967).

Reprinted from *An Introduction to Social Research,* 2nd ed., edited by John T. Doby, pp. 284–286. Copyright © 1967 by Meredith Publishing Company. Reprinted by permission of the authors and Appleton-Century-Crofts.

will provide rich and provocative data, while another will yield almost nothing. If the interviewer can find the more fruitful informants, he can save himself much time. Naturally, no rigid rules can be laid down; luck will always play a part.

There are several kinds of informants who are generally more helpful than the person selected by chance. These include:

1. *Informants who are especially sensitive to the area of concern.*

The *outsider,* who sees things from the vantage point of another culture, social class, community, etc.

The *rookie,* who is surprised by what goes on and notes the taken-for-granted things that the acclimated miss. And, as yet, he may have no stake in the system to protect.

The *nouveau statused,* who is in transition from one position to another where the tensions of new experience are vivid.

The naturally *reflective and objective person* in the field. He can sometimes be pointed out by others of his kind.

2. *The more-willing-to-reveal informants.* Because of their background or status, some informants are just more willing to talk than others.

The *naive informant,* who knows not whereof he speaks. He may be either naive as to what the field worker represents or naive about his own group.

The *frustrated person,* who may be a rebel or malcontent, especially the one who is consciously aware of his blocked drives and impulses.

The *"outs,"* who have lost power but are "in-the-know." Some of the "ins" may be eager to reveal negative facts about their colleagues.

The *habitué* or *"old hand,"* or *"fixture,"* who no longer has a stake in the venture or is so secure that he is not jeopardized by exposing what others say or do.

The *needy person,* who fastens onto the interviewer because he craves attention and support. As long as the interviewer satisfied this need, he will talk.

The *subordinate,* who must adapt to superiors. He generally develops insights to cushion the impact of authority, and he may be hostile and willing to "blow his top."

3. *Critical cases.* A case is critical when the variables one is not studying are held constant so that the causal influences of the others are more easily discerned. Thus, critical cases are selected where one or more of the important variables are equated. Youth recently moved from states that have segregated schools to a state that has integrated schools potentially would be good sources for information. But cities that are desegregating their schools would yield critical cases since the home and community environment of the school children would be held constant. Often the best informants for sociological studies are those with similar psychological and social characteristics placed in *different* sociological environments.

Where sample surveys have been made, one can use data already collected to isolate critical cases. Follow-up interviews with these critical cases will yield data of great testing relevance and permit "before-and-after" comparisons that may be especially helpful.

4. Trained persons in the field. In many field situations there will be persons with special training in social work, clinical psychology, or psychiatry who, by virtue of their present job, are closely in touch with those the researcher wishes to study. The researcher can sometimes profit enormously from their experience and familiarity with the field setting.

Selection of the best informants results in an unrepresentative sample, subject to bias. Therefore, the field worker should be cautious in his interpretations of the information he collects and corroborate it with data from systematically selected cases where this is feasible.

Turning now from techniques of theoretical sampling in generating hypotheses to those of *data analysis*, we shall find that fruitful analytic techniques vary widely in their scope, systematization, and point of application.

Perhaps the first technique applied in most participant observation studies is simply an analytic summary of one's field notes after the first few days in the field. The following selection by Blanche Geer describes the manner in which summary reviews typically point toward the working hypotheses and major themes of a study and, in addition, reveal much about one's developing field relations.

FIRST DAYS IN THE FIELD:
A CHRONICLE OF RESEARCH IN PROGRESS

BLANCHE GEER

Participant-observation studies, as we have been doing them,[1] follow a pattern of several years in the field, a period of analytic model-building, outlining, and drafting, and the final assembly of data in the form of description, evidence, and argument for the monograph. The beginning of the final stage, when we go back to the field notes to see if there is evidence for what we want to say, is a time of suspense and self-questioning. It brings up a point seldom mentioned in monographs but frequently discussed by field workers among themselves: the relationship of initial field experiences to our thinking before entering the field and after the field work has been completed. There is so much reiteration of findings in our work that we sometimes think we have always known what we find (everybody knows it; why bother to write a book?) and at other times that it all became clear in some magical way on the very first day in the field.

Reprinted from "First Days in the Field," by Blanche Geer, Chapter 11 of *Sociologists at Work,* edited by Phillip E. Hammond, Copyright © 1964 by Basic Books, Inc., New York, by permission of the author and publisher.

1.   See Howard S. Becker *et al., Boys in White* (Chicago, Ill.: The University of Chicago Press, 1961).

Most field workers include in their notes material which is not narration, quotation, or description, but comment. It occurred to me that I might use, as a partial answer to questions about what happens in initial field work, the comments recorded during my first days in the field on our current research. Do strategies and concepts change? By what mechanisms? How is subsequent field work affected, and how much of the first experience gets into a final monograph?

METHOD

Field work on our present study of undergraduates at the University of Kansas began during the summer orientation period for prospective freshmen in 1959.[2] At the end of a six-hour day in the field, I dictated an account of what I had seen and heard, occasionally inserting comments on the material or appending an interpretive summary. In this report, I shall use the thirty-four comments in the first eight days of field notes. They have been edited when in need of grammatical correction, and names have been changed. When comments duplicate each other, I use one but tabulate all of them as a rough measure of my initial interests.

In addition to the comments, I shall draw on letters and memoranda exchanged by project members before entering the field and the original proposal for a one-year pilot study. The full proposal and a memorandum written after the summer field work complete the documentation.

BEGINNINGS OF THE UNDERGRADUATE STUDY—THE PREVIEWS

Tentative arrangements for a study of undergraduates were made with the University of Kansas while we were still engaged on a study of the University's medical school. During the academic year 1958–1959, we met with members of the administration interested in the project. They provided a gradual introduction to the University and indicated what they wished it to become.

In November of 1958, we submitted a proposal to investigate the following question: What are the differing perspectives on academic work characteristic of an undergraduate college and how are these influenced by participation in student groups characterized by the possession of a student culture? Our method would be participant observation and interviews of a random sample of one or more subgroups of the student body, beginning with premedical students.

2. The study is financed by the Carnegie Corporation and directed by Everett C. Hughes. The field workers were Howard S. Becker (director), Blanche Geer, and Marsh Ray, then of Community Studies, Inc., Kansas City, Missouri.

On January 22, 1959, at a lunch meeting with members of the administration, the dean[3] mentioned that the University conducted summer orientation sessions, or previews, for prospective freshmen. In notes on the conversation I summarized what he said as follows:

▶   Throughout the month of July, groups of prefreshmen come to the University for talks by administrators and for a session of filling out forms. . . . Approximately half the prospective freshman class is processed in July to relieve the pressure at fall orientation time. Each preview group contains about two hundred students with an approximately equal number of boys and girls. The selection is first-come first-served, so that the groups are mixed in respect to the schools of the University (engineering, fine arts, liberal arts, and so forth) they plan to enter and the region from which they come. There is, however, some tendency for students in the same high school to send in their applications together so that sometimes there are groups that know each other at a preview, particularly from the larger high schools in the state. ◀

In June, I talked to the director of the previews, who agreed to supply me with the names and home towns of students attending, banquet tickets, and a schedule of events. There would be two previews a week—the first on Monday and Tuesday, the second on Thursday and Friday—for the first three weeks of July.

I arrived on campus on the morning of the first preview (July 6) and picked up the list of names from the director's office. At the Union, where orientation sessions were being held, I introduced myself to previewers and attended meetings with them to get their comments and make appointments to meet later on. In the afternoon, many students had free time which gave me a chance to talk to them at length in the Union or dormitories or to explore the campus with them. At six o'clock, everybody went to a social hour and banquet, and I received a name tag and table assignment along with the previewers. After dinner, the previewers again had free time (at some previews there was a dance) until the house meeting held after closing hours at ten thirty.

The second morning was taken up for most students by placement and physical examinations, which left me little time for interviewing. My best opportunities were during the afternoon free time, at dinner, and the dance.

This pattern of going to formal sessions and interviewing during free time followed our plans for the field work. It produced enough data on the previewers' backgrounds and their expectations of what college would be like to orient us. We did not anticipate one feature of the previews which materially changed our plans. No one had told us, thinking it unimportant perhaps, that college seniors acted as speakers, entertainers, and hosts at the dinner table. They were also dormitory counselors.

---

3.   The "dean" mentioned here and in subsequent comments is a general term for all administrators. There are so few that to give anyone a more precise title might identify him.

ANALYSIS OF FIELD COMMENTS

Data, no matter how you collect them, are recalcitrant. They will not always answer the questions you put to them. In this report, since I am dealing with my own work, I want to be particularly careful to stick to the data, to avoid reading more into the comments than is in them by interpreting them in the light of our subsequent findings. I have, therefore, subjected the comments, somewhat grandiosely, to the kind of analysis we use in regular studies, collecting all data in the notes that bear on a topic (in this case all comments), grouping them by subtopic, and then looking to see what I have. The thirty-four comments fall into five categories: the field worker's role, the problem of empathy, the solution of anticipated problems, the nature of working hypotheses, and the recognition of a major theme. I shall consider the categories in order, noting for each of them the number of comments included. Discussion of the relationship of the comments to our original planning of the study and the monograph we are now writing follows the analysis.

The Field Worker's Role. To those who have not done field work, the adoption of a role with informants presents a difficult problem. There is a large literature on the pitfalls of role and failures of rapport, but it is usually written with the interviewer rather than the observer in mind. The interviewer starts from scratch with an informant. He must rapidly establish himself securely enough in a relationship with another person to permit intimate questioning. The participant-observer establishes a relationship with a group. To a single informant, he is much less of a stranger because he moves freely in the informant's own setting and can be seen interacting with other members of the informant's group.

If the setting and the group are reasonably familiar to the observer, his problem in initiating a role is a matter of judicious negatives. He should not have the manner or appearance of any group which his informant group distinguishes sharply from itself. This does not mean forcing identity with the informant group; it does mean that the observer of students, if he wishes a good understanding with them, will avoid the manner of teacher and authoritative adult. Selecting a neutral, approachable role in the sense of acting and speaking in ways which are not threatening to informants smooths the first days of participant observation. But the field worker must soon become aware of the role he plays in more detail to assess its effect. The first comment in my field notes on role deals with this problem.

▶ 7/9/59: I am conscious that part of my role for [the previewers] is an educational one. I am somebody in a profession that they have not run up against before, and I have a lot of knowledge about universities that they could use. This is quite different from the role you play with medical students who are tolerant of you but not seeking anything. ◄

Occasioned by a previewer who wanted me to tell him whether he must study medicine to be a psychologist, the comment is a warning to myself: Don't wise up your informant! More subtly, the comment suggests the field worker's effort to uncover informants' concepts of who he is and what he wants to know, since such definitions govern what people tell him and how they say it, whether they will volunteer or must be questioned.

After this warning, role in the sense of presentation of self does not turn up in the confessional of the comments, but I become conscious of doing a number of things in the field not planned in our proposal or memoranda and of leaving other things undone. I am concerned about role in the sense of my function as coworker on the larger study of which the previews are a small part. After five days in the field, I evaluate this role as follows.

► 7/13/59: I want briefly to take a look at the kind of questions I have been asking and my general goals during this period of field work. First of all, I've been getting background data [on previewers]; this is necessary if we are to understand the types of students we are dealing with. Second, I've been trying, evidently, to pick up a tremendous body of facts and names, about campus organizations, slang, and customs. This is a natural thing for any field worker, trying to orient himself, to do, and I think it is particularly important in our study if we are to identify groups, as it is by these means that we are able to separate students from each other and recognize them easily and quickly. In other words, if we get all this stuff down we may be able to sort them out without going to such lengthy interviews as this [a three-hour talk with a senior].

I seem to have the feeling that information of this kind is necessary in order to be able to find [the boundaries of] groups. I also seem to be developing a technique for next fall in which I talk with a student long enough to get his confidence thoroughly and make plans to meet him next fall and attend some class or activity and get to know his friends. This, I think, will be quite a reasonable way of bounding groups, at the same time learning more about the actual activity.

I think I have developed an impatience as a result of our various theoretical and methodological innovations of last year. I apparently want to go right out and put data into perspectives and tables.[4] I am impatient with the mountain of background information that I must first learn before I can interpret any of this. . . . Of course, there are repeats and reiterations coming already, and these are the material of perspectives. At the same time, an outline of the place is forming in my mind, a kind of topographical map in which it becomes more and more easy to locate what the various students say to me. ◄

As I begin to see what we need to learn and ways of learning it, my conception of my role in the study rapidly expands from that of interviewer of prefreshmen to general spadeworker. I do not want to lose the opportunity presented by the previews of laying the groundwork for what we will do in the fall. Getting campus background, learning the lingo, and setting up future meetings with infor-

---

4.   For a discussion of our use of the term *perspective* and the type of tables we used, see Becker, *op. cit.*, pp. 33–45.

mants are important. Almost in spite of myself, I have embarked on an attempt to apprehend undergraduate culture as a whole.

Our proposal seems forgotten. Of course, there were not enough pre-medical students at the previews for me to concentrate on them. To limit my-self to our broader objective, the liberal-arts college student, was difficult. The previewers did not group themselves according to the school or college of the University they planned to enter. Out of ordinary politeness (at the dinner table, for instance), I found myself talking to prefreshmen planning careers in engineering, pharmacy, business, and fine arts, as well as the liberal arts. Perhaps it is impossible to stick to a narrow objective in the field. If, as will nearly always be the case, there are unanticipated data at hand, the field worker will broaden his operations to get them. Perhaps he includes such data be-cause they will help him to understand his planned objectives, but he may very well go after them simply because, like the mountain, they are there.[5]

Three comments in the field notes deal with role. I have quoted the one dealing with role as presentation of self and one of two extended discussions of my role as coworker in the undergraduate study.

The Problem of Empathy. Developing empathy with informants as a group often presents more of a problem to field workers planning a study, at least in anticipation, than the adoption of an interaction-facilitating role. Role in this sense is a public stance which all of us practice, but empathy is personal. Field workers are not free of prejudice, stereotypes, or other impediments to the un-derstanding of out-groups. But to study, as we proposed to do, the experience of going to college from the point of view of the student necessarily entails at least recognition of personal bias in order to achieve empathy with the infor-mant group.

Throughout the time the undergraduate study was being planned, I was bored by the thought of studying undergraduates. They looked painfully young to me. I considered their concerns childish and unformed. I could not imagine becoming interested in their daily affairs—in classes, study, dating, and bull sessions. I had memories of my own college days in which I appeared as a child: overemotional, limited in understanding, with an incomprehensible taste for milk shakes and convertibles.

Remembering my attitude as I began to sort out the thirty-four comments in the field notes on the prefreshmen, I expected to find evidence of this un-favorable adult bias toward adolescents. But on the third day in the field I am already taking the students' side.

---

5. I have been accustomed to think of the field worker's tendency to look at wholes as an important theoretical principle, maintaining that those who look at limited portions of a community or institution leave themselves open to serious misapprehension. On reflection, the interpretation offered here seems more likely. Compulsive or inelegant origins, however, do not make the "whole" any less necessary and important to under-stand.

► 7/9/59: Some of these statements by boys like Joe Ropes may sound over-dramatic, or self-conscious, or just plain foolish to an adult, and yet . . . when [you] see their serious and thoughtful faces you realize you [are] getting the best fruit of their experience and thoughts and you take them very seriously when they make statements like this. ◄

Humorless seriousness evidently does not fit the stereotype of college students I took with me into the field. In my own person, I might have kidded the students out of it, but as a field worker I must listen and record. My disbelief is reserved for the comment:

► 7/9/59: Here, again, this sounds just too fatuous but I can not do anything but repeat that these kids are speaking seriously from their hearts. They're not trying to be humorous, and they're really not trying to brag. They're explaining the world as they see it to me in [a] kind of man-to-man fashion, and they're not trying to be overearnest about it or anything. It's just apparently a normal conversation with a kid of this age, at least on such an important day in his life as his first day of a college preview. [This observer's comment comes after a student said, "I think getting into student politics here would be a good thing. You get to be well known and people get to like you. I guess that's an important thing if you want to have your place in the sun."] ◄

I have lost the adult tendency to laugh at such statements, but I think my colleagues will. (They are reading the field notes but are not yet on the scene.) To read what the students say is not as compelling as experiencing it in the flesh, hearing the voices, seeing the gesture and expression. Responding to the students with a solemnity equal to their own, I have fallen into empathy by acting it out.

Later in the field work, I attend a dance in the Trail Room of the Student Union and comment as follows.

► 7/16/59: I am amazed again, in starting the field work, at how quickly . . . you respond in quite other ways than you ordinarily would. I now react with a startled reaction when some dean or other says, as Dean Brown did the other day, "Isn't it boring, talking to all these children?" No, it is not boring when you are doing it, nor is the behavior odd. It has a great deal of inevitability. [What I am referring to here as not being odd is the shyness of the boys at the dance: great numbers of boys walking up and down and standing in groups and some sitting with their heads in their hands, looking at the girls and presumably wondering if they want to dance with them. One or two Romeos leaned nonchalantly against a pillar or two and surveyed the scene without becoming a part of it.] ◄

This comment is part of the notes for the last day of field work on the previews. My reaction to the dean's question suggests not only anger at his failure to understand my job (whatever field work is, it is not boring) but also anger on the student's behalf: why call them children? I am taking up cudgels on their side. Perhaps the rapid development of empathy for a disliked group does not surprise old hands at field work, since it seems to happen again and again. But it surprised me; I comment on it seven times in eight days. Three of the comments have been quoted here.

The Solution of Anticipated Problems. The development of empathy in the field is not the only surprise an observer experiences. Theory, other studies, and common sense make one anticipate difficulties which do not materialize. People one expects to be hostile are not; situations one expects to be incoherent reveal themselves as relatively easily grasped when one is in the midst of them; apparently difficult problems of finding subjects or grouping them in manageable categories are easier in the doing than in theoretical discussion. There are only three comments in the field notes on anticipated problems. One deals with the kind of continuing concern one seldom puts down on paper.

► 7/8/59: Throughout my contacts with administrative officials on this day I express surprise at their friendliness and my ease of access to them. I evidently expect them to ask me personal questions about students. ◄

Absence of one problem provokes anticipation of another. Friendly administrators may expect information about students it would be impossible for us to give while keeping students' confidence. To deal with this problem, we later began efforts to educate members of the administration in field workers' ethics.

In the medical-school study, student fraternity groups were a major variable, meaningfully related to academic perspectives in the freshmen year.[6] But we anticipated serious problems in identifying similar groups among nine thousand undergraduates. We thought and wrote on the formation of groups and the technical problems of observing them. Here is a comment intended to allay some of our fears.

► 7/6/59: I think that this one afternoon and evening has given us some idea of the friend-making process at the beginning of college. When you see it happening under your nose this way, it seems so natural that I wonder why we ever had any questions about it. I think you could make a typology somewhat as follows: There are the students who come from the same high schools or nearby towns and have some acquaintance with each other, and if there is a small number of these they get together and stay together, at least at the beginning of school. It is probable, for instance, that Tom, Dick, Harry . . . from [a small town] will room together in some combination. Those students who come from Kansas City can get together rather easily, although they have come from different schools, by placing each other by means of country clubs, addresses, and boys they have dated. All of these [cues], of course, [are] in addition to the obvious, immediately grasped detail of hair, manner, and clothing. Isolated students from different towns pair up with their assigned roommates for the preview, and they perhaps make a friend to room with the rest of the year or may simply take their chances on being assigned a good person. ◄

---

6.   There is extended discussion of friendship groups in relation to academic perspectives in Becker, *op. cit.*, chap. 9.

Watching people initiate friendships lessens the mystery. Seeing ten students choose a roommate is to begin to structure the activity. The observer now has a list of commonalities to look for: home town, country club, dress, and temporary propinquity.

Getting into the field disposed of another problem.

▶ 7/16/59: This is really a summary comment. I had the idea before I started this field work that because of the complete turnover in students each time it would be a rather disjointed affair in which the observer did not get a cumulative and continuing sense of growing knowledge of what college is all about. I find that I was quite mistaken in this and that this feeling is going on at a great rate and that I am already at the stage in which I quite falsely pretend to ignorance to get somebody's viewpoint on such things as the fraternity. ◀

Why do field workers so frequently anticipate problems that do not materialize? We do it on each new study. We underestimate people's trust in our neutrality, their lack of interest, perhaps, if we seem to be doing no harm. And we project theoretical problems into the field. Because the process of group formation is difficult to conceptualize, we suppose it will be difficult to observe. We expect ephemeral, unstructured situations like the previews to appear incoherent. Perhaps such mistakes are a necessary part of our efforts to design the study in advance.

The Nature of Working Hypotheses. Although the term *observer* suggests passivity, a participant-observer in the field is at once reporter, interviewer, and scientist. On the scene, he gets the story of an event by questioning participants about what is happening and why. He fills out the story by asking people about their relation to the event, their reactions, opinions, and evaluation of its significance. As interviewer, he encourages an informant to tell his story or supply an expert account of an organization or group. As scientist, he seeks answers to questions, setting up hypotheses and collecting the data with which to test them.

One type of hypothesis is drawn up before entering the field. Essentially a list of variables which theory or common sense suggests may be relevant to what the investigator wishes to study, the hypothesis, for the field worker, takes the practical form of kinds of people to see, places to go, and questions to ask. Although he spends a good part of his time just listening to informants or drifting along with a group to see what will happen, the observer also forms hypotheses during the field-work period. These are called working hypotheses. Some of them are so simple they can be tested immediately by having a look at a group or asking questions of informants. Others, usually based on an accumulation of data, predict an event or state that people will behave in specified ways under certain conditions. These undergo a prolonged process of testing and retesting, preferably by more than one field worker, over a period of months and years. There is no finality about them. They must be refined, expanded, and developed. Checking out may depend on the return of the organizational calendar to its beginning point or the election of a fresh group of officials.

The concept of working hypothesis is not difficult, but field workers often have trouble explaining it to others and sometimes to themselves. The concept is clear as a generality, but its mechanics, the doing of it, smacks of magic. Untrained observers, for instance, can spend a day in a hospital and come back with one page of notes and no hypotheses. It was a hospital, they say; everyone knows what hospitals are like. My comments in the field notes suggest that working hypotheses are a product of the field data itself and of whatever ideas the field worker can summon. The initial stimulus may come from repetition or anomalies in the data which catch the observer's attention so that he searches his mind for explanations. Or he may start from the opposite end—what is in his head—and search the data for evidence of stereotypes from the general culture or notions derived from discussions with colleagues, previous research, and reading.

I do not wish to dignify an impromptu process by formal discussion. My field-note comments are not technical. They are summaries, not of an entire day's work, but of parts of it drawn together into tentative statements of findings, often in quasi-quantitative language. A comment at the end of the first day's field work shows I have been using the general hypothesis: previewers will have concrete knowledge of academic arrangements in college. (We had drawn up a list of questions to test this proposition before I went into the field.) But:

▶ 7/6/59: The tremendous ignorance of the prefreshmen of college is somewhat startling. They don't know how many hours of classes there will be. I think they are going to get a big surprise when they find that they may have only one class in the morning and another late in the afternoon on a given day. They have many different notions of how many hours of study they are going to get in. ◀

One day's observation has shaken the prefield hypothesis—students have specific knowledge of the academic side of college before entrance—and substituted the hypothesis that they do not.

The comment continues with a statement about an area of college life we did not plan to study. We had no hypotheses about it, no list of questions prepared.

▶ 7/6/59 (continued): [The previewers] have very little notion of the tremendous numbers of organizations and activities open to them on the campus. Their ideas are rather limited to the advantages of learning manners, meeting girls, singing or other musical activities, and occasionally sports. ◀

It is not clear why I was struck by the fact that previewers do not talk about college activities. We had on hand University bulletins listing hundreds of organizations. I may have picked up the notion that activities were important from conversation with seniors even on this first day.

It is clear, however, that in the concluding portion of the comment I am drawing on stereotypes in the general culture.

▶ 7/6/59 (continued): Sports seem, so far, with this group to be a pretty minor undertaking. I wonder if by any chance there is some selective factor acting here and the athletes or even those interested in athletics do not even show up at previews? No freshman has mentioned big football week ends or college rah-rah shindigs in any connection. ◀

Athletes turned up at subsequent previews to lay my sampling doubt at rest, but at the time the hold on me of the tradition of collegiate sports and big week ends was strong. I very tentatively state the working hypothesis that they are not interested.

The first day in the field leaves me with three working hypotheses, each expressed, interestingly enough, in negative form. If I did my work well on subsequent days in the field, I was on the lookout for data to substantiate or disprove these propositions. Reading the educational literature, as we continued to do in the field, probably supplied me with another working hypothesis: college students are not interested in "culture" or religion. There is no comment on these points until July 16, perhaps because I was not getting much data.

▶ 7/16/59: They had no notion of "cultural advantages" in the way of concerts, lectures, and so on. I noticed again at the dinner the very solemn and attentive faces that watched the students playing the violin and piano. The faces of the dean's staff and the senior students wore that half-smile of gracious appreciation which particularly in the Middle West, I think, accompanies or encourages a performer—or perhaps what I'm describing is a middle-class phenomenon. All the faces of the freshmen that I could see as I ranged around the room with my eyes, however, were quite unsmiling. It was impossible to tell whether they liked it or didn't like it, but it was clear that they had no social conventions of the proper listener's face.

I haven't heard anybody talk down culture nor have I heard anybody talk it up. It is the same with religion. Those who are religious reveal it by their conversation about something else as very much a part of their lives and connected with their choice of a fraternity or a profession. ◀

The working hypothesis proposed is again negative but more complex than those about sports and knowledge of academic matters, which were relatively simple to test. In a group of x previewers, so many express interest in college sports; so many do not. It is a matter of asking the question and counting. The comment above suggests that previewers use their religion when making important decisions. This is a two-step hypothesis. It directs me to look for religious influences only under certain conditions. It is a statement of the logical type: if this, then that.

If some working hypotheses mercifully narrow the area the field workers must observe by specifying a relationship between variables, others ask him to broaden his perspective, to look at something small and apparently unimportant as a matter of regional history.

▶ 7/13/59: I had a conversation the other night with Mary and Dave Newell [sociologists], in which they asked me about the new field work, and I told them as an amusing anecdote about the stress in the fraternities on the teaching of manners. Mary was appalled and said she thought she should immediately leave the Middle West, at least before the great quantities of KU freshmen began to spread finger bowls on the streets of the Plaza. She seemed extremely upset [she is an English girl who has been over here about three years] and seemed to think that this sort of thing was the downfall of education and of America. David said that, on the contrary, he found it very heartening as it was clear the future generations of Kansas Citians would already know what to do with their finger bowls because their fathers, who had been to KU, would be able to teach them as children. And in this way the progress of the race would go on. I concurred in this.

The image of KU as a civilizer taking the grandchildren of the frontier at least one step along the path to a world comparable, at least at the dinner table, all over the world for "educated people," is a good perspective, I think, and one that we must not forget. In this way, it looks quite reasonable for a student whose parents have a grocery store in that distant Kansas town to spend four years acquiring the rudiments of manners that he was not taught at home, and with these he can go on to the real business of life and study in graduate school. ◀

Perhaps because my friends were not midwesterners, they suggested an important relationship to me, putting manners in a historical perspective. My working hypothesis expanded: look for evidence that training in the social graces is a major function of the University.

Inclusive hypotheses, of course, cannot be immediately tested in the field. If something is really important, we should expect to find it cropping out in many sectors of college life. Evidence for and against must be accumulated throughout the study; we must look for it in classes, living groups, and everyday activities. Detailed hypotheses derived from one's own or other people's work on similar institutions may also be useful models for the field worker, whether or not they can be immediately checked. In a long postscript to the summer field notes, I try to relate data on the previewers to a complex model of student development over time which we used for the medical school.[7]

▶ 7/16/59: No one so far has made any distinction between practical and impractical learning in the fashion of the medical students. I used this as a probe a couple of times and got uncomprehending looks. What there is in college is something to learn, and then in another compartment are their aspirations toward various positions and professions. . . .

---

7.   *Ibid.*, especially chaps. 8 and 10. Medical-school freshmen often thought they knew better than their teachers what they needed to know to practice medicine.

Again, [the previewers] have no smartalecky knowledgeableness about rules and regulations or how to beat the dean or the test or anything else. College is a very serious place, and at least at a preview you don't think about these things in connection with it. In this way, they are very similar to the medical-school freshmen, and it will be interesting to see if the conflict between learning for the professor and learning for yourself develops in these students. I know I certainly had an extremely acute case of it as a college student, to the point of wondering whether I should go on. ◄

Working with the hypothesis that previewers may have attitudes toward studying similar to those of medical-school upperclassmen, I find they have instead the idealistic acceptance of college of medical-school freshmen at entrance. Since the latter rapidly become test-wise, I tentatively advance the hypothesis that previewers will also, when they get into college. The basic hypothesis—attitudes toward academic work arise in response to some facet of college experience—is in two steps with a specific time condition. It can be tested only in the fall.

Although our plan was to talk to prefreshmen, I increasingly found myself with older students, present to direct the previews, who told me about the college in great detail. I was acquiring, as I continued to interview freshmen, an idea of what was ahead of them and the contrast in knowledge, interests, and manner between prefreshmen and upperclassmen. The seniors spoke frequently about activities and cultural advantages; previewers did not. The sense of contrast was an unanticipated consequence of what I regarded as a mistake in my field behavior. The next comment reflects information picked up from seniors and staff.

► 7/16/59: Here is an addition to the conversation with Betty Jones [Student Union staff]. She said, "There are some students here who spend practically all their time on activities. I don't know when they do any studying. And really I don't know sometimes what things are coming to. On Monday night they have house meetings in the dorms, and that takes two hours. On Wednesday night there's a dance, and on Thursday night there are all kinds of other meetings."

It is quite clear that the [preview] students are unprepared for this wealth of competition for their time, this wealth of choice, and I would say that probably only the ones with something very specific in mind are going to get over the realization of this variety as a painful and difficult thing when it comes to them after they arrive. This is really a prediction, I suppose, and I feel that it is reinforced by their earnestness and wanting to do well in their studying and have their family be proud of them, which is going to set up a conflict between all these fascinating things and their rather weak direction in themselves. They want to study, but they don't know what and they don't know how much. They are earnest and sincere, but they have no guideposts. They look to me at the moment like . . . a bunch of very sweet lambs being led into a slaughter of decisions to make, pressures to withstand, and moral fiber to reinforce. And yet many of them speak regretfully of their casual high-school years, and you get the strong flavor of missed opportunities and lack of foresight.

This is not true of all students, and I think I am right in saying that the ones from the small schools far out in the state are more apt to have experienced a studious atmosphere in high school. ◄

Provided by seniors with a view of college as full of decisions, pressures, and demands in addition to the academic (to be checked out later) and sufficient acquaintance with previewers to suggest that they do not see it this way, I am possessed of an elaborated hypothesis about change and major learning areas in college.

The five comments quoted in this section (four additional examples are omitted) suggest that the field worker makes constant use of working hypotheses from many sources. My use of hypotheses falls roughly into three sequential types. The first operation consisted of testing a crude yes-or-no proposition. By asking informants or thinking back over volunteered information in the data ("nearly all students today" or "no student"), I stated a working hypothesis in the comments and began the second operation of the sequence: looking for negative cases or setting out deliberately to accumulate positive ones. At the second stage, working with negatively expressed hypotheses gave me a specific goal. One instance that contradicts what I say is enough to force modification of the hypothesis. It is a process of elimination in which I try to build understanding of *what is* by pinning down *what is not.*

The third stage of operating with hypotheses in the field involves two-step formulations and eventually rough models. Hypotheses take the form of predictions about future events which may take place under specific conditions or changes in informants over time in conjunction with events. Needless to say, particularly in the first days in the field, the worker is never at the same stage with all his data; he may be operating at the yes-or-no level in one area and advancing to the model stage with another at any given time.

Recognition of a Major Theme. Participant-observers sometimes say that the major themes of a study appeared very early in the field of work, although they may have been unrecognized. The field comments present an opportunity to investigate the phenomenon—one case in what should be a larger study.

Is there early and sudden insight? If so, what brings it about? On what grounds can an observer predict that a major theme will be central to the study? To get at my reasoning retrospectively, I take the comments related to recognition of a possible major theme in chronological order. After the first day in the field, I tentatively suggest a relationship between two reiterated findings.

► 7/6/59: I had been probing very gently all day when I asked students about KU as to whether their image of it was a place where you did not study but just had a good time, but I had gotten no flavor of this from any of the students I've talked to. They seem to be very serious about college and, if they were not, were pretending to it or were simply overawed by its social challenge. I think this is part of their saying it is such a big place, certainly a place where you come with some trepidation and with respect. ◄

Since I talked to as many visibly different types of previewers as possible, I was interested that, even after probing, no student provided expected data. As statements on "bigness" were volunteered, I regarded them with added confidence.[8] Considering the comment now, we can say that my tentative statement of the relationship between the academic seriousness of the previewers and their notion that KU is a big place takes the form (following Polya) that *A* is made somewhat more plausible by *B*.[9]

The next day I comment on another form of seriousness.

▶ 7/7/59: Throughout this day there are small indirect references to the fact that I have found students more serious about academic affairs than I expected. From Dean Brown's conversation, I get the notion that the administration is just as serious about educating them in the social realm as are the students themselves. This is evidently a major change in my orientation to the college. ◀

While the increment is not great, if previewers are serious about social matters (*C*) as well as academic (*A*), *A* becomes more plausible. The dean's concern about the social realm helps still more.

On July 8, I announce "bigness" as a major theme because it is frequent and widespread.[10]

▶ 7/8/59: One major theme is evidently already coming out in today's field notes: KU is a very big place. I am already comparing coming to KU as similar to going to New York City [to Eastern kids]. ◀

If I think there is a relationship between academic seriousness (*A*) and "bigness" (*B*), to feel certain about *B*, in the primitive analysis I am conducting in the field, increases my confidence in *A* once more.

Later in the same day's notes, I speculate about the origins of seriousness.

▶ 7/8/59: In summary of these two days of field work, I feel frustrated at having talked to a very few students, and yet at the same time I feel that I have the beginning of some sound knowledge of how things are up here and that this will increase if I attend more previews. There already seems to be some repetition in the students' reasons for coming to KU, the amount they expect to study, and the general serious academic outlook that they have. They are more focused on academic matters here at the beginning than you would expect, but I have an idea this may be because these things appear manageable or more manageable to them than the great unspoken questions

8.   See Howard S. Becker, "Problems of Inference and Proof in Participant Observation," *American Sociological Review, XXIII* (1958) 655–656.

9.   George Polya, *Mathematics and Plausible Reasoning* (2 vols.; Princeton, N.J.: Princeton University Press, 1954), vol. 2. *Patterns of Plausible Inference*. On pages 18–54 and 109–141, he discusses a "calculus of plausibility" based on everyday reasoning.

10. See Howard S. Becker and Blanche Geer, "Participant Observation: The Analysis of Quantitative Data," in Richard N. Adams and Jack J. Preiss, eds., *Human Organization Research* (Homewood, Ill.: The Dorsey Press, Inc., 1960), pp. 283–285.

about whether they will make it socially. They have real fears about this last and very much of a do-or-die attitude, I think, although they did not express this to me directly. Real life has begun, and if you don't make it now perhaps you never will. ◄

The existence of seriousness about academic and social aspects of college (*A* and *C*) is made more understandable, hence plausible, if there is evidence of common cause: previewers think college is "real life" (*D*). We have an explanatory proposition: *D* leads to *A* + *C*.

On the third day in the field, taking a subgroup of the preview population—prospective graduate students—I explain their seriousness by the fact that for them college is a step in an irreversible career sequence.

► 7/9/59: Apparently the recent introduction of psychology into the high schools has had a great effect, and that, plus nuclear physics, is leading many students who probably would have before been at a loss if they did not want to be doctors, to think of graduate work and academic research careers. These kids are taking a really big jump in coming to college because they have no intention of going back to the small town which they came from, and they are aware that there would be no place for their knowledge there. ◄

Since an irreversible career sequence (D_1) is certainly "real life," we now have a proposition of the form $D_1 = A$. Plausible explanation of seriousness in a subgroup lends greater strength to the proposition $D \rightarrow A + C$ for the population as a whole.[11]

At the time of the fourth preview, although I do not use the phrase "major theme," I make a last statement associating the "bigness" of the University, academic seriousness, and seriousness about social life.

► 7/16/59: I have so far found absolutely nothing to contradict the image of KU students, prefreshmen that is, as very serious and in many cases academic-minded. Their fears are of its bigness, possible unfriendliness, and snobbishness and how hard the work will be. ◄

In the primitive analysis carried on during field work, I now seem to take it for granted that previewers define college as real life and that their seriousness toward it and reference to it as big express this definition ($A + B + C = D$).

In what sense can we say that I recognized a major theme in the eight days of field work? Certainly there is no flash of insight, no sudden revelation. The formulation proceeds slowly along lines of other working-hypothesis sequences, but the data bear up under elaboration. Unlike some of the working hypotheses mentioned earlier, the "seriousness" theme does not peter out. According to the comments, the field notes are full of it. I cannot turn up a

---

11. Hanan Selvin has called similar reasoning "internal replication." See his discussion in "Durkheim's *Suicide* and Problems of Empirical Research," *American Journal of Sociology*, LXIII (1958), 613–618.

negative case. As at least part of the data is volunteered, I am not afraid that my questioning has put it in my informants' heads. Insofar as I was able to identify visible groups or types of previewers, I found seriousness present in each. It characterized both of the two dimensions of college, academic and social, that previewers perceived.

Equally important in suggesting status as a major theme, seriousness has no rivals. It is easy to elaborate[12] and not trivial; if we find in subsequent field work that students consider college real life, it should prove important for understanding their behavior.

TABLE I CHANGES IN CONCEPTS DURING EARLY FIELD WORK

CONCEPT BEFORE PREVIEWS	COMMENTS SHOWING CHANGE	NO CHANGE	TOTAL
Role	2	1	3
Empathy	7	0	7
Anticipated problems	3	0	3
Hypotheses	9	0	9
Major theme	9	0	9
Miscellaneous	3	0	3
Total	33	1	34

DISCUSSION

The comments make clear that the answer to the question "Do strategies and concepts change in the first days of field work?" is emphatically *yes*. Furthermore, many of the changes are of such a nature as to affect subsequent field work radically. Table I summarizes the discussion.

Perhaps because of our experience with medical students of the same University, role as presentation of self to informants changes least. My role as coworker on the larger study changed rapidly from interviewer of pre-freshmen to general ground-breaker. Largely because of the unanticipated presence of college seniors, several of whom I interviewed at length, I became aware of students' interests in prestige rankings among living groups, extra-curricular activities, and politics. In the fall, we dropped our plan to interview students in order to map out important areas of interest to them and proceeded on the preview leads.

Three days of field work were enough to change my concept of college students dramatically. Before entering the field, I thought of them as irrespon-

12. The term *elaborate* is used to suggest the general similarity of the reasoning process with that described in Paul F. Lazarsfeld and Morris Rosenberg, eds., *The Language of Social Research* (Glencoe, Ill.: The Free Press, 1955), pp. 121–124.

sible children. But as I listened to their voices, learned their language, witnessed gesture and expression, and accumulated the bits of information about
them which bring people alive and make their problems real, I achieved a
form of empathy with them and became their advocate. The observers who
began work in the fall experienced the same change, but not until they got
into the field. Reading my field notes did not help.

Parenthetically, one might suppose that empathy for informants, once
developed, would become a problem in itself. It often feels like one in the
field but drops sharply on leaving it. After a few weeks on analysis, I won-
dered how I could stand those silly kids. Discussion with coworkers and
getting the faculty perspective later in the study also helped to restore a balance.

The problems we anticipated with the administration remained as illusory
in the fall as they were during the previews. Identifying student groups, which
we thought would be difficult, did not turn out to be a problem in the fall.
As at the previews, it was easy to meet individuals who then told us about
friends or fellow group-members; we could, over time, get at more of the
variables related to formation and maintenance.

Many of the hypotheses I took into the field at the previews did not check
out. Prefreshmen did not have concrete enough information about what
college would be like to answer our questions about studying, using time,
choosing courses or activities. Making the hypotheses and asking questions,
however, served to structure initial contacts and produced negative findings
which changed our concept of what previewers were like and what they would
experience as freshmen. The working hypotheses I used provided a similar
entree for work in the fall. The major theme I began to elaborate during the
previews—students take college very seriously as part of real life—was a
change, not so much from our prefield-work concepts as from the stereotype
in the general culture (which the comments suggest I shared) that finds college students, particularly at large state universities, frivolous and sports-
minded. This is the way they are in fiction and much of the literature. My
efforts to uncover frivolity in the previewers failed. Seniors swamped me
with complicated accounts of their activities. In the fall, we started out looking
for negative cases and continued to look throughout the field work without
much result. The theme should have a place in the monograph in a more differentiated form, along with others we developed later.

CONCLUSIONS

If early field work reaches few conclusions, it may nevertheless have far-
reaching effects on the rest of the study. Memoranda written after the previews
indicate that the idea of dealing only with premedical students in the fall has
gone by the board. We are aware that students in the different schools of the
University are so intermingled in living groups and activities that we must
deal with all of them. Our proposal to investigate only the academic aspects

of college no longer seems feasible. The academic is too closely tied to other aspects of students' lives.

Evidently the preview data—particularly those from the senior leaders—went beyond my comments in giving us a picture of the campus as we might expect to find it in the fall. In a memorandum based on discussion of the summer field notes written before entering the field in September, Becker states:

▶ The major units of the college in which students belong are based on residence and are contained in the following list: large fraternities, small fraternities, ... scholarship halls, other dormitories, married students' residences, and rooms in town ... each of these groups can be thought as a network of interconnected cliques ... essentially similar in their views of academic effort.[13] ◄

Becker goes on to hypothesize several student cultures on campus. He later wonders if all may not have the same general goals, but, à la Cohen, differential access to success.[14]

It is clear that while one may reasonably expect initial field work to settle questions of role, empathy, and anticipated problems and to lay the grounds of later work by developing hypotheses and beginning the elaboration of a major theme, the observer may fail to comment on important things. My comments were concerned almost entirely with the previewers. I let the long interviews with seniors speak for themselves. Having more than one person on a study lessens the danger that such leads will be missed. Practically, the early field work provided us with informants to follow up and previewers as foils for college students when we met them. Its most far-reaching result was our broadened objective. We would study all the students, abandon interviews in the formal sense, and take our chances in the field, trusting the students to be as articulate and helpful as previewers.

One must conclude that the first days of field work may transform a study, rightly or wrongly, almost out of recognition.

The procedures described by Geer are among the earliest and simplest of analytic techniques. As the mass of data obtained accumulates, more complex and systematic techniques become applicable and desirable. The most comprehensive review of their range is provided by Allen Barton and Paul Lazarsfeld, who describe and demonstrate with helpful details the various procedures. They also suggest the conditions under which each is most usefully applied and the limitations that confront each.

---

13. Memorandum entitled "Comments on Theory and Techniques for the Undergraduate Study," September 9, 1959. It begins, "This is written on the eve of going into the field. I am simply recording the more or less tentative conclusions that Ray, Geer, and I arrived at in discussing our preliminary strategy."

14. Albert E. Cohen, *Delinquent Boys* (Glencoe, Ill.: The Free Press, 1955).

SOME FUNCTIONS OF
QUALITATIVE ANALYSIS IN SOCIAL RESEARCH

ALLEN H. BARTON AND PAUL F. LAZARSFELD

THE METHODOLOGICAL PROBLEM

The advancement of research procedure in social science as elsewhere depends on making explicit what researchers actually do, and systematically analyzing it in the light of logic and of substantive knowledge. Such a "codification" of procedures points out dangers, indicates neglected possibilities, and suggests improvements. It makes possible the generalization of methodological knowledge—its transfer from one specific project or subject matter to others, from one researcher to the scientific community. Finally it makes possible a more systematic training of students, in place of simply exposing them to concrete cases of research in the hope that they will somehow absorb the right lessons.

Such a recording and analysis of procedures has gone quite far in certain parts of the social research process—in the design of experiments, in the analysis of survey data, in the scaling and measurement of social and psychological variables, and in sampling. But codification has been very unevenly applied; important parts of the research process have been neglected.

This is particularly true of the analysis of non-quantified data, "qualitative analysis," as it is often called. A great deal of social research operates with qualitative descriptions of particular institutions, situations or individuals, rather than with "largely quantified data accumulated by structured observation in empirical situations approximating (with specified deviations) the model of controlled experiment."[1] Not only is this type of research large in volume, but it plays important roles in the research process, by itself and in connection with quantitative research. This paper aims to make a start at the systematic analysis of "qualitative procedure."

The question which we would like to answer is: "What can a researcher do when confronted by a body of qualitative data—detailed, concrete, non-metric descriptions of people and events, drawn from direct observation, interviews, case-studies, historical writings, the writings of participants?" The methodologist's first step toward a systematic answer is to examine what

Reprinted from pp. 321–356 of Allen H. Barton and Paul F. Lazarsfeld, "Some Functions of Qualitative Analysis in Social Research," *Frankfurter Beiträge zur Soziologie* (1955), **1**, 321–361. Copyright 1955 by Europäische Verlagsanstalt, Frankfurt am Main, by permission of the authors and publisher.

1. Definition of quantitative research given by Daniel Lerner, " 'The American Soldier' and the Public," in: Robert K. Merton and Paul F. Lazarsfeld, Continuities in Social Research, Glencoe, Illinois, 1950, p. 220.

researchers in fact have been doing with qualitative material. About 100 studies were culled for characteristic examples. An effort was then made to organize these cases in order that the most characteristic types of qualitative work could be distinguished and documented. This paper presents the resulting organization.

The reader will have no difficulty in noting that this "guide through qualitative research" is itself guided by proceeding from simple to ever more complex procedures. We begin with a discussion of the value of simple observations. We then proceed to those studies which center on ordering and classification. Our next group of examples demonstrates the various ways in which several variables are interrelated through qualitative analysis. Next we discuss cases where the analyst wants to encompass such a great number of dimensions that he cannot make them all explicit, but tries to sum them up in a general "pattern." This is probably the point at which qualitative research is most creative, most controversial, and most difficult to describe. It will be seen that we had to use a special term ("matrix formula"), to bring into relief this means of seeing the social world in a new way. Finally, we touch on the role of qualitative data in the support of theory, a topic so large that we did not dare to pursue it to any extent.

It should also be kept in mind what this paper does not attempt to do. First of all, it does not describe how qualitative research should be done; it is restricted to an organized description of what is actually being done, without expressing any judgment. Secondly, this paper, but for one point, does not make any attempt at formalization. The exception is in Section II where the use of typologies is discussed. The logic of typologies is by now so well developed that it was simple to include it in this paper. Such formalizations have considerable advantages. They indicate the underlying assumptions in a given piece of qualitative work, what points the author might have overlooked, at what points he might have contradicted himself, and so forth. There is no doubt that additional formalizations will be needed. We have, for example, distinguished various ways in which a single observation can be fruitful; however, we have not tried to bring the different possibilities into a more general context from which they can be derived. As a matter of fact, one of the hopes for the present survey is that it will facilitate further work in this direction.[2] We have also not dealt with the problem of evidence. Under what conditions

---

2. The general idea of codifying existing methods of social research is now being carried out by a special project on Advanced Training in Social Research at Columbia University. Formalizations of specific pieces of qualitative writing are an essential part of this project. Available in monograph form so far are a formalization by Ernest Nagel of procedures of functional analysis in social research, and a formalization by Paul F. Lazarsfeld of certain problems of process analysis, the interaction of social variables through time. The present can be considered as the typical first step which has to precede a more full-fledged formalization. It is one of the documents developed by the Columbia project.

in the social sciences an assertion is proved is a very difficult question, not restricted to qualitative research. It seemed best not to touch on this issue, in a context in which all emphasis was placed on providing a picture of a kind of work which is usually considered so "private" that it defies all systematic presentation.

I. ANALYSIS OF SINGLE OBSERVATIONS

When one examines qualitative reports, one of the first types of material which catches our attention is the "surprising observation." Like the nets of deep-sea explorers, qualitative studies may pull up unexpected and striking things for us to gaze on. We find that there are people who believe that they are being educated by the unrelated and trivial information presented by quiz shows.[3] Interviews with people deprived of their newspaper by a strike disclose that some do not turn to alternative sources of news, but to reading anything which is lying around the house; a major function of newspaper reading seems to be simply to fill in "gaps" in the daily routine.[4] Observers of the underworld tell us that professional thieves constitute a rather exclusive social group, with exacting standards of membership strongly reminiscent of those of lawful professions.[5] Anthropological data of course are full of surprising observations: that Eskimos lend their wives to guests without any jealousy, that Fiji Islanders kill their chiefs when they grow old, and so on.[6]

These phenomena are of various levels: some are individual beliefs and behaviors, some are a matter of group standards and structures within a society, some involve the norms of a whole culture. In each case the qualitative researcher has simply disclosed that such-and-such a phenomenon exists. And in one way or another, to be told that such things exist has a strong impact on the reader. They all have an element of surprise.

In the next few pages we will try to clarify what this impact is, and what research functions are served by these qualitative observations which simply state the existence of something surprising. We can distinguish at least two different uses for such observations. First, the existence of a phenomenon may raise problems—that is, compel us to look for explanations, to explore its consequences, to try to fit it into our scheme of knowledge. Second, we may find in the qualitative observations an indicator of some general variable which we want to study, but cannot measure directly.

3.   Paul F. Lazarsfeld, Radio and the Printed Page, New York 1940, pp. 74 seq.

4.   Bernard Berelson, What "Missing the Newspaper" Means, in: Paul F. Lazarsfeld and Frank Stanton, Communications Research 1948–1949, New York 1949, pp. 122 seq.

5.   E. H. Sutherland, The Professional Thief, Chicago 1937.

6.   A variety of anthropological examples is given in Margaret Mead, Adolescence in Primitive and in Modern Society, in: Theodore M. Newcomb and Eugene L. Hartley, Readings in Social Psychology, New York 1947, pp. 6 seq.

Observations Which Raise Problems.   Some observations are surprising because they conflict with our expectations, either common-sense or theoretically derived.   Other observations surprise us by bringing to light phenomena which are simply new and unexplained, which challenge our curiosity.   Yet another type of problem-raising observations is that which brings together under a clear label a body of "familiar" experiences which had not previously been seen as a definite, generally occurring social phenomenon—which forms for the first time, so to speak, a "social object" to be studied.

In any of these cases the result is that a problem is raised.   Our attention is focussed on a phenomenon, and we are stimulated to seek explanations and inquire into consequences.   To make such a problematic observation is to initiate a research process which may lead to significant advancement of our understanding of social phenomena.   (Some kind of observations no doubt raise more significant questions and lead to more valuable findings than others. It would be of great value to develop "screening principles" which can direct our attention to the more significant of the surprising observations; this cannot however be gone into here.[7])

To give concrete meaning to the notion of a problematic qualitative observation, and to provide material for its further development, a number of examples can be given.

As is well known, the original experiments of the Western Electric researchers led to highly surprising quantitative results: the experimental changes in physical conditions of work in no way accounted for the changes in production in the experimental group or workers.   At this point the researchers decided to go back to the very first stage of the research process, and simply gather observations about what goes on in a normal working group in a factory.   This exploratory research turned up a number of surprising qualitative observations:[8]

▶ Some work groups were characterized by "a lack of ambition and initiative and a complacent desire to let well enough alone";

"The supervisory control which is set up by management to regulate and govern the workers exercises little authority . . ."

"They (the employees) firmly believe that they will not be satisfactorily remunerated for any additional work they produce over the bogey . . ." ◀

All of these facts were in conflict with what the management and the researchers had expected.   By following them up the researchers were led to their now well-known discovery of the importance of informal groups in formal organizations, and of the barriers to communication which exist between levels within organizations.

---

7.   A discussion of this point is found in Robert K. Merton, Social Theory and Social Structure, Glencoe, Illinois, 1949; Chapter III, The Bearing of Empirical Research on Sociological Theory.

8.   F. J. Roethlisberger and William J. Dickson, Management and the Worker, Cambridge, Mass., 1946, Chapter XVII.

Communications research offers many examples of surprising qualitative observations.   We have already mentioned the discovery of unexpected motives—for listening to quiz programs and for reading newspapers.   Unexpected responses to communications are another important example.   A broadcast warning the public to patronize X-ray operators and avoid "quacks" left some listeners afraid of any X-ray treatments, and others doubting whether there could be any X-ray machines in the hands of incompetent operators.[9] A film designed to impress Americans with the British war-effort left some more convinced than ever that America was bearing all the burden.[10] The discovery of such anomalous responses led to more detailed investigations of the communications process, which turned up some important general principles —for example, about the need to relate the message to the experience-world for the audience, which may be quite different from that of the communicator.

A study of how prejudiced people respond to cartoons ridiculing prejudice found an unexpected type of response.[11] Some people were neither shamed out of their prejudices nor insulted; they simply did not understand what the cartoons were driving at.   When this response was investigated in detail, the "derailment mechanism" of motivated misunderstanding was revealed (see p. 185 below).

Listeners to Kate Smith's war-bond "marathon broadcast" placed remarkable emphasis on her "sincerity."[12] Considering that other professional entertainers drew no such response, and that the respondents were generally suspicious of advertising and propaganda manipulation, this seemed worth investigating.   Further study suggested the importance of "the propaganda of the deed" in a propaganda-wary society—in this case, Kate Smith's presumed strain and sacrifice in making the 18-hour broadcast.

The examples so far have involved unexpected phenomena which stimulated a search for causal explanations.   In other instances the problem which is raised is in the other direction—an investigation of the consequences of a certain phenomenon is stimulated.   Thus one researcher interested in problems of the profession noted an "obvious" fact as raising a problem: while all professionals meet a certain proportion of failures, the trial lawyers as a group necessarily lose half their cases.[13] What must be the consequences of such a high rate of failure for these professionals, and how do they deal with it?

9.   Paul F. Lazarsfeld and Patricia L. Kendall, The Listener Talks Back, in: Radio and Health Education, New York 1945.

10.   Robert K. Merton and Patricia L. Kendall, The Boomerang Response, in: Channels, Vol. XXI, No. 7 (June 1944).

11.   Patricia L. Kendall and Katherine M. Wolfe, The Analysis of Deviant Cases in Communications Research, in: Lazarsfeld and Stanton, l.c., pp. 158 seq.   Also E. Cooper and M. Jahoda, The Evasion of Propaganda, Journal of Psychology, Vol. XXIII, 1947, pp. 15 seq.

12.   Robert K. Merton, Mass Persuasion, New York 1946, pp. 82 seq.

13.   Wagner Thielens, research in progress, Columbia University, Department of Sociology.

The answers to these problems might throw light on some important problems of the professional role. The ability to take a commonplace fact and see it as raising problems is important because it can lead ultimately to such enlightenment.

Another such observation was made by Merton in his study of the Kate Smith war-bond marathon. In the content of the broadcast there was no reference to the real economic purpose of war bond buying as an anti-inflation measure. Merton saw this fact as raising problems of consequences: an opportunity to educate a large and attentive audience in economic realities had been neglected, and reliance had been placed instead upon "large delusive statements" playing upon the anxieties of those with loved ones overseas. What were "the further, more remote but not necessarily less significant effects of these techniques upon the individual personality and the society?" "Does the unelaborated appeal to sentiment which displaces the information pertinent to assessing this sentiment blunt the critical capacities of the listeners?"[14]

An example of the forming of commonplace experiences into a clearly labelled social phenomenon, and thereby creating a new object for investigation, is Adler's formulation of the concept of the inferiority complex.[15] Everyone at one time or another has experienced feelings of being inadequate, unworthy, etc., but until these private sensations had been pointed out and labelled, they could not be investigated by social science. Other examples which might be called to mind are Veblen's formulation of the concept of conspicuous consumption,[16] or Sutherland's labelling of certain categories of business behavior as "white collar crime."[17] Without having actually discovered any new facts, simply by directing attention to familiar facts placed for the first time within a distinctive category, these investigators were able to raise important problems and initiate fruitful study.

The reader may have noticed that some of the examples of "surprising observations" cited are no surprise at all to him. This is as it should be. The point is that one time they were surprising, and initiated further investigation which has been sufficiently successful to render them familiar and understandable today. Another problem is that an observation may be surprising to the particular researchers, while other social scientists have known about it all along. Thus the Western Electric researchers made the "surprising discovery" that informal social organization existed among workers. Other sociologists had long been aware of the problem of informal groups; however, the special preconceptions of American industrial sociology up to that time had kept it unaware of this whole realm of phenomena. In a still more extreme

---

14. Merton, Mass Persuasion, l.c., pp. 188 seq.
15. Alfred Adler, The Neurotic Constitution, New York 1926.
16. Thorstein Veblen, The Theory of the Leisure Class, Modern Library, New York 1934.
17. Edwin H. Sutherland, White-Collar Criminality, in: American Sociological Review, Vol. V, February 1940, No. 1, pp. 1 seq.;—White Collar Crime, New York 1949.

case, a finding may be new only to one particular researcher; in which case it might better be termed "self-education" than a scientific discovery.

Is there anything which a researcher can do toward making "surprising observations" other than to maintain an alert state of mind? It may seem contradictory to speak of giving instructions for making surprising observations. However, there are ways in which one can at least increase the probability of making such observations. Some of these are discussed by Jahoda, Deutsch, and Cook under the heading, "The Analysis of 'Insight-Stimulating Cases'."[18] Strangers or newcomers to a community or a country, it is suggested, may be able to pick out problematic facts which are simply taken for granted by those accustomed to the locale. Marginal individuals, or cases in transition from one stage or status to another, may present much more clearly certain problematic features of a personality-type of social system. Deviants, extreme cases, or "pure, ideal-typical" cases may have a relatively high efficiency in indicating problematic facts.

Observations Which Serve Indicators. The first type of surprising observations discussed were those which were anomalous and unexplained, which served the function of stimulating a search for explanations. Another type of qualitative observations are challenging because we see in them indications of some large-scale phenomenon which we cannot perceive directly. Thus the occurrence of riots and protest meetings in the North during the Civil War serves as an indication that opposition to Lincoln's war policy existed; bits of shell or pottery found in graves mark the routes of trade and cultural contact in the prehistoric world; a peculiar military custom indicates the caste-like nature of army organization; modes of speech may indicate complex mental patterns or cultural emphases.

Three situations can be pointed out in which one pays particular attention to qualitative indicators. They are distinguished in terms of the kind of obstacle which prevents direct observation and measurement of the underlying variable:

1. Situations in which qualitative evidence substitutes for otherwise simple statistical information relating to past ages or inaccessible countries.

2. Situations in which qualitative evidence is used to get at psychological data which are repressed or not easily articulated—attitudes, motives, assumptions, frames of reference, etc.

3. Situations in which simple qualitative observations are used as indicators of the functioning of complex social structures and organizations, which are difficult to subject to direct observation.

---

18. Marie Jahoda, Morton Deutsch and Stuart W. Cook, Research Methods in Social Relations, New York 1951, pp. 42 seq.

The underlying assumption in all these cases is that a phenomenon which cannot be directly observed will nevertheless leave traces which, properly interpreted, permit the phenomenon to be identified and studied. A great historical movement, a basic personality characteristic, an essential characteristic of organizational structure, should all leave their imprint on almost any documentary material, accounts by observers, or even physical refuse, which they leave behind.

Examples of the first class (qualitative substitutes for unavailable statistical or descriptive material) would include the use of newspaper stories or other contemporary records of public demonstrations as indications of public opinion in past times of crisis;[19] Frazer's use of advertisements for slaves in ante-bellum Southern newspapers to find out about the structure of the slave family;[20] the use of reports of refugees, Soviet press materials, and the contents of Soviet literature to provide information about life in the Soviet Union;[21] the use of archeological remains to indicate culture contacts or religious beliefs in prehistoric times.

Examples of the second class (qualitative indicators of psychological variables) include formal projective testing, the psychological analysis of personal documents or artistic works, the analysis of items of literature or entertainment as presumed projections of the traits of their audience,[22] and of course the analysis of qualitative interviews or records of participant observation. A good example of the use of indicators for a psychological concept is found in the study of anti-prejudice cartoons mentioned earlier:

▶ "In tracing the process through which these 68 respondents arrived at their misunderstanding, we find our starting point in the fact that most of them *identified* with Mr. Bigott. (Footnote:) By 'identification' we mean the mental process through which a subject assumes the role of another person to such an extent that actions, either verbal or behavioral, directed toward the object of identification are experienced as directed toward the identifying person. Evidence of identification with Mr. Bigott was manifested by the subject's acting in one or more of the following ways: (a) explicitly affirming identification, saying, for example, 'I guess I'm a Mr. Bigott'; (b) consistently and openly sympathizing with Mr. Bigott, expressing sorrow, for example, that Mr. Bigott

---

19. For a number of examples, see Paul F. Lazarsfeld, The Obligations of the 1950 Pollster to the 1984 Historian, in: Public Opinion Quarterly, Vol. 14, No. 4 (Winter 1950–51).

20. E. F. Frasier, The Negro Family in the United States, Chicago 1939, pp. 55 seq. This and other examples are discussed in: Robert Bower, Training Guide on the Qualitative Use of Documentary Material, New York, Bureau of Applied Social Research, 1950; mimeographed.

21. For example: Barrington Moore, Jr., Soviet Politics: the Dilemma of Power, Cambridge, Mass., 1950; Alexander Gerschenkron, A Neglected Source of Economic Information on Soviet Russia, in: American Slavic and East European Review, Vol. IX (February 1950).

22. For one example: Donald V. McGranahan and Ivor Wayne, German and American Traits Reflected in Popular Drama, in: Human Relations, Vol. I, No. 4 (August 1948), pp. 429 seq.

looked so weak and sick in the 'transfusion' cartoon; (c) interpreting a threat to or criticism of Mr. Bigott as referring to himself, as, for example, becoming emotionally upset by the cobweb on Mr. Bigott's head."[23] ◄

A single conversation reported by the authors of *Deep South* bears witness to the depth of feeling involved in white attitudes toward Negroes in this deeply prejudiced area: A social worker described a poor-white family in which two girls

► "'are having babies and are not married . . . That isn't the end by any means . . . Somebody told me that this older girl was sleeping with the father . . .' After the recitation of the case, when the social worker was out of the room, a woman whispered to the interviewer: 'Mrs. Wilson says *those girls have Negro men too,* but Miss Trent (the supervisor) won't let me say anything about that . . . *Isn't that awful?'* It is significant to note from this interview that the incest situation was viewed with less horror than the infraction of the caste sex taboos."[24] ◄

On the basis of his long participant observation, William Whyte was able to report the following striking indicator of the complete acceptance of gambling in Cornerville:

► "When a mother sends her small child down to the corner for a bottle of milk, she tells her to put the change on a number."[25] ◄

Investigators studying the effects of unemployment on the psychology of the people of an Austrian village had the school children write essays on the theme, "My Future Occupation." The pervasiveness of the insecurity of the children of the unemployed, its corrosive effect on planning for the future, was indicated among other things by the very language used. Children of employed workers would write, "I will be . . ." or "I want to become . . ." Children of the unemployed tended to use phrases like "I might become" or "I would like to be . . ." In the same study a small boy remarked to one of the investigators that he would like to be an Indian chief, "But I am afraid it will be hard to get the job."[26]

The third situation—the use of simple qualitative indicators to show the attributes of complex social structures—is very clearly exemplified in Blumenthal's study of a small mining community. The speed and inclusiveness of interpersonal communication in the community was indicated

► "by the fact that should a death occur at nine o'clock in the morning and the information not reach a resident until late in the afternoon, his usual

---

23. Kendall-Wolfe, l.c., p. 163.

24. Allison Davis, Buleigh B. Gardner and Mary R. Gardner, Deep South, Chicago 1943, p. 116.

25. William F. Whyte, Street Corner Society, Chicago 1943, p. 116.

26. M. Jahoda and H. Zeisel, Die Arbeitslosen von Marienthal, Leipzig 1932, quoted in: Jahoda, Deutsch and Cook, l.c., pp. 298 seq.

expression is, 'I can't understand why I didn't hear that sooner,' and others say to him, 'Where have you been? Everybody knew that by noon.'"[27] ◀

At another point Blumenthal notes the existence of conflicting qualitative indicators of the social contact between Mineville and its nearest neighbor, and concludes that one has the greater weight:

▶ "During the heyday of Crystal her people and those of Mineville were not so well acquainted as might be supposed ... Hotly contested baseball games and the communities having celebrated together on the main day of festivities for each—Miner's Union Day—were not indications of far-reaching personal relations. This is shown by the measure of social distance evidenced by the fact that a young man whose reputation was such in one town that its 'respectable' girls refused to associate with him could go to the other and fraternize with its 'best' young woman."[28] ◀

The existence of primary group relations within smaller units of the American army can be inferred from the following qualitative indications drawn from an interview:

▶ "We bunked together, slept together, fought together, told each other where our money was pinned in our shirts ... If one man gets a letter from home the whole company reads it."[29] ◀

The authors of *The American Soldier*, wanting an indicator for the complex notion of the "Army caste system," pointed to an institutionalized symbolic act:

▶ "Enlisted men selected for officer candidate school were first discharged from the Army and then readmitted in their new and very different status." ◀

Just as it is impossible to move from one caste to another in an ethnic case situation, so an enlisted man about to become an officer must leave the Army system before reentering in his new status. The continuation of this custom is a certain indication of the continuation of the attitudes of a "caste system" in the Army.[30]

In discussing the family structure found in Middletown's various classes, the Lynds suggest a possible indicator of the position of the husband in the family:

▶ "It may not be wholly fantastic to surmise that there may be some significance for the understanding of local marital association in the hierarchy of

27. Albert Blumenthal, Small Town Stuff, Chicago 1932, pp. 136 seq.

28. l.c., p. 30.

29. Samuel Stouffer et al, The American Soldier, Princeton 1949, Vol. II, p. 99.

30. l.c., Vol. I, p. 56, fn. 2. This example and others are discussed by Patricia L. Kendall and Paul F. Lazarsfeld, Problems of Survey Analysis, in: Merton and Lazarsfeld, l.c., pp. 183 seq.

terms by which local women speak of their husbands. There is a definite ascent of man in his conjugal relations as one goes up in the social scale, from 'my old man' through 'the man', 'he' (most frequent), 'the mister', 'John', 'my husband', to 'Mr. Jones'. The first four are the common terms among the working class families, and the last two among business class families."[31] ◄

The indicators which have been referred to are of many different forms. Some are linguistic, some are symbolic acts, some are documentary, some are physical objects. As substantive knowledge of linguistics, social organization, and technology are applied to the problem, one may expect ever more sensitive and reliable interpretations of such qualitative indicators. To what extent interpretation of indicators will have to remain an art, and to what extent it can be made a science, is one of the important problems of qualitative research which we cannot attempt to discuss here.

II. CONSTRUCTION OF DESCRIPTIVE SYSTEMS

The previous section discussed what can be done with a single "point" of qualitative data; the present section considers what one does when confronted by a whole array of qualitative observations. As a first step toward understanding a field of human activity, one must organize the raw observations into a descriptive system. In some cases one has only to apply categories already set up by previous investigators or by the society itself, and proceed with the further stages of analysis. In other cases previously existing categories are clarified and revised by the attempt to apply them to a concrete body of data. And in some cases the researcher must create his own classification system for the material under study. It is this latter case which will be particularly considered here.

In terms of their formal structure, the descriptive systems created by investigators can range from crude lists of "types," each defined individually without clear logical relationship to the others, to fully systematic typologies in which each type is a logical compound of a small number of basic attributes. Between these end points are all intermediate degrees of "partial" systematization, including some sets of types which include in their definition virtually all the logical elements necessary to set up a multi-dimensional "attribute space," but in which the logical analysis has not been explicitly made. Descriptive systems may also vary in terms of their degree of concreteness or generality. A fully systematic typology may be based on dimensions of a highly limited, concrete nature, while a preliminary classification can be broad and general.

Preliminary Classifications. A classification which falls toward the unsystematized end of the continuum can be called a preliminary one, since it

---

31. Robert S. and Helen Merrell Lynd, Middletown, New York 1929, p. 118, fn. 2.

represents an essential first step toward the ideal of a fully systematic one. The importance of this first step from completely unordered data to a preliminary classification must never be underestimated. Until the data are ordered in some way, the analysis of relationships cannot begin; more refined categories normally develop out of the attempt to analyze relationships between preliminary categories; there is an interacting process between refinement of classification and the analysis of relationships.

A good preliminary classification must provide a workable summary of the wealth of elements in the original data, and include—even if in unsystematic form—the basic elements necessary for understanding the situation. A bad preliminary classification is one which is poor in elements and suggestiveness, which omits so many important aspects of the situation that analysis reaches a dead end, and one must go back to the original data for a new start. So long as the essential elements are suggested somewhere in the initial classification, they can be picked and recombined more logically as the analysis proceeds. The question of what it takes to make fruitful preliminary categories—whether the process can be systematized and taught, or whether it is wholly an individual art—is one of those which most needs exploring. The present discussion can only raise this question, and present a number of examples of the process.

Good examples of the use of this form of qualitative analysis—the formation of relatively unsystematized but fruitful classifications of people and situations—can be found in the work of the Chicago urban sociologists. Such an instance is Louis Wirth's suggestive notes on "Some Jewish Types of Personality." Wirth defines his purpose in using this technique as follows:

▶ "The sociologist, in transforming the unique or individual experience into a representative or typical one, arrives at the social type, which consists of a set of attitudes on the part of the person toward himself and the group and a corresponding set of attitudes of the group toward him . . . The range of personality types in a given social group is indicative of the culture of that group."[32] ◀

Wirth's gallery of "characteristic and picturesque personalities that are met with in the average community" includes:

▶ the *Mensch,* a person of superior economic status who has "achieved his success without sacrificing his identity as a Jew";
the *allrightnick,* who "in his opportunism, has thrown overboard most of the cultural baggage of his group";
the *Schlemihl,* who belies the stereotype of the Jew as "the personification of the commercial spirit" by being "quite shiftless and helpless, failing miserably in everything he undertakes";

---

32. Louis Wirth, Some Jewish Types of Personality, in: Ernest W. Burgess, The Urban Community, Chicago 1926, p. 106.

the *Luftmensch,* who moves easily from one unsuccessful project to another, and whose "only apparent means of subsistence is the air he breathes";

the *Yeshiba Bochar,* literally the talmudical student, the young man whose learning gives prestige irrespective of wealth or origin;

the *Zaddik,* the "pious, patriarchal person . . . whose exemplary conduct is pointed to as an example"; and so on.[33] ◄

The purpose of presenting these types, drawn largely from the folklore and literature of the subject group, lies in the fact that

► "they are as complete an index as any at present obtainable of the culture traits . . . and the culture pattern of the group . . . Together they constitute the personal nuclei around which the fabric of the culture of the group is woven. A detailed analysis of the crucial personality types in any given area or cultural group shows that they depend upon a set of habits and attitudes in the group for their existence and are the direct expressions of the values of the group."[34] ◄

Starting from these types, therefore, one can derive a classification of the values, habits and attitudes which are important to the explanation of the behavior of the group.

In much the same way, from folklore and literature as well as personal observation, C. Wright Mills draws a gallery of "white-collar types." There are types of managers:

► the "glum men" on the top of the white-collar pyramid, harrassed, cautious, careful to stay in line with the aims of the employers or other higher ups;

the "old veterans" just below the top, who seek security in closely following explicit instructions, and strive for deference from those below;

the "live wire," the younger man on his way up;

the "new entrepreneur," who prospers as a fixer and go-between in a world of huge and complicated organizations, mass manipulation, and general insecurity.[35] ◄

There are types of intellectuals,[36] of academic men,[37] and—all the way down at the bottom of the white-collar pyramid—of salesgirls: "the wolf," "the charmer," "the ingenue," "the social pretender," and so on.[38]

There is a serious purpose in pin-pointing these picturesque types:

► "By examining white-collar life, it is possible to learn something about what is becoming more typically 'American' than the frontier character probably ever was. What must be grasped is the picture of society as a great sales-

---

33. l. c., paraphrased, pp. 108 seq.

34. Ibid.

35. C. Wright Mills, White Collar, New York 1951, pp. 92 seq.

36. l. c., pp. 144 seq.

37. l. c., pp. 131 seq.

38. l. c., pp. 174 seq.

room, an enormous file, an incorporated brain, a new universe of management and manipulation. By understanding these diverse whitecollar worlds, one can also understand better the shape and meaning of modern society as a whole, as well as the simple hopes and complex anxieties that grip all the people who are sweating it out in the middle of the twentieth century."[39] ◄

The general run of preliminary categories will not be as colorful and rich in suggestions as these just quoted, but they will be of the same formal nature: a simple list of discrete "types." Thus we will have lists of "types" of comic-book readers,[40] types of client-professional relations, types of appeals in a certain propaganda broadcast,[41] types of communities, etc., representing a preliminary ordering of material into a simple list of headings. As the analysis progresses, either within the original study or in the work of replication or secondary analysis, these simple lists may be developed into more systematic and more general descriptive systems.

Somewhat further along the road to generality and systemization are the kinds of "types" found in the great deal of the speculative and theoretical literature. Typical examples here are Spranger's six "value types"—the theoretical, economic, aesthetic, social, political, and religious[42]—or von Wiese's four types of religious organizations—the ecclesia, the denomination, the sect and the cult.[43] Merton, in discussing the forms of interpersonal influence, lists the following types: coercion, domination, manipulation, clarification, provision of prototypes for imitation, advice, and exchange.[44] Kingsley Davis classifies social norms in traditional categories: folkways, mores, law, custom, morality, religion, convention, and fashion.[45] Lasswell sets up eight basic categories of values which he uses to classify institutions and leaders;[46] Malinowski sets up seven "basic needs" in terms of which cultural phenomena can be classified;[47] and so on.

All of the above mentioned sets of categories are of far greater generality than those which arise in the analysis of a single empirical study of limited

---

39. l. c., Introduction, p. xv.

40. Katherine M. Wolfe and Marjorie Fiske, The Children Talk About Comics, in: Lazarsfeld and Stanton, l. c.

41. For examples: Merton, Mass Persuasion, l. c., pp. 50 seq.

42. Eduard Spranger, Types of Men, Halle 1928; for an attempt to develop measuring instruments for Spranger's concepts, see P. E. Vernon and G. W. Allport, A Test for Personal Values, in: Journal of Abnormal and Social Psychology, Vol. 26 (1931), pp. 231 seq.

43. Leopold von Wiese and Howard Becker, Systematic Sociology, New York 1932, pp. 624 seq.

44. Robert K. Merton, Patterns of Influence, in: Lazarsfeld and Stanton, l. c., p. 218.

45. Kingsley Davis, Human Society, New York 1950, Ch. III.

46. Harold D. Lasswell and Abraham Kaplan, Power and Society, New Haven 1950, pp. 55 seq.

47. Bronislaw Malinowsky, The Group and the Individual in Functional Analysis, in: American Journal of Sociology, Vol. XLIV, No. 6 (May 1939), pp. 938 seq.

scope. They are the result of attempts at general analysis of a wide range of situations. On the other hand, in their formal aspect, they are similar to the other forms of preliminary categories discussed earlier. Some of them are quite unsystematized; others include in their definition most of the elements required to set up a logical structure of basic attributes from which they could be derived, but this has not been explicitly done.

A special kind of descriptive system which might be mentioned under this heading consists of ordered categories, which are set up as developmental stages or degrees along a continuum. Thus Piaget distinguished the stages of development of children's attitudes toward the rules of conduct, from "moral realism" in which the letter of the rule is absolute to "autonomous rationality" in which blind acceptance "withdraws in favor of the idea of justice and of mutual service."[48] Scheler sets up seven categories of knowledge which he orders along the dimension of increasing "artificiality;" (1) myth and legend; (2) knowledge implicit in the natural folk-language; (3) religious knowledge; (4) the basic types of mystical knowledge; (5) philosophical-metaphysical sciences; (7) technological knowledge.[49] In such sets of categories an ordering along one dimension is explicitly stated, while the other attributes characterizing the categories are simply listed or suggested without any systematization.

Systematic Typologies. The most highly developed form of descriptive system which can arise in a qualitative analysis is one in which each type is explicitly derived from the logical combination of basic attributes or dimensions. A simple example is the logical scheme set up by Riesman in his study of political participation.[50] By examining a set of concrete "type cases" Riesman was led to break the concept of participation into two basic elements: emotional involvement and competence, or more simply, "caring" and "knowing." Taking each of these elements as a simple dichotomy, Riesman obtained four types of relations to politics:

	COMPETENCE	
	+	−
+	"involved"	"indignants"
AFFECT		
−	"inside-dopesters"	"indifferent"

Merton employs this technique in his typology of prejudice and discrimination. He starts from the usual formulation of two types of people: people

---

48. Jean Piaget, The Moral Judgement of the Child, New York 1932.

49. Max Scheler, Die Wissensformen und die Gesellschaft, Leipzig 1926, p. 62. The list given here is adapted from Merton's discussion of Scheler, in: Social Theory and Social Structure, l. c., pp. 230 seq.

50. David Riesman and Nathan Glazer, Criteria for Political Apathy, in: Alvin W. Gouldner, Studies in Leadership (1950), New York: Russell & Russell, 1965, pp. 535 seq.

who live up to the American creed of non-discrimination, and people who violate it. Merton suggests a further elaboration: that people be distinguished on one hand by whether they personally believe in the creed or not, and, on the other hand, by whether they practice discrimination or not.

▶ "... This is the salient consideration: conduct may or may not conform with individuals' own beliefs concerning the moral claims of all men to equal opportunity. Stated in formal sociological terms, this asserts that attitudes and overt behavior vary independently. Prejudicial attitudes need not coincide with discriminatory behavior. The implications of this statement can be drawn out in terms of a logical syntax whereby the variables are diversely combined, as can be seen in the following typology."[51] ◀

A TYPOLOGY OF ETHNIC PREJUDICE AND DISCRIMINATION

	ATTITUDE DIMENSION	
	Non-prejudiced	Prejudiced
Non-discrimination BEHAVIOR DIMENSION	Type I: "The All-Weather Liberal"	Type III: "The Fair-Weather Illiberal"
Discrimination	Type II: "The Fair-Weather Liberal"	Type IV: "The All-Weather Illiberal"

A mere list of the "folk-labels" of each type would appear superficially like one of the preliminary lists of categories; they are fundamentally different, however, since they are systematically derived from the cross-tabulation of two basic dimensions.

The most elaborate use of systematic typologies is found in Talcott Parsons' recent works.[52] Parsons sets forward five dichotomous attributes:

1. Affectivity—Affective neutrality;
2. Self-orientation—Collectivity orientation;
3. Universalism—Particularism;
4. Ascription—Achievement;
5. Specificity—Diffuseness.

By combining these five "pattern variables" Parsons has been able to construct general categories for describing social relations, cultural systems, and personality systems.

---

51. Robert K. Merton, Discrimination and the American Creed, in: R. M. MacIver, Discrimination and National Welfare, New York 1949.—Table is adapted from Merton's, p. 103. See also Merton's Appendix to that paper: A Note on the Use of Paradigms in Qualitative Analysis.

52. Talcott Parsons and Edward A. Shils, Toward a General Theory of Action, Cambridge, Mass., 1951, Part 2.

The process of constructing systematic typologies need only be briefly summarized here. The starting point is often a good preliminary set of categories. By examining them one derives a small number of attributes which seem to provide the basis for the distinctions made, and sets these attributes up as a multidimensional system (an "attribute-space"). This operation has been termed the "substruction" of an attribute space to a typology. One can then examine all of the logically possible combinations of the basic attributes. This serves to locate the original set of categories within the system; it often shows that some combinations have been ignored (appear as blank cells), while in other bases distinctions have been missed (the original category will overlap several cells). Of course not all of the logically possible combinations may be important or even empirically possible; it will often be necessary to restrict the combinations to be studied, or to recombine several categories to simplify the analysis. Such a recombination has been termed a "reduction," and is closely related to the operation of index formation.[53]

Partial Substructions. There remains to be mentioned a type of operation which is very frequent in qualitative analyses: the partial systematization of a concept or a set of categories. A good introduction to this operation is the well-known discussion by Simmel of envy and jealousy.[54] The situations in which these feelings arise are quite complex, and Simmel does not give an exhaustive account of them. What he does, however, is to indicate one important aspect in which the two attitudes differ: in the case of jealousy the person feels that he has a claim on the object of his desire, while in the case of envy he has no claim, only desire for the object. Simmel has thus partially substructed the attribute-space by which envy and jealousy could be systematically defined; he has not done so completely, but rather only enough to make one major distinction.

A more elaborate but still partial substruction is presented in Werner Landecker's discussion of "Types of Integration and Their Measurement." Landecker begins by indicating his discontent with the undifferentiated concept of "social integration." To study the relation of integration to other variables, to find its necessary conditions and its consequences, the broad abstraction must be broken down:

▶ "Early in the exploration of a type of phenomena it seems advisable to break it up into as many subtypes as one can distinguish and to use each subdivision as a variable for research. This appears to be a more fruitful procedure than to attempt immediately to generalize about the generic type as a whole. The main advantage of subclassification in an initial phase of research

---

53. A more detailed discussion will be found in Paul F. Lazarsfeld and Allen H. Barton, Qualitative Measurement in the Social Sciences, in: Daniel Lerner and Harold D. Lasswell, The Policy Sciences, Stanford, California, 1951, pp. 169 seq.

54. Georg Simmel, The Sociology of Conflict, in: American Journal of Sociology, Vol. IX, No. 4 (January 1904), pp. 521 seq.

is that it leads to problems of relationship among subtypes which would evade the attention of the investigator if he were to deal with the broader type from the very beginning. Generalizations on the higher level of abstraction will suggest themselves as a matter of course once regularities common to several subtypes are discovered."[55] ◄

In analyzing the concept of social integration, Landecker first breaks down society into two types of elements: cultural standards, on the one hand, and persons and their behavior, on the other. The logical interrelations among these two elements give him three types of integration:

"Cultural integration": integration within the realm of cultural standards;
"Normative integration": integration between cultural standards and the behavior of persons;
"Integration among persons": integration within the realm of behavior.

This last type in turn is broken down in terms of two types of human behavior: the interchange of ideas and the interchange of services. Integration within the realm of communication is termed "communicative integration;" integration within the realm of services is termed "functional integration."

Since "integration" is a relational concept, Landecker's types can be easily represented by a relational matrix—a table, along each side of which we list the elements involved in interrelationships. The interior cells of the table then indicate the logically possible connections, including, in the main diagonal, the internal relationship within each element:

	CULTURAL STANDARDS	PERSONS AND THEIR BEHAVIOR: COMMUNICATION	WORK
CULTURAL STANDARDS	1. Cultural integration	2. Normative integration	
COMMUNICATION		3. Communicative integration	5. ?
WORK			4. Functional integration

This relational scheme allows us to locate all of the types of integration proposed by Landecker. It also raises the question of further relationships not discussed and distinctions not made: e.g. the possible subdivision of "normative integration" in terms of the two spheres of behavior, the relationship between the two forms of behavior themselves, and indeed the possibility of distinguishing still other major spheres within the realm of behavior, for example the sphere of government, religion, or family life. For this reason we refer to Landecker's scheme as a "partial" substruction, one which is not fully worked through in all its logical possibilities.

---

55. Werner S. Landecker, Types of Integration and Their Measurement, in: American Journal of Sociology, Vol. LVI, No. 4 (January 1951), p. 332.

An even more elaborate relational scheme is implicit in a discussion of "craftsmanship" by C. Wright Mills:

▶ "Craftsmanship as a fully idealized model or work gratification involves six major features: (1) There is no ulterior motive in work other than the product being made and the processes of its creation. (2) The details of daily work are meaningful because they are not detached in the worker's mind from the product of the work. (3) The worker is free to control his own working action. (4) The craftsman is thus able to learn from his work; and to use and develop his capacity and skills in its prosecution. (5) There is no split of work and play, or work and culture. (6) The craftsman's way of livelihood determines and infuses his entire mode of living."[56] ◀

In effect, Mills proposes six attributes by which a job situation can be described. If all six of these attributes have the values indicated above, we have the ideal-type situation of "craftsmanship." The situation of the modern industrial or office worker, Mills implies, is the opposite of the idealized craftsman in all these respects. Actually the six attributes give 64 logically possible combinations of values; the intermediate, mixed combinations however do not enter into Mills' present discussion, which deals only with the idealtype cases and not with the whole attribute-space.

In this case each of the six attributes actually refers to a relationship— between a worker's capacities and his work, between work and leisure, etc. They can be derived from a relational matrix consisting of four elements: the worker (his capacities, his character); the work activity; the final product; and the worker's leisure activities (his "play," "culture," "general mode of living"). Each of these can act on any of the others, as summarized in the relational scheme below:

ACTING ON:	WORKER	WORK ACTIVITY	FINAL PRODUCT	LEISURE
WORKER	—	1) Gratifies 4) Develops	1) Gratifies	
WORK ACTIVITY	3) Freely controls	—		5, 6) Contributes to
FINAL PRODUCT		2) Visibly related to	—	
LEISURE		5, 6) Contributes to		—

This scheme might suggest additional dimensions of the man-job relationship to be taken into account, to make for a more systematic classification of work situations. Still more elements might also be added—for instance, the "external rewards" which are not supposed to dominate the craftsman's approach to his work but which are obviously primary for many kinds of jobs.

---

56. Mills, l. c., p. 220.

Formal devices such as attribute-space and relational matrices can often help to clarify concepts which are not systematically presented; sometimes they can even suggest significant possibilities not originally considered. They are not, however, a substitute for careful study and sensitive thinking about a problem. There are any number of possible relationships or attributes which might be picked out and put into a formal scheme; the strategic act is to "feel out" those which are important, which will ultimately help to solve the problems in which we are interested. Formal analysis can then be used to clarify, develop, and communicate the results of qualitative insights.

III. QUALITATIVE DATA SUGGESTING RELATIONSHIPS

The only fully adequate way to test the existence of a relationship between two variables is through statistical analysis; to test cause-and-effect relations requires either a controlled experiment, or a rather large number of cases of "natural change" observed over time. But research which has neither statistical weight nor experimental design, research based only on qualitative descriptions of a small number of cases, can nonetheless play the important role of suggesting possible relationship, causes, effects, and even dynamic processes. Indeed, it can be argued that only research which provides a wealth of miscellaneous, unplanned impressions and observations can play this role. Those who try to get suggestions for possible explanatory factors for statistical results solely from looking at tabulations of the few variables which were deliberately included in the study in advance often can make no progress; sometimes even a single written-in comment by a respondent will provide a clue to additional factors.

Finding "Factors" Influencing Action. A classic case of the use of qualitative observation to disclose possible factors influencing behavior is the Western Electric study.[57] When the experimental group of workers maintained their high production even when physical conditions were made worse than before the experiment began, it was clear that something else was affecting their production. What the real factors were was first suggested by informal conversations with and observations of the experimental group, and from then on the main research effort was focussed on qualitative interviewing and observation to discover social factors and processes.

A recent study, the main focus of which was to uncover possible factors rather than strictly to test them, is Merton's Mass Persuasion.[58] Here some 75 people were selected who were known to have bought bonds through a Kate Smith war-bond "marathon" broadcast, and interviewed in such a way as to reconstruct their experience during the broadcast as spontaneously as

---

57. Roethlisberger and Dickson, l. c.
58. Merton, Mass Persuasion, l.c.

possible. Among the factors which stood out as possibly influential were the fact that "the all-day series of appeals emerged as a dramatic event . . . a single unified pattern"; "There was reciprocal interplay, for the audience was not only responding to Smith, but she was also responding to her audience and modifying her subsequent comments as a result"; "there was considerable qualitative evidence that belief in Smith's disinterestedness and altruism played an integral role in the process of persuasion"; "the audience's images of Smith, the class structure of our society, the cultural standards of distinct strata of the population, and socially induced expectations, feelings, tensions were all intricately involved in the patterns of response to the bond drive"; "but the cumulation of affect and emotion was not the major function of the marathon broadcasts. Above all, the presumed stress and strain of the eighteen-hour series of broadcasts served to validate Smith's sincerity . . . for an understanding of the process of persuasion, the most significant feature of these responses to the marathon is the effectiveness of this propaganda of the deed among the very people who were distrustful and skeptical of mere exhortation."

A study applying the same technique to a broader historical situation was that of Elizabeth Zerner on the factors in recent history which influenced attitudes toward Jews in France.[59] By a very small number of detailed interviews with people who were presumed to be good observers (about half concierges of apartment houses, the other half intellectuals), it was suggested that there were four main events influencing attitudes toward Jews in one manner or another: the persecutions outside France, which made people more aware of the Jews as a special group; the appearance of Jewish refugees from other countries, who were a clearly visible, different group in French society; the persecution of the French Jews during the occupation, which aroused certain feelings of guilt and a certain real danger for those who helped the Jews; the restoration of Jewish jobs and property after the Liberation, which obviously caused loss and disturbance to some non-Jews.

One special technique for discovering additional factors relevant to a given type of behavior is the examination of cases which deviate from the behavior expected in terms of known factors. Thus a purely economic-interest explanation of voting leaves poor Republicans and rich Democrats as "deviants"; by qualitative interviewing one may be able to get some idea of the factors other than economic interest which motivate voting. In the "Mr. Bigott" study of the response of prejudiced people to anti-prejudice cartoons, it was expected that the prejudiced would misunderstand the message of the cartoons—as indeed almost 2/3 did. But there remained deviant cases who understood the "hostile" meaning. To explain these cases, qualitative interviews were used. It appeared that such factors were involved as the degree of security in one's

59. Elizabeth Zerner (with Robert T. Bower), German Occupation and Anti-Semitism in France, in: Public Opinion Quarterly, Vol. 11, No. 2 (Summer 1948), pp. 258 seq.

attitudes, the feeling that one's beliefs were socially caused and not a personal responsibility, the fact that the subject totally disidentified himself from the caricatured figure of "Mr. Bigott" and therefore were under no threat.[60]

Qualitative Suggestions of Process. The simplest form of a "process" analysis is that which looks for an intervening variable which "explains" the correlation between two other variables. In his study of an East-coast slum neighborhood, William Whyte arrived (on a qualitative basis) at the following relationship: the socially aspiring "college boys" clubs seemed to be more unstable and subject to internal conflict than those of the non-mobile "corner-boys." To explain this relationship (which could be considered quite "upside-down" from a middle-class viewpoint) Whyte introduced a third variable, "informal organization." The corner boy clubs could draw for cohesion on already existing informal organization:

▶ "The daily activities of the corner boys determined the relative positions of members and allocated responsibilities and obligations within the group." ◀

Among the college boys on the other hand,

▶ "Outside club meetings the members seldom associated together except in pairs. Since there was no informal organization to bind the men together, there was also no common understanding upon matters of authority, responsibility, and obligation."[61] ◀

To be able to assert this explanation with any certainty, it would be necessary for Whyte to have observed corner boy clubs which were weak in informal organization and college boy groups which were strong in it; if the former were also unstable, while the latter were stable, it would constitute a certain test of the hypothesis. Whyte does not record whether he sought out such "test situations" or was familiar with a range of such cases.

In the same way the relation between membership in a corner gang and failure to rise economically was explained in terms of the impact of group relations on saving and spending habits. Whyte denies that preexisting differences in intelligence and ability explain the whole relation (again on the basis of qualitative observations which presumably held ability constant for a number of cases in each group). Whyte goes on to suggest:

▶ "The pattern of social mobility in Cornerville can best be understood when it is contrasted with the pattern of corner-boy activity. One of the most important divergences arises in matters involving the expenditure of money. The college boys fit in with an economy of savings and investment. The corner boys fit in with a spending economy. The college boy must save his money in order to finance his education and launch his business or professional

60. Kendall-Wolfe, l. c., pp. 166 seq.

61. Whyte, l. c., 96 seq.

career. He therefore cultivates the middle-class virtue of thrift. In order to participate in group activities, the corner boy must share his money with others. If he has money and his friend does not, he is expected to do the spending for both of them . . . Prestige and influence depend in part upon free spending."[62] ◄

This observation indicates some of the factors in the process of social mobility. Of course behind each such factor uncovered are other factors—the variables which for instance determine who sticks with the boys and spends, and who breaks away, saves money, and rises.

The uncovering of possible processes can go much further than inserting a third variable in a chain. The study of anti-prejudice cartoons mentioned previously suggested a whole chain which led up to misunderstanding among the non-deviant two thirds of the prejudiced people who misunderstood:

1. Identification with Mr. Bigott and momentary understanding;

2. Desire for escape from identification;

3. Disidentification mechanism (caricaturing Mr. Bigott, making him intellectually or socially inferior);

4. Derailment of understanding: absorbtion in the derogatory characteristics of Mr. Bigott to the exclusion of understanding the point of the cartoons.[63]

In the Whyte study one finds the process of the rise of a local corner boy to political leadership traced out through a series of steps, with interacting forces noted.[64] To get a start, the corner boy must demonstrate his loyalty and ability to get results for his immediate circle of friends. Yet "if he concentrates on serving his own group, he will never win widespread support." "In order to win support he must deal with important people who influence other groups." Since he has only limited resources in terms of energy and access to official favors, he must "betray" his original friends by neglecting their interests and using his resources to help outsiders and big-shots. The result is a widespread cynicism toward "politicians" among the rank and file, which might be expected to cause constant turnover. However, according to Whyte, the politician is normally able to "trickle down" enough benefits to his followers in the district as a whole to prevent a revolt, even though his closest original friends who had the highest expectations may be badly disillusioned. The process reaches a kind of equilibrium, presumably at a level determined by the political abilities, initial "connections," and good luck of the individual politician.

In exploring for possible factors affecting some given variable, or for chains of causes and effects constituting a "process," there appear to be two basic tech-

---

62. l. c., p. 106.

63. Kendall-Wolfe, l. c., pp. 163 seq.

64. Whyte, l. c., pp. 209 seq.

niques. The first attempts to obtain objective information about the sequence of events, particularly what events preceded the response under investigation.[65] The typical questions, whether addressed to a subject or used by an observer to guide his observations, are: "What happened before X? What happened just before the subject made his decision to move, vote, buy, steal, etc.? What was the frame of mind? What had been going on in the family, neighborhood, nation, world? Had he been talking with anyone, reading anything, listening to anything?" Some responses will look like causal factors immediately, on the basis of our past experience or general hypotheses about human behavior. Others will only become prominent when we notice an apparent correlation between them and the criterion behavior in several cases.

The second technique is to ask people themselves to explain what happened and to give their reasons for acting as they did.[66] The basic question here is always "Why?" This technique has obvious limitations: people are often unaware of the real motives, of indirect influences, of the precise chain of causes and effects, of underlying necessary conditions. On the other hand it stands to reason that the participant knows a good deal about his own behavior, particularly about attitudes, motives, influences, "trigger events," and so on, and often can tell the outside investigator about things which he would never have guessed by himself. "Reasons" may not be the whole story, but they are an important source of information on possible factors, and in some cases a quite indispensable source, especially in the early stages of investigation. By adding to the general "why" query a set of more specific questions, focussing the respondent's attention on each of several basic aspects of the situation, reason questions can obtain more adequate coverage, although still limited to what the respondent himself is in a position to know.

Both of these techniques are combined in a technique of qualitative exploration of causal relations known as "discerning." This has been carefully described in Mirra Komarovsky's study of the effect of unemployment on the family status of the husband.[67] With only 59 case-studies to analyze, it was not possible to undertake a full-scale statistical analysis of the interrelations between all the possible variables. What was done was to take each case of apparent change due to the husband's unemployment and subject it to systematic checks: Had the change already begun before the unemployment? Did other factors arise concurrently with unemployment which might have been

---

65. Robert K. Merton and Patricia L. Kendall, The Focussed Interview, in: American Journal of Sociology, Vol. LI (1946), pp. 541 seq.; Herta Herzog, Training Guide on the Techniques of Qualitative Interviewing, New York, Bureau of Applied Social Research, 1948; mimeographed.

66. Paul F. Lazarsfeld, The Art of Asking Why, in: National Marketing Review, Vol. I, pp. 26 seq.

67. Mirra Komarovsky, The Unemployed Man and His Family, New York 1940; especially pp. 135 seq.

the real cause? Are the participants able to trace the step-by-step development of the change, the detailed links between unemployment and the altered role of the husband? If the respondents believe that unemployment was the reason for a certain change, on what evidence do they base their opinion? By these techniques it was possible to isolate with considerable promise of validity the causal relations between unemployment and family structure. The search for "possible factors" and "possible consequences" was made systematic; within the limitations of the data real precautions were taken against spurious relations.

Quasi-Statistics. Previous sections have dealt with operations of qualitative analysis which are essentially prior to quantitative research: observations which raise problems, the formulation of descriptive categories, the uncovering of possible causal factors or chains of causation for a particular piece of behavior. These operations stimulate and focus later quantitative research, and they set up the dimensions and categories along the "stub" of the tables, into which quantitative research may fill the actual frequencies and measurements.

However, one encounters very frequently in social science literature studies which do not use the mechanism of quantitative data-collection and statistical analysis, and still make the kind of statements which quantitative research makes. These statements may be simple frequency distributions (i.e. "most Trobrianders" or even "the Trobriander" knows or believes or does so-and-so); they may be correlations (corner boys have a spending economy, while college boys have a saving economy); they may be statements of causal relationships ("If [the politician] concentrates upon serving his own group, he will never win widespread support . . . In order to win support, he must deal with important people who influence other groups"). Such statements, based on a body of observations which are not formally tabulated and analyzed statistically, may be termed "quasi-statistics." They include "quasi-distributions," "quasi-correlations," and even "quasi-experimental data."

Non-quantitative research of this sort is no longer logically prior to statistical research. It rather directly substitutes for statistical research, making the same kind of statements but on the basis of a recording and analysis of cases which takes place largely within the mind of the observer. This kind of research has obvious shortcomings, but it also has a place in the research process, viewed as a continuing and increasingly refined pursuit by the whole community of social scientists.

An example of the dangers of impressionistic "quasi-statistics" is given by Bernard Barber in an article on participation in voluntary associations:

▶ "American observers themselves were overwhelmed by what they did not fully understand: instance the following from Charles and Mary Beard's *The Rise of American Civilization:* 'The Tendency of Americans to unite with their fellows for varied purposes . . . now became a general mania . . . It was a rare American who was not a member of four or five societies . . . Any citizen who refused to affiliate with one or more associations became an object of curiosity, if not suspicion.' Although in comparative perspective the United States may well be a 'nation of jóiners,' a survey of the available data on the number of people with memberships in voluntary associations reveals the little-known fact that many have not even a single such affiliation. This uniformity too holds for all types of areas in the United States, whether urban, suburban, small city, small town or rural."[68] ◄

Barber then quotes statistics showing that in these various areas and strata of the population from one third to over two thirds of the people do not belong to any voluntary associations. As one proceeds from simple frequency distributions to correlations and then to systems of dynamic relationships between several variables, impressionistic "quasi-statistics" become steadily less adequate.

On the other hand it is argued that a careful observer who is aware of the need to sample all groups in the population with which he is concerned, who is aware of the "visibility bias" of the spectacular as opposed to the unspectacular case, who becomes intimately familiar with his material over a long period of time through direct observation, will be able to approximate the results of statistical investigation, while avoiding the considerable expense and practical difficulty of quantitative investigation. It has been claimed, for instance, that to provide a fully statistical basis for the conclusions which Whyte was able to draw from his observation of corner gangs and college boys groups, would require hundreds of observers studying hundreds of gangs and neighborhoods over many years.

There are some situations in which formal quantitative methods are apparently less necessary than others. When one is dealing with primitive groups with a nearly homogeneous culture, in which one set of prescribed roles is just about universally carried out by the population, it may require only the observation and interviewing of relatively few cases to establish the whole pattern. The same argument can be applied to studies of a quite homogeneous subculture within a civilized society. These methods seem to have succeeded in presenting a good first approximation at least in the description of the culture and behavior of such groups. When anthropologists now call for formal sampling, data-recording, and statistical analysis it is either to catch up finer details—the small number of deviant individuals, for instance—or to deal with situations of culture groups with less homogeneity—with groups in process of acculturation, breakdown of old norms, or the development of strong internal differentiation.

In situations of less homogeneity and simplicity, it is doubtful that quasi-statistics are anything like a full substitute for actual statistics. However they can still play an important "exploratory" function. Statistical research is too expensive and time-consuming to be applied on all fronts at once; like the 200-inch telescope it must focus on a few areas of particular interest for inten-

---

68. Bernard Barber, Participation and Mass Apathy in Associations, in: Gouldner, l. c., pp. 481 seq.

sive study. Quasi-statistical studies can run ahead of the more cumbersome quantitative procedures to cover wide areas of social phenomena, and to probe into tangled complexes of relationship in search of possible "processes." They serve as a broad scanner and "finder" like the wideangled but less powerful Schmidt telescope of Mount Wilson and Palomar. Moreover the gathering and analysis of "quasi-statistical data" can probably be made more systematic than it has been in the past, if the logical structure of quantitative research at least is kept in mind to give general warnings and directions to the qualitative observer.

Systematic Comparison.   There is one special form of research into relationship which stands on the border between statistical and quasi-statistical methods. This involves the systematic comparison of a relatively small number of cases. It differs from quasi-statistics in that the cases are proceeds along lines closely approximating those of a statistical survey or controlled experiment. However it involves too few cases to actually apply statistical tests, and it involves natural situations in which one cannot be certain that "other factors are equal" for the various cases beyond those factors specifically analyzed. It is as though one set up the tables for a statistical or experimental research, but had only one or two cases to fill in each cell, and perhaps had to leave some entirely empty.

This form of "comparative research" is the only possible when the "cases" to be studied are social phenomena of a high order of complexity, such as wars, revolutions, large-scale social systems, forms of government. There do not exist very many cases in recorded history of such phenomena. Toynbee faced this problem in his classic "comparative analysis" of "Great Civilisations"—there were only about twenty-one such civilisations, along with a number of abortive or arrested civilisations.[69] Weber faced the same situation in dealing with the role of religious systems in the development of society.[70] Besides the total number of available cases being small, each is a very large and complex unit which requires great time and effort to analyze. Even where there are a large number of cases, this factor may compel the researcher to restrict himself to the systematic comparison of a few. This situation arises in studying communities or large institutions. To describe any one community's social structure is such a large job that most studies have been of single cases. Only after different researchers over a generation have produced a dozen or so such studies can a "secondary analyst" undertake a comparative analysis. In the long run, it is to be hoped that data-gathering procedures on such complex "cases" can be so simplified that statistical studies will become possible. Then the intensive

---

69. Arnold Toynbee, A Study of History, Abridgement by D. C. Somerville, New York 1947.

70. Max Weber, Gesammelte Aufsätze zur Religionssoziologie, Tübingen 1920–21. A brief outline is presented in: Talcott Parsons, The Structure of Social Action, Glencoe, Illinois, 1949, Ch. XV.

study of one community, factory, union, government agency, or voluntary association can give way to a quantitative study of a sample of such cases, testing the hypotheses derived from single-case studies. Of course, where the difficulty lies in the fact that there is only a handful of cases at all, the comparative method is the best we can do.

An example of systematic comparison of a small number of cases is offered by Lipset's study of the Canadian province of Saskatchewan. [Seymour M. Lipset, *Agrarian Socialism*, Berkeley, 1959] The population of the province, mainly wheat farmers, had a remarkably high level of participation in political affairs and in collection for this unusual behavior, comparisons were first made with areas where participation was known to be low.

The amount of participation in public affairs in the large cities of Canada and the U. S. is notoriously low. This is true even of cities like Toronto and Vancouver, which resemble Saskatchewan in giving a large vote to the new, radical C. C. F. party. Comparing Saskatchewan with these large cities, Lipset was struck by the smallness of political units in Saskatchewan and the large number of offices to be filled in each. The average rural municipality had fewer than 400 families, with over 50 elective posts on municipal council and school boards to be filled, while most large cities elect no more officials than that to represent their hundreds of thousands of families.

Besides the small size of Saskatchewan communities, they were relatively lacking in social stratification—almost everyone was a working farmer. In this respect too Saskatchewan is at the opposite pole from the cities, with their wide differences in incomes and their staffs of specialists for performing normal public services. In the cities the positions of responsibility which are available tend to be monopolized by upper-class people and professionals; in Saskatchewan school boards, telephone companies, marketing agencies, etc. had to be staffed by ordinary farmers, who thereby acquired organizational and political skills unknown to the average city dweller.

Certain rural areas also are highly stratified, and in such areas the rate of mass participation is also low:

▶ "Within the rural areas of the Southern States or in parts of California, where significant social and economic cleavage exists within the rural community, the wealthier and upperclass farmers are the formal community leaders, and the bulk of the poorer farmers are politically apathetic." (p. 202) ◀

A third structural factor distinguishing Saskatchewan is its exposure to extreme economic fluctuations, due to the unstable price of its one main crop and to the recurrence of drought. In this it can be contrasted with its eastern neighbor, Manitoba, which has more diversified crops, stable markets, and more reliable weather. And it is notable that Manitoba today has much less community and political activity. Low participation is also found in the Maritime Provinces, where the farmers generally have a low standard of living, but do not experience the chronic alternation between wealth and poverty of the farmers of Saskatchewan.

Having isolated these possible sources of high participation by comparing the social structure of Saskatchewan with that of areas of low participation, we can now look for other areas which have equally favorable patterns of social characteristics. The neighboring wheat-belt areas of North Dakota and Alberta have virtually the same characteristics: small political units, little social stratification, and highly unstable economies. And both these areas have widespread community participation through local government and cooperatives, and a readiness to develop new political movements when confronted by economic crisis. The same structural characteristics were found in Manitoba in the 1890's, at which time the Manitoba agrarian political movement evoked widespread participation. When Manitoba's society changed through the development of a large urban center with an upper-class and specialized services, and through the diversification of agriculture which ended the complete dependence on the wheat crop, mass participation in politics fell off. Manitoba thus provides a natural "before-and-after" experiment.

Lipset notes that the same pattern of structural characteristics which exists in Saskatchewan can also be found in communities far removed from the specific conditions of the wheat belt. Merton studied an American industrial community, "Craftown," which was small in size, relatively unstratified, being mainly inhabited by workers, and faced with a series of pressing social and economic problems. This community was found to be much more politically active than neighboring urban areas; its widerspread political participation resembled that of the Saskatchewan farmers (pp. 303–304). The generalization of explanatory factors from "the wheat economy" to attributes applicable to any community obviously opens up a much wider range of cases for use in comparative analysis.

This comparative analysis of areas of high and low participation can be summarized in the following scheme:

SCHEME OF FACTORS ACCOUNTING FOR POLITICAL PARTICIPATION

(Attributes in parantheses were not explicitly discussed in the comparisons)

ECONOMIC FLUCTUATIONS	SMALL SOCIAL UNITS	LITTLE STRATIFICATION	CASES	PARTIC-IPATION
+	+	+	Saskatchewan North Dakota Alberta Manitoba, 1890–1910 "Craftown"	High " " " "
(+)	(+)	−	Rural South Rural California	Low "
(+)	−	−	Large cities in U.S. and Canada	"
−	(+)	(+)	Maritime Provinces	"
−	−	−	Manitoba today	"

In the study just discussed it appears that comparisons were used not only to suggest explanatory factors but also to offer supporting evidence, as a kind of quasi-experimental test. One of the most celebrated instances of such quasi-experimental tests is found in Malinowski's study of the use of magic in the Trobriand Islands.[71] Malinowski wanted to test the old theory that primitive man uses magic because of a childlike confusion of the real and the imaginary or because of some instinctive belief in the supernatural. He found the Trobrianders engaging in some activities—for instance, fishing within the lagoons —for which their technology was adequate to permit certain economic returns and personal safety. Other activities—for instance fishing in the open sea— involved uncertainty of return and risks to life which could not be eliminated by available technological means. In the safe and certain activities, no magic was used; in the unsafe and uncertain ones, magic was used a great deal. This supported Malinowski's contention that magic was not a substitute for rational techniques, but a supplement to them when dealing with situations beyond the power of available rational technology, which created severe emotional strain.

Of course the use of comparisons of small numbers of cases as tests requires great caution; care must be taken to see that other significant factors are in fact equal, and that cases are selected in an unbiased manner.

IV. MATRIX FORMULATIONS

Sometimes the analysis of qualitative observations confronts a mass of particular facts of such great number and variety that it seems quite unworkable to treat them individually as descriptive attributes or in terms of their specific interrelationships. In such a situation the analyst will often come up with a descriptive concept on a higher level which manages to embrace and sum up a great wealth of particular observations in a single formula. Take for instance, Ruth Benedict's description of the Zuni Indians, which mentions their avoidance of drugs and alcohol, their lack of personal visions, their placid response to divorce, their "mild and ceremonious" relation to their gods, and so on. After presenting a great many such particular facts, Benedict is able to sum them up in a single formula: The Zuni culture has an Apollonian pattern— that is, a central theme of avoidance of emotional excess. This pattern or theme permeates every aspect of Zuni life.[72] Such a formula capable of summing up in a single descriptive concept a great wealth of particular observations may be called a matrix formulation. This definition covers the notion of a "Basic pattern" of a culture, a "theme," an "ethos," a "zeitgeist" or "mentality of the time," a "national character," and on the level of the individual person a "personality type."

---

71. Bronislaw Malinowski: Magic, Science and Religion. A brief outline is presented in Talcott Parsons, l. c., Ch. XV.

72. Ruth Benedict, Patterns of Culture, New York 1946, Ch. IV.

Matrix formulations may be applied to complex units at any level. In a study of an unemployed village in Austria, the researchers made a collection of separate "surprising observations." Although they now had more time, the people read fewer library books. Although subject to economic suffering, their political activity decreased. Those totally unemployed showed less effort to look for work in other towns than those who still had some kind of work. The children from the unemployed village had more limited aspirations for jobs and for Christmas presents than children of employed people. The researchers faced all kinds of practical difficulties because people often came late or failed to appear altogether for interviews. People walked slowly, arrangements for definite appointments were hard to make, "nothing seemed to work any more in the village."

Out of all these observations there finally arose the over-all characterization of the village as "The tired Community." This formula seemed clearly to express the characteristics which permeated every sphere of behavior: although the people had nothing to do, they acted tired—they seemed to suffer from a kind of general paralysis of mental energies.[73]

In a study of a particular group—people who had been designated as "influentials" in an American community—Merton confronted the problem of explaining their diverse behaviors. Various classifications proved of no avail in accounting for the wide range of observations available. The particular behavior on which the research was focussed—the reading of news magazines—remained unexplained. In trying to order the "welter of discrete impressions not closely related one to the others," the researchers finally came up with one general "theme" which distinguished the influentials: some were "cosmopolitan," primarily interested in the world outside the local community, while others were "local," primarily interested in the local community itself. Merton clearly indicates the typical function of such a matrix formulation when he declares:

▶ "All other differences between the local and cosmopolitan influences seem to stem from their difference in basic orientation . . . The difference in basic orientation is bound up with a variety of other differences: (1) in the structures of social relations in which each type is implicated; (2) in the roads they have travelled to their present positions in the influence-structure; (3) in the utilization of their present status for the exercise of interpersonal influence; and (4) in their communications behavior."[74] ◀

The bulk of the article is then taken up with an elaboration of this dual matrix formulation in terms of all the specific behaviors which fit into one or the other type of orientation, the local or the cosmopolitan.

Matrix formulations can thus vary in the level of the unit which they describe, from a whole culture to a community and to a status group within a

73. Jahoda and Zeisel, l. c.

74. Merton, Patterns of Influence, l. c., p. 191.

community. They are used right down to the level of individual personalities, where, for instance, a great variety of particular behaviors will be summed up in the matrix formula of an "anal personality" or a "cerebrotonic temperament." At the personality level they are often referred to as "syndromes," a term arising out of the physiological level where it refers to just the same kind of complex of individual facts all of which can be summed up in one single formula.

Another way in which the matrix formulations can vary is in terms of the relations between the elements. The elements which went into Benedict's formulation of an Apollonian culture were all alike in terms of the variable "emotional tone"—their emotional tone was low in intensity. They all went together in the same sense that one can classify in a single group all regions with a very even temperature, or all people with a high blood pressure. In a matrix formulation such as Tönnies' "Gemeinschaft," the elements seem to be involved in causal relations and processes with one another.[75] The element of "reciprocal trust" for example can be considered as growing out of the element of "prolonged face-to-face association with the same people," as can a great many of the other characteristics of a "Gemeinschaft"-situation. In the matrix formulation of an "anal personality," the behavior characteristics are thought of as all arising out of a single basic factor, the fixation of the erotic development at a certain childish stage. In many of the culture-pattern formulations since Benedict's purely descriptive ones, we find the idea that all of the elements in the pattern are products of the pattern of child training—or even of a single element in the child training pattern. Some matrix formulations involve a mixture of descriptively related and causally related elements.

Yet another way in which matrix formulae can be differentiated could be called their "projective distance." The following examples should indicate what is meant by this dimension. In Merton's study of *Mass Persuasion,* it was found that a wide variety of remarks made by the Kate Smith devotees could be summed up in the notion of "submissiveness to the status quo."[76] They believed that it was right for some to be poor and others rich, they accepted their position in the system of stratification, they rationalized that the rich had so many troubles that it was just as well to be poor. The more general descriptive concept follows very directly from the manifest content of the respondent's statements; they could almost have made the generalization themselves.

In Cantril's study of the *Psychology of Social Movements,* he confronted a collection of interviews and observations of people who join all sorts of marginal political cults like the Townsend groups, Moral Rearmament, the Coughlinites, and so on.[77] Out of the welter of characteristics there emerged the general notion that all of these people were suffering from a lack of orientation in

75. Ferdinand Tönnies, Gemeinschaft und Gesellschaft, Leipzig 1887. A brief summary is found in Parsons, l. c., pp. 686 seq.

76. Merton, Mass Persuasion, l. c., pp. 152 seq.

77. Hadley Cantril, The Psychology of Social Movements, New York 1941.

the complexities of the modern world, a need for a frame of reference within the events of their lives and for world affairs could be understandable. The matrix formulation of "need for orientation" seemed to tie together a great many diverse forms of behavior, attitudes and beliefs on the part of the members of these groups. Now this matrix formulation is further removed from the manifest content of the material than was the formulation in the previous example. There is a greater gap between the formula and what the people actually said, in talking about troubles they had and how good it made them feel that their movement told them what was wrong with the world and how it could be corrected. Here the statements and observations collected by the field work are interpreted as projections of a somewhat complex psychological state, which very few of the respondents themselves could directly articulate.

A still greater distance between the manifest content of the material and the matrix formulation which is constructed to express its basic pattern is often found in the characterization of personality types or of the ethos of a culture. In these cases, guided by general theoretical orientations, one may use subtle indicators as a basis for a formulation which appears in some ways contradictory to the manifest content of the material. Verbal expressions and actual behavior patterns apparently indicative of feelings of superiority are interpreted, when seen in the context of more subtle indicators, as evidence of quite the opposite basic outlook. In Benedict's characterization of the Zuni as basically Apollonian, she has to explain away—on the basis of looking beneath the surface—various apparently "Dionysian" elements.[78]

There is a good deal of similarity between the rationale of the matrix formulation and Parson's discussion of the place of "secondary descriptive systems" in his scheme of social systems based on the unit act:

▶ "When a certain degree of complexity is reached, however, to describe the system in full in terms of the action scheme would involve a degree of elaboration of details which would be very laborious and pedantic to work out. This is true even if description is limited to 'typical' unit acts and all the complex detailed variations of the completely concrete acts are passed over. Fortunately, as certain degrees of complexity are reached, there emerge other ways of describing the facts, the employment of which constitutes a convenient 'shorthand' that is adequate for a large number of scientific purposes.

". . . It has been seen that the acts and action systems of different individuals, in so far as they are mutually oriented in one another, constitute social relationships. In so far this interaction of the action systems of individuals is continuous and regular these relationships acquire certain identifiable, relatively constant properties or descriptive aspects . . . It is not necessary to observe all the acts of the parties to a relationship, or all their attitudes, etc., but only enough to establish what is for the purpose in hand the relevant 'character' of the relationship . . .

"Thus the primary function of such a secondary descriptive scheme as that of social relationship is one of scientific economy, of reducing the amount of

---

78. Benedict, l. c., see p. 80, 83, 85, 94, 107, 112 for instances.

labor of observation and verification required before adequate judgements may be arrived at. A second function . . . (is) to state the facts in a way that will prevent carrying unit analysis to a point where it would destroy relevant emergent properties."[79] ◄

Parsons gives as examples of secondary descriptive schemes typologies of social relationships, personality types, and descriptive categories applied to groups. While Parsons' concept is not entirely identical with that of the matrix formulation, it illustrates much of the reasoning behind such complex descriptive concepts, which sum up and render manageable a large and varied body of individual points of data.

Some of the latter techniques described by Barton and Lazarsfeld border closely on truly statistical analysis. The one technique of hypothesis-generation which historically has been most frequently linked with participant observation is likewise an essentially statistical procedure. This technique of "analytic induction" has been used not only to generate and reformulate hypotheses, but also, simultaneously, to afford proof for these hypotheses. Such twofold employment has given rise to considerable controversy, as described by W. S. Robinson in the following selection.

THE LOGICAL
STRUCTURE OF ANALYTIC INDUCTION

W. S. ROBINSON

Since Znaniecki stated it in 1934,[1] the method of analytic induction has come into important use. Angell used it in his *The Family Encounters the Depression*.[2] Sutherland refined the method and recommended it for general use in studying the causes of crime.[3] Lindesmith used it in his well-known study

---

79. Parsons, l. c., pp. 743 seq.

Reprinted from *American Sociological Review* (1951), **16**, 812–818, by permission of the author and publisher.

Author's note: I am indebted for assistance in preparing this paper to Donald R. Cressey. Gloria F. Roman, Wendell Bell, and the members of my seminar in the logic of social inquiry, all of whom helped me shape some rather vague intitial ideas into this present form.

1.   *The Method of Sociology*, New York, 1934, pp. 249–331.

2.   New York, 1936, pp. 296–297.

3.   *Principles of Criminology*, New York, 1939, pp. 66–67.

of opiate addiction.[4] Cressey has used it most recently in his study of the causes of embezzlement,[5] and the method is probably in current use by others also.

Znaniecki holds that analytic induction is the true method of the physical and biological sciences, and that it ought to be the method of the social sciences too.[6] He contrasts analytic induction with what he calls enumerative induction, which is the ordinary statistical way of studying relationships with correlations. He holds that analytic induction gives us universal statements, of the form "All S are P," instead of mere correlations to which there are always exceptions.[7] He holds that analytic induction gives us exhaustive knowledge of the situation under study, so that further study will not and cannot reveal anything new.[8] Finally, he holds that analytic induction leads us to genuinely causal laws.[9]

There is, however, some confusion as to the real nature and function of analytic induction. The purpose of this paper is to clarify this confusion by exploring the logical structure of analytic induction. It will be convenient to take up the problem in three steps: to discuss analytic induction first as a research procedure directing activity in the field, second as a method of causal analysis, and third as a method of proof.

ANALYTIC INDUCTION AS RESEARCH PROCEDURE

Cressey has given the most explicit and systematic statement of analytic induction as a research procedure, as follows:[10] "(1) A rough definition of the phenomenon to be explained is formulated. (2) An hypothetical explanation of that phenomenon is formulated. (3) One case is studied in the light of the hypothesis with the object of determining whether the hypothesis fits the facts in that case. (4) If the hypothesis does not fit the facts, either the hypothesis is reformulated or the phenomenon to be explained is re-defined, so that the case is excluded. (5) Practical certainty may be attained after a small number of cases has been examined, but the discovery by the investigator or any other investigator of a single negative case disproves the explanation and requires a

---

4. *Opiate Addiction,* Bloomington, Indiana, 1947. Completely revised version published under title *Addiction and Opiates* (Chicago: Aldine Publishing Co., 1968).

5. *Criminal Violation of Financial Trust,* a dissertation at Indiana University, 1950. Cressey's findings are reported in his article with the same title in the *American Sociological Review,* 15 (Dec., 1950), 738–743. References to Cressey, unless otherwise stated, will be to the first-named source.

6. Znaniecki, *op. cit.,* pp. 236–237.

7. *Op. cit.,* pp. 232–233.

8. *Op. cit.,* p. 249.

9. *Op. cit.,* pp. 305–306.

10. Cressey, *op. cit.,* p. 31. Cressey's statement, however, differs little from Sutherland's.

re-formulation. (6) This procedure of examining cases, re-defining the phenomenon and re-formulating the hypothesis is continued until a universal relationship is established, each negative case calling for a re-definition or a re-formulation."

Lindesmith provides an illustration of the procedure in describing how he successively revised his hypothesis: "The first tentative, and obviously inadequate hypothesis formulated was that individuals who do not know what drug they are receiving do not become addicted and, on the positive side, that they become addicted when they know what they are getting and have taken it long enough to experience withdrawal distress when they stop. This hypothesis was destroyed almost at once by negative evidence. . . . In the light of [additional cases], the second hypothesis of the investigation was that persons become addicts when they recognize or perceive the significance of withdrawal distress which they are experiencing, and that if they do not recognize withdrawal distress they do not become addicts regardless of any other considerations.

"This formulation proved to be much more significant and useful than the first one, but like the first one it did not stand the test of evidence and had to be revised when cases were found in which individuals who had experienced and understood withdrawal distress, though not in its severest form, did not use the drug to alleviate the distress and never became addicts. The final revision of the hypothesis involved a shift in emphasis from the recognition of withdrawal distress, to the use of the drug after this insight has occurred for the purpose of alleviating the distress."[11]

In terms of procedure, then, the method of analytic induction begins with an explanatory hypothesis and a provisional definition of something to be explained. The hypothesis is then compared with facts, and modifications are made in two ways: (1) The hypothesis itself is modified so that the new facts will fall under it, and/or (2) the phenomenon to be explained is re-defined to exclude the cases which defy explanation by the hypothesis. Let us consider these two modifications in turn.

1. The first, that of altering the hypothesis, is well-known as the method of the working hypothesis.[12] Scientists have long known that even a false hypothesis may be useful, for it does direct our observation, and in checking it against facts we usually get ideas as to how to bring it better into accordance with the facts. "The logical procedure of verification or disproof is intimately bound up with the procedure of discovery, and the character of the observations that bring about the disproof of one hypothesis often suggests the sort of modification that ought to be made to create a better hypothesis."[13]

---

11. Lindesmith, *op. cit.,* pp. 7–8.
12. *Cf.* Homer H. Dubs, *Rational Induction,* Chicago, 1930, p. 128.
13. *Loc. cit.*

The fact that the method of analytic induction formalizes and systematizes the method of the working hypothesis is probably one reason why it has been so fruitful in applications such as Angell's, Lindesmith's, and Cressey's. The method performs an important service in emphasizing the need for study of deviant cases in a situation in which the explanation is not complete.

However, this insistence upon analysis of deviant cases is not logically different from the similar insistence of the sophisticated practitioner of enumerative induction. The practitioner of enumerative induction phrases it differently. He says that he looks for a new variable correlated with his residuals, so as to include it in a new multivariate analysis; but it amounts to the same thing. The point is that he keeps modifying his hypothesis to account for the failures of his original relation to predict infallibly. The fact that few statistically oriented investigators actually do this is regrettable, but the fact that they *might* do it indicates no basic difference between analytic and enumerative induction on this count. It is a particular excellence of the method of analytic induction, however, that it insists upon this knowledge-building, self-corrective procedure of the analysis of deviant cases.

2. The second modification which may come about in applying the method of analytic induction is that of re-defining the phenomenon so as to exclude cases which contradict the hypothesis. This is what Dubs calls "limiting the universal," limiting the range of applicability of the explanatory hypothesis.[14] "An exception, even though it is a real and not an apparent exception, may not overthrow a hypothesis, but may merely indicate that the hypothesis in question is a limited universal. . . . If, then, a universal is only true within limits, it is important to know what are those limits and to consider the limits as well as the universal."[15]

This limitation of the universal in analytic induction is to insure causal homogeneity in the cases to be explained, to insure that the same process functions in all the cases to be examined. Thus Lindesmith found it necessary to distinguish between true addiction and habituation, "in which the physiological factors occur in isolation, without arousing the self-conscious desire for the drug which characterizes the addict and around which he organizes his life."[16] Similarly, Cressey found it necessary to restrict himself to a study of persons who had violated a financial trust undertaken in good faith, for the process involved was very different from that involved when a person accepted a trust for the express purpose of violating it.[17]

Such limitation of universals has occurred not infrequently in the history of science, and is now a matter of common acceptance. The relation between

---

14. *Op. cit.,* p. 260.
15. *Op. cit.,* pp. 260 and 282.
16. Lindesmith, *op. cit.,* p. 45.
17. Cressey, *op. cit.,* pp. 33–40.

Newtonian physics and the relativity theory is a case in point.[18] The failure of Newton's laws to account for the observed motion of Mercury and the failure of the Michelson-Morley experiment reduced Newtonian physics to a limited universal, restricted its application to cases in which velocities did not approach the velocity of light. The usual history of limited universals in the physical sciences is that they are eventually shown to be special cases of more general universals. The relativity theory includes all of Newtonian physics as a special case, and considerably more besides. This might well be the case with the limitation of universals by the method of analytic induction. It would be the case, for example, were Cressey to develop a more general explanation which would include trust violations in both good faith and bad faith as special cases.

ANALYTIC INDUCTION AS METHOD OF CAUSAL ANALYSIS

It is easy to show that the method of analytic induction *as described* gives only the necessary and not the sufficient conditions for the phenomenon to be explained. The method calls for studying only those cases in which the phenomenon occurs,[19] and not cases in which it does not occur. To study cases in which the phenomenon does not occur would involve us in enumerative induction, the comparative method, for which Znaniecki would substitute the method of analytic induction.[20]

What analytic induction does *as described* can be shown most easily with the accompanying fourfold table (Table 1), in which P stands for instances in which the phenomenon occurs, and $\bar{P}$ for instances in which it does not occur. Thus all instances in which the phenomenon occurs fall in the left column, and all instances in which it does not occur fall in the right column.

TABLE 1

	P	$\bar{P}$
C	X	?
$\bar{C}$	0	X

The method of analytic induction consists in taking a number of instances in which the phenomenon occurs, a number of instances in the left column, and finding a set of conditions which always accompany that phenomenon and without which it does not occur. Let C in Table 1 stand for instances in which these conditions are present, and $\bar{C}$ for instances in which not all of them are present. Thus the first row of the table contains instances in which the conditions C are present, and the second row contains instances in which not all of them are present.

---

18. *Cf.* Dubs, *op. cit.,* pp. 278–280.
19. Cressey, *op. cit.,* p. 31, quoted *supra.*
20. Znaniecki, *op. cit.,* pp. 225–227.

As the method is described, it consists in studying cases in the left column of Table 1 and then so defining C, the conditions, as to make all these cases fall in the upper cell of the column, as indicated by an X in the upper cell and the zero in the lower cell. We may go further, moreover, and point out that all of the cases in the lower row must fall in the right column. There are certainly instances at large in which the conditions C are not all present, and since we know that these do not occur in the P-column they must occur in the $\bar{P}$-column, as indicated in the table by an X in the lower right cell.

The relation between analytic and enumerative or statistical induction is now clear. A statistician would study cases in all four cells of the table. He would hope, but not insist, that there would be zeroes in the lower left and upper right cells—and there he would stop. A person practicing analytic induction, however, would study cases only in the left column of the table, and would insist that he get a zero in the lower cell of that column. By an additional argument he could then show, if he wanted to, that all cases in the lower row fell in the right column. But he could not determine whether or not there were cases in the upper right cell, as indicated by the ? in that cell.

This argument shows why the method of analytic induction as described by Sutherland and Cressey cannot enable us to predict. It cannot because it gives us only the necessary and not the sufficient conditions for the phenomenon to be explained. Only if we know that the phenomenon never fails to occur in the presence of the conditions C, only if we know that the upper right cell in the table contains a zero, can we predict the occurrence of the phenomenon from C.

This argument also shows that the explanation provided by the method of analytic induction is only a partial explanation. It is now well established that prediction and explanation have identically the same logical form. "It may be said . . . that an explanation is not fully adequate unless . . . [it] . . . , if taken account of in time, could have served as a basis for predicting the phenomenon under consideration. The logical similarity of explanation and prediction, and the fact that one is directed towards past occurrences, the other towards future ones, is well expressed in the terms 'postdictability' and 'predictability' used by Reichenbach. . . ."[21] We have an adequate explanation, in other words, only when we have both the necessary and the sufficient conditions for the phenomenon to be explained, *i.e.*, only when we have zeroes in both the lower left and the upper right cells of Table 1.

Both Lindesmith and Cressey have sensed this inadequacy of analytic induction as stated, and neither has applied it in the form in which it is stated. Lindesmith made a systematic study of non-addicts to determine whether addiction ever failed to occur when his conditions were present.[22] Cressey did not study persons who had not violated a financial trust at the time he inter-

---

21. Carl G. Hempel and Paul Oppenheim, "Studies in the Logic of Explanation," *Philosophy of Science*, 15 (April 1948), 138.

22. Lindesmith, *op. cit.*, p. 14.

viewed them, but he has pointed out that he actually did study non-violators as well, because each of his subjects was a non-violator before his defection. Cressey therefore systematically studied the history of each subject to determine whether the conditions had been present in the past without a violation. Cressey, that is, assumed that before their defection his violators were representative of all non-violators, *i.e.*, of all the cases in the right column of Table 1. His assumption is open to question and should be tested, but his intention to include non-violators as well as violators is unmistakable.

Thus in practicing the method of analytic induction both Lindesmith and Cressey found it necessary for adequacy to study the cases in the right column of Table 1, *i.e.*, to determine that the ? was actually a zero. This leads to the interesting conclusion that the method of analytic induction *in practice* leads directly to the use of the comparative method, the method of enumerative induction, which it is designed to supplant.

The only evident difference between enumerative induction and analytic induction in practice is that analytic induction insists upon zeroes in two cells of Table 1, and provides a procedure for trying to get them there, while enumerative induction is satisfied with relatively small frequencies. Choose a sophisticated approach to enumerative induction, one that realizes that a perfect explanation is the ultimate goal, and there is no difference between an analytic and an enumerative induction except that the latter is incomplete. Or imagine that someone practicing analytic induction has failed to achieve perfection and publishes his results as a progress report: he has made an enumerative induction. The success of analytic induction in producing complete explanations is due to its procedure, to its systematization of the method of the working hypothesis, and not to its logical structure. The qualitative contrast which Znaniecki sets up between analytic and enumerative induction as methods of causal analysis is thus only a quantitative contrast and is not basic. The difference is in how far you push your study before you publish your results.

ANALYTIC INDUCTION AS METHOD OF PROOF

Analytic induction is regarded by Znaniecki as a special and *certain* way of proving that the generalizations to which it leads will apply to all instances of the phenomenon under study, whether they have yet been examined or not. "The analysis of data is all done before any general formulations; and if well done, there is nothing more of importance to be learned about the class which these data represent by any subsequent investigation of more data of the same class."[23] Sutherland follows in this line also, though with characteristic canniness he remarks that *practical* certainty may be attained after the examination of a few instances.[24] This anti-probabilistic insistence is found in Angell

---

23. Znaniecki, *op. cit.*, p. 249.
24. Sutherland, *op. cit.*, p. 67.

too.[25] No sampling considerations are involved, and no merely probable generalizations are admitted; the method leads to certainty.

Lindesmith and Cressey do not follow here in word, for each points out that future instances may necessitate revision of his hypothesis. But they do follow in deed, for neither shows particular concern for the coverage of his sample, and both seem to rely implicitly upon Znaniecki's claim to extend their generalizations to as yet unenumerated instances. It will be instructive, therefore, to examine Znaniecki's claim for analytic induction as a method of proof, and then to consider the possibility of integrating analytic induction with the probabilistic approach of modern science.

Znaniecki argues that analytic induction leads to certainty without benefit of representative cases because it isolates the "essential" characters which determine the phenomenon under study. The method leads to certainty because the characters C in Table 1 are "essential" to the phenomenon P. ". . . Analytic induction ends where enumerative induction begins; and if well conducted leaves no real and soluble problems for the latter. . . . Analytic induction abstracts from the given concrete case characters that are essential to it and generalizes them, presuming that in so far as essential, they must be similar in many cases. This is why the method of analytic induction has been also called the *type* method. . . . Thus, when a particular concrete case is being analyzed as typical or eidetic, we assume that those traits which are essential to it, which determine what it is, are common to and distinctive of all the cases of a class."[26]

Znaniecki's belief that there are "essential" characters which determine phenomena is reminiscent of Aristotelian ontology, in which "the membership of an object in a given class was of critical importance, because for Aristotle the class defined the essence or essential nature of the object and thus determined its behavior in both positive and negative respects."[27] But Znaniecki denies that his belief in "essential" characters has any ontological implications.[28] We therefore still have the problem of trying to assess the claims of analytic induction as a method of proof, operating through its isolation of the "essential" characters which determine phenomena.

We can attack this problem by considering what analytic induction actually does. Znaniecki clearly holds (though not in these terms) that analytic induction is an operational definition of essentiality, that the method is a way of isolating the essential characters which determine a phenomenon. But we have already seen that the method as stated leads merely to the necessary conditions for the phenomenon, to conditions which must be in existence before the phenomenon occurs but which are not shown to be sufficient to produce the

25. Angell, *op. cit.,* p. 7.

26. Znaniecki, *op. cit.,* pp. 250, 251–252.

27. Kurt Lewin, "The Conflict between Aristotelian and Galileian Modes of Thought in Contemporary Psychology," in *A Dynamic Theory of Personality,* New York, 1935, p. 4.

28. Znaniecki, *op. cit.,* p. 231.

phenomenon, and we should hardly consider these conditions essential in the sense of determining what the phenomenon is.

We have also seen that the method leads in practice to the isolation of the necessary and sufficient conditions for the phenomenon. It leads to the isolation of characters of such a nature that when the characters are all present the phenomenon occurs, and when the characters are not all present the phenomenon does not occur. However, the method does not lead us to the conclusion that these characters are "essential" apart from the fact that they are necessary and sufficient as operationally defined.

We are, in fact, in a situation which has a well known philosophical analogue. When Hume looked at instances of causal relations he was never able to discover any "necessary connection." All he could conclude was that one event invariably followed the other.[29] Considering analytic induction as an operational definition of essentiality, then, leads us to the conclusion that those characters which are essential to a phenomenon are those whose appearance is followed by the phenomenon and whose non-appearance is not followed by the phenomenon. This is perhaps as good a definition of essentiality as any—except that it makes the essentiality superfluous. It does not provide a basis for saying that when we have located the "essential" characters for a phenomenon *we may be sure* that those characters will appear in any future instance of the phenomenon.

There is no real reason, however, why analytic induction cannot be integrated with the probabilistic approach characteristic of other research procedures in modern science. In fact the integration has already been made, though implicitly, by Lindesmith and Cressey. We know how to set fiducial limits to an observed zero frequency of exceptions, and we know that the lower of these limits will be zero and that the upper will be some small fraction.

Frankly to espouse the probabilistic viewpoint would enhance the already valuable contribution of analytic induction to scientific procedure. It would point up the necessity for representative sampling. Practitioners of analytic induction would then no longer have to cling with anxiety to the ontologically based essentiality argument, but could openly state the confidence limits for the proportion of exceptions which might occur in the future. It is almost superfluous to add that the occurrence of future exceptions would then be a focal point for a new attack by the method; for as Znaniecki has so usefully pointed out, and as his method itself manifests, "The exception is . . . an essential instrument of scientific progress."[30]

Robinson's criticisms of analytic induction are primarily aimed at its inadequacies in establishing clear-cut causal determination and at its neglect of sampling proce-

---

29. David Hume, *An Enquiry Concerning Human Understanding*, LaSalle, Illinois, 1945, p. 64.

30. Znaniecki, *op. cit.*, p. 233.

dures. Although he finds analytic induction useful in guiding research and hypothesis formulation, Robinson also points out its essential similarity in this respect to the "deviant case analysis" procedures of the survey analyst.[2]

Ralph Turner, on the other hand (see selection below) finds a special use for analytic induction in constructing theoretical categories which permit the logical *deduction* of the causal hypothesis from the properties of the categories themselves. Although Turner is basically in agreement with Robinson's criticism of the causal efficacy of analytic induction, Turner views a relationship established by analytic induction as a particularly important intervening relationship in terms of which merely statistical relationships may be theoretically interpreted.[3]

THE QUEST FOR
UNIVERSALS IN SOCIOLOGICAL RESEARCH

RALPH H. TURNER

In a book which has maintained attention and perhaps increased in influence over two decades, Florian Znaniecki describes the method he names "analytic induction," and designates it as *the* method which should be adopted in all sociological research.[1] Analytic induction is merely a special name for one formulation of a basic philosophy that research must be directed toward generalizations of *universal* rather than *frequent* applicability.[2] But Znaniecki's statement is unusually unequivocal and is specifically oriented toward sociological research. Hence it makes an excellent point of departure for a study of contrasting methodologies.

Znaniecki's position has recently been challenged by W. S. Robinson, who depicts analytic induction as an imperfect form of the method Znaniecki calls enumerative induction.[3] Robinson's contentions are further discussed by Al-

---

2. Lazarsfeld and Rosenberg (1955), pp. 167–174.

3. Neither Robinson's nor Turner's views have met with complete acceptance among the major figures identified with the use of analytic induction. See Lindesmith, Weinberg, and Robinson (1952) and Angell and Turner (1954).

Reprinted from *American Sociological Review* (1953), **18**, 604–611, by permission of the author and publisher.

Author's note: This paper has benefited from discussion with W. S. Robinson's seminar in methodology and from a critical reading by Donald R. Cressey.

1. Florian Znaniecki, *The Method of Sociology,* New York: Farrar and Rinehart, 1934.

2. This point is brought out by Alfred R. Lindesmith in his comments in the *American Sociological Review,* 17 (August, 1952), p. 492.

3. W. S. Robinson, "The Logical Structure of Analytic Induction," *American Sociological Review,* 16 (December, 1951), pp. 812–18. Robinson's argument may not altogether escape a logical pitfall. He first makes a careful description of the analytic induction procedure, but does it by describing its elements within the framework of statistical method. Any such operation necessarily slights any aspects of the first framework which lack counterparts in the second. The conclusion that analytic induction is a special but imperfect form of statistical procedure would then be inherent in the operation itself rather than a legitimate finding.

fred Lindesmith and S. Kirson Weinberg in replies to his paper.[4] The three discussions extend our understanding of the method, but leave some questions unanswered.

Methodological advance requires more than the mere tolerance of alternative methods. Any *particular* methodology must be examined and assessed in the light of the total process of research and theory formulation.[5] Accordingly, the objective of the present paper is to offer a definition of the place of the search for universals in the total methodology for dealing with non-experimental data. The procedure will be to examine specific examples of empirical research employing the analytic induction (or similar) method, to note what they do and do not accomplish, to establish logically the reasons for their distinctive accomplishments and limitations, and on these grounds to designate the specific utility of the method in relation to probability methods.

EMPIRICAL PREDICTION

Robinson's contention that actual studies employing the method of universals do not afford a basis for empirical prediction appears sound. However, it is only when the method is made to stand by itself that this limitation necessarily applies. Furthermore, the reason for the limitation is more intimately linked to the intrinsic logic of the method than the incidental fact that investigators using the method have tended to neglect the right-hand side of the fourfold table.[6] These statements may be substantiated and elaborated by an examination of selected studies.

Lindesmith's well-known study of opiate addiction will serve as a useful first case. The causal complex which is essential to the process of addiction involves several elements. The individual must use the drug, he must experience withdrawal distress, he must identify these symptoms or recognize what they are, he must recognize that more of the drug will relieve the symptoms, and he must take the drug and experience relief.[7]

From the standpoint of predicting whether any given individual will become an addict or not, the formulation has certain limitations. First, it does not tell who will take the drug in the first place, nor give any indication of the rela-

---

4. "Two Comments on W. S. Robinson's 'The Logical Structure of Analytic Induction,'" *American Sociological Review*, 17 (August, 1952), pp. 492–95.

5. Lindesmith's statement that, "Statistical questions call for statistical answers and causal questions call for answers within the framework of the logic of causal analysis" (*ibid.*, p. 492), seems to be an evasion of the problems of *why* and *when* each type of question should be asked. "Methodological parallelism" is of dubious fruitfulness.

6. W. S. Robinson, *op. cit.*, pp. 814–16. The writer doubts that this limitation inheres logically in the conception of analytic induction as described by Znaniecki.

7. Alfred R. Lindesmith, *Opiate Addiction*, Bloomington: Principia Press, 1947, pp. 67–89, *et passim*.

tive likelihood of different persons taking the drug.[8] Second, the thesis itself affords no cue to variability in intensity of withdrawal symptoms, nor any guide to instances in which the symptoms will be mild enough not to result in addiction. Third, the theory does not provide a basis for anticipating who will recognize the symptoms and the means of securing relief. Fourth, personal and social factors involved in taking or not taking the drug to relieve the identified distress are not indicated. We cannot predict in an empirical instance unless there is some way of anticipating which people, given exposure to the drug, will recognize the nature of the withdrawal symptoms, will identify the means of relief, and will take that means of relief.[9] Finally, Lindesmith's theory does not indicate to us what will be the pattern of the addict's behavior, since this is determined by the cultural definition and treatment of the drug and its addicts. In sum, Lindesmith provides us with a causal complex which is empirically verified *in retrospect,* but which does not in itself permit prediction that a specific person will become an addict nor that a specific situation will produce addiction.

Donald R. Cressey's statement regarding the violation of financial trust likewise is posited as a system of universal generalizations and is similar to Lindesmith's in format.[10] Three elements are essential to trust-violation. The person who will violate a financial trust has, first, a "non-sharable financial problem," a difficulty which he feels he cannot communicate to others. Second, he recognizes embezzlement as a way of meeting this problem. And third, he rationalizes the prospective embezzlement, justifying it to himself in some way.

First, the points at which Lindesmith's and Cressey's statements are parallel and points at which they are not parallel may be noted. The withdrawal symptoms and the non-sharable problem can be equated as the conditions which require some relief which cannot be secured through conventional channels. There is also a parallel between recognition that the drug will relieve the distress and recognition of embezzlement as a possible solution to the non-sharable problem. On the other hand, because drug addiction ensues from but one type of problem, withdrawal distress, Lindesmith can specify the taking of an

---

8. Some of Lindesmith's argument with current theories of drug addiction (*ibid.,* pp. 141–64) rest upon a difference of purpose. Some of the theories he criticizes can be defended if reworded in terms of likelihood of first taking the drug in other than a medical treatment situation, rather than in terms of the likelihood of becoming addicted.

9. Lindesmith does not overlook these considerations in his descriptive treatment of the process. However, his treatment of them remains anecdotal and impressionistic rather than systematic and they are not integrated into the rigorous statement of his theory. The nearest he comes to a systematic statement concerning one of these variables is his observation that, "as long as a patient believes he is using the drug solely to relieve pain, and regards it as a 'medicine,' he does not become an addict." (*Ibid.,* p. 56). Weinberg suggests the use of measurement in some of these connections (*op. cit.,* p. 493).

10. *Other People's Money,* Glencoe: The Free Press, 1953. A brief statement of the theory also appears as, "Criminal Violation of Financial Trust," *American Sociological Review,* 15 (December, 1950), pp. 738–43.

opiate as essential. Cressey can specify no specific "first step" because of the variety of problems which may come to be non-sharable. The rationalization stage is absent from Lindesmith's formulation though he discusses it as a *frequent* phenomenon.

It is difficult to find a logical reason why rationalization should be *essential* in the one instance and merely *frequent* in the other. Perhaps the explanation lies, not in the logic of the phenomena themselves, but in the conditions necessary for a sense of closure on the part of the investigators. Since Lindesmith is explaining the existence of a continuing psychological state, it is sufficient for his purposes that the prospective addict be carried from a particular state of recognition (the symptoms and role of the drug) to an overt act with specific psychological consequences (relief by taking the drug). Cressey, however, is explaining a single action and so he seeks to fill the gap more fully between the particular state of recognition (that embezzlement will solve a non-sharable problem) and the act of embezzling, which he does with the rationalization.[11]

In light of the parallels between the two schemes, it is not surprising that the same limitations with regard to empirical prediction apply to Cressey's statement as did to Lindesmith's. The theory does not indicate who will have non-sharable problems, what specific conditions will make a problem non-sharable and in what circumstances a problem may cease to be non-sharable. Nor do we have a guide to the circumstances surrounding recognition of embezzlement as a solution to the problem. And, finally, there are no systematic indicators of who will be able to rationalize and who will not.

There are perhaps two general reasons why the Lindesmith and Cressey studies do not produce empirical prediction, reasons which are applicable because of the very specifications of their method itself. One of these reasons has already been extensively illustrated, namely, that there is no basis for determining beforehand whether the conditions specified as necessary will exist in a particular instance.

The second general reason for lack of empirical prediction is that the alleged *preconditions* or essential causes of the phenomenon under examination cannot be fully specified apart from observation of the condition they are supposed to produce. In any situation in which variable "A" is said to cause variable "B," "A" is of no value as a predictor of "B" unless we establish the existence of "A" apart from the observation of "B." This limitation is in particular applicable to Cressey's study. Is it possible, for example, to assert that a problem is non-sharable *until* a person embezzles to get around it? If a man has not revealed his

---

11. Perhaps there is an object lesson indicated by this comparison. If the perspective of the investigator can determine what will be necessary for inclusion as the *essential* elements, there may be no theoretical limit to the number of such perspectives and consequently to the variations in what is considered essential. Such an observation would make Znaniecki's dictum that the investigator can arrive at a point beyond which no new knowledge about a class can be added difficult to defend. (Cf. Znaniecki, *op. cit.*, p. 249).

problem to others today, can we say that he will not share it tomorrow? The *operational* definition of a non-sharable problem is one that has not been shared up to the time of the embezzlement. Similarly, Cressey must be referring to some *quality* in the recognition of embezzlement as a solution which may not be identifiable apart from the fact that under appropriate conditions it eventuates in embezzlement. With embezzlement techniques and tales of successful embezzlement a standard part of the folklore of banks, offices handling public and private payrolls, and the like, mere recognition of embezzlement as a solution to problems is probably a near-universal characteristic of persons in a position to be able to embezzle. Similarly, rationalizations of embezzlement are part of the folklore and their use is standard joking behavior among persons in such positions. Consequently both recognition of embezzlement as a potential solution and ability to rationalize the act only become discriminating conditions when some sort of qualitative or quantitative limitation is imposed upon them. But under the present formulation it is only possible to identify what is a sufficient recognition or a sufficient ability to rationalize by the fact that they eventuate in embezzlement.

Lindesmith's theory, though less subject to this limitation, reveals the same vulnerability. Since withdrawal distress varies in degree according to size of dose and the number of shots taken, and since several shots may precede the existence of addiction as Lindesmith defines it, definition of the point at which the individual is taking the drug *to relieve withdrawal distress* as distinct from the point at which he is simply taking another shot must be arbitrary in some cases. But the distinction is crucial to Lindesmith's theory, since before this point the individual is not addicted and presumably may interrupt the process, while after this point he is addicted and the process is complete. Hence, the identification of what constitutes an effective recognition of the relief the drug will bring can only ultimately be determined by the fact that addiction follows such recognition.[12]

As a final case, we shall refer to a study which is in important respects rather different, but which is couched in terms of a parallel logic. In Robert C. Angell's well-known study of fifty families that suffered a serious reduction in income during the Depression, he attempted to work out a set of categories which could be applied to a family before the Depression which would predict how it would respond to the drop in family income. On the basis of assessments of "integration" and "adaptability," Angell "predicts" the response to financial crisis in terms of a "vulnerability-invulnerability" continuum and a "firm-readjustive-yielding" continuum.[13] Through his designation of a presumably comprehen-

---

12. Lindesmith admits some vagueness on the matter of what genuinely constitutes knowledge that an opiate will relieve withdrawal distress, but regards the vagueness as a present limitation of his knowledge rather than an intrinsic limitation of his method. Cf. *op. cit.*, p. 77.

13. Robert C. Angell, *The Family Encounters the Depression*, New York: Scribner's Sons, 1936.

sive pair of concepts for describing those characteristics of the family which are essential in predicting his post-crisis variables, Angell follows an analytic induction model, though his variables are not simple attributes as are those of Lindesmith and Cressey.

On the surface, Angell's formulation looks a good deal more like a device for empirical prediction since he provides categories which can be assessed before the process of responding to the Depression gets under way and without reference to the consequences. A careful examination of the nature and manner of assessment of the two essential variables will indicate whether the impression is justified.

The idea of integration seems to refer to the degree to which a family is a unit, which is a fact not observable in the same direct sense as the fact of taking a drug, for example. Integration conveys a meaning or feeling which is recognized by a number of symptoms, such as affection, common interests, and sense of economic interdependence. Integration in practice, then, is identified by an impressionistic assessment of several observable variables.[14] Of these variables there is no single one by which alone integration can be identified, nor is there any single "symptom" which may not be lacking in families classified as highly integrated.

The prediction which is provided by this scheme is *theoretical* prediction according to an analytic induction model. But the theoretical prediction cannot be converted into empirical prediction unless integration can be assessed beforehand. The assessment is made by an implicitly statistical operation, a mental weighting of several items of observation. In order, then, to gain *empirical* prediction the investigator shifts over to an "enumerative induction" procedure.

The concept of adaptability is both more important[15] and more complex, combining two elements as Angell uses the term. First, if a family has been flexible in the face of minor crises or problems that have occurred in the past, it is said to be adaptable and the prediction that it will maintain its unity in the face of a larger crisis is consequently made. This, of course, is merely an application of the principle that there is a constancy in the response of a given system to situations of the same sort, and has no causal significance. The other aspect of adaptability consists of a number of criteria, such as commitment to material standards, concerning which the same comments apply as in the case of integration.

---

14. Not only is the weighting of the various data of observation impressionistic but these criteria are themselves impressionistic. The implicitly statistical nature of Angell's operation has been noted before and his documents subjected to a restudy under Social Science Research Council auspices. In the restudy, scales for the measurement of integration and adaptability were devised to objectify ratings and translate them into numerical values. Ruth Cavan, *The Restudy of the Documents Analyzed by Angell in "The Family Encounters the Depression."* Unpublished.

15. Reuben Hill, *Families Under Stress*, p. 132, citing Cavan, *op. cit.*

Thus in the three cases cited empirical prediction is not provided by statements of universally valid relationships taken alone. What, then, do such efforts accomplish?

ANALYTIC INDUCTION AS DEFINITION

What the method of universals most fundamentally does is to provide definitions. Not all definitions are of equal value for deriving scientific generalizations, and the definitions produced by the analytic induction procedure are intended to be characterized by causal homogeneity.

The effort at causal homogeneity is evident in the refinements of definition that accompany the method. In the process of attempting to generalize about addiction Lindesmith had to distinguish between those drugs that produce withdrawal distress and those that do not. Early in his work he concluded that it would be futile to seek a single theory to explain both types. Cressey points out that he could not study everyone who is legally defined as an embezzler. Unless he restricted his subjects, for example, to those who entered the situation in good faith, he could not form valid generalizations having universal applicability. Angell also rules out certain types of families. He recognized that some of his families were units merely in a formal sense, and that he could not observe uniform principles which would be applicable to the latter.

Saying that the principal accomplishment of the search for universals is to make definitions depends upon showing that the generalizations which it produces are deducible from the definitions. This is clearest in the case of Lindesmith's theory. In Lindesmith's presentation he has outlined the essential stages in becoming addicted by the time that he has arrived at his full definition of the phenomenon. The essential stages are implicit in the concept of addiction as he presents it.[16]

In place of the empirical attributes viewed essential by Lindesmith, Angell constructs two theoretical categories to which he ascribes the character of essentiality. But Angell is really getting the definition of his causal variables from the dependent or effect variables which he sets up. Adaptability seems to correspond to the firm-yielding dimension and integration to the vulnerability dimension. Adaptability and integration are the logically deducible counterparts to the dependent variables.

Cressey's formulation is less completely amenable to this interpretation. The recognition of embezzlement as a solution is a logically deducible component, since one cannot perform a purposive self-conscious act unless its possibility is recognized. By definition the subjects of Cressey's study possessed long standing conceptions of themselves as law-abiding individuals, and were socially recognized as such at the time of the offense. While perhaps not from

16. W. S. Robinson has suggested this in his "Rejoinder to Comments on 'The Logical Structure of Analytic Induction,'" *American Sociological Review*, 17 (August, 1952), p. 494.

the definition alone, at least from the body of established theory which is implicit in the definition, it follows that the individuals must at the time of the crime in some way reconcile their behavior with their law-abiding self-conception. Indeed, we cannot help wondering whether failure to report rationalization could be entirely independent from the criteria by which an investigator would exclude some subjects from his study on grounds of doubting the honesty of their initial intentions.

The non-sharable problem, however, is probably only partially deducible. Given the fact that all people have problems that might be solved by stealing, given the fact that these subjects were mature individuals, and recognizing that they must, by definition, have resisted situations in the past which could have been improved by stealing, then it would seem to follow that a very distinctive type of problem would be required for people to deviate from their established life-patterns. The non-sharability of the problem might be deducible as a *frequent* characteristic, but probably not as a universal characteristic.

Thus, with the exception of non-sharability, the theories that have been examined serve chiefly to delimit a causally homogeneous category of phenomena, the so-called essential causes of the phenomenon being deducible from the definition.

It is, of course, not accidental but the crux of the method that these generalizations should be deducible. It is through the causal examination of the phenomenon that its delimitation is effected. The operation in practice is one which alternates back and forth between tentative cause and tentative definition, each modifying the other, so that in a sense closure is achieved when a complete and integral relation between the two is established. Once the generalizations become self-evident from the definition of the phenomenon being explained, the task is complete.

THE INTRUSIVE FACTOR

The next step in our argument must be to ask why the search for universals does not carry us beyond formulating a definition and indicating its logical corollaries, and why it fails to provide empirical prediction. The answer may be that there are no universal, uniform relations to be found except those which constitute logical corollaries of conceptual definition. The positing of operationally independent causal variables, empirically assessible prior to the existence of the postulated effect, always seems to result in relationships of statistical probability rather than absolute determination.[17]

---

17. These remarks and some of the subsequent observations must be qualified by noting that Cressey's "non-sharable problem" is an apparent exception. If the statements in this paragraph are correct we should expect further research to eventuate either in some modification of the concept, "violation of financial trust," or in the reevaluation of the non-sharable problem as a *frequent* rather than essential characteristic.

A minor reason for these limited findings is the fact of multiple determination, with which analytic induction is rather ill-equipped to cope. When such complex phenomena as family integration, rather than individual behavior, are examined, the method very rapidly shifts into the ideal-type technique, which is no longer subject to the sort of straight-forward empirical verification as analytic induction. As in Angell's study, the logic of the method is preserved but the empirical problems become quite different.

But as the central thesis of this paper we shall call attention to another explanation for the absence of universal, uniform relations which are not logical corollaries of definitions. The "closed system," which is the core of Znaniecki's statement and whose isolation is the objective and accomplishment of the method, is a causally self-contained system. As such, it is not capable of activation from within, but only by factors coming from outside the system. While, by definition, uniform relations exist within closed causal systems, uniform relations do not exist *between* any causal system and the external factors which impinge on it. *External variables operating upon any closed system do not have a uniform effect because they have to be assimilated to the receiving system in order to become effective as causes.* The outside variable has to be translated, in a sense, into a cause relevant to the receiving system. Normally there will be alternate ways in which the same external variable may be translated depending upon the full context within which it is operative. The situation in which a man finds himself, for example, can only activate the closed system of the embezzlement process when it becomes translated into a nonsharable problem. Cressey finds no type of problem, phenomenologically speaking, which necessarily and uniformly becomes a non-sharable problem.

The external factor which activates a system may be referred to as an *intrusive* factor. This idea is taken from Frederick Teggart's discussion of what he calls an "event." "We may then define an event as an intrusion from any wider circle into any circle or condition which may be the object of present interest."[18] There are always intrusive factors which are accordingly not predictable in terms of the causal system under examination, but which serve to activate certain aspects of the system. The same idea may be thought of as levels of phenomena. There are no uniform relations between levels of phenomena, only within levels.

Empirical prediction always concerns the way in which one closed system is activated by various intrusive factors. Hence empirical prediction always requires some statistical or probability statements, because there is some uncertainty or lack of uniformity in the *way* in which the intrusive factors will activate the causal system and even in *whether* they will activate the system.

---

18. Frederick J. Teggart, *Theory of History,* New Haven: Yale University Press, 1925, p. 149. Quoted by Clarence Marsh Case, in "Leadership and Conjuncture: A Sociological Hypothesis," *Sociology and Social Research,* 17 (July, 1933), p. 513.

UNIVERSALS AND STATISTICAL METHOD

The utility of defining universals within closed systems lies in the translation of *variables* into *concepts*. A variable is any category which can be measured or identified and correlated with something else. A concept is a variable which is part of a theoretical system, implying causal relations. That correlations among variables, of themselves, do not provide a basis for theory, or even for anticipating future correlations, is well known. Analytic induction fails to carry us beyond identifying a number of closed systems, and enumerative induction fails to go beyond the measurement of associations. The functions of the two methods are not only distinct; they are complementary. When the two methods are used together *in the right combination*,[19] they produce the type of findings which satisfies the canons of scientific method.

What the identification of closed systems does is to provide a basis for organizing and interpreting observed statistical associations. For example, valid research would probably reveal some correlation between liking-to-run-around-with-women and embezzlement. Cressey's findings do not discredit such an observation but afford a basis for interpreting it. In the light of certain American mores such a behavior pattern is likely, in some circumstances, to create a problem which would be difficult to discuss with others. The crucial aspect of this behavior for the determination of embezzlement would be its creation of a non-sharable problem.

With the closed system described it is possible to take the various correlations and get order from them. Identification of the closed system also gives us guides to significant variables, correlations that would be worthy of test. At the present point it should be profitable to search for the kinds of situations which most often become non-sharable problems, the characteristics which are correlated with the ability to rationalize an activity which would normally be regarded as contrary to the mores of society, the personal and situational characteristics associated with taking opiates (other than by medical administration) sufficiently to experience withdrawal symptoms. A study of correlations between certain sex patterns and the acquisition of non-sharable problems would build cumulatively in a way that a study of correlation between the former and embezzlement would not do. Some quantitative measure of such correlation would in turn provide the basis for using the closed system formulation for empirical prediction.[20]

---

19. In no sense can those research reports which devote a section to statistical findings and another section to case study findings be said to illustrate the thesis of this paper. In most cases such contrasting categories refer only to the method of data *collection,* the method of *analysis* being enumerative in both cases, but precise in the former and impressionistic in the latter.

20. Cressey proposes a study of such related conditions in much the same manner as is indicated here, but does not clarify whether this should be by a further extension of the method he has used or by the measurement of probabilities. Cf. *Other People's Money,* Chap. V.

One useful indication of the way in which a statement of universals can function in the total research operation is afforded by Edwin Sutherland's "differential association" theory of criminality.[21] While this theory is not the product of a specific empirical research operation of the sort that Lindesmith or Cressy undertook, the form of Sutherland's proposition is that of the analytic induction model. He employs a felicitous term in stating his theory. Differential association, he says, is "the specific causal process" in the genesis of systematic criminal behavior. He does not say that differential association is *the* cause or the *only* one; poverty and the like may be in some sense causes. But differential association is the specific causal process through which these other factors, or more removed causes, must operate. Poverty and other correlated factors only facilitate criminal behavior because they affect the person's likelihood of learning a pattern of criminality from a model of criminality which is presented to him. The differential association theory identifies a hypothesized closed system, in terms of which the many correlated variables gain their meaning.

There are many theories already extant which have this same character, but which have not always been viewed as logical counterparts to the analytic induction method: Edwin Lemert's proposition that, "The onset of insanity coincides with the awareness of one's behavior as being invidiously different from that of all other people's," points to the same sort of *specific causal process* in the genesis of insanity, or "secondary psychotic deviation."[22] And Sorokin's interpretation of Durkheim's theory of suicide follows the same form.[23]

Statements of this sort are devices for placing in bold outline the meaningful components of the phenomenon under study. In order to achieve the form of a universally valid generalization the investigator either states his causes as inferential variables (Angell), or states empirically continuous variables as attributes (Lindesmith, Cressey). In the latter case, the dividing point between the two phases of the crucial attribute is identifiable only retrospectively on the basis that the specified sequence is or is not completed. But if the essential components of the causal complex are viewed as continuous variables, capable of measurement independently of completion of the hypothesized sequence, the *essential degree* of the components will vary from instance to instance. Hence, in the process of designating the essential causes in a manner susceptible to empirical identification prior to their expected effect, the investigator must recast his thesis in terms of probability rather than uniform and universal relations.

---

21. Edwin H. Sutherland, *Principles of Criminology*, Chicago: J. B. Lippincott Co., 1939, pp. 4–9. The third edition of Sutherland's work is cited here because he has modified the features of his theory most relevant to the argument of this paper in his fourth edition (1947).

22. Edwin M. Lemert, *Social Pathology*, New York: McGraw-Hill, 1951, p. 428.

23. Pitirim A. Sorokin, *Society, Culture and Personality*, New York: Harper, 1947, pp. 8–13.

A danger of the search for universals lies in the inadequate utilization of much valuable data. Cressey has information on the types of backgrounds his subjects came from, but because these are not universals the information has been filed away, or handled impressionistically. Lindesmith likewise secured abundant information which he uses only to demonstrate that absolute uniformity does not exist. Angell describes the frequent characteristics of the integrated and the adaptable family, but he does not systematize this material because such aspects of it are not universals. In these cases the imposition of particular methodological restrictions has limited what can be found out about the phenomenon under examination.

Analytic induction or some logical counterpart of the method is an essential aspect of research directed toward accumulating an ordered body of generalizations. But, for the reasons developed in this paper, Znaniecki's statement that, "analytic induction ends where enumerative induction begins; and if well conducted, leaves no real and soluble problems for the latter,"[24] represents an untenable position. It is through conceiving the "essential" conditions in a closed system as the avenues through which correlated factors can operate as causes, that generalizations about closed systems can escape their self-containment and probability associations may be organized into meaningful patterns.

Turner's criticism—that analytic induction fails to use much of the data, concentrating upon a single relationship between theoretical categories—is particularly emphasized by Barney Glaser. An alternate analytic technique for generating hypotheses is proposed by Glaser with emphasis on proliferating rather than restricting the properties of categories. Because Glaser's technique of constant comparison is unconcerned with the provisional testing of hypotheses, his procedure can avoid many of the criticisms of analytic induction. Much of the tedium of having to classify every case is also eliminated.

THE CONSTANT COMPARATIVE
METHOD OF QUALITATIVE ANALYSIS

BARNEY G. GLASER

Research into social problems, problems of deviation, of control and of crisis, and the like—the general subject matter to which the journal, *Social Problems* is devoted—is still mainly feasible through methods which yield qualitative data. Because these areas raise problems of secrecy, sensitivity,

---

24. Florian Znaniecki, *The Method of Sociology*, p. 250.

Reprinted from *Social Problems* (1965), **12**, 436–445, by permission of the author and publisher.

taboo topics, stigma, and legality, and because people in these situations are usually adept at covering the facts when necessary, often the only way a researcher can obtain any data, or data that is accurate, is some combination of observing what is going on, talking in rather loose, sharing, fashion with the people in the situation, and reading some form of document that they have written. These methods best allow the researcher either to gain the trust of the people in the situation or, if necessary, to accomplish clandestine research. In view of this *distinctive relevance* of qualitative data collection and analysis for many areas of social problems, the constant comparative method of qualitative analysis will in particular, I trust, increase the battery of alternative approaches useful to researchers in these areas.

My other purpose in presenting the constant comparative method may be stated by a direct quotation from Robert K. Merton—a statement he made in connection with his own qualitative analysis of locals and cosmopolitans as community influentials.

▶ This part of our report, then, is a bid to the sociological fraternity for the practice of incorporating in publications a detailed account of the ways in which qualitative analyses *actually* developed. Only when a considerable body of such reports are available will it be possible to *codify* methods of qualitative analysis with something of the clarity with which quantitative methods have been articulated.[1] ◀

SOME DIVERSE APPROACHES TO QUALITATIVE ANALYSIS

Two general current approaches to the analysis of qualitative data are as follows: (1) If the analyst wishes to convert qualitative data into crudely quantifiable form in order to test provisionally an hypothesis, he codes the

Author's note: This paper developed out of problems of analysis arising during the study of terminal care in hospitals; particularly the interaction of staff and dying patients. The study is sponsored by the National Institutes of Health, Grant GN9077. Anselm Strauss, Fred Davis, and Stewart Perry have been strong sources of encouragement in the preparation of this paper. I am particularly indebted to the extensive editorial work of Robert K. Merton. Substantive papers from this study are: Anselm Strauss, Barney G. Glaser, and Jeanne Quint, "The Non-Accountability of Terminal Care," *Hospitals,* 36 (Jan. 16, 1964), pp. 73–87; Barney G. Glaser and Anselm Strauss, "The Social Loss of Dying Patients," *American Journal of Nursing,* 64 (June, 1964) pp. 119–121; Barney G. Glaser and Anselm Strauss, "Awareness Contexts and Social Interaction," *American Sociological Review,* 29 (Oct. 1964), pp. 669–678; Barney G. Glaser and Anselm Strauss, "Temporal Aspects of Non-Scheduled Status Passage," (to be published in the *American Journal of Sociology*); and a forthcoming book, Barney G. Glaser and Anselm Strauss, *Awareness of Dying: A Study of Social Interaction,* Chicago: Aldine Press.

1.   Robert K. Merton, *Social Theory and Social Structure,* New York: Free Press, 1957, p. 390. This is, of course, also the basic position of Paul F. Lazarsfeld. See Allen H. Barton and Paul F. Lazarsfeld, "Some Functions of Qualitative Analysis in Social Research," in Seymour M. Lipset and Neil J. Smelser (eds.), *Sociology: The Progress of a Decade,* Englewood, N.J.: Prentice-Hall, 1961. It is the position that has stimulated the work of Becker and Geer, and Berelson cited in footnote 2.

data first and then analyzes it. An effort is made to code "all relevant data [that] can be brought to bear on a point," and then the assemblage, assessment, and analysis of this data is accomplished systematically in a fashion that will "constitute proof for a given proposition."[2]

(2) If the analyst wishes only to generate theoretical ideas—new concepts and their properties, hypotheses and interrelated hypotheses—the analysis cannot usefully be confined to the practice of coding first and then analyzing the data, since the analyst, in direct pursuit of his purpose, is constantly re-designing and reintegrating his theoretical notions as he reviews his material.[3] Not only would analysis after a coding operation unnecessarily delay and inter-fere with his purpose, but explicit coding itself often seems an unnecessary, burdensome task. As a result, the analyst merely inspects his data for new properties of his theoretical categories and writes memos on the properties.

In this paper, I wish to suggest a third approach to the analysis of qualitative data, combining, by an analytic procedure of constant comparison, the explicit coding procedure of the first approach and the style of theory development of the second. The purpose of the constant comparative method of joint coding and analysis is to generate theory more systematically than allowed by the second approach by using the explicit coding and analytic procedures. At the same time, it does not forestall the development of theory by adhering completely to the first approach which is designed for provisional testing, not discovering, of hypotheses.

Systematizing the second approach by this method does not supplant the skills and sensitivities required in inspection. Rather the constant comparative method is designed to aid analysts with these abilities in generating a theory which is integrated, consistent, plausible, close to the data, and in a form which is clear enough to be readily, if only partially, operationalized for testing in quantitative research. Depending as it still does on the skills and sensitivities of the analyst, the constant comparative method is *not* designed (as methods of quantitative analysis are) to guarantee that two analysts working indepen-

---

2.   Howard S. Becker and Blanche Geer, "The Analysis of Qualitative Field Data" in *Human Organization Research,* edited by Richard N. Adams and Jack J. Preiss, Home-wood: Dorsey Press, Inc., 1960, pp. 279–289. See also Howard S. Becker, "Problems of Inference and Proof in Participant Observation," *American Sociological Review,* Dec., 1958, pp. 652–660, and Bernard Berelson, *Content Analysis,* Glencoe: Free Press, 1952, Chapter III, and page 16.

3.   Constantly redesigning the analysis is a well known normal tendency in qualita-tive research (no matter what the approach to analysis) which occurs throughout the whole research experience from initial data collection through coding to final analysis and writing. It has been noted in Becker and Geer, *op. cit.,* 270, Berelson, *op. cit.,* 125; and for an excellent example of how it goes on, see Robert K. Merton, *Social Theory and Social Structure,* New York: Free Press, 1957, pp. 390–392. However, this tendency may have to be suppressed in favor of the purpose of the first approach, but in the second approach and the approach to be presented here, it is used purposefully as an analytic strategy.

dently with the same data will achieve the same results; it *is* designed to allow, with discipline, for some of the vagueness and flexibility which aid the creative generation of theory.

If the person applying the first approach wishes to discover some or all of the hypotheses to be tested, his discoveries are typically made by using the second approach of inspection and memo-writing along with explicit coding. In contrast, the approach presented here *cannot* be used for provisional testing as well as discovering theory, since the collected data, as will be seen in the foregoing description, are not coded extensively enough to yield provisional tests, as they are in the first approach. The data are coded only enough to generate, hence, to suggest, theory. Partial testing of the theory, when necessary, is left to more rigorous, usually quantitative, approaches which come later in the scientific enterprise.

The first approach differs in another way from that presented here. The first approach is usually concerned with a few hypotheses at the same level of generality, while the constant comparative method is concerned with many hypotheses synthesized at different levels of generality. The reason for this difference is that the first approach must keep the theory tractable for provisional testing in the same presentation. Of course, the analyst using the first approach might, after either proving or disproving his hypotheses, attempt to explain his findings with some more general ideas suggested by his data, thus achieving some synthesis at different levels of generality.

Another approach to qualitative analysis is "analytic induction," which combines the first and second approaches in a manner different from the constant comparative method.[4] Analytic induction is concerned with generating and proving an integrated, limited, precise, universally applicable theory of causes accounting for a *specific* phenomenon, e.g., drug addiction or embezzlement. Thus, in line with the first approach, it tests a limited number of hypotheses with *all* available data, which are numbers of clearly defined and carefully selected cases of the phenomena. In line with the second approach, the theory is generated by the reformulation of hypotheses and redefinition of the phenomena forced by constantly confronting the theory with negative cases.

In contrast to analytic induction, the constant comparative method is concerned with generating and plausibly suggesting (not provisionally testing) many properties and hypotheses about a *general* phenomenon, e.g., the distribution of services according to the social value of clients. Some of these properties may be causes; but unlike analytic induction others are conditions, consequences, dimensions, types, processes, etc., and, like analytic induction, they should result in an integrated theory. Further, no attempt is made to ascertain either the universality or the proof of suggested causes or other

---

4.   See Alfred R. Lindesmith, *Opiate Addiction,* Bloomington: Principia, 1947, pp. 12–14, and Donald R. Cressey, *Other People's Money,* New York: Free Press, 1953, p. 16 *et passim.*

TABLE 1 USE OF APPROACHES TO QUALITATIVE ANALYSIS

| | | PROVISIONAL TESTING OF THEORY | |
		YES	NO
GENERATING THEORY	YES	2) Inspection for hypotheses along with (1) coding for test, then analyzing data 4) Analytic Induction	2) Inspection for hypotheses 3) Constant Comparative Method
	NO	1) Coding for test, then analyzing data	Ethnographic Description

properties. Since no proof is involved, the constant comparative method, in contrast to analytic induction, does not, as will be seen, require consideration of *all* available data, nor is the data restricted to one kind of clearly defined case. The constant comparative method may be applied for the same study to any kind of qualitative information, including observations, interviews, documents, articles, books, and so forth. As a consequence, the constant comparisons required by both methods differ with respect to breadth of purpose, extent of comparing, and what data and ideas are compared.

Clearly the purposes of both these methods for generating theory supplement each other as well as the first and second approaches in providing diverse alternatives to qualitative analysis. Table 1 locates the uses of these approaches to qualitative analysis and provides a scheme for locating other approaches according to their purposes.

THE CONSTANT COMPARATIVE METHOD

The constant comparative method can be described in four stages: (1) comparing incidents applicable to each category, (2) integrating categories and their properties, (3) delimiting the theory, and (4) writing the theory. Although this method is a continuous growth process—each stage after a time transforms itself into the next—previous stages remain in operation throughout the analysis and provide continuous development to the following stage until the analysis is terminated.

1. Comparing incidents applicable to each category. The analyst starts by coding each incident in his data in as many categories of analysis as possible.[5] To this procedure I add the basic, defining rule for the constant comparative method: *while coding an incident for a category, compare it with the previous incidents coded in the same category.* For example, as the analyst codes an

---

5. I follow the procedure for selection and coding of categories given in Becker and Geer, *op. cit.,* pp. 271–82.

incident in which a nurse responds to the potential "social loss"—loss to family and occupation—of a dying patient, he compares this incident with others previously coded in the same category before further coding.[6] Since coding qualitative data takes some study of each incident, this comparison can often be based on memory. There is usually no need to turn back to every previous incident for each comparison.

This constant comparison of the incidents very soon starts to generate theoretical properties of the category. One starts thinking in terms of the full range of types or continua of the category, its dimensions, the conditions under which it is pronounced or minimized, its major consequences, the relation of the category to other categories, and other properties of the category. For example, in constantly comparing incidents on how nurses respond to the social loss of dying patients, we saw that some patients are perceived as a high social loss and some as a low social loss and that patient care tended to vary positively with degree of social loss. It was also apparent that some of the social attributes which nurses combine to establish a degree of social loss are seen immediately (age, ethnic, social class) and some are learned after a time with the patient (occupational worth, marital status, education). This further led us to the realization that perceived social loss can change as new attributes of the patients are learned. It also became apparent under what conditions (types of wards and hospitals) we would find clusters of patients with different degrees of social loss.

After coding for a category perhaps three or four times, the analyst will experience a conflict in emphasis of thought. He will both muse over these theoretical notions and try to concentrate on the study of the next incident to determine the alternate ways in which it should be coded and compared. At this point, the second rule of the constant comparative method is: *stop coding and record a memo on ideas.* This rule is designed to tap the initial freshness of the analyst's theoretical notions and to relieve the conflict in thought. In doing so, the analyst should take as much time as necessary for reflecting and taking his thinking to its most logical (grounded in the data, not speculative) conclusions. If one is working on a team, it is also a good idea to sit down with a teammate and discuss theoretical notions with him. The teammate can help bring out points missed, add points he has run across in his own coding and data collection, and crosscheck points. He, too, begins to compare the analyst's notions with his own ideas and knowledge of the data, which generates more theoretical ideas. With clearer ideas on the emerging theory systematically recorded, the analyst then returns to the data for more coding and constant comparison.

2. *Integrating categories and their properties.* This process starts out in a small way; memos and possible conferences are short. But as the coding continues the constant comparative units change *from* comparison of incident

---

6.   Illustrations in the paper will refer to "The Social Loss of Dying Patients," *op. cit.*

with incident *to* incident with properties of the category which resulted from initial comparison of incidents. For example, in comparing incident with incident we discovered the property that nurses are constantly recalculating a patient's social loss as they learn more about him. From then on each incident on calculation was compared to accumulated knowledge on calculating, not to all other incidents of calculation. Thus, once we found that age was the most important characteristic in calculating social loss, we could discern how age affected the recalculation of social loss as the nurses found out more about the patient's education. We found that education was most important in calculating the social loss of a middle year adult, since at this time in life education was likely to be of most social worth. This example also shows that the accumulated knowledge on a property of the category—because of constant comparison —readily starts to become integrated; that is, related in many diverse ways, resulting in a unified whole.

In addition, the diverse properties of the category start to become integrated. We soon found that calculating and recalculating social loss was related to the development of a social loss "story" about the patient. When asked about a patient, nurses would tell what amounted to a story about a dying patient, the ingredients of which were her continual balancing out of social loss factors as she learned more about the patient. We also found that the calculus of social loss and the social loss story were related to her strategies for coping with the upsetting impact on her professional composure of say, a dying patient with a high social loss (e.g., a mother with two children). This example further shows that the category becomes integrated with other categories of analysis: the social loss of the dying patient is related to nurses' maintaining their *professional composure* while attending his dying. Thus the theory develops as different categories and their properties tend to become integrated through constant comparisons which force the analyst to make some related theoretical sense of each comparison.

3. Delimiting the theory. As the theory develops, various delimiting features of the constant comparative method set in to curb what could otherwise become an overwhelming task. This delimiting occurs at two levels: (1) the theory and (2) the original list of categories proposed for coding. First, the theory solidifies in the sense that major modifications become fewer and fewer as one compares the next incidents of a category to properties of it. Later modifications are mainly on the order of logical clarity; paring off non-relevant properties; integrating elaborating details of properties into the major outline of interrelated categories; and most important, reduction. By reduction I mean that a higher level, *smaller* set of concepts, based on discovering underlying uniformities in the original set of categories or their properties, might occur to the analyst by which to write the theory, hence, delimiting its terminology and text. An illustration showing both integration of more details into the theory and some consequent reduction is the following. We decided to elaborate the theory by adding detailed strategies which the nurses used to maintain their professional composure while taking care of patients with varying degrees of social loss.   We discovered that the rationales which they used among themselves could all be considered "loss rationales."   The underlying uniformity was that all rationales indicated why the patient, given his degree of social loss, would, if he lived, now be socially worthless; in spite of the social loss, he would be better off dead. (For example, he would have brain damage, be in constant, unendurable pain, or have no chance for a normal life.)

By further reduction of terminology we were also discovering that our theory could be generalized to one which concerns the care of all, not just dying, patients by all staff, not just nurses. Even more generally, it could be a theory of how social values of professionals will affect the distribution of their services to clients: for example, how they decide who among many waiting clients should next receive a service and what calibre of the service to give him. Thus, with reduction of terminology and consequent generalizing which are forced by constant comparisons—some of which can now be based on incidents found in the literature of other professional areas—the analyst starts to achieve two foremost requirements of theory: (1) *parsimony* of variables and formulation and (2) *scope* in the applicability of the theory to a wide range of situations,[7] while keeping a close correspondence of the theory to data.

Second, delimiting the theory results in a delimiting of the original list of proposed categories for coding. As the theory grows, reduces, and increasingly works better in ordering a mass of qualitative data, the analyst becomes committed to it. This commitment now allows him to delimit the original list of categories for coding according to the boundaries of his theory. In turn, his consideration, coding, and analyzing of incidents become more select and focused. He can devote more time to the constant comparison of incidents clearly applicable to a smaller set of categories.

Another factor, which then further delimits the list of categories for coding, is that categories become *theoretically saturated.* After one has coded incidents for the same category a number of times, it becomes a quick operation to see whether or not the next applicable incident points to a new aspect of the category. If yes, then the incident is coded and compared. If no, the incident is not coded, since it only adds bulk to the coded data and nothing to the theory.[8] For example, once we had established age as the base line for calculat-

---

7.   Merton, *op. cit.,* p. 260.

8.   If the purpose of the analyst, besides developing theory, is also to count incidents for a category to establish provisional proofs, then he must code the incident. Furthermore, Professor Merton has made the additional point in correspondence that counting for establishing provisional proofs may also feed back to the development of theory, since frequency and cross-tabulation of frequencies can also generate new theoretical ideas. See Berelson on conditions under which one can justify time consuming, careful counting, *op. cit.,* pp. 128–134. See Becker and Geer for a new method of counting frequency of incidents, *op. cit.,* pp. 283–287.

ing social loss, it was no longer necessary to code incidents referring to age in calculating social loss. However, if we came across a case where age did not appear to be the baseline (a negative case), it was coded and then compared. In the case of an 85-year-old, dying woman who was considered a great social loss, we discovered her "wonderful personality" outweighed her age as the most important factor in calculating her social loss.

The fact that categories become theoretically saturated can be employed as a strategy in coping with another problem: new categories will emerge after hundreds of pages of coding. The question is whether or not to go back and re-code all previously coded pages. The answer for large studies is "no," not until starting to code for the new category at the page when it occurs, and waiting for a few hundred pages of coding, or when the remaining data have been coded to see whether or not the new category has become theoretically saturated. If yes, then it is not necessary to go back because theoretical saturation suggests that what has been missed will in all probability have little modifying effect on theory. If the category does not saturate, then it is necessary to go back and try to saturate it, if the category is central to the theory.

Theoretical saturation helps solve another problem concerning categories. If the analyst has also collected the data, then he will be remembering from time to time other incidents he observed or heard that were not recorded. What does he do? If the unrecorded incident applies to an established category, it can, after comparison, either be neglected as a saturated point or, if it is a new property of the category, it can be added into the next memo and thus integrated into the theory. If the remembered incident generates a new category, both incident and category can be included in a memo bearing on their place in the theory. This may be enough data if the category is minor. However, if the category becomes a central part of the theory, the memo becomes a directive either for returning to the notes for more coding, or for returning to the field or library for more data or for future research.

The universe of data used in the constant comparative method is based on the reduction of the theory and the delimination and saturation of categories. Thus, the collected universe of data is theoretically delimited and, if necessary, carefully extended by a return to data collection according to theoretical requirements. This theoretical delimiting of the universe economizes research resources, since it forces the analyst to spend his time and effort on data relevant only to his categories. For large field studies with long lists of possibly useful categories and thousands of pages of notes embodying thousands of incidents, each of which could be coded a multitude of ways, theoretical criteria are of great necessity in paring down an otherwise monstrous task to the resources of the people and the project's allotted time and money. Without these criteria the delimiting of a universe of collected data if done at all, can become very arbitrary, less likely to yield an integrated product; and the analyst is more likely to waste time on what might later prove to be irrelevant incidents and categories.

4. Writing theory.   At the end of this process the analyst has coded data, a series of memos, and a theory. The discussions in the memos provide the content behind the categories, which are the major themes of the theory as written in papers or books. For example, the major themes (section titles) for our paper on social loss are "calculating social loss," "the patient's social loss story," and "the impact of social loss on the nurse's professional composure." To start writing one's theory, it is first necessary to collate the memos on each category, which is easy since the memos have been written according to categories. Thus, all memos on calculating social loss were brought together for summarizing and, perhaps, further analyzing before writing about it. The coded data is the resource to return to when necessary for validating a suggested point, "pinpointing" data behind an hypothesis or gaps in the theory,[9] and providing illustrations.

DISCUSSION

Conveying credibility.   A perennial problem with qualitative analysis is conveying the credibility of a theory.[10] The standard approach to this problem is presenting data as evidence for conclusions, thus indicating the way by which the analyst obtained the theory from his data. However, since qualitative data do not lend themselves to ready summary, the analyst usually presents characteristic illustrations and, if also attempting provisional proofs, accompanying crude tables. If the theory encompasses a multitude of ideas, it becomes too cumbersome to illustrate each idea and, even if space were allowed, too burdensome to read many illustrations which interrupt the flow of general ideas.[11] Thus qualitative analysts will usually present only enough material to facilitate comprehension, which is typically not enough data to use in evaluating all suggestions.

Another way to convey credibility of the theory along with the use of illustrations is to use a codified procedure for analyzing data, such as presented here, which allows readers to understand how the analyst obtained his theory from the data. In qualitative analyses the transition from data to theory is hard, if not impossible, to grasp when no codified procedure is used.[12]

---

9.   On "pinpointing" see Anselm Strauss, Leonard Schatzman, Rue Bucher, Danuta Ehrlich and Melvin Shabshin, *Psychiatric Ideologies and Institutions,* New York: Free Press of Glencoe, 1964, Chapter 2, "Logic, Techniques and Strategies of Team Fieldwork."

10.   Becker, *op. cit.,* p. 659.

11.   See detailed discussion on this point in Strauss, et al., *op. cit.*

12.   Following Merton's quotation (page 217), we need more descriptions of methods of transition from qualitative data to qualitative analysis. Barton and Lazarsfeld (*op. cit.*) delimiting the various functions of qualitative analysis indicate a full range of purposes for which other methods of transition can be developed. In focusing discussion on these purposes they hit upon what might be considered elements of possible such methods. To analyze a purpose and the analytic operations involved in its final achievement is *not,* however, to be construed as a method of transition that guides one the full route from raw qualitative data to accomplished purpose.

And in his turn the reader is likely to feel that the theory is somewhat impressionistic, even if the analyst strongly asserts he has based it on hard study of data gathered during months or years of field or library research.

Even such codified procedures as a search for negative cases or a consideration of alternative hypotheses[13] will leave a reader at a loss, since these analytic procedures are not linked with procedures for using qualitative data. They do not specify how and how long to search for negative cases or how to find alternative hypotheses given a specified body of qualitative data. Thus the analyst can still be suspect in making his theory appear credible by biasing his search for negative cases or his reasonable alternative hypotheses. The constant comparative method joins standard analytic procedures with directives for using the data systematically.

In addition, keeping track of one's ideas, as required by the constant comparative method, raises the probability that the theory will be well integrated and clear, since the analyst is forced to make theoretical sense of each comparison. Making sure the categories and their properties of the theory are meaningfully interrelated is difficult enough; keeping all the interrelations clearly delineated is an added difficulty. The integration and clarity of the theory will in turn raise the probability that it will be understood and believed credible by colleagues.

Properties of the theory. The constant comparative method raises the probability of achieving a complex theory which corresponds closely to the data, since the constant comparisons force consideration of much diversity in the data. By diversity, I mean that each incident is compared to other incidents or to properties of a category by as many of its similar and diverse aspects as possible. This way of comparing may be seen in contrast to coding for crude proofs, which only establishes whether or not an incident indicates the few properties of the category which are being counted.

The constant comparisons of incidents on the basis of as many of their similarities and differences as possible tend to result in the analyst's creating a developmental theory.[14] In comparing incidents, the analyst learns to see his categories as having both an internal development and changing relations to other categories. For example, as the nurse learns more about the patient, her calculations of social loss change; and recalculations change her social loss stories, her loss rationales and her care of the patient. Thus, while this method can be used to generate static theories, it especially facilitates the generation of theories of process, sequence, and change which pertain to organizations, positions, and social interaction.

---

13. Becker, *op. cit.,* p. 290.

14. Recent calls for more developmental, as opposed to static, theories have been made by Wilbert Moore, "Predicting Discontinuities in Social Change," *American Sociological Review,* June, 1964, p. 332; Howard S. Becker, *Outsiders,* New York: Free Press, 1962, pp. 22–25; and Barney G. Glaser and Strauss, Awareness Contexts and Social Interaction, *op. cit.*

This is an inductive method of theory development. In making theoretical sense of much diversity in his data, the analyst is forced to develop ideas on a level of generality which is higher than the qualitative material being analyzed. He is forced to bring out underlying uniformities and diversities and to account for differences with single, higher level concepts. He is forced to engage in reduction of terminology, as discussed above, to achieve mastery of his data. If the analyst starts with raw data, he will at first end up with a substantive theory: a theory for the substantive area on which he has done research—for example, patient care or gang behavior. If the analyst starts with the findings from many studies which pertain to an abstract sociological category, he will end up with a formal theory for a conceptual area such as stigma, deviance, lower class, status congruency, or reference groups. To be sure, the level of generality of a substantive theory can be raised to a formal theory (our theory of social loss of dying patients could be raised to the level of how professional people give service to clients according to their social value). This requires additional analysis of one's substantive theory, and the analyst should include material from other studies with the same formal theoretical import, however diverse the substantive content.[15] The analyst should be aware of the level of generality at which he starts in relation to the level at which he wishes to end up.

The constant comparative method can yield either property or propositional theory. The analyst may wish to proliferate many properties of a category or he may wish to write propositions about a category. Property theory is often sufficient at the exploratory stage of theory development and can easily be translated into propositions if the work of the reader requires a formal hypothesis. For example, two related properties of a dying patient are his social loss and the amount of attention he receives from nurses. This can easily be restated as a proposition: patients considered a high social loss compared to those considered a low social loss will tend to receive more attention from nurses.

The selection by Glaser raises important considerations for the participant observer concerning the relationships among the various hypotheses generated by the techniques described in this chapter. Since the distinguishing feature for scientific understanding of social dynamics is its systematic character, it is somewhat misleading to speak of the researcher as seeking to generate hypotheses; he must seek to

---

15. "... the development of any one of these coherent analytic perspectives is not likely to come from those who restrict their interest exclusively to one substantive area," Erving Goffman, *Stigma: Notes on the Management of Spoiled Identity*, Englewood Cliffs, N.J.: Prentice-Hall, Inc., 1963, p. 147. See also Reinhard Bendix, "Concepts and Generalizations in Comparative Sociological Studies," *American Sociological Review*, August, 1963, pp. 532–539.

generate *theory*. But because the problems of linking hypotheses into systematic theory and of seeking the appropriate level of theoretical abstraction are not at all peculiar to participant observation (they are quite general for all scientists), we must reluctantly refer the reader to the wider methodological literature for further discussion of these topics.[4]

---

4. Glaser and Strauss (1967); Zetterberg (1963); Homans (1964).

CHAPTER SIX

THE
EVALUATION
OF
HYPOTHESES

Although we noted in the previous chapter that the invention of systematic procedures for evaluating hypotheses had far outstripped that of comparable procedures for generating hypotheses, this is much more true for the social sciences in general than for participant observation. Given the general trend of the social sciences, it is surprising that very few procedures for evaluating hypotheses have been put forward in the participant observation literature, whereas a number of procedures for generating such hypotheses have been described (see Chapter 5).

The few discussions of hypothesis-testing center around the difficulties of applying ordinary testing procedures to the data that stem from the peculiar designs of participant observation studies.[1] These discussions do suggest the application of the basic canons of evaluation, and therefore, these canons may provide the best starting point for a consideration of possible procedures.

There are basically two distinct types of scientific hypotheses or, as we shall refer to them throughout this chapter, *propositions*. There are *descriptive propositions* (for example, the farther South an American community, the greater is its discrimination against Negroes) and *causal propositions* (for example, poverty causes crime).

Since the criteria for evaluating these two basic types of proposition differ importantly, we shall discuss them separately.

Descriptive Propositions

Descriptive propositions assert either that (1) some single property or variable is distributed in a particular fashion among the members of a specified population, or that (2) two or more specified variables are associated in a particular fashion among the members of a population. An example of the first form is as follows: medical students come to school to acquire practice in recognizing and treating the common diseases likely to confront a general practitioner, not to learn about exotic diseases seen primarily by specialists. An example of the second form of descriptive proposition is as follows: the greater the formal education of persons, the greater their political liberalism.

In either case, the primary criterion of evaluation is to determine whether or not the variable(s) is indeed distributed among that population in the manner indicated by the proposition. This determination requires (1) accurate classification of population members in terms of the variable(s), (2) adequate sampling of the entire population,

---

1.   Zelditch (1962); Becker and Geer (1960); Stavrianos (1950).

for purposes of such classification, and (3) an assessment of the pattern of the results of such classification as compared with that asserted in the proposition.

Accuracy of Classification. The classification of members of the population (be these persons, events, organizations, or whatever) in terms of a given variable demands that (1) true differences among members be reflected in their classification, and (2) such classification be relatively unaffected by other empirical factors.

The reflection of the true differences means, for the researcher, that he must be able to recognize, by means of some research technique, the earmarks or indicators of that variable in the actual behavior or characteristics of the population members. Moreover, he must be able to demonstrate to other scientists that he has succeeded in this task. Alternate approaches to such demonstration, with special reference to participant observation research, are discussed in the following selection.

THE PROBLEM OF INDICATORS
IN PARTICIPANT OBSERVATION RESEARCH

GEORGE J. MCCALL

Owing to the relative lack of structure of participant observation studies,[1] the relationships between the obtained data and the theoretical constructs (or concepts) purported to be reflected in these data has been a very difficult one to establish. In fact, the paucity of discussions of this problem underlines the magnitude of its complexity.[2]

In the core methodological literature of the social sciences, certainly, the central importance of establishing the relations between constructs and their empirical indicators has been amply emphasized.[3] For virtually all the standard techniques, problems of the validity and reliability of measurement have stimulated the invention of suitable checks and assessments.[4]

Author's note: Prepared especially for this volume.

1.   See Anselm Strauss *et al., Psychiatric Ideologies and Institutions,* New York: Free Press, 1964, pp. 18–37; Howard S. Becker and Blanche Geer, "Participant Observation: The Analysis of Qualitative Field Data," in R. N. Adams and J. Preiss, editors, *Human Organization Research,* Homewood: Dorsey Press, 1960, pp. 267–289; Melville Dalton, "Preconceptions and Methods in *Men Who Manage,"* in P. E. Hammond, editor, *Sociologists at Work,* New York, Basic Books, 1964, pp. 50–95.

2.   Becker and Geer, *op. cit.;* Morris Zelditch, Jr., "Some Methodological Problems of Field Work," *American Journal of Sociology* (1962), **67,** 566–576.

3.   Lee J. Cronbach and Paul E. Meehl, "Construct Validity in Psychological Tests," *Psychological Bulletin* (1955), **52,** 281–302; Donald T. Campbell and D. W. Fiske, "Convergent and Discriminant Validation by the Multitrait-Multimethod Matrix," *Psychological Bulletin* (1959), **56,** 81–105; Hans Zetterberg, *On Theory and Verification in Sociology,* Totowa: Bedminster Press, 1963.

4.   See any textbook in research methods, such as Claire Selltiz *et al., Research Methods in Social Relations,* New York: Holt, 1959.

However, it is the thesis of this paper that the absence of the term "measurement," which is standard with other research techniques, provides a major clue as to the lack of discussion of the construct-indicator problem in participant observation literature. Indeed, I believe that most participant observation studies make very little use of measurement *per se* but use instead an alternate and poorly conceptualized approach to constructs and indicators. Before examining this alternate approach, however, let us review the measurement approach.

MEASUREMENT OF PROPERTIES OF UNITS

Measurement[5] is an essentially deductive approach to the construct-indicator problem. That is, the researcher begins with a more or less well defined theoretical construct and, given the conditions of his chosen substantive context, logically deduces a number of empirical properties of pertinent unit-objects that would be entailed by the existence of that construct. These properties serve as indicators of the construct. For example, given the contemporary American values on education, youth, and family responsibility, these properties of persons may quite reasonably be deduced as indicators of the theoretical construct, "the social value of a person."

Education, youth, and family responsibility do not exhaust the universe of possible indicators, of course, and one of the first problems in measurement is to justify the selection of this particular sample of indicators. The standard procedure for such justification is to select other samples of indicators and to determine, for some sample of persons, whether or not the first set of indicators differentiates among persons in very much the same fashion as the other sets of indicators. A positive result serves to establish that the chosen set of properties is a reasonable sample from the universe of indicators.

These properties, however, might also serve as indicators of other constructs, for it is possible to derive a given conclusion from a number of different premises. Therefore, it is important to determine whether persons grouped together by these indicators display certain other common properties of quite different sorts which might also be theoretically predicted. For example, theory might predict that the greater the social value of a dying patient, the more he is catered to by the nursing staff of hospitals. If an examination of persons classified by the chosen indicators confirms this prediction, the researcher derives further confidence that these properties are indeed functioning as indicators of the theoretical construct.[6] The larger the number and the greater the diversity of such confirmations, the greater the confidence.

---

5. This discussion follows the general approach described in Cronbach and Meehl, *op. cit.,* and in Campbell and Fiske, *op. cit.*

6. If, on the other hand, the prediction is not confirmed, it may be the case that the measure was adequate but the theory was incorrect.

Each of these properties—education, youth, and family responsibility—itself has multiple manifestations in the empirical world, and some selection from these manifestations must be made if measurement is to proceed. Number of years of education, for example, could be found in hospital patient records, school records, casual conversation of patients or their acquaintances, or in answers to direct questions concerning years of education. Some sampling of such manifestations must be made, and the equivalence of this sample to other possible samples must be established.

The *number* of manifestations of each of the three properties, and the *combinations* (of such manifestations) that will be regarded as equivalent, must also be determined. Each set of equivalent combinations is then regarded as a distinct category of the theoretical construct, i.e., "social value of the person."

Care should also be taken to establish that the categories defined in this fashion yield equivalent, or "reliable," classifications of persons from one occasion to the next, whether executed by one researcher or several.

Subsequent to all these steps, the category system is at last accepted as a measure of the theoretical construct and may be employed in systematic research. Such research takes the form of classifying all the unit-objects under study in terms of such measures for two or more constructs and examining the relationships between these classifications.

INTERPRETATION OF INCIDENTS

As mentioned earlier, such measurement procedures are seldom employed in participant observation research. Rather, the problem of constructs and indicators is approached in a more inductive fashion through the theoretical interpretation of empirical incidents.

Typically, the participant observer does not begin his work with well defined theoretical constructs but with very general and poorly specified concepts of what may be important in the functioning of broad classes of social organizations. Under the loose guidance of such orienting concepts, the researcher begins accumulating data on the structure and dynamics of the organization under study. These data generally take the form of descriptive accounts of actual events, of participants' thoughts, dispositions, reactions, and of established practices and trends.

As such accounts accumulate, the researcher carefully sifts them to sort out accounts with similar contents, and he then attempts to make theoretical sense of these. Such interpretative attempts are typically tentative formulations of

---

7.   W. S. Robinson, "The Logical Structure of Analytic Induction," *American Sociological Review* (1951), **16,** 812–818; Ralph H. Turner, "The Quest for Universals in Sociological Research," *American Sociological Review* (1953), **18,** 604–611; Barney G. Glaser, "The Constant Comparative Method of Qualitative Analysis," *Social Problems* (1965), **12,** 436–445.

theoretical categories or, more often, propositions.[7] As an example, the following incidents might be noted:

▶ "Nurses X and Y seemed to be spending quite a bit of time today just chatting with the young boy in 7C who is thought to be dying of cancer."

"Nurse S was unusually prompt in responding to buzzes from the lawyer in 4G. He appears to be in terminal phase, but no particular emergency in most of his calls. Nurse S is usually so cavalier about answering these things."

"Many of the nurses again observed dropping into 7C, with little medical purpose for many of the visits."

"More pitiful cries audible in hall from the geriatric case in 7K. Though he seems to be slipping pretty fast, nurses seem reluctant to answer his calls, which don't strike me as particularly cranky."

"Nurse D made two special trips to the kitchen today to get ice cream for 4J. The fellow is parched and enjoys the cold stuff. Nurse D is particularly concerned about his poor prognosis and worries about what might become of his large family—six kids. Family is evidently in very shaky financial condition, as wife is reported unable to work." ◀

Having pulled together these incidents bearing upon differences in nurses' mobilization for patients, the researcher may see a common thread running through them. The special concern of nurses for a young boy, a professional, and a man with heavy family responsibilities, as contrasted with the lack of concern for a worn-out geriatric case, may suggest to the researcher the proposition that patients whose death would represent unusual social loss receive greater responsiveness from the nursing staff.

The researcher then endeavors to sharpen his definitions of the constructs of "social loss" and "responsiveness." As these definitions become elaborated, he compares them with each of the relevant incidents to determine the "goodness of fit" between definition and incident. He may, for example, initially define social loss primarily in terms of socio-economic status, but discover, in attempting to apply this definition to his collection of incidents, that his proposition accounts for more incidents if he defines social loss primarily on the basis of youth and only secondarily on socio-economic status. In this fashion, his changing definitions of the construct may lead him to reclassify the incidents, deciding that some particular incident which at first seemed similar to the others does not share the properties of the emerging construct and is thus irrelevant to the proposition.

These procedures serve to establish a significant number of features of the relationships between the construct and its indicators, though fewer than the procedures of measurement can establish. The feature most firmly established is the *relevance of the indicators* to the content of the theoretical construct, for the latter is shaped and modified to fit the properties of the actual incidents. Moreover, it will often be the case that phrases in these incidents will directly employ the construct itself; for example, nurses may themselves say, "What a terrible loss his death would be to his family."

A second feature established by these procedures is the *adequacy of weighting of indicators,* for at least one sample of cases. That is, given the set of incidents, it has been established in this instance that giving primary consideration to youth and only secondary consideration to socio-economic status yields positively useful results. (However, the participant observer will seldom adequately detail the weighting, as, for example, just how great socio-economic status must be to override the effects of a particular age.)

A third feature of the relationship between construct and indicators, which is established by the above procedures, is the *confirmation of a theoretical proposition,* for the proposition ("the greater the social loss of a dying patient, the more responsive is the nursing staff") has been carefully reformulated to ensure that the majority of relevant incidents bear out this relationship.[8] (Note that this proposition is not necessarily proved thereby, but that the empirical support for it affords greater confidence in the applicability of the constructs to these data.)

The demonstration to readers that in any given case these features have been established by inductive procedures, however, is more difficult than with measurement procedures, where a paragraph or two describing the details of checks and the resulting correlation coefficients will suffice. This problem of demonstration, though important, is beyond the bounds of the present paper.

Let us turn instead to certain features of the construct-indicator relations which are *not* established by the inductive techniques described. First of all, a useful construct will ordinarily suggest pertinent indicators beyond those employed for any one application of the construct. For example, one would certainly suppose, given the American value systems, that persons of great fame, public importance, or wonderful personality might be considered persons whose death would represent unusual social loss. The inductive techniques described do not provide a means for establishing the *equivalence of the indicator set* employed in the study (e.g., wealth and youth) with other potential sets (e.g., fame and warmth of personality).

- Similarly, inductive techniques do not establish the *equivalence of manifestations of indicators.* For example, in one case the observer may judge a patient's socio-economic status on the basis only of having overheard a nurse mention his occupation, while in another case the observer may judge it by interviewing the patient on his education and income. In addition to using different manifestations of one indicator for different cases, it often happens that no manifestations at all are available in a given incident with respect to one or more of the indicators.

By and large, participant observers seem to confront their inability to establish an equivalence of indicators or of their manifestations with an implicit reliance on the well-known "equivalence of indices" discovered in survey

---

8.   *Ibid.* Too often in these procedures the construct appears in only one such proposition, thus limiting the validation of theory, although the technique suggested by Glaser, *op. cit.,* provides for multiple propositions.

research.[9] That is, there seems to be a certain confidence that the use of *any* indicator or manifestation of it will do roughly as well as any other, so long as it is truly relevant to the content of the construct.

The question of *reliability of classification* of incidents in terms of the construct or its indicators is seldom dealt with. The tacit philosophy of many veteran participant observers seems to be that the greater the number and range of indicators or manifestations employed in classifying a particular incident, the greater the reliability. This view is, of course, much like the measurement theory, that the greater the number of items employed, the more reliable the classification. Participant observers seldom present (or indeed employ) any check on the reliability of the classification of incidents, such as correlating the independent results of two or more coders, although it would be simple and very useful to do so.

All in all, the problems of the inductive procedures described in this section resemble those of all inductive procedures, such as factor analysis, for example.[10] These procedures examine commonalities in a delimited corpus of data and these commonalities are theoretically construed. The fit between construct and data is pretty much insured by such procedures. The major problem arises when one asks whether, and how, the construct can be meaningfully applied in other contexts.[11] If the construct has been adequately conceptualized, specified, and elaborated in a theoretical system, the validity of the original classification of incidents may be confirmed by positive results in other studies, employing alternative indicators and manifestations and confirming additional theoretical propositions.

For empirical research it is somewhat meaningful, therefore, to contrast the measurement approach, which requires the establishment of validity of the construct-indicator relations *before* carrying out a study, with the interpretation of incidents approach, which requires the establishment of validity *during and after* the study. Despite the heuristic utility of this contrast, it remains true that, even in the measurement approach, construct validity can never be finally established but must depend upon positive results in a great number of studies.

PINPOINTING

Although I have talked thus far as though the measurement approach were used only in traditionally structured studies and that the interpretation of incidents approach were, therefore, the sole recourse of participant observation, this allocation is not entirely correct.

9.   Paul F. Lazarsfeld, "Evidence and Inference in Social Research," in Daniel Lerner, editor, *Evidence and Inference,* New York: Free Press, 1959, pp. 107–138, especially pp. 113–117.

10. H. H. Harman, *Modern Factor Analysis,* Chicago: University of Chicago Press, 1960.

11. Benjamin Fruchter, *Introduction to Factor Analysis,* Princeton, N. J.: Van Nostrand, 1954, pp. 149–154; 192–208.

Increasingly, the best participant observation studies make use of both approaches, with only the early phases of field work being characterized primarily by the inductive, interpretation of incidents approach. At later points in such studies, solidly based constructs and propositions, formulated on the basis of the early phases, are rigorously elaborated and are then employed in an essentially measurement approach.[12]

This second phase, which has been termed "pinpointing of specific propositions,"[13] seeks actually to *measure* the relevant phenomena. That is, quite uniform and specific combinations of indicators are formulated and applied to all cases which enter into the final evidence for and against a proposition. By necessity, most such cases must be collected *after* the measure has been constructed, so that late data collection operations tend to assume quite pointed direction. However, the early data are not discarded. Attempts are made to salvage as many as possible by going back to the field to seek supplementary information on these early cases so that they may be rigorously classified in terms of the new measure.

In addition to uniformity of indicators in the pinpointing phase, more nearly uniform sets of manifestations of those indicators are also sought to increase comparability of measurement.

Because the pertinent cases are then very nearly comparable in terms of the essential data, the conventional tabular techniques for presentation of evidence, supplemented by brief descriptions of the measures employed, are quite plausible even in participant observation studies.[14]

Despite these quite important advances, however, even pinpointing operations typically fail to establish all the features of the construct-indicator relations which the true measurement approach demands. Most importantly, pinpointing fails to investigate the equivalence of the chosen set of indicators with other possible sets. Second, pinpointing fails to demonstrate the equivalence of the chosen manifestations of the selected indicators with other possible manifestations of those particular indicators. Third, it fails to demonstrate the reliability of data collection and classification procedures.

These, it should be noted, are largely failures in practice rather than failures in principle. To a considerable extent, it would certainly be possible to remedy each of these failures of pinpointing within the bounds of a participant observation study by hewing to the procedures established for measurement. For most of the large number of constructs and propositions which emerge in the typical study, the exigencies of the field make it impractical to insist on appropriate remedial measures. Pinpointing is a quite reasonable compromise. For the key propositions, however, the inconvenience and cost of achieving true mea-

---

12. Strauss *et al., op. cit.;* Becker and Geer, *op. cit.;* Barney G. Glaser and Anselm L. Strauss, *Awareness of Dying,* Chicago: Aldine, 1965.

13. Strauss *et al., op. cit.,* Chapter 2.

14. Howard S. Becker *et al., Boys in White,* Chicago: University of Chicago Press, 1961.

surement would often be more than repaid by the greatly increased acceptance which the data would receive from the scientific public.

I suggest, then, that there are three types of propositions which occur in the typical participant observation study and that for each there is an appropriate approach to the problem of constructs and indicators:

1. *Propositions discovered after the conclusion of data collection.* Some propositions are discovered only upon inspection of field notes after the researcher has left the field and is digesting his data, or are discovered after it is effectively too late to carry out any further major data collection. Typically, such propositions are not central to the researcher's conclusions. For these propositions, the researcher has little choice other than the *interpretation of incidents* approach;

2. *"Mine-run" propositions discovered while in the field.* The bulk of the researcher's interesting propositions will ordinarily be discovered with sufficient time remaining for *pinpointing operations* but will not be so critical as to justify still more rigorous procedures;

3. *Central propositions.* The key propositions of a study will usually emerge long before the conclusion of the fieldwork and may often justify the labors and precautions inherent in the *measurement* approach.

After the researcher has demonstrated that his classifications do in fact reflect true differences among population members in terms of his variable(s), the researcher must yet demonstrate that his classifications are relatively unaffected by other empirical factors. This problem was discussed at length in Chapter 4, and we saw there that the participant observer faces serious difficulty in demonstrating that his data are relatively uncontaminated. One procedure described there by McCall (pp. 128–141) suggests that, for each proposition, the researcher include a data quality profile indicating the proportion of relevant data which have been judged to be free of a number of common contaminating influences.

TABLE 1   SAMPLE TABLE FOR TESTS OF CONTAMINATION OF PROPOSITION

| | | SUPPORTS PROPOSITION | |
		Yes	No
CATEGORY OF	A		
CONTAMINATION	$\bar{A}$		

In the present context, a somewhat different use of the data quality profile, suggested by Naroll, may be more nearly adequate.[2] Taking the data bearing upon a given proposition, a series of statistical tests may be run, cross-classifying the data for and against the proposition as being either contaminated or clean in the specified category of the data quality profile. A measure of relationship, such as ϕ or Q, is computed for each table and this relationship is evaluated by means of Fisher's exact test.[3]

---

2.   Naroll (1962).

3.   Siegel (1956), pp. 96–104.

If Fisher's test reveals the relationship to be statistically significant at the .10 level, and the relationship is negative in direction, the researcher may conclude that his *contaminated* data are obscuring his variables and may properly discard these data with respect to the given proposition. Such an event is rather unlikely but greatly favors the proposition. If it occurs for one category of possible contamination, its occurrence in other categories is somewhat more likely, but almost always the result will be to discard the very same items previously discarded, along with a few others.

If Fisher's test is significant but the relationship is positive in direction, the researcher may conclude that his variables are hopelessly confounded with the contaminating influence. At this point, he will do well to abandon all his data on the proposition as being uninterpretable.

If, on the other hand, Fisher's test is *not* significant, the researcher may conclude that his variables are not significantly contaminated by that particular influence. However, if data quality profiles are to be made available for the proposition in question, it would be extremely useful to add two columns to the profile, giving the magnitude and direction of the various test relationships and the probability values for those relationships as determined by Fisher's test.

Adequacy of Sampling. If the researcher is to evaluate a descriptive proposition concerning some population, it would obviously be ideal to classify all members of the population in terms of each variable. This is seldom possible for any scientist, and he must resort to a *sample* of that population. If his sample is an accurate reflection of the larger population, his conclusions will be the same as he would have obtained had he studied the entire population.

The first step is to define and delineate the population relevant to his proposition. For the participant observer, who typically studies some type of social organization, the relevant population is usually the members of that organization (or some part of it), the parts of the organization themselves, or some category of events pertinent to the organization.

In structured research, the relevant population is first delineated and then an adequate sample is deliberately designed. The optimal procedure here is some variety of random sampling, although other systematic sampling designs are sometimes used.

As discussed in Chapter 3, sampling in participant observation is not completely planned in advance, for in the beginning the researcher cannot know what the relevant populations might be. That is, in the early phases of field work, his sampling is theoretical, with the goal of *generating* propositions rather than providing evidence for or against them.

When, however, the researcher later seeks evidence regarding some proposition, he broadens his sample, attempting to get a more accurate picture. At this point, the participant observer, too, has recourse to systematic sampling procedures, although these are seldom probability procedures, due to limitation of access. Very often he designs what might be described as a quota sample without randomization. Perhaps even more frequently, he attempts to sample every person or every event (during some time span) with respect to his proposition.

Under the circumstances, the samples obtained in seeking evidence for a proposition are often surprisingly good, *where he has been able adequately to conceptualize and enumerate his population.* Because the sample was not drawn according to traditional probability methods, however, the participant observer is typically reluctant to attempt to describe his sample. Very often, he has managed to obtain data on nearly the entire population, or nearly every member within each set of subpopulations. The participant observer should bear in mind that if a sufficiently large proportion of the population is classified, it will rarely happen that those missed would alter the results.

At any rate, in evaluating descriptive propositions, the researcher should be certain to describe as accurately as possible just what sort of sample he did manage to obtain. Even if it was not designed in any of the fashions described in sampling manuals, it *was* his sample and may have been very adequate. Without a description of the sample used to study *this* proposition, other scientists have no choice but to be skeptical of the researcher's results.

Distribution of Evidence. If the classifications and the sampling employed in a study are more or less adequate, the major criterion employed in evaluating the validity of a proposition is the distribution of the empirical evidence bearing on the proposition. Has the pattern of classification of the population members (or of a justifiable sample) been shown to follow basically the pattern described in the proposition?

Particularly when only a sample has been studied, one is seldom able to *prove* unequivocally that even a simple, descriptive proposition is correct. Certain patterns of distribution of empirical data can, however, render the proposition so eminently probable that only the most steadfast skeptics could doubt its validity. In general, the greater the range, number, and proportion of classifications which follow the pattern described in the proposition, the more credible the proposition becomes.

But how can such evidence be communicated to other scientists, so that they too are led to extend greater credibility to the proposition?

One useful approach, too seldom employed, is the paradigms of plausible inference described by Polya.[4] These paradigms, representing essentially probabilistic modifications and interpretations of the classic syllogistic forms of demonstrative proof, such as *modus ponens* and *modus tollens,* allow inference of the credibility of one assertion based upon the established credibility of some other assertion of fact. Resembling the classic, three-sentence syllogisms, these paradigms provide a concise and convenient form for summarizing one's pattern of evidence for a proposition.

A more traditional approach is the use of data tables in their various forms to summarize the distribution of classified cases. The simplest and least adequate means of presenting evidence regarding a proposition is to directly provide the reader with a number of pertinent cases and to allow him to form his own implicit tabular summary. This procedure, though crude, can furnish a certain degree of plausibility for the proposition as Allen Barton and Paul Lazarsfeld demonstrate in the following selection.

QUALITATIVE SUPPORT OF THEORY

ALLEN H. BARTON AND PAUL F. LAZARSFELD

So far we have mainly discussed ways in which qualitative data can contribute to the formulation of problems, classifications, and hypotheses. Qualitative materials are particularly suitable for this exploratory phase of research: their wealth of detailed descriptive elements gives the analyst the maximum

---

4.   Polya (1954).

Reprinted from pp. 356–361 of Allen H. Barton and Paul F. Lazarsfeld, "Some Functions of Qualitative Analysis in Social Research," *Frankfurter Beiträge zur Soziologie* (1955), **1,** 321–361. Copyright 1955 by Europäische Verlagsanstalt, Frankfurt am Main, by permission of the authors and publisher.

opportunity to find clues and suggestions. For testing hypotheses, on the other hand, the ideal model would be the controlled experiment, with precise measurements on a limited number of preselected variables.

The use of controlled experiments in social science is increasing, but it remains severely limited. Recent years have also seen a great development of quantitative research, employing such rough approximations of the experimental design as the controlled observation of natural processes, or the correlational analysis of cross-sectional surveys. These techniques provide tests for certain theories. There remain, however, major areas in which theories are supported mainly by qualitative data.

The General Problem of Qualitative Support. The word "theory" has actually a number of different meanings, ranging from broad general orientations to precise propositions.[1] The theories for which qualitative support is most often used are relatively large-scale, wide-ranging systems or relationships. For example, large-scale theories of social change must rely upon the qualitative data of historical records; theories of the functioning of organizations and institutions are based largely on qualitative descriptions; theories of personality development grow out of clinical case materials. One calls to mind at once the historical theories of Marx, Weber's institutional analysis, Freud's personality theory, and the later work in their traditions.

In discussing the use of qualitative data to support theory, it should be made clear that more is involved than mere illustration. For illustration, intended to help the writer communicate the meaning of his concepts, purely imaginary examples can be used. Durkheim, for instance, in describing types of suicide, drew on examples from literature as well as real case-histories.[2] But for the use we have in mind it is important that the examples are real. Since they are not systematically samples or precisely measured, they do not offer rigorous proof in any statistical or experimental sense. Yet according to their number, range, and relation to the reader's own experience they offer varying degrees of support or corroboration. It is this function which we wish to examine.

Psychoanalysis, Marxism, and other theories of history in general or of overall personality development are large and complicated structures. The use of qualitative data in supporting such complex theoretical systems is one of the major undeveloped areas for methodological analysis. In order to find manageable illustrations of the use of qualitative data to support theory, we will restrict ourselves to a much simpler type, which may be called "trend theories." These are theories which call attention to one particular trend in

---

1. Robert K. Merton, Social Theory and Social Structure, New York: Free Press, 1957, Chapter II.

2. Emile Durkheim, Suicide, Glencoe, Illinois, 1951; Book Two, Ch. 6.

society, usually derived from some underlying change in the economic or demographic structure.

We will consider three such theories. Erich Fromm has suggested that a major tendency in our time is "self-alienation," resulting from the insecurities and disruption of social bonds brought about by the rise of the market economy and industrialization. C. Wright Mills suggests that the rise of the big city and the standardization of tastes subjects increasing numbers of people to status-insecurity. Lasswell proposes the "developmental construct" of the garrison state, which attempts to work out the logical implications of the tendency toward an increasing reliance on military force in international relations.

"Signs of the Times"; Qualitative Observations Supporting Trend Theories. Fromm's theory as a whole is relatively complicated, dealing with the interaction of economic structure, personality, and systems of belief.[3] We will consider one particular aspect of that theory: that the individual, rendered isolated and powerless in the face of impersonal market forces, monopolies, mass organization and recurring wars, develops "automaton conformity" as a mechanism of escape:

▶ "This particular mechanism is the solution that the majority of normal individuals find in modern society. To put it briefly, the individual ceases to be himself; he adopts entirely the kind of personality offered to him by cultural patterns; and he therefore becomes exactly as all others are and as they expect him to be."[4] ◄

Let us see how Fromm goes about supporting this contention derived from his trend theory. First of all, he wants to demonstrate that it is at all possible for a person to think thoughts and feel feelings which are not his own, but induced from outside. This he does by describing a common hypnotic experiment where it is suggested to a subject that he will do certain things and have certain feelings upon awakening from the hypnotic sleep. This establishes that the phenomenon can exist; however it involves very special conditions.

Fromm then attempts to show that the same kind of behavior occurs in the daily life of many individuals. To specify what this would involve, he gives a hypothetical example of "pseudo-thinking" in daily life: the man who makes a weather prediction which he believes to be his own thinking, when he is simply repeating what he heard on the radio. He then proceeds to actual observations:

▶ "Many persons looking at a famous bit of scenery actually reproduce the pictures they have seen of it numerous times, say on postal cards . . . Or, in

---

3.   Erich Fromm, Escape From Freedom, New York 1941; Appendix: Character and the Social Process.

4.   l. c., pp. 185 seq. Quoted by permission of Routledge & Kegan Paul, Ltd.

experiencing an accident which occurs in their presence, they see or hear the situation in terms of the newspaper report they anticipate."

"The average person who goes to a museum and looks at a picture by a famous painter, say Rembrandt, judges it to be a beautiful and impressive picture. If we analyze his judgement, we find that he does not have any particular inner response to the picture but thinks it is beautiful because he knows that he is supposed to think it beautiful."[5] ◀

Fromm gives a number of other observations of pseudo-thinking and feeling: the man whose face goes solemn after he leaves a party where he was "gay," children who say they "like" to go to school every day, people who believe they are marrying because they want to, while they are only conforming to other people's expectations, the case of a man who "voluntarily" follows the career set by his father, but suffers strange difficulties.

Of course Fromm's examples do not provide rigorous proof of the assertion that "the majority of normal individuals" are self-alienated. What Fromm has done is, first, to establish thoughts and feelings. Then he presented a hypothetical example to show how this might happen in daily life. Finally he mobilized a wide range of common observations to show that it actually does occur frequently.

Let us take another example. C. Wright Mills holds that the white-collar worker in urban, mass-production society suffers from an increasing ambiguity and insecurity of social status; he or she is unable to develop a stable self-esteem or a secure prestige-status in the eyes of others.[6] Mills presents qualitative observations from various sources. Strategically-placed specialists—e.g. personnel directors—report such surprising behavior as the following: a girl typing in a large office was deeply hurt when her chair was replaced with a new one, because the old one had her nameplate on the bottom; office workers attach great importance to objectively meaningless changes in the location of desks, etc. This suggested to Mills the intensity of the effort to retain some identity and status in a standardized environment.

Detailed interviews found other phenomena which fitted in with the notion of a "status panic": Routine clerical workers tried to conceal the nature of their own work, and borrow prestige from the firm or industry, by identifying themselves with such phrases as "I am with Saks," or "I work at Time." They saved up their salaries and spent them for an evening at expensive places of entertainment, or for a vacation at a costly resort, in order to "buy a feeling, even if only for a short time, of higher status." A salesgirl dealing with "Park Avenue" customers will try to behave with greater dignity and distinction in her off-the-job contacts than the girl who works on 34th Street.

Such qualitative observations provide support for a theory in several ways. Aside from their own weight, they may call the reader's attention to certain

---

5. l. c., pp. 192 seq.

6. C. Wright Mills, *White Collar*, New York: Oxford University Press, 1951, Ch. 11, The Status Panic.

areas of his own experience, which may provide much additional support. Furthermore, when the observations cover many different areas of behavior they gain additional weight, because they indicate that the theory has the ability to account for a wide range of phenomena.

The notion of the "garrison state" as formulated by Lasswell also suggested a trend growing out of basic social changes; however it was unusual in being formulated not ex post facto but at a very early stage in the process. This is what Lasswell meant in describing it as a "developmental construct"—a trend theory referring not only to the immediate situation but to the future. The substance of Lasswell's theory was a set of consequences which could be expected if the world situation stimulated modern great powers, with modern economies and technology, to all-out development of military strength. Some of these consequences were relatively logical and obvious: the entire labor force would be put to work, political conflicts will be minimized in the interests of national unity, the government will become involved in more and more previously private activities. Others were more of a symbolic nature:

▶ "The distinctive frame of reference in a fighting society is fighting effectiveness. All social change is translated into battle potential.

"The military are therefore compelled to become competent in the skills of technology, administration, and public relations; there is a 'merging of skill' between the professional soldier and the manager of large-scale civilian enterprise.

"There is intense concern with public morale and its manipulation; the military 'are compelled to consider the entire gamut of problems that arise in living together under modern conditions.'"[7] ◀

If one wanted in 1953 to see to what extent the predicted trend had become a reality, the developmental construct provides a guiding framework for observation. "All social change is translated into battle potential"—a study of illiteracy in America is discussed mainly in terms of "how many divisions" it costs the army. "The merging of skills"—generals appear on boards of directors of large corporations, and large corporation executives appear in the defense departments. "Intense concern with public morale"—the traditional concern with the morality of school-teachers in terms of smoking, drinking, and sex shifts to a concern with treasonable ideas. In politics the traditional charges of corruption and inefficiency against opponents are replaced by charges of treason, or of failure to build enough air groups.

One or two of these might be isolated events; taken together they begin to build up a "pattern," giving some plausibility to the theory. At this point it becomes important to undertake more systematic studies of the actual extent and degree of militarization, to distinguish its progress in different spheres, etc.

---

7.   Harold Lasswell, The Garrison State and Specialists on Violence, in: American Journal of Sociology (January 1941).   Reprinted in: Lasswell, The Analysis of Political Behavior, London: Routledge & Kegan Paul, Ltd.—Archon Books, 1966, p. 146 seq.

From the few examples presented here, it is hoped that the reader has been able to get an idea of the intermediate role played by qualitative observations in relation to theory—as more than simply illustration, but less than definitive proof. It is likely that there are several degrees or stages of qualitative support, ranging from an initial encouragement to go on with a certain line of speculation, to a systematic examination of case material which offers some approximation to the classical canons of proof. There also may be differences in function according to the type of "theory" involved. The present analysis is only a tentative beginning; there is a great need for intensive work on additional examples of qualitative support of theory.[8]

Now that we are at the end of our survey, it is necessary to add that some of the areas we have distinguished inevitably overlap at their borders. It would be easy to find examples in which it would be difficult to decide whether they have the complexity of a matrix formula. Another set of uncertainties will sometimes arise when we have to decide whether the writer is arguing for a relationship between a few variables or whether he is supporting a rather general theory. Even the very notion of qualitative research has its haziness on the fringes; it would not be easy, e.g., to say when the comparative analysis of a few cases shades over into statistical treatment.

The present discussion is a beginning only. It has started from a simple position: that there exists this area of research which is generally considered important but which has not been analyzed methodologically. It has set forward a collection of examples both as an extensional definition of "qualitative analysis" and as material for further study. Besides collecting this material, it has made a preliminary organization of it. There are many problems left unsolved in the discussion.[9] The tentative classifications set forward here need to be tried out on additional materials; more good cases need to be collected and examined. Only after many successive phases of logical formulation and attempted application will the methodology of qualitative techniques come to possess the same usefulness to the research worker which is today possessed by quantitative methodology.

In the case of a descriptive proposition dealing with the distribution of a single variable within some population (e.g., that status panic is frequent among white-collar workers), the presentation of a number of diverse and striking incidents of status panic

---

8. Paul F. Lazarsfeld, Remarks on Administrative and Critical Communications Research, in: Studies in Philosophy and Social Science, Vol. IX (May 1941), gives a number of further examples in the field of mass communications, especially from the work of Max Horkheimer and T. W. Adorno. In another field, Thorstein Veblen, Theory of the Leisure Class, offers a classic example of the use of qualitative observations.

9. The authors are indebted to Professor Merton and the members of his seminar in the Sociology of Occupation for raising many of these problems in discussing an earlier draft of this paper.

among such workers does serve to demonstrate that the variable (status panic) does exist, that it exists in a number of manifestations, and that some of these manifestations have been observed among white-collar workers of various sorts. Note, however, that this procedure does *not* demonstrate that the variable is particularly frequent in that population, absolutely or relatively. The evidence only makes this conclusion more plausible by casting greater doubt on the opposite proposition (that the variable is infrequent in that population), since a number of cases have here been presented.

In the following selection, Howard Becker discusses a somewhat more powerful elaboration of this same procedure.

PROBLEMS OF INFERENCE AND PROOF IN PARTICIPANT OBSERVATION

HOWARD S. BECKER

The participant observer gathers data by participating in the daily life of the group or organization he studies.[1] He watches the people he is studying to see what situations they ordinarily meet and how they behave in them. He enters into conversation with some or all of the participants in these situations and discovers their interpretations of the events he has observed.

Let me describe, as one specific instance of observational technique, what my colleagues and I have done in studying a medical school. We went to lectures with students taking their first two years of basic science and frequented the laboratories in which they spend most of their time, watching them and engaging in casual conversation as they dissected cadavers or examined pathology specimens. We followed these students to their fraternity houses and sat around while they discussed their school experiences. We accompanied stu-

Reprinted from pp. 652–657 of Howard S. Becker, "Problems of Inference and Proof in Participant Observation," *American Sociological Review* (1958), **23,** 652–660, by permission of the author and publisher.

Author's note: This paper developed out of problems of analysis arising in a study of a state medical school. The study is sponsored by Community Studies, Inc., of Kansas City, Missouri. It is directed by Everett C. Hughes; Anselm Strauss is also a member of the research team. Most of the material presented here has been worked out with the help of Blanche Geer, who has been my partner in field work and analysis in this study. I am grateful to Alvin W. Gouldner for a thorough critique of an earlier draft.

Substantive papers on the study, whose findings are made use of throughout, include: Howard S. Becker and Blanche Geer, "The Fate of Idealism in Medical School," *American Sociological Review,* 23 (February, 1958), pp. 50–56, and "Student Culture in Medical School," *Harvard Educational Review,* 28 (Winter, 1958), pp. 70–80. Another paper on participant observation by the same authors is "Participant Observation and Interviewing: A Comparison," *Human Organization,* 16 (Fall, 1957), pp. 28–32.

1. There is little agreement on the specific referent of the term *participant observation*. See Raymond L. Gold, "Roles in Sociological Field Observations," *Social Forces,* 36 (March, 1958), pp. 217–223, for a useful classification of the various procedures that go by this name. Our own research, from which we have drawn our illustrations, falls under Gold's type, "participant-as-observer." The basic methods discussed here, however, would appear to be similar in other kinds of field situations.

dents in the clinical years on rounds with attending physicians, watched them examine patients on the wards and in the clinics, sat in on discussion groups and oral exams. We ate with the students and took night call with them. We pursued internes and residents through their crowded schedules of teaching and medical work. We stayed with one small group of students on each service for periods ranging from a week to two months, spending many full days with them. The observational situations allowed time for conversation and we took advantage of this to interview students about things that had happened and were about to happen, and about their own backgrounds and aspirations.

Sociologists usually use this method when they are especially interested in understanding a particular organization or substantive problem rather than demonstrating relations between abstractly defined variables. They attempt to make their research theoretically meaningful, but they assume that they do not know enough about the organization *a priori* to identify relevant problems and hypotheses and that they must discover these in the course of the research. Though participant observation can be used to test *a priori* hypotheses, and therefore need not be as unstructured as the example I have given above, this is typically not the case. My discussion refers to the kind of participant observation study which seeks to discover hypotheses as well as to test them.

Observational research produces an immense amount of detailed description; our files contain approximately five thousand single-spaced pages of such material. Faced with such a quantity of "rich" but varied data, the researcher faces the problem of how to analyze it systematically and then to present his conclusions so as to convince other scientists of their validity. Participant observation (indeed, qualitative analysis generally) has not done well with this problem, and the full weight of evidence for conclusions and the processes by which they were reached are usually not presented, so that the reader finds it difficult to make his own assessment of them and must rely on his faith in the researcher.

In what follows I try to pull out and describe *the basic analytic operations carried on in participant observation,* for three reasons: to make these operations clear to those unfamiliar with the method; by attempting a more explicit and systematic description, to aid those working with the method in organizing their own research; and, most importantly, in order to propose some changes in analytic procedures and particularly in reporting results which will make the processes by which conclusions are reached and substantiated more accessible to the reader.

The first thing we note about participant observation research is that analysis is carried on *sequentially,*[2] important parts of the analysis being made while

---

2.   In this respect, the analytic methods I discuss bear a family resemblance to the technique of *analytic induction.* Cf. Alfred Lindesmith, *Opiate Addiction* (Bloomington: Principia Press, 1947), especially pp. 5–20, and the subsequent literature cited in Ralph H. Turner, "The Quest for Universals in Sociological Research," *American Sociological Review,* 18 (December, 1953), pp. 604–611.

the researcher is still gathering his data. This has two obvious consequences: further data gathering takes its direction from provisional analyses; and the amount and kind of provisional analysis carried on is limited by the exigencies of the field work situation, so that final comprehensive analyses may not be possible until the field work is completed.

We can distinguish three distinct stages of analysis conducted in the field itself, and a fourth stage, carried on after completion of the field work. These stages are differentiated, first, by their logical sequence: each succeeding stage depends on some analysis in the preceding stage. They are further differentiated by the fact that different kinds of conclusions are arrived at in each stage and that these conclusions are put to different uses in the continuing research. Finally, they are differentiated by the different criteria that are used to assess evidence and to reach conclusions in each stage. The three stages of field analysis are: the selection and definition of problems, concepts, and indices; the check on the frequency and distribution of phenomena; and the incorporation of individual findings into a model of the organization under study.[3] The fourth stage of final analysis involves problems of presentation of evidence and proof.

SELECTION AND DEFINITION OF
PROBLEMS, CONCEPTS, AND INDICES

In this stage, the observer looks for problems and concepts that give promise of yielding the greatest understanding of the organization he is studying, and for items which may serve as useful indicators of facts which are harder to observe. The typical conclusion that his data yield is the simple one that a given phenomenon exists, that a certain event occurred once, or that two phenomena were observed to be related in one instance; the conclusion says nothing about the frequency or distribution of the observed phenomenon.

By placing such an observation in the context of a sociological theory, the observer selects concepts and defines problems for further investigation. He constructs a theoretical model to account for that one case, intending to refine it in the light of subsequent findings. For instance, he might find the following: "Medical student X referred to one of his patients as a 'crock' today."[4] He may then connect this finding with a sociological theory suggesting that occupants of one social category in an institution classify members of other categories by criteria derived from the kinds of problems these other persons raise in the relationship. This combination of observed fact and theory directs him to look

---

3.   My discussion of these stages is abstract and simplified and does not attempt to deal with practical and technical problems of participant observation study. The reader should keep in mind that in practice the research will involve all these operations simultaneously with reference to different particular problems.

4.   The examples of which our hypothetical observer makes use are drawn from our own current work with medical students.

for the problems in student-patient interaction indicated by the term "crock." By discovering specifically what students have in mind in using the term, through questioning and continued observation, he may develop specific hypotheses about the nature of these interactional problems.

Conclusions about a single event also lead the observer to decide on specific items which might be used as indicators[5] of less easily observed phenomena. Noting that in at least one instance a given item is closely related to something less easily observable, the researcher discovers possible shortcuts easily enabling him to observe abstractly defined variables. For example, he may decide to investigate the hypothesis that medical freshmen feel they have more work to do than can possibly be managed in the time allowed them. One student, in discussing this problem, says he faces so much work that, in contrast to his undergraduate days, he is forced to study many hours over the weekend and finds that even this is insufficient. The observer decides, on the basis of this one instance, that he may be able to use complaints about weekend work as an indicator of student perspectives on the amount of work they have to do. The selection of indicators for more abstract variables occurs in two ways: the observer may become aware of some very specific phenomenon first and later see that it may be used as an indicator of some larger class of phenomena; or he may have the larger problem in mind and search for specific indicators to use in studying it.

Whether he is defining problems or selecting concepts and indicators, the researcher at this stage is using his data only to speculate about possibilities. Further operations at later stages may force him to discard most of the provisional hypotheses. Nevertheless, problems of evidence arise even at this point, for the researcher must assess the individual items on which his speculations are based in order not to waste time tracking down false leads. We shall eventually need a systematic statement of canons to be applied to individual items of evidence. Lacking such a statement, let us consider some commonly used tests. (The observer typically applies these tests as seems reasonable to him during this and the succeeding stage in the field. In the final stage, they are used more systematically in an overall assessment of the total evidence for a given conclusion.)

The Credibility of Informants. Many items of evidence consist of statements by members of the group under study about some event which has occurred or is in process. Thus, medical students make statements about

---

5.   The problem of indicators is discussed by Paul F. Lazarsfeld and Allen Barton, "Qualitative Measurement in the Social Sciences: Classification, Typologies, and Indices," in Daniel Lerner and Harold D. Lasswell, editors, *The Policy Sciences: Recent Developments in Scope and Method,* Stanford: Stanford University Press, 1951, pp. 155–192; "Some Functions of Qualitative Analysis in Sociological Research," *Sociologica,* 1 (1955), pp. 324–361 (this important paper parallels the present discussion in many places); and Patricia L. Kendall and Paul F. Lazarsfeld, "Problems of Survey Analysis," in R. K. Merton and P. F. Lazarsfeld, editors, *Continuities in Social Research,* Glencoe: Free Press, 1950, pp. 183–186.

faculty behavior which form part of the basis for conclusions about faculty-student relations. These cannot be taken at face value; nor can they be dismissed as valueless. In the first place, the observer can use the statement as evidence *about the event*, if he takes care to evaluate it by the criteria an historian uses in examining a personal document.[6] Does the informant have reason to lie or conceal some of what he sees as the truth? Does vanity or expediency lead him to mis-state his own role in an event or his attitude toward it? Did he actually have an opportunity to witness the occurrence he describes or is hear-say the source of his knowledge? Do his feelings about the issues or persons under discussion lead him to alter his story in some way?

Secondly, even when a statement examined in this way proves to be seriously defective as an accurate report of an event, it may still provide useful evidence for a different kind of conclusion. Accepting the sociological proposition that an individual's statements and descriptions of events are made from a perspective which is a function of his position in the group, the observer can interpret such statements and descriptions as indications of the individual's perspective on the point involved.

Volunteered or Directed Statements.   Many items of evidence consist of informants' remarks to the observer about themselves or others or about something which has happened to them; these statements range from those which are a part of the running casual conversation of the group to those arising in a long intimate tete-a-tete between observer and informant. The researcher assesses the evidential value of such statements quite differently, depending on whether they have been made independently of the observer (volunteered) or have been directed by a question from the observer. A freshman medical student might remark to the observer or to another student that he has more material to study than he has time to master; or the observer might ask, "Do you think you are being given more work than you can handle?", and receive an affirmative answer.

This raises an important question: to what degree is the informant's statement the same one he might give, either spontaneously or in answer to a question, in the absence of the observer? The volunteered statement seems likely to reflect the observer's preoccupations and possible biases less than one which is made in response to some action of the observer, for the observer's very question may direct the informant into giving an answer which might never occur to him otherwise. Thus, in the example above, we are more sure that the students are concerned about the amount of work given them when they mention this of their own accord than we are when the idea may have been stimulated by the observer asking the question.

---

6.   Cf. Louis Gottschalk, Clyde Kluckhohn, and Robert Angell, *The Use of Personal Documents in History, Anthropology, and Sociology,* New York: Social Science Research Council, 1945, pp. 15–27, 38–47.

The Observer-Informant-Group Equation. Let us take two extremes to set the problem. A person may say or do something when alone with the observer or when other members of the group are also present. The evidential value of an observation of this behavior depends on the observer's judgment as to whether the behavior is equally likely to occur in both situations. On the one hand, an informant may say and do things when alone with the observer that accurately reflect his perspective but which would be inhibited by the presence of the group. On the other hand, the presence of others may call forth behavior which reveals more accurately the person's perspective but would not be enacted in the presence of the observer alone. Thus, students in their clinical years may express deeply "idealistic" sentiments about medicine when alone with the observer, but behave and talk in a very "cynical" way when surrounded by fellow students. An alternative to judging one or the other of these situations as more reliable is to view each datum as valuable in itself, but with respect to different conclusions. In the example above, we might conclude that students have "idealistic" sentiments but that group norms may not sanction their expression.[7]

In assessing the value of items of evidence, we must also take into account the observer's role in the group. For the way the subjects of his study define that role affects what they will tell him or let him see. If the observer carries on his research incognito, participating as a full-fledged member of the group, he will be privy to knowledge that would normally be shared by such a member and might be hidden from an outsider. He could properly interpret his own experience as that of a hypothetical "typical" group member. On the other hand, if he is known to be a researcher, he must learn how group members define him and in particular whether or not they believe that certain kinds of information and events should be kept hidden from him. He can interpret evidence more accurately when the answers to these questions are known.

CHECKING THE FREQUENCY AND DISTRIBUTION OF PHENOMENA

The observer, possessing many provisional problems, concepts, and indicators, now wishes to know which of these are worth pursuing as major foci of his study. He does this, in part, by discovering if the events that prompted their development are typical and widespread, and by seeing how these events are distributed among categories of people and organizational sub-units. He reaches conclusions that are essentially quantitative, using them to describe the organization he is studying.

Participant observations have occasionally been gathered in standardized form capable of being transformed into legitimate statistical data.[8] But the

---

7. See further, Howard S. Becker, "Interviewing Medical Students," *American Journal of Sociology,* 62 (September, 1956), pp. 199–201.

8. See Peter M. Blau, "Co-operation and Competition in a Bureaucracy," *American Journal of Sociology,* 59 (May, 1954), pp. 530–535.

exigencies of the field usually prevent the collection of data in such a form as to meet the assumptions of statistical tests, so that the observer deals in what have been called "quasi-statistics."[9] His conclusions, while implicitly numerical, do not require precise quantification. For instance, he may conclude that members of freshmen medical fraternities typically sit together during lectures while other students sit in less stable smaller groupings. His observations may indicate such a wide disparity between the two groups in this respect that the inference is warranted without a standardized counting operation. Occasionally, the field situation may permit him to make similar observations or ask similar questions of many people, systematically searching for quasi-statistical support for a conclusion about frequency or distribution.

In assessing the evidence for such a conclusion the observer takes a cue from his statistical colleagues. Instead of arguing that a conclusion is either totally true or false, he decies, if possible, how *likely* it is that his conclusion about the frequency or distribution of some phenomenon is an accurate quasi-statistic, just as the statistician decides, on the basis of the varying values of a correlation coefficient or a significance figure, that his conclusion is more or less likely to be accurate. The kind of evidence may vary considerably and the degree of the observer's confidence in the conclusion will vary accordingly. In arriving at this assessment, he makes use of some of the criteria described above, as well as those adopted from quantitative techniques.

Suppose, for example, that the observer concludes that medical students share the perspective that their school should provide them with the clinical experience and the practice in techniques necessary for a general practitioner. His confidence in the conclusion would vary according to the nature of the evidence, which might take any of the following forms: (1) *Every* member of the group said, *in response to a direct question,* that this was the way he looked at the matter. (2) *Every* member of the group *volunteered* to an observer that this was how he viewed the matter. (3) *Some given proportion* of the group's members either *answered* a direct question or *volunteered* the information that he shared this perspective, but none of the others was asked or volunteered information on the subject. (4) Every member of the group was asked or volunteered information, but *some given proportion said* they viewed the matter from the differing perspective of a prospective specialist. (5) No one was asked questions or volunteered information on the subject, but *all members were observed to engage in behavior* or to make other statements from which the analyst *inferred* that the general practitioner perspective was being used by them as a basic, though unstated, premise. For example, all students might have been observed to complain that the University Hospital received too many cases of rare diseases that general practitioners rarely see. (6) *Some given proportion* of the group *was observed* using the general practitioner perspective as a basic premise in their activities, but *the rest of the group* was

9.   See the discussion of quasi-statistics in Lazarsfeld and Barton, "Some Functions of Qualitative Analysis . . .," *op. cit.,* pp. 346–348.

not observed engaging in such activities. (7) *Some proportion* of the group *was observed* engaged in activities implying the general practitioner perspective while *the remainder* of the group was observed engaged in activities implying the perspective of the prospective specialist.

(In a later, collaborative work Becker continues:)

We have found it useful to present the findings of this kind of analysis in the following tabular form, presenting in each cell both frequencies and the appropriate percentages:

		Volunteered	Directed by the Observer	Total
Statements	To observer alone			
	To others in every-day conversation			
Activities	Individual			
	Group			
Total				

We have not developed any formulas for interpretation of a table of this kind, but we can state a few ground rules. In the first place, the number of directed statements should be small in comparison to the volunteered statements. Secondly, in the "volunteered" column, the proportion of items consisting of statements made to the observer alone should not be overwhelming. This, of course, begs the question of just what proportion would be large enough to cause us to doubt our proposition that the perspective is collective. We are inclined now to think that any proportion over 50 per cent would necessitate another look at the proposition, but we cannot state any rationale for this inclination. Third, there should be a reasonable proportion of activities as well as statements by students. Again, we cannot state any rigid formula, but we are inclined to think that somewhere in the neighborhood of 20 or 25 per cent would be an appropriate figure.

A table like this makes possible summary presentation of a great deal of material and is thus very useful. It gives the reader much of the grounds for

Reprinted from pp. 43–45 of Howard S. Becker, Blanche Geer, Everett C. Hughes, and Anselm L. Strauss, *Boys in White,* Chicago: University of Chicago Press, 1961, by permission of the authors and publisher.

concluding that the perspective is shared by students and regarded by them as legitimate, and allows him to see the basis on which that conclusion was formed.

The final step in our analysis of perspectives was a consideration of those cases found in the field notes which run counter to the proposition that the students shared a particular perspective. Because the statement of the perspective had been refashioned many times in the course of the field work and later analysis in order to take into account as many of the negative cases as possible,[10] this number was usually quite small. We considered each one carefully; whatever revisions it suggested were incorporated in the analysis. Two generic types of negative instances were noted, and we deal with each type differently. In one type, we found individuals not making use of the perspective because they had not yet learned it. Negative cases of this kind typically consisted of a student's taking action contrary to the perspective and being corrected by his fellows. Such an instance required no change in our proposition except to note that not everyone knows the perspective at first and that people acquire it in the course of their experience in the situation we were studying.

The second kind of negative case consisted of observations indicating that a few people had a perspective other than that which we postulated as the common one, or of cases in which students were observed to behave according to the perspective publicly but to deviate from it privately. In these cases, our most likely revision was to say that there apparently exists confirmed deviance in the social body or that there may be marginal areas in which the perspective is not necessarily applied, even though our evidence indicated that in most kinds of situations it was usual.

This second kind of negative case in fact afforded an opportunity for additional confirmation of the proposition that the perspective is a collective phenomenon. Where it could be shown that the person who acted on a different perspective was socially isolated from the group or that his deviant activities were regarded by others as improper, unnecessary, or foolish, we could then argue that these facts indicated use of the perspective by all but deviants, hence its collective character.

Through the kind of analysis just described, we demonstrate that students customarily operated in terms of a given perspective. Such a conclusion is, of course, descriptive. However, our analyses go a step further, by suggesting the conditions under which given kinds of perspectives arise. Ordinarily, the propositions about the genesis of perspectives take this form: students with this kind of initial perspective, faced with this set of environmental problems under conditions allowing for mutual interaction, will develop this kind of

---

10. We thus make use, in some sense, of the method of analytic induction. See Alfred R. Lindesmith, *Opiate Addiction* (Bloomington: Principia Press, 1947), especially pp. 5–20, and the subsequent literature cited in Ralph H. Turner, "The Quest for Universals in Sociological Research," *American Sociological Review*, XVIII (December, 1953), 604–11.

perspective. We are not able to provide any demonstration for such propositions, other than the prima facie plausibility and reasonableness of the connections we postulate. The reason for our inability to provide any more conclusive
assessment of the proposition is simple. Conclusive demonstration would
require, at a minimum, comparison of at least two cases in which the postulated conditions varied and the perspectives developed by students also varied.
But, as we shall see, the students we observed had remarkably similar initial
perspectives and faced the same set of environmental problems. Thus, there
were no alternative collective perspectives—only isolated cases of deviance—
developed among the student body, and we had no opportunity for a systematic comparison. More compelling demonstration of these propositions on the
genesis of perspectives of various kinds must necessarily wait on the study of
more cases in which the consequences of differing conditions can be observed.

Becker, Geer, Hughes, and Strauss quite reasonably contend that an examination
of the relative frequency of incidents which *do* and incidents which *do not* manifest
the variable in question, provides fairly convincing evidence for the plausibility of the
proposition that medical students are oriented toward learning to deal primarily with
common rather than unusual diseases. Again, the evidence does not so much directly
support this proposition as it casts doubt on the opposite proposition—that orientation toward learning common diseases is relatively infrequent. The incidents summarized largely contradict this opposite proposition.

Becker *et al.*'s procedure falls short of proof in that they cannot demonstrate
that they have examined all possible incidents or even a sample that would provide an
accurate representation of the larger population of incidents. Had they obtained
similar results with all possible incidents (and adequate classification procedures), the
proposition would be considered proved. Similar results with a demonstrably adequate sample would have removed virtually all doubt of the proposition's validity.

Let us now examine various distributions of evidence for a descriptive proposition
involving *two* variables, e.g., the assertion that variable *A* is positively related to variable *B*, taking the simplest case in which *A* and *B* are only qualitative attributes.

TABLE 2 DUMMY TABLE FOR PATTERNS
OF DISTRIBUTION OF EVIDENCE

	B	$\bar{B}$
A	1	2
$\bar{A}$	4	3

In Table 2, the procedure analogous to that described above by Barton and
Lazarsfeld would be to present directly a sprinkling of incidents classifiable in cells
1 and 3. Let us take, for an example, the proposition that white-collar workers (*A*)
are insecure about their status (*B*) whereas blue-collar workers ($\bar{A}$) are more secure
about their status ($\bar{B}$). In this case, the researcher might present a few incidents
documenting cases of status insecurity on the part of white-collar workers as well as

a few incidents showing cases of status security on the part of blue-collar workers. This procedure would serve to increase the plausibility of the proposition by demonstrating that A, $\bar{A}$, B, and $\bar{B}$ do exist in the population, that these exist in a number of manifestations, and that B has sometimes occurred with A and $\bar{B}$ with $\bar{A}$. Again, however, this procedure does not establish that either of these occurrences is particularly frequent, relatively or absolutely.

A procedure for two-variable propositions analogous to that described above by Becker *et al.* would be to summarize the frequency of incidents classifiable in cells 1 and 3, supporting the proposition, relative to the frequency of incidents classifiable in cells 2 and 4, which contradict the proposition. If the combined frequencies of cases in cells 1 and 3 considerably exceed those for cells 2 and 4, the proposition is rendered considerably more credible.[5]

Note that once more this increased credibility stems not so much from direct support of the proposition as from the preponderance of evidence contradicting the opposite proposition. If the entire population of pertinent incidents had been classified with such results, however, the proposition would have been demonstratively validated. If even an assuredly adequate sample of the population of incidents had been employed with comparable results, virtually all doubt of the proposition would have been eliminated.

Two conclusions should be obvious from this discussion. First, that the credibility of a descriptive proposition is a variable feature determined by the possible distributions of evidence. Some degree of credibility (often considerable) can be established even in the absence of complete proof. Second, that adequacy of sampling is of tremendous importance in evaluating descriptive propositions, regardless of the distribution of evidence.

Causal Propositions

A causal proposition, as the term implies, asserts that the distribution of some variable B is determined by the effects of some other variable (or variables) A. Three criteria are of primary importance in evaluating the validity of such a proposition: concomitant variation of A and B, proper time relations between the occurrence of A and B, and elimination of the possible effects of other variables upon B. The relevance of these criteria will be elaborated below.[6]

Concomitant Variation. If the values of variable A are determining the values of variable B, an examination of actual cases must therefore reveal that certain values of B occur most frequently in the presence of the associated values of A. If they do not, there is little evidence that A is affecting B in any manner at all.

To establish for such actual cases that A and B are differentially associated is simply to validate (in reasonable degree) the descriptive proposition that A and B are related in a specified fashion. The criteria and procedures for such validation have been rather thoroughly discussed in the preceding section of this chapter, centering on accuracy of classification of cases, adequacy of sampling, and patterns of distribution of evidence of the two variables.

---

5.   If the opposite pattern should obtain, the proposition is of course rendered considerably less credible.

6.   An admirably concise discussion of these criteria can be found in Selltiz, Jahoda, Deutsch, and Cook (1959), pp. 80–88.

A few additional comments on the patterns of distribution are in order at this point. To say that A determines B is to assert that A is a condition for the occurrence of B. Various patterns of distribution of evidence signify different manners in which A may be a condition for B.

Referring once more to Table 2, if A is a *necessary condition* for the occurrence of B, no cases should be classifiable in cell 4, but some should occur in each of the other cells. If A is a *sufficient condition* in itself for the occurrence of B, no cases should be observed to fall in cell 2, but some should fall in each of the others. If A is both a *necessary and sufficient condition* for the occurrence of B, all cases should be observed to fall in cells 1 and 3. If the occurrence of A is neither necessary nor sufficient but is yet a partial or *contributing condition* for B, some cases should be classifiable in each of the cells with the majority occurring in cells 1 and 3.[7]

Note that the occurrence of any of these patterns of distribution does not in itself demonstrate that A actually is a condition for the occurrence of B, but a pattern of this sort is a necessary part of any such demonstration.

Time Order of Variables. Having established an empirical relationship between A and B of the sort specified by the proposition, the researcher must also demonstrate that the occurrence of B did not precede in time the occurrence of A. Given contemporary views of determinism, A cannot be said to have determined B if B had already taken place before A. It will not always be possible to show that A actually preceded B, and it is sometimes conceivable that A might have affected B even if these were simultaneous occurrences. To make more credible one's claim that A could have affected B, therefore, one can at least present evidence making less plausible the assertion that B preceded A. Even this is often quite difficult, however, when the nature of the variables is such that conceptualization of a time of occurrence is basically indeterminate.[8]

Eliminating Effects of Other Variables. If the two previous criteria have been satisfied, any causal proposition has a strong presumptive claim to validity. This validity cannot be directly demonstrated, but once again its plausibility can be increased by presenting evidence diminishing the credibility of rival hypotheses. That is, the researcher is unable to prove that A determines B, but he may be able to show that B could scarcely have been determined by X, Y, or Z, thus leaving A as the most reasonable determinant.

The rival hypothesis that can be most systematically eliminated is that the observed relationship between A and B was the result of chance errors in sampling cases. A statistical test of the significance of this rival hypothesis is necessary, and any good statistics text describes the procedures appropriate to the type of data involved. Because many of these statistical tests require that the cases be randomly sampled, a condition seldom met in participant observation research, it has often been argued that statistical tests are inappropriate. Some statisticians, however, have made the case that such tests are useful and in considerable degree justifiable even though the condition of random sampling has not been met.[9] Thus, the time has passed in which the participant observer could justify excusing himself from the beneficial effects of statistical tests of significance.

---

7. *Ibid.* See also Francis (1961).
8. Hyman (1955).
9. Selvin (1957); McGinnis (1957); D. Gold (1959).

Certain other rival hypotheses, pertinent to any causal evaluation, are not easy to deal with, however. These include:[10]

1. *History*, or the effects of unspecifiable events other than the occurrence of *A*;
2. *Maturation*, the effects of autochthonous processes within the research subjects, such as growing older, etc.;
3. *Testing*, the effects of having been observed or interviewed with respect to *B*, on subsequent observation of *B*;
4. *Instrumentation*, the effects of changes in the participant observer such that his earlier observations or interviews are systematically different from later ones;
5. *Statistical regression*, where cases have been selected on the basis of their extreme previous values of *B*;
6. *Selection*, where biased operations of various sorts (including self-selection) have influenced the classification of cases in terms of *A*;
7. *Mortality*, where cases in the various categories of *A* differentially drop out of the study before the observation of *B*;
8. *Reactive effect of testing*, in which prior observation of cases with respect to *B* increases or decreases their sensitivity to the effects of *A*; and
9. *Interaction of selection and the independent variable.*

If evidence is not presented to suggest rather strongly that each of these and similar rival hypotheses was unlikely to have affected *B*, the credibility of the *A–B* proposition is considerably diminished. By and large, these rival hypotheses can be effectively dealt with only by means of careful design in the collection of data on *A* and *B*. Campbell and Stanley (1966) present and evaluate a great variety of such designs, a surprising number of which might feasibly be employed in pinpointing or measurement operations in participant observation. Particular attention should be paid to their discussion of various pre-experimental and quasi-experimental designs, many of which are often quite unwittingly used by participant observers. It will also sometimes happen that true (field) experiments can be executed under favorable conditions.[11]

A final category of rival hypotheses to be considered are *substantive* variables which might on theoretical grounds be thought to have some effect on *B* independent of or in conjunction with *A*. Appropriate multivariate techniques, such as those of partial association or multiple and partial correlation, have been widely discussed in the general methodological literature of the social sciences.[12] By means of such analytic techniques, a rival substantive hypothesis may be shown to have no effect on the *A–B* relationship, to render it causally spurious, to constitute a link in the causal chain between *A* and *B*, or to constitute a contingent condition for the effect of *A* on *B*.[13]

It will seldom be possible in participant observation, or in any social research, to muster strong evidence discounting all possible rival hypotheses, but it is important that the researcher realize that the credibility of his causal proposition is the greater, the larger the proportion of rival propositions he can justifiably discredit.

---

10. Campbell (1957); Campbell and Stanley (1966).
11. J. R. P. French (1953); Lofland and Lejeune (1960).
12. Lazarsfeld (1959); Blalock (1960).
13. Lazarsfeld (1959).

CHAPTER SEVEN

PUBLICATION
OF
RESULTS

In participant observation studies, the writing up of results is not a clear-cut phase of the research process, as it tends to be in more tightly structured studies. That is to say, write-ups of considerable magnitude are undertaken *throughout* the study. These write-ups summarize the masses of incoming data and sharpen the researcher's thinking, often serving to somewhat refocus the ongoing data collection activities. Many of these write-ups undertaken *in media res* are more than just working memos and actually appear virtually intact as important sections of final reports of the study. The process and problems of writing up results are not, thus, matters that can be deferred until everything else has been completed when the sheer press for closure might carry the researcher through the grueling work of writing and rewriting.

Even in participant observation studies, however, final reports do not write themselves. The numerous substantive memos and position papers are not simply pieces of a jigsaw puzzle, precut and interlocking. Rather, these intermediate write-ups tend to overlap greatly in some areas, yet leave noticeable gaps in others. Some will be cryptically compressed and others excessively wordy; some will be rashly sweeping and others overly hedged and qualified. Many pieces will simply be missing.

The writing of final reports is, then, despite the availability of intermediate reports which serve as drafts of many sections, a laborious and painstaking task. In fact, many participant observers feel that writing up such studies presents special difficulties not found to comparable degrees in writing up more conventional types of studies. These difficulties tend to be of two general types—technical problems and ethical problems.

Technical Problems

Perhaps the most frequently mentioned difficulty encountered in presenting the results of participant observation research is that it demands excessive space to present the typically rather large number of conclusions, along with the pertinent qualitative evidence for these.[1]

This complaint is in part, we feel, somewhat ill-conceived. The situation confronting the participant observer is very much like that confronting the director of a systematic *program* of structured research, in that many small studies must be fitted together in order to communicate the full significance of the research. A participant observation study is comprised of many specific propositions, each of which is in effect a small study with a research design of its own but each of which is importantly related to

---

1. Strauss, Schatzman, Bücher, Ehrlich, and Sabshin (1964), pp. 36–37; Becker and Geer (1960).

others. The researcher thus finds it difficult to present any one of these "sub-studies" in isolation from those others with which it is importantly connected. Consequently, comparatively few participant observation studies of substantial scale become journal articles because space restrictions impose stringent limits on the number of propositions that can be entertained and evaluated.

Such eschewal of journal outlets has unfortunate consequences for one's professional career, since many social scientists doubt the soundness of work which does not (and thus by inference is not *qualified* to) appear in the major professional journals. This result is rather distressing, for few scientists are willing to make such an inference in the case of conventionally structured program research, which, like participant observation research, is confined mostly to the only reasonable format—a large monographic volume—for its reporting of a large number of closely interrelated conclusions.

Similarly, we question the participant observer's complaint that his reliance on *qualitative* (hence verbally described) evidence confronts him with unusual problems of bulkiness in reporting, if he is to present impressive evidence rather than mere examples.

In earlier chapters we have argued that the major conclusions of a participant observation study should be studied in terms of true measurement of the variables involved, or at least in terms of pinpointing operations (see pp. 230–237 above). Where such approaches have been adopted, tabular summaries of the evidence can be employed very effectively and concisely, as in the study *Boys in White.*[2] With such tabular devices, the same compression found in more conventional studies can be readily achieved and the participant observer is certainly no worse off than, for example, the content analyst.

Many participant observers are unwilling to resort entirely to such tables and to abandon the richness and indirect plausibility gains afforded by the presentation of very telling, discrete, qualitative incidents (see pp. 239–244 above), nor is there any reason that these should be entirely abandoned. On the other hand, the use of such qualitative data is not at all peculiar to participant observation for it lies at the core of clinical case studies in psychology and of historical analyses. Yet the clinical or historical analyst does not complain of the spatial demands of reliance on qualitative material.

In fact, the monographic reports of the anthropologist, historian, or clinician tend to be somewhat slimmer than those of the sociological participant observer but at least equally persuasive. Part of the reason for this difference may well lie in the fact that these other scientists are superior stylists, less prone to inflated clauses and excessive repetition, weaving their incidents more artfully into a coherent large pattern. The *dis*advantage of such artful weaving may, on the other hand, account for the somewhat greater bulk of the sociological monograph. That is, the sociologist may well have a fussier methodological conscience, with the result that he feels he must mention more loose ends, qualifications, and discrepancies than the presentationally less patient clinician, historian, or anthropologist.

At any rate, though the participant observer may in fact be limited to the bulky monograph for his major presentational format, we must question (1) whether this format is so unjustifiable and (2) whether it need be quite so bulky in order to avoid sacrificing evidential adequacy.

---

2.   Becker, Geer, Hughes, and Strauss (1961).

Ethical Problems

The other major problem in writing reports of participant observation research is an ethical one. What facts or interpretations does the researcher have the right to make public about the subjects of his study?

This question is quite pertinent to all social research, but it assumes a particularly sharp edge in participant observation due to the human ties the researcher has developed with his subjects, ties which he has developed in order to gain access to his data. What he has learned in confidence may be painful to the subjects when immortalized and analyzed in public print. What, and how much, of this ought the researcher to divulge, given his indebtedness to the subjects? What are the responsibilities of the researcher to the canons of science, to his subjects, to the general public, and to the future research possibilities of his colleagues?[3]

Such questions, along with ethical questions concerning field relations during the study itself (cf. Chapter 2), have contributed greatly to the agitation for a defined code of ethics for social researchers.[4] Many social scientists, however, accept broad ethical precepts aimed at minimizing abrogations of the researcher's various responsibilities, but they reject the idea that any set of concrete specifiable rules can be laid down which will invariably exemplify these precepts.[5] This is the position put forward by Howard Becker in the following selection, after reviewing the substance of many of the major discussions of ethical problems that have appeared in the sociological literature.

PROBLEMS IN THE PUBLICATION OF FIELD STUDIES

HOWARD S. BECKER

THE PROBLEM

Publication of field research findings often poses ethical problems. The social scientist learns things about the people he studies that may harm them, if made public, either in fact or in their belief. In what form and under what conditions can he properly publish his findings? What can he do about the possible harm his report may do?

---

3. See, for example, Dexter (1964) on the last mentioned responsibility.

4. See the official reports of the American Sociological Association Committee on Professional Ethics in the *American Sociological Review*—(1962), **27,** 925; (1963), **28,** 1016; (1964), **29,** 904.

5. Becker and Freidson (1964).

Reprinted from Howard S. Becker, "Problems in the Publication of Field Studies," in Arthur J. Vidich, Joseph Bensman, and Maurice R. Stein, editors, *Reflections on Community Studies,* New York: Wiley, 1964, pp. 267–284, by permission of the author and publisher.

Author's note: I am indebted to Blanche Geer, William Kornhauser, and Arthur Vidich for their comments on an earlier version of this paper.

Although many social scientists have faced the problem, it seldom receives any public discussion. We find warnings that one must not violate confidences or bring harm to the people one studies, but seldom a detailed consideration of the circumstances under which harm may be done or of the norms that might guide publication practices.

Let us make our discussion more concrete by referring to a few cases that have been discussed publicly. Most thoroughly discussed, perhaps, is the "Springdale" case, which was the subject of controversy in several successive issues of *Human Organization*.[1] Arthur Vidich and Joseph Bensman published a book—*Small Town in Mass Society*—based on Vidich's observations and interviews in a small, upstate New York village. The findings reported in that book were said to be offensive to some of the residents of Springdale; for instance, there were references to individuals who, though their names were disguised, were recognizable by virtue of their positions in the town's social structure. Some townspeople, it is alleged, also found the "tone" of the book offensive. For instance, the authors used the phrase "invisible government" to refer to people who held no official position in the town government but influenced the decisions made by elected officials. The implication of illegitimate usurpation of power may have offended those involved.

Some social scientists felt the authors had gone too far, and had damaged the town's image of itself and betrayed the research bargain other social scientists had made with the townspeople. The authors, on the other hand, felt they were dealing with problems that required discussing the facts they did discuss. They made every effort to disguise people but, when that was impossible to do effectively, felt it necessary to present the material as they did.

In another case John F. Lofland and Robert A. Lejeune[2] had students attend open meetings of Alcoholics Anonymous, posing as alcoholic newcomers to the group. The "agents" dressed in different social-class styles and made various measurements designed to assess the effect of the relation between the social class of the group and that of the newcomer on his initial acceptance in the group. Fred Davis[3] criticized the authors for, among other things,

---

1.   The discussion of the Springdale case began with an editorial, "Freedom and Responsibility in Research: The 'Springdale' Case," in *Human Organization*, 17 (Summer 1958), pp. 1–2. This editorial provoked comments by Arthur Vidich and Joseph Bensman, Robert Risley, Raymond E. Ries, and Howard S. Becker, *ibid.*, 17 (Winter 1958–1959), pp. 2–7, and by Earl H. Bell and Urie Bronfenbrenner, *ibid.*, 18 (Summer 1959), pp. 49–52. A final statement by Vidich appeared in *ibid.*, 19 (Spring 1960), pp. 3–4. The book whose effects are discussed is Arthur Vidich and Joseph Bensman, *Small Town in Mass Society*, Princeton, N.J.: Princeton University Press, 1958.

2.   John F. Lofland and Robert A. Lejeune, "Initial Interaction of Newcomers in Alcoholics Anonymous: A Field Experiment in Class Symbols and Socialization," *Social Problems*, 8 (Fall 1960), pp. 102–111.

3.   Fred Davis, "Comment," *Social Problems*, 8 (Spring 1961), pp. 364–365.

failing to take into account the effect of publication of the article on the attitudes of A. A. toward social science in view of its possible consequences on the A. A. program. (A. A. groups might have refused to cooperate in further studies had the authors reported, for instance, that A. A. groups discriminate on the basis of social class. That their finding led to no such conclusion does not negate Davis' criticism.)

Lofland[4] suggested in reply that the results of the study were in fact not unfavorable to A. A., that it was published in a place where A. A. members would be unlikely to see it, and, therefore, that no harm was actually done. Julius Roth,[5] commenting on this exchange, noted that the problem is not unique. In a certain sense all social science research is secret, just as the fact that observers were present at A. A. meetings was kept secret from the members. He argued that we decide to study some things only after we have been in the field a while and after the initial agreements with people involved have already been negotiated. Thus, even though it is known that the scientist is making a study, the people under observation do not know what he is studying and would perhaps (in many cases certainly would) object and refuse to countenance the research if they knew what it was about.

When one is doing research on a well-defined organization such as a factory, a hospital, or a school, as opposed to some looser organization such as a community or a voluntary association, the problem may arise in slightly different form. The "top management" of the organization will often be given the right to review the social scientist's manuscript prior to publication. William Foote Whyte describes the kinds of difficulties that may arise.

▶ I encountered such a situation in my research project which led finally to the publication of *Human Relations in the Restaurant Industry*. When members of the sponsoring committee of the National Restaurant Association read the first draft of the proposed book, some of them had strong reservations. In fact, one member wrote that he had understood that one of the purposes of establishing an educational and research program at the University of Chicago was to raise the status of the restaurant industry. This book, he claimed, would have the opposite effect, and therefore he recommended that it should not be published. In this case, the Committee on Human Relations in Industry of that university had a contract guaranteeing the right to publish, and I, as author, was to have the final say in the matter. However, I hoped to make the study useful to the industry, and I undertook to see what changes I could make while at the same time retaining what seemed to me, from a scientific standpoint, the heart of the study. . . . The chief problem seemed to be that I had found the workers not having as high a regard for the industry as the sponsoring committee would have liked. Since this seemed to me an important part of the human relations problem, I could hardly cut it out of the book. I was,

---

4. John F. Lofland, "Reply to Davis," *ibid.,* pp. 365–367.

5. Julius A. Roth, "Comments on Secret Observation," *Social Problems,* 9 (Winter 1962), pp. 283–284.

however, prepared to go as far as I thought possible to change offensive words and phrases in my own text without altering what seemed to me the essential meaning.[6] ◀

It should be kept in mind that these few published accounts must stand for a considerably larger number of incidents in which the rights of the people studied, from some points of view, have been infringed. The vast majority of such incidents are never reported in print, but are circulated in private conversations and documents. In discussing the problem of publication I am, somewhat ironically, often prevented from being as concrete as I would like to be because I am bound by the fact that many of the cases I know about have been told me in confidence.

Not much is lost by this omission, however. Whether the institution studied is a school for retarded children, an upper-class preparatory school, a college, a mental hospital, or a business establishment, the story is much the same. The scientist does a study with the cooperation of the people he studies and writes a report that angers at least some of them. He has then to face the problem of whether to change the report or, if he decides not to, whether to ignore or somehow attempt to deal with their anger.

CONDITIONS AFFECTING PUBLICATION

Fichter and Kolb have presented the most systematic consideration of ethical problems in reporting.[7] They begin by suggesting that several conditions, which vary from situation to situation, will affect the problem of reporting. First, the social scientist has multiple loyalties: to those who have allowed or sponsored the study, to the source from which research funds were obtained, to the publisher of the research report, to other social scientists, to the society itself, and to the community or group studied and its individual members. These loyalties and obligations often conflict. Second, the group under study may or may not be in a position to be affected by the published report. A historical study, describing the way of life of a people who never will have access to the research report, poses few problems, whereas the description of a contemporary community or institution poses many. Third, problems arise when the report analyzes behavior related to traditional and sacred values, such as religion and sex, and also when the report deals with private rather than public facts. Fourth, when data are presented in a statistical form, the problem

---

6. William Foote Whyte, *Man and Organization: Three Problems in Human Relations in Industry,* Homewood, Ill.: Irwin, 1959, pp. 96–97. Reprinted by permission from the publisher.

7. Joseph H. Fichter and William L. Kolb, "Ethical Limitations on Sociological Reporting," *American Sociological Review,* 18 (October 1953), pp. 96–97.

of identifying an individual does not arise as it does when the mode of analysis is more anthropological.

Fichter and Kolb distinguish three kinds of harm that can be done by a sociological research report. It may reveal secrets, violate privacy, or destroy or harm someone's reputation.

Finally, Fichter and Kolb discuss four variables that will affect the social scientist's decision to publish or not to publish. First, his conception of science will affect his action. If he regards social science simply as a game, he must protect the people he has studied at any cost, for his conception of science gives him no warrant or justification for doing anything that might harm them. He will feel a greater urgency if he believes that science can be used to create a better life for people.

The social scientist's decision to publish will also be affected by his determination of the degree of harm that will actually be done to a person or group by the publication of data about them. Fichter and Kolb note that there is a difference between imaginary and real harm and that the subjects of studies may fear harm where none is likely. On the other hand, it may be necessary to cause some harm. People, even those studied by social scientists, must take responsibility for their actions; a false sentimentality must not cause the scientist to cover up that responsibility in his report.

Fichter and Kolb further argue that the scientist's decision to publish will be conditioned by the degree to which he regards the people he has studied as fellow members of his own moral community. If a group (they use the examples of Hitler, Stalin, Murder Incorporated, and the Ku Klux Klan) has placed itself outside the moral community, the social scientist can feel free to publish whatever he wants about them without worrying about the harm that may be done. They caution, however, that one should not be too quick to judge another group as being outside the moral community; it is too easy to make the judgment when the group is a disreputable one: homosexuals, drug addicts, unpopular political groups, and so on.

Fichter and Kolb conclude by suggesting that the urgency of society's need for the research will also condition the scientist's decision to publish. Where he believes the information absolutely necessary for the determination of public policy, he may decide that it is a lesser evil to harm some of the people he has studied.

Although the statement of Fichter and Kolb is an admirable attempt to deal with the problem of publication, it does not do justice to the complexities involved. In the remainder of this paper I will first consider the possibility that the relationship between the social scientist and those he studies contains elements of irreducible conflict. I will then discuss the reasons why some reports of social science research do not contain conflict-provoking findings. Finally, I will suggest some possible ways of dealing with the problem.

Before embarking on the main line of my argument, I would like to make clear the limits of the area to which my discussion is meant to apply. I assume that the scientist is not engaged in willful and malicious defamation of character, that his published report has some reasonable scientific purpose, and therefore do not consider those cases in which a scientist might attempt, out of malice, ideological or personal, to destroy the reputation of persons or institutions. I further assume that the scientist is subject to no external constraint, other than that imposed by his relationship to those he has studied, which would hinder him in reporting his results fully and freely. In many cases this assumption is not tenable. Vidich and Bensman argue[8] that a researcher who does his work in the setting of a bureaucratic research organization of necessity must be unable to report his results freely; he will have too many obligations to the organization to do anything that would harm its interests in the research situation and thus cannot make the kind of report required by the ethic of scientific inquiry. Although I do not share their belief that bureaucratic research organizations necessarily and inevitably restrict scientific freedom, this result certainly occurs frequently. (One should remember, however, that the implied corollary of their proposition—that the individual researcher will be bound only by the ethic of scientific inquiry—is also often untrue. Individual researchers on many occasions have shown themselves to be so bound by organizational or ideological commitments as to be unable to report their results freely.) In any case my argument deals with the researcher who is encumbered only by his own conscience.

THE IRREDUCIBLE CONFLICT

Fichter and Kolb seem to assume that, except for Hitler, Stalin, and others who are not members of our moral community, there is no irreconcilable conflict between the researcher and those he studies. In some cases he will clearly harm people and will refrain from publication; in others no harm can be done and publication is not problematic. The vast majority of cases will fall between and, as men of good will, the researcher and those he studies will be able to find some common ground for decision.

But this analysis can be true only when there is some consensus about norms and some community of interest between the two parties. In my view that consensus and community of interest do not exist for the sociologist and those he studies.

The impossibility of achieving consensus, and hence the necessity of conflict, stems in part from the difference between the characteristic approach of the social scientist and that of the layman to the analysis of social life. Everett Hughes has often pointed out that the sociological view of the world— abstract, relativistic, generalizing—necessarily deflates people's view of

---

8. Arthur Vidich and Joseph Bensman, "The Springdale Case: Academic Bureaucrats and Sensitive Townspeople," in Arthur J. Vidich, Joseph Bensman, and Maurice R. Stein, editors, *Reflections on Community Studies,* New York: Wiley, 1964, pp. 345–348.

themselves and their organizations. Sociological analysis has this effect whether it consists of a detailed description of informal behavior or an abstract discussion of theoretical categories. The members of a church, for instance, may be no happier to learn that their behavior exhibits the influence of "pattern variables" than to read a description of their everyday behavior which shows that it differs radically from what they profess on Sunday morning in church. In either case something precious to them is treated as merely an instance of a class.

Consensus cannot be achieved also because organizations and communities are internally differentiated and the interests of subgroups differ. The scientific report that pleases one faction and serves its interests will offend another faction by attacking its interests. Even to say that factions exist may upset the faction in control. What upsets management may be welcomed by the lower ranks, who hope the report will improve their position. Since one cannot achieve consensus with all factions simultaneously, the problem is not to avoid harming people but rather to decide which people to harm.

Trouble occurs primarily, however, because what the social scientist reports is what the people studied would prefer not to know, no matter how obvious or easy it is to discover. Typically, the social scientist offends those he studies by describing deviations, either from some formal or informal rule, or from a strongly held ideal. The deviations reported are things that, according to the ideals of the people under study, should be punished and corrected, but about which, for various reasons that seem compelling to them, nothing can be done. In other words the research report reveals that things are not as they ought to be and that nothing is being done about it. By making his report the social scientist makes the deviation public and may thereby force people to enforce a rule they have allowed to lapse. He blows the whistle both on those who are deviating but not being punished for it and on those who are allowing the deviation to go unpunished.[9] Just as the federal government, by making public the list of persons to whom it has sold a gambling-tax stamp, forces local law-enforcement officials to take action against gamblers whose existence they have always known of, so the social scientist, by calling attention to deviations, forces those in power to take action about things they know to exist but about which they do not want to do anything.

Certain typical forms of blowing the whistle recur in many studies. A study of a therapeutic organization—a mental hospital, a general hospital, a rehabilitation center—may show that many institutional practices are essentially custodial and may in fact be antitherapeutic. A study of a school reveals that the curriculum does not have the intended effect on students, and that many students turn out to be quite different from what the members of

---

9. I have discussed the role of the person who makes deviation public, the rule enforcer, at some length in *Outsiders: Studies in the Sociology of Deviance*, New York: Free Press of Glencoe, 1963, pp. 155–163.

the faculty would like them to be. A study of a factory or office discloses that many customary practices are, far from being rational and businesslike, irrational and wasteful. Another typical situation has already been mentioned: a study reveals that members of the lower ranks of an organization dislike their subordinate position.

Nor is this phenomenon peculiar to studies that depend largely on the techniques of anthropological field work, though it is probably most common among them. Any kind of social science research may evoke a hostile reaction when it is published. Official statistics put out by communities or organizations can do this. For example, remember the indignation when the 1960 Census revealed that many major cities had lost population, the demands for recounts by Chambers of Commerce, and so on. By simply enumerating the number of inhabitants in a city, and reporting that number publicly, the Bureau of the Census deflated many public-relations dreams and caused a hostile reaction. The statistics on admissions and discharges to hospitals, on salaries and similar matters kept by hospitals and other institutions can similarly be analyzed to reveal great discrepancies, and the revelation can cause much hostile criticism. The results of survey research similarly can cause trouble as, for instance, when a survey of students reveals that they have reactionary political or cultural attitudes. A program of testing can produce the same result by showing that an organization does not recruit people of as high a caliber as it claims, or that a school does not have the effect on its students it supposes it has. Any kind of research, in short, can expose a disparity between reality and some rule or ideal and cause trouble.

That the sociologist, by publishing his findings, blows the whistle on deviance whose existence is not publicly acknowledged may explain why the poor, powerless, and disreputable seldom complain about the studies published about them. They seldom complain, of course, because they are seldom organized enough to do so. Yet I think further reasons for their silence can be found. The deviance of homosexuals or drug addicts is no secret. They have nothing to lose by a further exposure and may believe that an honest account of their lives will counter the stereotypes that have grown up about them. My own studies of dance musicians and marihuana users bear this out.[10] Marihuana users, particularly, urged me to finish my study quickly and publish it so that people could "know the truth" about them.

It may be thought that social science research exposes deviations only when the scientist has an ax to grind, when he is particularly interested in exposing evil. This is not the case. As Vidich and Bensman note:

▶ One of the principal ideas of our book is that the public atmosphere of an organization or a community tends to be optimistic, positive, and geared to the public relations image of the community or the organization. The public

---

10. The studies are reported in Becker, *Outsiders, op. cit.,* pp. 41–119.

mentality veils the dynamics and functional determinants of the group being studied. Any attempt in social analysis at presenting other than public relations rends the veil and must necessarily cause resentment. Moreover, any organization tends to represent a balance of divergent interests held in some kind of equilibrium by the power status of the parties involved. A simple description of these factors, no matter how stated, will offend some of the groups in question.[11] ◄

Unless the scientist deliberately restricts himself to research on the ideologies and beliefs of the people studied and does not touch on the behavior of the members of the community or organization, he must in some way deal with the disparity between reality and ideal, with the discrepancy between the number of crimes committed and the number of criminals apprehended. A study that purports to deal with social structure thus inevitably will reveal that the organization or community is not all it claims to be, not all it would like to be able to feel itself to be. A good study, therefore, will make somebody angry.

SELF-CENSORSHIP: A DANGER

I have just argued that a good study of a community or organization must reflect the irreconcilable conflict between the interests of science and the interests of those studied, and thereby provoke a hostile reaction. Yet many studies conducted by competent scientists do not have this consequence. Under what circumstances will the report of a study fail to provoke conflict? Can such a failure be justified?

In the simplest case, the social scientist may be taken in by those he studies and be kept from seeing the things that would cause conflict were he to report them. Melville Dalton states the problem for studies of industry.

► In no case did I make a formal approach to the top management of any of the firms to get approval or support for the research. Several times I have seen other researchers do this and have watched higher managers set the scene and limit the inquiry to specific areas—outside management proper—as though the problem existed in a vacuum. The findings in some cases were then regarded as "controlled experiments," which in final form made impressive reading. But the smiles and delighted manipulation of researchers by guarded personnel, the assessments made of researchers and their findings, and the frequently trivial areas to which alerted and fearful officers guided the inquiry—all raised questions about who controlled the experiments.[12] ◄

This is probably an uncommon occurrence. Few people social scientists study are sophisticated enough to anticipate or control what the researcher

---

11. Vidich and Bensman, "Comment," *op. cit.*, p. 4.

12. Melville Dalton, *Men Who Manage: Fusions of Feeling and Theory in Administration*, New York: Wiley, 1959, p. 275.

will see. More frequently, the social scientist takes himself in, "goes native," becomes identified with the ideology of the dominant faction in the organization or community and frames the questions to which his research provides answers so that no one will be hurt. He does not do this deliberately or with the intent to suppress scientific knowledge. Rather, he unwittingly chooses problems that are not likely to cause trouble or inconvenience to those he has found to be such pleasant associates. Herbert Butterfield, the British historian, puts the point well in his discussion of the dangers of "official history." He talks of the problems that arise when a government allows historians access to secret documents.

▶ A Foreign Secretary once complained that, while he, for his part, was only trying to be helpful, Professor Temperley (as one of the editors of the British Documents [On the Origins of the War of 1914]) persisted in treating him as though he were a hostile Power. Certainly it is possible for the historian to be unnecessarily militant, and even a little ungracious in his militancy; but what a satisfaction it is to the student if he can be sure that his interests have been guarded with unremitting jealousy! And if we employ a watchdog (which is the function the independent historian would be expected to perform on our behalf), what an assurance it is to be able to feel that we are served by one whom we know to be vigilant and unsleeping! The ideal, in this respect, would certainly not be represented by the picture of a Professor Temperley and a Foreign Secretary as thick as thieves, each merely thinking the other a jolly good fellow; for the historian who is collecting evidence—and particularly the historian who pretends as an independent authority to certify the documents or verify the claims of the government department—must be as jealous and importunate as the cad of a detective who has to find the murderer amongst a party of his friends. One of the widest of the general causes of historical error has been the disposition of a Macaulay to recognize in the case of Tory witnesses a need for historical criticism which it did not occur to him to have in the same way for the witnesses on his own side. Nothing in the whole of historiography is more subtly dangerous than the natural disposition to withhold criticism because John Smith belongs to one's own circle or because he is a nice man, so that it seems ungracious to try to press him on a point too far, or because it does not occur to one that something more could be extracted from him by importunate endeavor. In this sense all is not lost if our historian-detective even makes himself locally unpopular; for (to take an imaginary case) if he communicates to us his judgment that the Foreign Office does not burn important papers, the point is not without its interest; but we could only attach weight to the judgment if he had gone into the matter with all the alertness of an hostile enquirer and with the keenly critical view concerning the kind of evidence which could possibly authorise a detective to come to such a conclusion. And if an historian were to say: "This particular group of documents ought not to be published, because it would expose the officials concerned to serious misunderstandings," then we must answer that he has already thrown in his lot with officialdom—already he is thinking of their interests rather than ours; for since these documents, by definition, carry us outside the framework of stories somebody wants to impose on us, they are the very ones that the independent historian must most desire. To be sure, no documents can be published without laying many people open to grievous misunderstanding. In this connection an uncommon significance must attach therefore to the choice of the people who are to be spared. The only way to reduce misunderstanding is to keep up the clamour for more and more of the strategic kinds of evidence. . . .[13]

It is essential for everybody to be aware that the whole problem of "censorship" to-day has been transformed into the phenomenon of "auto-censorship"—a matter to be borne in mind even when the people involved are only indirectly the servants of government, or are attached by no further tie than the enjoyment of privileges that might be taken away. It is even true that where all are "pals" there is no need for censorship, no point where it is necessary to imagine that one man is being overruled by another. And in any case it is possible to conceive of a State in which members of different organizations could control or prevent a revelation with nothing more than a hint or a wink as they casually pass one another amidst the crowd at some tea-party.[14] ◀

Although Butterfield is speaking of the relations of the social scientist to a national government, it takes no great leap of imagination to see the relevance of his discussion to the problem of the sociologist who has studied a community or organization.

Finally, even if he is not deceived in either of the ways so far suggested, the social scientist may deliberately decide to suppress conflict-provoking findings. He may suppress his findings because publication will violate a bargain he has made with those studied. If, for example, he has given the subjects of his study the right to excise offensive portions of his manuscript prior to publication in return for the privilege of making the study, he will feel bound to honor that agreement. Because of the far-reaching consequences such an agreement could have, most social scientists take care to specify, when reaching an agreement with an organization they want to study, that they have the final say as to what will be published, though they often grant representatives of the organization the right to review the manuscript and suggest changes.

The social scientist may also suppress his findings because of an ideological commitment to the maintenance of society as it is now constituted. Shils makes the following case.

▶ Good arguments can be made against continuous publicity about public institutions. It could be claimed that extreme publicity not only breaks the confidentiality which enhances the imaginativeness and reflectiveness necessary for the effective working of institutions but also destroys the respect in which they should, at least tentatively, be held by the citizenry.[15] ◀

---

13. Herbert Butterfield, "Official History: Its Pitfalls and Criteria," in his *History and Human Relations,* London: Collins, 1951, pp. 194–195. Reprinted by permission of A. D. Peters & Co.

14. *Ibid.,* pp. 197–198.

15. Edward A. Shils, "Social Inquiry and the Autonomy of the Individual," in Danier Lerner, Ed., *Meaning of the Social Sciences,* New York: Meridian Books, 1959, p. 137. I am indebted to William Kornhauser for calling this article to my attention.

He believes that the first of these considerations is probably correct and thus constitutes a legitimate restriction on scientific inquiry, whereas the second, although not entirely groundless ethically, is so unlikely to occur as not to constitute a clear danger.

It is only in the case of deliberate suppression that an argument can be made, for in the other two cases the scientist presumably reports all his findings, the difficulty arising from his failure to make them in the first place. I will discuss the problem of the research bargain in the next section, in the context of possible solutions to the problem of publication. It remains only to consider Shils' argument before concluding that there is no reasonable basis for avoiding conflict over publication by failing to include the items that will provoke conflict.

Shils rests his case on the possibility that the publicity generated by research may interfere with the "effective working of institutions." When this occurs the scientist should restrict his inquiry. We can accept this argument only if we agree that the effective working of institutions as they are presently constituted is an overriding good. Shils, in his disdain for the "populistic" frame of mind that has informed much of American sociology (his way of characterizing the "easy-going irreverence toward authority" and the consequent tendency to social criticism among social scientists), is probably more ready to accept such a proposition than the majority of working social scientists. Furthermore, and I do not know that he would carry his argument so far, the right of public institutions to delude themselves about the character of their actions and the consequences of those actions does not seem to me easily defended.

POSSIBLE SOLUTIONS

An apparently easy solution to the dilemma of publishing findings and interpretations that may harm those studied is to decide that if a proper bargain has been struck at the beginning of a research relationship no one has any right to complain. If the researcher has agreed to allow those studied to censor his report, he cannot complain when they do. If the people studied have been properly warned, in sufficient and graphic detail, of the consequences of a report about them and have still agreed to have a study done, then they cannot complain if the report is not what they would prefer. But the solution, from the point of view of either party, ignores the real problems.

From the scientist's point of view, the problem is only pushed back a step. Instead of asking what findings he should be prepared to publish, we ask what bargain he should be prepared to strike. Considering only his own scientific interests, he should clearly drive the hardest bargain, demanding complete freedom, and should settle for less only when he must in order to gain access to a theoretically important class of institutions that would otherwise be closed to him.

When we look at the problem from the side of those studied, reaching a firm bargain is also only an apparent solution. As Roth pointed out,[16] the people who agree to have a social scientist study them have not had the experience before and do not know what to expect; nor are they aware of the experience of others social scientists have studied. Even if the social scientist has pointed out the possible consequences of a report, the person whose organization or community is to be studied is unlikely to think it will happen to him; he cannot believe this fine fellow, the social scientist with whom he now sees eye to eye, would actually do something to harm him. He thinks the social scientist, being a fine fellow, will abide by the ethics of the group under study, not realizing the force and scope of the scientist's impersonal ethic and, particularly, of the scientific obligation to report findings fully and frankly. He may feel easy, having been assured that no specific item of behavior will be attributed to any particular person, but will he think of the "tone" of the report, said to be offensive to the inhabitants of Springdale?

Making a proper research bargain, then, is no solution to the problem of publication. Indeed, with respect to the question of *what to publish*, I think there is no general solution except as one may be dictated by the individual's conscience. But there are other questions and it is possible to take constructive action on them without prejudicing one's right to publish. The social scientist can warn those studied of the effect of publication and help them prepare for it. When his report is written he can help those concerned to assimilate what it says and adjust to the consequences of being reported on publicly.

It is probably true that the first sociological report on a given kind of institution sits least well, and that succeeding studies are less of a shock to those studied, creating fewer problems both for the researcher and those he studies. The personnel of the first mental hospital or prison studied by sociologists probably took it harder than those of similar institutions studied later. Once the deviations characteristic of a whole class of institutions have been exposed they are no longer secrets peculiar to one. Subsequent reports have less impact. They only affirm that the deviations found in one place also exist elsewhere. Those whose institutions are the subject of later reports can only suffer from having it shown that they have the same faults, a lesser crime than being the only place where such deviations occur. The difference between "In this mental hospital attendants beat patients" and "In this mental hospital *also*, attendants beat patients" may seem small, but the consequences of the difference are large and important.

By having those he studies read earlier reports on their kind of institution or community, the social scientist can lead them to understand that what he reports about them is not unique. By making available to them other studies, which describe similar deviations in other kinds of institutions and communi-

16. Roth, *op. cit.*

ties, he can teach them that the deviations whose exposure they fear are in fact characteristic features of all human organizations and societies. Thus a carefully thought out educational program may help those reported on come to terms with what the scientist reports, and spare both parties unnecessary difficulties.

The program might take the form of a series of seminars or conversations, in which the discussion would move from a consideration of social science in general to studies of similar institutions, culminating in a close analysis of the about-to-be published report. In analyzing the report the social scientist can point out the two contexts in which publication will have meaning for those it describes.

First, is can affect their relations with other groups outside the institution: the press, the public, national professional organizations, members of other professions, clients, citizens' watchdog groups, and so on. By describing facts about the organization that may be interpreted as deviations by outside groups, the social scientist may endanger the institution's position with them. Second, the publication of descriptions of deviation may add fuel to internal political fires.[17] The social scientist, by discussing the report with those it describes, can help them to face these problems openly and warn them against one-sided interpretations of his data and analyses. For instance, he can help them to see the kinds of interpretations that may be made of his report by outside groups, aid them in assessing the possibility of serious damage (which they are likely to overestimate), and let them test on him possible answers they might make to adverse reaction.

If he confers with institutional personnel, he will no doubt be present when various people attempt to make use of his work in a selective or distorted way for internal political advantage, when they cite fragments of his conclusions in support of a position they have taken on some institutional or community issue. He can then, at the moment it takes place, correct the distortion or selective citation and force those involved to see the issue in more complete perspective.

In conferring with representatives of the institution or community, the social scientist should keep two things in mind. First, although he should be sensitive to the damage his report might do, he should not simply take complaints and make revisions so that the complaints will cease. Even with his best efforts, the complaints may remain, because an integral part of his analysis has touched on some chronic sore point in the organization; if this is the case, he must publish his report without changing the offending portions. Second, his conferences with representatives of the organization should not simply be attempts to softsoap them into believing that no damage will occur

---

17. The danger of exposure to external publics is most salient in studies of institutions; the danger of exposure of deviation within the group studied is most important in studies of communities.

when, in fact, it may. He must keep this possibility alive for them and make them take it seriously; unless he does, he is only postponing the complaints and difficulties to a later time when reactions to the report, within and outside the organization, will bring them out in full strength. In this connection it is useful to make clear to those studied that the preliminary report, if that is what they are given, is slated for publication in some form, even though it may be substantially revised; this fact is sometimes forgotten and many criticisms that would be made if it were clear that the document was intended for publication are not made, with the result that the process must be gone through again when the final version is prepared.

People whose organizations have been studied by social scientists often complain that the report made about them is "pessimistic" or "impractical," and their complaint points to another reason for their anger. Insofar as the report gives the impression that the facts and situations it describes are irremediable, it puts them in the position of being chronic offenders for whom there is no hope. Although some social science reports have such a pessimistic tone, it is more often the case that the report makes clear that there are no easy solutions to the organization's problems. There are solutions, but they are solutions that call for major changes in organizational practice, and for this reason they are likely to be considered impractical. The social scientist can explain that there are no panaceas, no small shifts in practice that will do away with the "evils" his report describes without in any way upsetting existing arrangements, and thus educate those he has studied to the unpleasant truth that they cannot change the things they want to change without causing repercussions in other parts of the organization.[18] By the same token, however, he can point to the directions in which change is possible, even though difficult, and thus relieve them of the oppressive feeling that they have no way out.

A regime of conferring with and educating those studied may seem like an additional and unwelcome job for the social scientist to take on. Is it not difficult enough to do the field work, analyze the data, and prepare a report, without taking on further obligations? Why not finish the work and leave, letting someone else bear the burden of educating the subjects of the study? Although flight may often seem the most attractive alternative, the social scientist should remember that, in the course of working over his report with those it describes, he may get some extremely useful data. For instance, in the course of discussions about the possible effect of the report on various audiences, it is possible to discover new sources of constraint on the actors involved that had not turned up in the original study. One may be told about sources on inhibition of change that are so pervasive as to never have been

18. See the discussion of panaceas in Howard S. Becker and Blanche Geer, "Medical Education," in Howard E. Freeman, Leo G. Reeder, and Sol Levine, Eds., *Handbook of Medical Sociology*, Englewood Cliffs, N.J.: Prentice-Hall, 1963, pp. 180–184.

mentioned until a discussion of change, occasioned by the report, brings them to light. The desire for further data, coupled with simple altruism and the desire to avoid trouble, may prove sufficiently strong motive for an educational effort.

CONCLUSION

In discussing the several facets of the problem, I have avoided stating any ethical canons. I have relied on those canons implicit in the scientific enterprise in suggesting that the scientist must strive for the freest possible conditions of reporting. Beyond that I have said only that it is a matter of individual conscience. In so restricting my remarks and in discussing the problem largely in technical terms, I have not meant to indicate that one need have no conscience at all, but only that it must remain a matter of individual judgment.

I ought properly, therefore, to express my own judgment. Briefly, it is that one should refrain from publishing items of fact or conclusions that are not necessary to one's argument or that would cause suffering out of proportion to the scientific gain of making them public. This judgment is of course ambiguous. When is something "necessary" to an argument? What is "suffering"? When is an amount of suffering "out of proportion"? Even though the statement as it stands cannot determine a clear line of action for any given situation, I think it does suggest a viable vantage point, an appropriate mood, from which decisions can be approached. In particular, it suggests on the one hand that the scientist must be able to give himself good reasons for including potentially harmful material, rather than including it simply because it is "interesting." On the other hand, it guards him against either an overly formal or an overly sentimental view of the harm those he studies may suffer, requiring that it be serious and substantial enough to warrant calling it "suffering." Finally, it insists that he know enough about the situation he has studied to know whether the suffering will in any sense be proportional to gains science may expect from publication of his findings.

The judgment I have expressed is clearly not very original. Nor is it likely that any judgment expressed by a working social scientist would be strikingly original. All the reasonable positions have been stated long ago. The intent of this paper has been to show that a sociological understanding of what we do when we publish potentially harmful materials may help us make the ethical decisions that we must, inevitably, make alone.

Becker suggests, then, that publication of results entails not simply an ethical problem but also a political problem. The former arises from the researcher's obligation to observe at once the scientific ethic of seeking uncompromised truth and the general ethic of not causing harm to others. Becker maintains, however, that the nature of sociological research itself is such that harm, real or feared, will always be done to some subjects. Therefore, the essentially political question arises "To whom shall harm be done in this study, in what magnitude?"

Given this perspective, Becker suggests that any solutions to the problem of what to publish are political adjudications of interests (though guided by the conflicting ethical principles previously mentioned).

This insight is elaborated in the following selection by Lee Rainwater and David Pittman, which shifts the focus from the study of a group or association to the study of a politically sensitive *community*. The selection is of additional interest in that it deals not only with publication of results in ordinary scientific media but with publicity in the broadest sense.

ETHICAL PROBLEMS IN STUDYING A
POLITICALLY SENSITIVE AND DEVIANT COMMUNITY

LEE RAINWATER AND DAVID J. PITTMAN

INTRODUCTION

Ethical issues have meaning only in relation to their human contexts; and the ethically relevant decisions that social scientists make can best be understood by a self-conscious awareness of the interaction between the abstract principles brought to bear and the concrete social situation in which they must be acted upon. This paper deals with a set of ethical issues that have arisen during the conduct of a research dealing with various forms of deviant and problem behavior in a public housing project on which the spotlight of publicity and political interest has shone for over ten years. From such a case study certain more general implications concerning ethical issues in social problems can be drawn. Rather than attempt an inventory of the ethical issues that have arisen during the two years the study has been in progress, we will choose issues that we feel are neither completely familiar nor part of the conventional wisdom of our profession. The issues dealt with are, also, ones that have seemed crucial to the direction and continuation of the research.

Reprinted from Lee Rainwater and David J. Pittman, "Ethical Problems in Studying a Politically Sensitive and Deviant Community," *Social Problems* (1967), **14,** 357–366, by permission of the authors and publisher.

Author's note: This paper is based in part on research aided by a grant from the National Institute of Mental Health, Grant No. MH-09189, "Social and Community Problems in Public Housing Areas," to the Social Science Institute of Washington University. Many of the ideas presented stem from discussion with the senior members of the Pruitt-Igoe Research Staff—Alvin W. Gouldner and Jules Henry—and with the research associates and research assistants on the project.

THE ORIGIN OF THE PRUITT-IGOE RESEARCH

The Pruitt-Igoe Housing projects were planned in the early 1950's and first occupied in 1954.   Originally the plan was to build two segregated projects, Pruitt for Negroes, and Igoe, across the street, for whites.   This plan was ruled unconstitutional, however, and after a short period of integration the project became all-Negro.   Currently, there are some 2,762 apartments in forty-three eleven-story buildings near the downtown area of St. Louis.   The project has the highest vacancy rate of any public housing complex in the country; twenty-seven per cent of the available units are vacant.   Sixty-two per cent of the households receive some kind of welfare assistance, and forty-five per cent of the households with minors are supported by ADC.   It should be clear from such a very brief description that this is a neighborhood in which social problems and deviant behavior abound.   We will indicate below why the housing project is also subject to a great deal of political interest.

By 1959 the Project had become a community scandal both because of certain unattractive design features (for example, the elevators stop only on the fourth, seventh and tenth floors), and as a result of the wide publicity given to crimes (rape, murder, robbery) and accidents (people fell down elevator shafts and children fell out of windows in the Project).   In response to the steady unfavorable publicity and a grand jury investigation of the project, former Mayor Tucker of St. Louis appointed in 1960 a Committee on Public Housing and Social Services that included representatives of business, labor, and the general public as well as the various private and public agencies whose services and facilities were available to public housing residents.[1]   The Committee directed its primary attention to Pruitt-Igoe, "because it had been much in the public eye and because the tangle of needs and services present and potential, could be grappled with in the smaller area first."   By February, 1961, the Committee had presented both its findings of fact and its recommendations.

About the same time in Washington the Federal Government's concern with urban problems was quickening.   The President's Committee on Juvenile Delinquency and Youth Crime, which had been the main instrumentality of Federal interest, had been supplemented by a Joint Task Force of the Public Housing Administration and the Department of Health, Education, and Welfare, which came to be most centrally concerned with "Community Planning for Concerted Services in Public Housing."   Concerted services meant that special efforts would be made in selected demonstration areas to maximize the input of social services and to maximize the coordination of these services.   St. Louis, because considerable interest at the local level had been evidenced in the problems of public housing and welfare services, was selected as the first city for a

---

1.   See Nicholas J. Demerath, "St. Louis Public Housing Study Sets Off Community Development to Meet Social Needs," *Journal of Housing*, Vol. XIX, No. 8, October 15, 1962.

demonstration of the concerted services program. It was planned that accompanying the concerted services program would be a research project to study the community and to evaluate the effectiveness of the concerted services. To fund this research the Joint Task Force in Washington drew on the Special Projects Branch of the National Institute of Mental Health, and negotiations were begun with the Social Science Institute of Washington University. In the course of these negotiations the original principal investigators (Gouldner, Pittman and Gilbert Shapiro) expressed considerable doubt about the possibility of systematically evaluating the proposed concerted services program since no one knew exactly what the program would involve, or indeed whether it would involve anything more than a slight increase of activity by the social welfare professions in the project. In the end, therefore, the research was designated as a basic social science research and was "not conceived primarily as an engineering task to measure the effectiveness of such actual programs as might be instituted by federal or local agencies." Instead, the primary objective was "diagnostic." The research would seek to perform a "basic analysis of the conditions underlying the pathological behavior currently found in urban public housing, and hopefully, in new proposals for social remedies for these pathologies." In other words, the research was not to be tied to the activities of the concerted services program but would be independent of them. The basic charter of the research project was, then, that of a broad community study in the social anthropological tradition.[2]

COMMUNITY INTEREST IN THE RESEARCH

There was a high level of public interest and dismay concerning the Pruitt-Igoe project. This interest was kept alive by constant newspaper publicity, first about crime and other difficulties in the project, later by the efforts of Mayor Tucker and his Committee to come to terms with the problem, and still later by the Federally-sponsored Concerted Services Program. When the research project grant of three-quarters of a million dollars was announced in the

---

2.   In the course of two years' work we have made use of some ten research assistants to carry out intensive participant observation and open ended interviewing with the residents of the project and, in particular cases, slum inhabitants who live outside the project. Through time, the overall study has been broken down to substudies dealing with particular institutions. These substudies include: studies of the history of the administration and management of public housing in St. Louis; of internal family dynamics of tenant families; of the street system or peer group system of young adults in the project; of the elementary schools in the area; and of a Missionary Baptist Church which many of the tenants attend. In addition, other substudies are concentrating on particular kinds of behavior; on drinking behavior, on how men go about finding jobs and what they do when they're unemployed, on female homosexuality, and on voluntary association activity within the project.

Spring of 1963, it, too, made the front pages. (After all, before the War on Poverty began that was a lot of money.)

From the time the research grant was announced, then, we were called by various agencies and the press for information. Even before we had been in the field three months we were being asked by the Housing Authority and various welfare agencies to provide consultation and to discuss our findings about whatever matters concerned the agency making the request. The newspapers and television stations were interested in whatever we might have to say about the housing projects and their problems; their desire for "juicy" copy was ill-concealed each time they called.

It was clear from the way many of these requests were made that there was involved not only the question of a desire for information or advice, but also a concern about how our research, and the findings it would produce, would affect the vested interests of the agencies calling. To a considerable extent this stemmed from a general misapprehension that we were evaluating the concerted services program, but behind that was an awareness that what we found about the project community, and the way it related to the larger world, would inevitably bring up questions about whether each agency was doing its job as it should.

THE RESEARCH AND THE PRESS

The problem of coping with pressure from news media proved a fairly simple one. We established a policy of not discussing the research with the press, telling them that we would rather not be drawn into premature statements about the housing project and its problems, nor would we give any newspaper or television interviews in which Pruitt-Igoe was likely to be discussed. It was not easy to convince the press that we really meant this and at the same time not antagonize them; since one of the principal investigators (Pittman) has for several years been very much involved in consulting with various local governmental agencies, St. Louis newsmen are used to calling on him for a social science view of community welfare and racial problems. After repeated statements to various members of the press continuing over several months' time, the request for material about the Pruitt-Igoe Study decreased significantly.

From our point of view, this policy of not talking to the press about the research represented a solution to both an ethical and a practical issue. Ethically, we did not want to be in a position of asserting findings before we were really sure of what we knew, and, practically, we did not want to have anything said that would have repercussions either in the field work or on the maintenance of necessary cooperation with various institutions connected with the Housing Project.

ETHICS IN RELATION TO SPONSORSHIP

While many ethical issues cut across the question of sponsorship and one's charter for conducting the research, some of the most difficult ones stem from the effort to reconcile the legitimate demands of professional standards, the sponsor's needs, and the elusive public interest. In our case, the pressure of various groups for access to our findings forced us to think through the questions of exactly the nature of our sponsorship and of who the "client" to whom we were responsible was.

As we have said, many agencies wanted consultation and access to our findings—the Housing Authority felt it had a legitimate need to know, other welfare agencies were calling at the rate of at least one or two a month. Student social action groups wanted help in their efforts to solve some of the problems of the Project neighborhood, and a church action group accused us of "suppressing findings" which they felt we had. We very much needed the cooperation of some of these people, and we are closely identified with some goals of the action groups. Therefore, there was a strong temptation to be selectively accommodating to these various requests. Yet we felt uncomfortable about communicating findings and ideas which we felt sure would become matters of controversial interest. Since we were not ready to make our findings public and generally available, we felt uneasy about talking to some groups and giving them information not available to others.

The only way out of the day-to-day dilemmas that these requests presented seemed to be to enunciate to ourselves and then to others a clear statement of the implications of the sponsorship of the study. We told ourselves that this research was sponsored by the National Institute of Mental Health as a basic social science study that hopefully would have some practical relevance. Since our charter came from a grant to carry out a basic research, we felt it was clear that our "client" was the public in general, anyone who wished to learn what we had learned. This meant that we had no right to communicate our findings selectively. Since we could not communicate our findings and implications about these crucial public issues until we were very sure of our findings, we established as an ethical principle that we would not give formal presentations to any group until we were ready to publish our findings in an appropriate way and to discuss them with anyone who was interested. This is the way we responded to requests for written summaries of our findings by organizations or to requests from individuals who were active in the area. For example, we said that we were not willing to give written materials to the Housing Authority until we were able to report formally and to discuss our findings with other groups.

It was necessary to backslide from this principle a little in connection with the Housing Authority. We needed their cooperation; we wanted to meet with them to ask questions about the operation of their Authority, and we wanted their permission to observe management processes. We felt bound by the norm of reciprocity to consult with them verbally and informally, and to make tentative statements about how tenants felt about problems in return for their cooperation beyond the level that could be formally required of them, given our sponsorship by the Housing and Home Finance Agency. However, the fact that we spelled out to ourselves and to them the ethical principle involved went a long way toward reducing the requests for specific kinds of information, and in guiding us as to just how far to go in our discussions with them. In addition, this ethical principle guided us in deciding not to request assistance and information from some agencies because we did not want to reciprocate. Thus, although we very much wanted leads into drug-using groups in the Project, we did not ask the Police Narcotics Squad for such leads since we knew that they would expect in return information about what we were learning. (We had to wait about a year before we were able to obtain access to drug-users on our own.)

It is important to note that under a different kind of sponsorship some of these issues would not have arisen. If the Housing Authority had been our sponsor, we could ethically have talked only to them without specific permission to do otherwise. If we had been doing a contract study for the Public Housing Administration, then we could ethically report only to them. And the same would have been the case if we had been carrying out the study for a tenant action group. But, it seemed to us that sponsorship by the public requires that, although the researcher has a right to take sides in controversy surrounding the subject of his research and to work actively for one side, he nevertheless has the responsibility to communicate his findings in forms that make them essentially equally available to all sides.

The social context in which we formulated this ethical guide for our research, and communicated it to relevant others, brought home to us a general truth about ethical principles that we think is important. This is that one's statement of an ethical *obligation* inevitably also involves an assertion of a *right* to fulfill that obligation. Others may be reluctant to grant that right and they may advance diverse notions about what is ethical in the situation. This happened in our case. Some agencies were reluctant to accept our statement that we could not communicate with any one group until we were ready to communicate with all groups. Viewed sociologically, with the doubting eyes of an Everett Hughes, our concern with ethics can be seen as also a concern with our rights, and an effort to legitimate those rights in the eyes of other institutions and the public. This can create a very sticky situation if others are not willing to recognize our right to behave ethically (for example, by preserving confidential relations with our informants).

ETHICS AND THE DAMAGE TRUTH MAY DO

Another ethical aspect of the public interest in our study arose not in relations with outsiders but within our own group. Some of the fifteen faculty and graduate student researchers expressed concern early in the study over the effect a really penetrating analysis of the style of life of poor Negroes might have on the public dialogue about race relations and poverty. That is, if one describes in full and honest detail behavior which the public will regard as immoral, degraded, deviant, and criminal, will not the effect be to damage the very people we hope our study will eventually help? We have heard such views offered by others, by eminent social scientists in universities and in government. The question is generally phrased something along the following line, "How do you know that the constructive effect of our research will outweigh the damage to the reputations of the people we study? Our science isn't that good yet. Maybe all that will happen is that we will strengthen prejudices and provide rationalizations for bigotry."

This is a knotty issue, and one which perhaps can only be resolved by an act of faith. If you believe that in the long run truth makes men freer and more autonomous, then you are willing to run the risk that some people will use the facts you turn up and the interpretations you make to fight a rear guard action. If you don't believe this, if you believe instead that truth may or may not free men depending on the situation, even in the long run, then perhaps it is better to avoid these kinds of research subjects. We say perhaps it is better, because it seems to us that a watered-down set of findings would violate other ethical standards, and would have little chance of providing practical guides to action; thus it would hardly be worth the expenditure of one's time and someone else's money.

At the level of strategy, however, this concern for the effect of findings on public issues sensitizes one to the question of how research results will be interpreted by others, and to his responsibility to anticipate probable misuses, and from this anticipation attempt to counteract the possibility of misuse. That is, though we do not feel a researcher must avoid telling the truth because it may hurt a group (problems of confidentiality aside) we do believe that he must take this possibility into account in presenting his findings and make every reasonable effort to deny weapons to potential misusers.

For example, several years ago one of us published a study analyzing the problems of motivation and marital role difficulty that lead lower class women to be poor family planners.[3] The study was commissioned by the Planned Parenthood Federation of America in hope of learning how to operate their clinics more effectively. The findings indicated that most lower class women could not sustain the kinds of habits required to practice contraception effectively with the then existing methods (this was before the introduction of the "pill" and the intrauterine device). During the two years after the study appeared, there was considerable agitation in several cities and states to establish family planning services in public health and welfare facilities. In

---

3. Lee Rainwater, *And the Poor Get Children: Sex, Contraception, and Family Planning in the Working Class,* Chicago: Quadrangle Books, Inc., 1960.

the course of the controversy that ensued several officials who opposed the establishment of family planning services in this way quoted the study to support their contention that lower class women really did not want help in limiting their families. In examining what he had written, the author realized that he had not taken this possibility into account at all, although knowing the strong feelings people have about family planning and contraception he should have known better. He had not made crystal clear that there was no question but that these lower class women wanted fewer children, even though they needed a good deal of help in realizing that desire. In his desire to get at the problems that created difficulties in Planned Parenthood's clinic organization, he had not sufficiently emphasized the wishes that lower class women have for some kind of really effective help in family limitation.

Another example of the misuse of social science findings can be found in controversies dealing with problems of integration and segregation. Much recent research on the problems of slums and ghettos has emphasized the destructive effects of lower class family and neighborhood systems. The authors of these studies clearly hope that by understanding the dynamics of slum living it will be possible to develop programs that do not fail as present housing, welfare, and retraining programs seem to be failing. However, since these researchers deal with the internal dynamics of the ghetto, their findings can prove quite attractive to individuals and institutions that seek to perpetuate containment of Negroes in segregated areas. Recently Rainwater testified for the National Association for the Advancement of Colored People in a de facto segregation suit against the Cincinnati School Board. In direct testimony he said some very elementary things about the destructive effects of going to a ghetto school and thus contributed to the plaintiff's case that de facto segregation, as much as legal segregation, affects negatively the "hearts and minds" of Negro children and therefore violates the due process clause of the Fourteenth Amendment. However, on cross-examination he found himself exposed to a fairly sophisticated line of questioning that sought to have him "admit" that the low achievement scores and high drop-out rate of Negro children in ghetto schools have nothing to do with the fact that these schools are "racially imbalanced" but rather is due to the home and neighborhood environment. The Board of Education obviously felt that it had a defense against the plaintiff's charges which was validated by social science research on Negro slum family and neighborhood behavior. This is apparently a popular defense by boards of education in several parts of the country. They seek to substantiate the view that ghetto schools do not damage Negro children but that the damage is instead done by the family and the neighborhood over which the schools have no control. Indeed, we have heard of one other social scientist expert witness in a de facto segregation case who was cross-examined for five days along exactly this line. In that case the court was not impressed and found for the plaintiffs, but given the jaundiced eyes with which courts view social science testimony anyway, it seems likely that more often the effect of such "conflicting" findings will be beneficial to the case of those who wish to maintain a segregated school system.

It probably would have been difficult to anticipate such a sophisticated misuse of research findings before the fact. After all, that families may damage their children says nothing about whether schools do or do not also damage the same children. But once we know that such misuse is being made of the products of our discipline, perhaps we have a responsibility to try to do something about it, much as psychologists have done with the misuses of intelligence test data on racial groups. Perhaps we need some kind of "intelligence service" which appraises us of this kind of misuse so that in our subsequent writings we can make it less easy for people to misuse the findings and also so that as a group we can make efforts to counteract this kind of misinterpretation.

More generally, it seems evident that as sociology is more and more accepted as of relevance to the important issues the country must cope with, what sociologists have to say will be increasingly fateful in the lives of individuals and groups. It behooves us then, not only to study significant problems and report our findings accurately, but also to be sensitive to the way these findings are used, particularly to whether or not they are used in ways that seem illegitimate, given the findings. In this respect sociologists will come increasingly to have the same kinds of problems that historians, political scientists, economists, and psychologists have had for some time.

PROBLEMS OF CONFIDENTIALITY

Confidentiality is perhaps the most familiar ethical question in our business. Confidentiality for our informants is our stock in trade, as it is for journalists. The question of confidentiality in research is of a rather different order, however, from the confidentiality that physicians, priests, and lawyers offer their clients. They are *asked* for help; the right of privileged communication is deemed necessary if they are to be able to serve their clients. The right involved is essentially that of the client and by extension only, that of the professional. In our case we use the promise of confidentiality as an *inducement* to informants for their cooperation. This places a double kind of responsibility on us; we are bound by the right of privacy of the informant *and* by the fact that we made a commitment as an inducement to gain cooperation and are ethically bound to honor that commitment.

The simplest problem of confidentiality is that of protecting the identity of individual informants. We maintain that, once having given the promise of confidentiality, we have an obligation not to reveal any information we possess which could identify an individual or connect him with what he has told us. Most of the time this is a simple, routine matter—one deals with large samples of more or less anonymous members of a collectivity; the variability within the group makes it impossible to attribute particular behavior to any one member so long as his identity is concealed. The main practical issue is that one must not take this principle so much for granted that he forgets to honor it. Typically, in survey work, names and other identifying information are left on questionnaires because we assume that no one outside the research group will have access to the information. That is, we believe we have the right to, and can, control access to documents which could identify the individuals we have talked to. But, suppose our interviews were subpoenaed by some authority (and this is not an idle speculation)? If this is a possibility, or becomes a possibility in the course of a research, then we are bound to think of ways of protecting the identity of our informants.

We might wish to claim a legal right to privileged communication—but apparently we have no such right and little reason to believe we might be granted it since journalists have made no progress on this score. Being aware of the possibility of having our records subpoenaed, however, we can take precautions. We can arrange to obliterate identifying information on records. We can obtain a clear legal definition of who can and who cannot subpoena us and exactly what kind of control they can exercise over our records. Also, it seems to us, we must face up to the necessity if all else fails of having to engage in one or another kind of "hanky panky" to preserve the informant's anonymity where the courts will not sustain that right. In short, we are saying that if other people will leave you alone the ethical task of maintaining the anonymity of informants is a fairly simple one of being careful. However, where others have an interest in reducing the confidentiality you want to maintain, and are prepared to buttress this with legal sanctions, it becomes a difficult and uncomfortable problem—one which we present more for discussion than as something we have solved.

The problem of confidentiality becomes much more complicated when the group one studies is small, and when the individuals in it are necessarily considered responsible for the behavior of all the other members as well as their own. In such a situation there is really no way of presenting findings about the group and at the same time protecting their identities.

Much as we dislike the idea of sociologists following the same well-trod road of professionalism followed by our colleagues, the psychologists, it seems to us that the whole question of confidentiality in politically sensitive situations may be one that needs attention from the profession.

IS A CONFIDENTIAL RELATION
WITH THE INFORMANT ALWAYS DESIRABLE?

The traditions of our field emphasize anonymity as necessary and desirable in research. We generally think of ourselves as studying social behavior about which our informants are protective. They may be protective because their deepest interests are involved, or for reasons that are less vital, but it is traditional to honor our subjects' wish that what we learn about them not be communicated to a larger public in any way that will affect their interests or identify them. Confidentiality is deemed technically necessary, and once it is offered we are ethically bound to honor our promise.

However, there are some situations for which the offer of confidentiality may be both unnecessary and technically a bad choice. In some situations the applicability of research findings to applied goals will be rendered almost impossible if true confidentiality is maintained. And in some other situations it may be impossible to communicate the findings once the informants have been told that what we see and hear will be kept confidential.

It seems to us that we should rethink our automatic assumption that we offer to maintain the privacy of our informants. The question of whether or not to make such an offer demands a conscious and thoughtful decision that is made in the light of needs and goals of a particular research. Let us offer a couple of examples of situations in which confidentiality has not been offered and then suggest a principle which underlies these examples.

In our Pruitt-Igoe research, we have not made promises of confidentiality to anyone in the Housing Authority management. We have not done so since we feel that were the information we collect from them regarded as confidential it would not be possible to publish a sensible report of our findings. This applies both to individual functionaries in the Housing Authority and to the Authority as an organization. We cannot possibly conceal the identity of this particular Project when we publish our results. We must be free to identify the organization and its various constituent units. Similarly we could not possibly discuss the role of the Executive Director of the Housing Authority or of the Project Managers without their being identified as particular persons. While in the end we might adopt some cover of pseudonyms it would be more to avoid becoming enmeshed in questions of personality than to prevent the identification of the actual persons involved. Thus, while we feel that no useful purpose would be served by not concealing the identities of the tenants in the Project and of the low level employees, at the higher reaches of the organization our presumably useful purpose can be served only by openness about the identities of the organization and the top level executives involved. These persons know that it is possible that our study will have unpleasant repercussions on them, but they also are used to being exposed to the light of publicity.

An excellent example of this point is provided by David Sudnow's study of public defenders.[4] It would not be too hard for someone in the San Francisco Bay Area to identify which particular city's public defenders are being described, and a newspaper editor might easily pick up the study to accomplish quite a bit of social, or at least personnel, change. Indeed, given the findings of

---

4. David Sudnow, "Normal Crimes: Sociological Features of the Penal Code in a Public Defender Office," *Social Problems*, Vol. XII, No. 3, 1965.

the study, that would be a very worthwhile thing to have happen. Yet if Sudnow had promised his public defenders anonymity, he could hardly have presented his findings as fully as he did; indeed, it would have been hard for him to present any findings at all. Yet, the research has a great deal of social value as well as intrinsic basic sociological interest; we imagine that one would not even think of the issue of confidentiality were he not already sensitive to the problem.

The decision not to promise confidentiality makes explicit our claim to a *right* to study social behavior in certain situations. Obviously we do not claim the right to study all kinds of behavior in non-confidential ways and to make public our findings, but we do and should study certain kinds of behavior in this way. As an initial formulation, we suggest that sociologists have the right (and perhaps also the obligation) to study publicly accountable behavior. By publicly accountable behavior we do not simply mean the behavior of public officials (though there the case is clearest) but also the behavior of any individual as he goes about performing public or secondary roles for which he is socially accountable—this would include businessmen, college teachers, physicians, etc.; in short, all people as they carry out jobs for which they are in some sense publicly accountable. One of the functions of our discipline, along with those of political science, history, economics, journalism, and intellectual pursuits generally, is to further public accountability in a society whose complexity makes it easier for people to avoid their responsibilities.

We would suggest that, in principle, anyone is publicly accountable for the actions which it is his duty to perform. Most of the time, however, since sociologists are not muckrakers, it is not necessary or desirable to single out individuals or even clearly identifiable small groups. In such situations one may reasonably use confidentiality as an inducement to cooperation. In other situations, however, this is clearly unwarranted. If one wishes to study the functioning of courts, or of a mayor's office, or of General Motors, or of unions, it is perhaps better to put up with the difficulties of only doing what one can do without promising to keep information confidential. Since publicly accountable individuals often recognize the fact of their accountability and the useful purposes that might be served by sociologists studying them, one can often gain a good deal of cooperation without the promise of confidentiality.[5]

We are suggesting that sociologists in this respect have the same rights that journalists have. Our understanding of the social process may be such that we do not use this right in the same way as journalists, because we are not interested in momentary sensations but in developing an understanding of the persisting tendencies of social systems, large or small.

---

5. Clearly the question of methodology is also involved here. It is easier to maintain the position we have outlined if the methods used are primarily observational (as was true of Sudnow's work) than it is with interviewing methods where the interaction of the interviewer and respondent may more easily generate expectations of confidentiality which must be dealt with in some forthright fashion.

This observed trend toward broadening ethical concerns to include political aspects is demonstrated in the excellent volume, *Ethics, Politics, and Social Research.*[6] Among the many issues dealt with in Sjoberg's book, three represent important continuities with the Rainwater and Pittman selection above; rethinking of the confidentiality promise;[7] community political pressures,[8] and relations between researchers and their sponsors.[9]

---

6.   Sjoberg (1967).
7.   Colvard (1967).
8.   Brymer and Faris (1967).
9.   Orlans (1967); Record (1967); Goldner (1967).

CHAPTER EIGHT

COMPARISON
OF
METHODS

Throughout this book participant observation has been compared and contrasted, explicitly and tacitly, to other research procedures in the social sciences in order to define and illuminate its distinctive characteristics. Because these other procedures have been well codified while participant observation has not, such comparison has been useful in locating the major issues regarding participant observation.

In this concluding chapter, however, we wish to broaden the considerations upon which such comparison might be made. The methodological literature contains a number of important papers which compare participant observation to other research procedures, not with regard to specific operational differences, but with regard to overall results of their applications.

Some of these papers seek to *evaluate the validity* of participant observation results by showing that they sustain conclusions identical to those derived from the more conventional procedures. Such comparison is certainly valuable in light of the many unusual features we have found to be characteristic of participant observation and in light of its lack of methodological codification. The following selection by Donald Campbell, comparing the results of participant observation with those of survey research, is particularly important because Campbell is perhaps the leading methodologist in experimental psychology.

THE INFORMANT IN
QUANTITATIVE RESEARCH

DONALD T. CAMPBELL

Among the several contributions of anthropology to general social science methodology, the technique of utilizing informants has received relatively little systematic attention. The present report deals with an exploratory use of informants in research focused upon the evaluation of morale as an adjunct to a study in naval leadership.[1]

Reprinted from *American Journal of Sociology* (1955), **60,** 339–342, by permission of the author and The University of Chicago Press.

1. This study was supported by a contract from the Office of Naval Research to Ohio State University, N6ori-17 T.O. 111 NR 171 123. It has been more fully reported in the research report issued by the Personnel Research Board, Ohio State University, "A Study of Leadership among Submarine Officers" (1953).

There are at least two ways in which the use of the informant may be interpreted as a general social science tool. On the one hand, it may be considered as a sampling technique, in which any normal participant in the society could substitute for any other. The use of only one or a few individuals is justified where the culture is homogeneous and where there are no relevant individual differences in the knowledge or behavior in question. Were this interpretation of the technique to be generalized for rigorous application to complex Western cultures, it would take the form of opinion-survey procedures with methodological emphasis upon representativeness of the sample employed and statistical sampling techniques employing randomness as the most feasible means of achieving representativeness on all possible relevant grounds.[2]

In contrast, an alternative interpretation of the technique of the informant seems to offer something new to the other social sciences in the way of explicitly formalized methodology. As understood in the present study, the technique of the informant means that the social scientist obtains information about the group under study through a member who occupies such a role as to be well informed but who at the same time speaks the social scientist's language. It is epitomized by the use of one or a few *special* persons who are extensively interviewed and upon whose responses exceptional reliance is placed and, thus, is to be most clearly distinguished from randomly or representatively sampled interviews. The requirement that the informant speak the language of the social scientist epitomizes this difference. For the general public opinion survey there is typically no procedure for placing special credence upon the answers of those who intelligently understand the interview questions; rather there is an attempt to describe the state of information and opinion among a universe which includes those who comprehend and can verbalize adequately as well as those who lack comprehension or expressive skill. By the requirement of speaking the scientist's language we mean not only the literal sharing of a common tongue (which can, of course, be the informant's native tongue if the social scientist is so trained) but also the capacity to share, in some degree at least, the scientist's frame of reference and his interest in abstract generalized and comparative aspects of culture. As Paul, for one, has pointed out, more often than not the informant is himself an amateur or self-developed social scientist with a genuine curiosity about cultural phenomena and the capacity to verbalize his observations.[3]

But the seeking-out of the exceptionally observant and communicatively gifted person as an informant raises a number of methodological problems.

---

2.   This interpretation seems implied by Margaret Mead in her paper on "National Character," in A. L. Kroeber *et al.* (eds.), *Anthropology Today: An Encyclopedia Inventory* (Chicago: University of Chicago Press, 1953), p. 648.

3.   Benjamin D. Paul, "Interview Techniques and Field Relationships," in A. L. Kroeber *et al.* (eds.), *Anthropology Today*, pp. 443–44.

The very backgrounds which would stimulate in the potential informant an interest in observing social custom and would develop perspectives making verbalization possible are likely also to produce eccentricities of personality and asymmetries of social locus which are possible sources of bias. To quote Paul: "Those who are willing to enter into novel relationships rather than to remain within familiar grooves, to examine culture rather than express it in action, are likely, almost by definition, to diverge from the normal." While to some extent bias can be reduced by using several informants, the danger cannot be corrected by recourse to representative sampling without at the same time losing the special character of the technique. If the use of informants as a social science research tool is to be developed, it seems likely that principles for optimal selection will have to be developed. Paul has made suggestions along this line, and the present study can be considered as a small contribution in this direction.

The problem was the ranking of ten ships in a squadron of submarines in terms of their morale, for the purpose of helping evaluate the quality of leadership. A good informant for this purpose had to be one who had access to all ten ships. Such could be found in the personnel of the squadron headquarters. For each of the major types of billet aboard the submarine there were parallel numbers in the squadron headquarters. Thus there were officers and enlisted men with responsibilities for engine maintenance on each submarine and in the squadron headquarters. The same held for other functions such as communication, electronics, supply, and so on. The personnel from the squadron headquarters had opportunity to visit with their parallel numbers from the ships when the latter came in to the headquarters office, and they frequently took short cruises with them or at least found an opportunity to eat with them when they were alongside dock. The squadron headquarters personnel had all had extensive and recent shipboard experience. Thus within the personnel of the squadron headquarters there were some at least who had the opportunity to be expert informants in the comparison of the ships.

Morale, for the purposes of this study, was considered primarily as an attribute of the enlisted personnel, that is, the 90 per cent of the crews who were not commissioned officers. For this reason the best informants would probably come from the enlisted personnel in the squadron headquarters, if one assumes some barrier to communication between officers and enlisted personnel. In addition, the ideal informants had to be observant of the symptoms of morale and be willing and able to talk of them. This latter requirement would tend to rule out some of the enlisted personnel of the more mechanically oriented specialties, many of whom found it hard to speak with any confidence about social-psychological intangibles. For such reasons, as well as for reasons of expediency, the informants were selected from the yeoman (rated enlisted personnel performing secretarial duties) of the squadron headquarters company. Three of these men were willing to rank the ten ships in terms of which were the "happiest." A ranking based upon the average of the three individual rankings was the basis of our elementary quantification.

Similar rankings of the ships were obtained from officers of varying duty in the squadron headquarters. None of them was in the direct line of command, and none had in the normal course of his duties the administrative responsibility of making comparative evaluations of ships or their personnel.

In addition to the rankings of the ships, the informants provided anecdotal material about specific episodes and persons, guesses as to the source of poor morale, and so on. These materials are perhaps more characteristic of what would be obtained in the typical anthropological use of informants, but they are not the aspects of the data receiving emphasis here. In the quantification of material from informants, two basic procedures seem to be open. First of all, the free-response verbal material provided by them may be coded, categorized, and then counted, as in public opinion surveys. Second, the informant may agree to participate in a procedure which provides some quantification at the onset. Of the possible ways of achieving this, the method of ranking here employed is probably the most flexible; it is one which probably could be employed for informants at any degree of civilization. While the level of quantification is primitive by mathematical or physical standards, it does provide that rudiment of quantification necessary for checking the data against other sources of information. In some situations the use of rating-scale procedures, which have been elaborately evolved by psychologists, would also be possible.

The study employed several other techniques for the evaluation of the relative morale of the ten ships, the most expensive and extensive of which was a "morale ballot." This was a questionnaire containing prepared statements to be answered "Yes" or "No" and administered anonymously to the enlisted personnel in rooms off the ship, none of the ship's commissioned officers being present. It contained thirty questions dealing with a variety of potential complaints or expressions of dissatisfaction. Representative questions are:

▶ Will you ship over and request duty on the same ship when your present enlistment is up?
On the whole, does everyone get a square deal aboard this ship?
Is there a better bunch of fellows here than aboard most ships?
Is the commanding officer aboard this ship a better leader than most skippers?
Do the officers play favorites and give certain fellows the breaks?
Do all hands get enough information on ship's plans?
Would you like to see more recreational activities aboard this ship? ◀

While there is considerable topical variation among the thirty items, statistical analysis showed that they shared enough variance in common to justify the computation of an over-all morale score for the ship, based upon the total of answers in the direction of high morale. Although this questionnaire is in a sense the most direct approach to morale used, it should not necessarily be regarded as a "criterion," inasmuch as it, like any other approach, is potentially subject to error. For example, it might have been that the questions employed did not cover the actual sources of discontent, although their development from earlier interviews had attempted to achieve this. It might also have been that the research setting did not provide convincing anonymity and that the degree of distortion due to distrust and caution varied significantly from ship to ship. While probably not the case, such possibilities must be kept in mind.

A Spearman rank-order correlation has been used to describe the degree of agreement between the various approaches used to rank the ships in terms of morale. With only ten observations, a high degree of correlation is required before we can be certain that the relationship is other than a chance sampling error. A rank-order correlation of .6 is required before the 5 per cent level of confidence is reached. That is, through sampling error alone the value of .6 would be reached in a series of samples of ten cases less than 5 per cent of the time if the "true" correlation in the universe of samples was zero. The value of .8 is required for significance at the 1 per cent level. The small number of cases must make the study exploratory rather than definitive from the statistical point of view.

The correlation between the ranking of the ships by the enlisted informants and the ranking of ships by morale ballot is .9, showing an impressive amount of agreement, considering the independence and dissimilarity of the two methods. The correlation between the officer informants and the morale ballot is .7. The correlation between these two groups of informants is .8. These values, all substantially high, serve collectively to reinforce our confidence in each of the techniques. While it is impossible to claim that the superiority of the enlisted informants over the officer informants in degree of correlation with the morale ballot is statistically significant, it is certainly in the anticipated direction. The major advantage of the enlisted over the officer informants turns out upon more detailed inspection to involve the placement of a single ship, rated relatively high in morale by the enlisted personnel and low in morale by the squadron headquarters officers. The commanding officer of this particular ship had a cavalier and arrogant manner which made him unpopular with his junior officers and with the squadron headquarters officers (except possibly his immediate superiors) but which apparently did not create discontent among the enlisted personnel. The ship had recently been assigned to a new duty. There had also recently been a concentration of requests for transfer from the personnel of the ship. The squadron officers tended to interpret this flurry of requests for transfer as reflecting on the morale of the ship and the adequacy of its leadership. The alternative interpretation in terms of the kind of duty involved and the likelihood of the ship remaining in its home port was overlooked by them, although utilized to explain away similar increases of requests for transfer on other ships of the squadron. Probably because of the increased contact with the enlisted personnel of the ship, the enlisted headquarters informants were not misled by these superficial symptoms of discontent. While the difference gives some slight evidence of the anticipated barrier to communication between officer and enlisted strata in the naval service, the correlations also provide clear evidence of substantial communication across it. It seems probable, considering the conditions of service in the submarine study, that the barrier to communication is slight in this setting.

One other approach to the comparative morale on the ships seems worthy of attention. This is the ship's reputation for morale with other ships. At the time of taking the secret ballot, each enlisted crewman of the ten ships of the squadron was given the opportunity to name other ships in answer to the question, "Which of the ships in this squadron would you most like to serve on for peacetime duty?" The ships were ranked in terms of the number of times mentioned by the personnel of other ships. This may be described as an opinion survey on a reputational topic or as the utilization of informants in an exhaustive and nondiscriminative fashion. It should be pointed out that, while all the ships were in the same squadron and had roughly the same kind of duty, they were on separate annual schedules which kept them out of their home port for periods up to two or three months during the year. At the moment of the survey, all the ships were in the home port, but some had only recently arrived from extended tours. In addition, a great bulk of the men were married and went directly from ship to home, thus not availing themselves of the opportunity for mass recreational intermingling that might have characterized the personnel of such a squadron in a foreign port. The ranking of the ships on reputation for morale correlated .8 with the morale-ballot ranking. In this instance, at least, such exhaustive sampling of opinion proves inferior to the careful selection of a few informants. Reputation for morale with other ships correlates with the data from both enlisted informants and officer informants at the level of .7.

It seems fair to conclude from these data that the use of the informants in quantitative studies may be successfully carried out and may produce findings of validity and generality. Further methodological research seems justified on a number of grounds. From a standpoint of research cost, the expense of obtaining ship rankings and of securing data by the morale ballot might easily be in the ratio of 1 to 100. In addition, there will be many situations in which procedures for the morale ballot will be out of the question but in which informants might be effectively used.

Campbell's favorable conclusion, on empirical grounds, concerning the validity of participant observation results is corroborated by other studies.[1] One of the best is the selection by Arthur Vidich and Gilbert Shapiro, again comparing participant observation with survey research, but on a broader scale. This study seeks to discover reasons for the discrepancies which are observed.

---

1.   In addition to the study reprinted above, see Henry and Spiro (1953); Vidich and Bensman (1954); L. R. Dean (1958).

A COMPARISON OF PARTICIPANT
OBSERVATION AND SURVEY DATA

ARTHUR J. VIDICH AND GILBERT SHAPIRO

There has been considerable discussion in the literature concerning the validity of data secured by the informal anthropological research technique designated as "participant observation." The question at issue is to what extent a lone and frequently foreign observer is capable of observing or "absorbing" the culture of a group well enough to render a correct account of its beliefs, attitudes, values and practices. It is clear that any answer to this question must presume some standard of judgment—preferably the results of some different method of investigation—against which the anthropological report can be compared. There would be no problem for the social scientist if he could be thoroughly convinced of the absolute validity of the research method used as a standard for the test of participant observation. All discrepancies between the two sets of results could be attributed to the anthropological method. Unfortunately, any alternative procedure for the study of culture and social behavior is also subject to serious questions of validity.

In this study, an observer's perception of a community will be compared with data obtained by sample survey techniques. Two distinct approaches are possible for the evaluation of either of the research methods. The most common approach (continually used by the best practitioners in both methods) is the test of internal consistency. The careful anthropologist, for example, will cross-check the reports of one informant against those of another, and will pay careful attention to discrepancies between avowals in one context and facts which are allowed to "slip out" in another. These are "internal" consistency checks because they compare, within the confines of the same method, one observation with another. In a very similar fashion, careful survey technicians check the results they receive on one attitude question by comparison with results on a different question which is supposed to measure the same variable. The various scaling procedures are, in part, designed to test the data for "internal consistency" in our general sense. While such tests of the internal consistency of each method are an admirable first step, we might ask further questions about the *external* validity of each of the methods. For it is perfectly conceivable that either method may present us with a thoroughly *consistent* picture which has little relationship to "reality." One valuable way of testing the external validity of both methods is to examine the degree to which their results correspond to one another in areas where the two methods can be made to yield comparable data.

Reprinted from *American Sociological Review* (1955), **20**, 28–33, by permission of the authors and publisher.

We see the problem of the validity of the two methods, for present purposes, as twofold; as involving the degree of correspondence between the results and the direction of selectivity introduced in each. While it would be ideal to compare results of the two methods on a large number of variables, we have available measures of only one variable by both methods. The prestige of community members was measured by an anthropological field worker's ratings and by sociometric-type questions in a sample survey of the same community. By "prestige" we mean the generalized attitude of respect and admiration, or disdain and condemnation extended by individuals to each other. We feel that the comparison of the prestige measures resulting from the two techniques will throw some light on the correspondence of the methods and the direction of selectivity of each.

The research was conducted in "Springdale," a rural New York state community with a total adult population of about 1500.[1] A sample of the adults in the community was drawn by choosing at random one person between the ages of 20 and 80 from each household in the survey area. Due to lack of cooperation and availability, illness, language barriers and deaths, schedules were not completed in about two hundred households. The "achieved sample" consisting of 547 community residents was, therefore, unrepresentative to some extent, lacking proportional representation of the ill, the busy, and the intransigent. The participant observer's knowledge of the community was based upon one year of intensive contact as a resident, interviewing and observation, and the experience gained in the administration of the survey. Prior to his work in Springdale, he had had previous anthropological field experience in two other cultures and in another rural American community.

The participant observer was assisted in making the prestige ratings by a graduate student who had done field work in Springdale. The task was undertaken to provide a measure of prestige for the purpose of testing a theory of primary social integration.[2] In presenting the task, Shapiro attempted to instruct the raters in such a fashion as to minimize his own influence upon the criteria of rating to be used. A set of cards containing the names of the household heads of the community was given to the raters, and they were asked to classify them according to the "prestige, respect, standing, or general reputa-

---

1. The Springdale research is sponsored by the Department of Child Development and Family Relationships in the New York State College of Home Economics at Cornell University. This report is a by-product of a larger study of the social and psychological correlates of community activity. The research is supported in part by grants from the National Institute of Mental Health, United States Public Health Service, and the Committee on the Early Identification of Talent of the Social Science Research Council with the aid of funds granted to the council by the John and Mary R. Markle Foundation. Mr. Vidich acted as the participant observer and Mr. Shapiro analyzed the sociometric data introduced in this report.

2. Gilbert Shapiro, "The Formulation and Verification of a Theory of Primary Social Integration." Ph.D. Thesis, Cornell University, 1954.

tion" of the individuals in the "eyes of the community." All further questions about the meaning of these terms were met by asking that the raters use those criteria which, in their experience, were commonly used by community members in evaluating one another. In addition, no effort was made to determine in advance the number of categories or prestige groupings. This effort to keep the task unstructured was intended to utilize to the fullest extent the informal, unconscious understanding of the community developed by the judges over the period of their field experience. The groupings isolated by this method are described below.

DESCRIPTIONS OF THE PRESTIGE GROUPINGS
PROVIDED BY THE JUDGES IMMEDIATELY AFTER THE
RATING PROCESS, IN ORDER FROM LOW TO HIGH PRESTIGE

1. Non-entities, on the bottom rung of the financial and social ladder. Many without kin in community. Frequently their existence is unrecognized, at least publicly, by the town. Includes physical and mental wrecks, degenerates, "deadbeats," and the like.

2. Only slightly higher in prestige than Group 1. More contact with the rest of the community. Economically marginal, unskilled. Includes some moral degenerates, such as alcoholics, as well as some widows with large families.

3. The lowest group which has a steady income; respectable working folk. Some have risen to this status from Groups 1 and 2; others have fallen to it from higher Groups described below.

4. Only slightly higher in prestige than Group 3. These are more often recruited from *migration* rather than higher or lower local groups. They are still unskilled occupationally, but are striving to enter the semiskilled ranks, and to improve their lot generally more than Group 3. The wives of the families in this group sometimes participate in formal organizations (a form of behavior much rarer in lower groups). Includes marginal entrepreneurs, such as a freelance trucker, as well as part-time farmers with jobs.

5. Almost equal in prestige with Group 4. These, however, are people who have risen or fallen to lower middle class respectability and have close kinship ties in the community with relatives in higher and lower positions.

6. A large, intermediate, and indeterminate catch-all grouping. Neither disdained nor admired by the community. Frequently have both pretensions to much higher standing and skeletons in the family closet.

7. The lowest group which can be properly considered as having higher than median prestige. Their prestige is based primarily on non-economic characteristics (such as high moral standards, temperance, community activity, church support and membership) although they may, in addition, have money.

These are continually striving for and exhibiting their respectability. Extremely conscious of community attitudes towards them. Includes some newcomers.

8. A separate category for school teachers, including only those teachers who have no community ties other than their jobs and those social activities incumbent upon them because of their occupation. They have positive prestige as teachers. All of their actions, and the evaluation of them by the community, are focused upon their occupation. Prestige slightly higher than Group 7, lower than 9.

9. Relatively powerless professionals and holders of new wealth deriving from the post-war prosperity. Includes also a scattering of "old names" maintaining their prestige without the income or power which used to buttress it. Some non-professionals (larger farmers, business operators) in this group are hard working "money makers."

10. The highest ranking group of any size. All of the qualifications of an "upper-upper" in the usual sense, except that they lack the extreme of power, prestige, and money characteristic of the small "X-Family" group described below. Active in organizations, frequently as powers behind the scenes, sometimes openly the leaders of the community. Most economically well off (in terms of local standards). Includes prosperous businessmen and farmers, as well as the upper group of professionals.

11. The Springdale equivalent of the Middletown X-Family; *the* powers, highest in money, prestige, and political control (*always* behind the scenes).

12. Unknown. People whom the raters did not know well enough to classify. This group includes about a third of the total population. Their characteristics will be examined in detail in the discussion of selectivity below.

The survey questions used for the measurement of prestige were in the form of five sociometric type queries:

1. If some one person were to be selected to represent this particular part of town at a special meeting of the town board, who would *you personally* want to go?

2. What person do you think most of the people around here would choose to represent them?

3. When you think of the over-all leadership in this community, who are the three or four people you would think of first?

4. Are there any women (men) you would think of as leaders in this community? (Asked with reference to sex opposite the respondent's.)

5. Are there any other people you think have a good deal of influence in the community?

The total number of these five types of choices received is interpreted here as an index of each individual's prestige in the community. It is clear that this

TABLE 1   Correspondence between Anthropologist's Prestige Ratings
and Prestige as Indicated by Number of Choices Received

NUMBER OF CHOICES RECEIVED	PER CENT OF PRESTIGE GROUPING								
	1–2	3	4	5	6	7	8–9	10–11	NOT KNOWN
0	100	87	79	63	64	54	36	7	88
1	0	7	15	21	18	14	10	7	4
2–4	0	7	4	8	14	18	21	27	5
5 or more	0	0	2	8	4	14	33	60	2
(N)	(20)	(61)	(53)	(24)	(72)	(56)	(39)	(15)	(207)

interpretation of the score is not immediately given to us by the manifest meaning of the questions asked. In this sense, the sociometric score described is a more *indirect* prestige index than the observer's ratings. The interpretation, on the other hand, is not wholly arbitrary. It is at least reasonable in a rural American context that those most frequently mentioned as "community leaders," or as desirable neighborhood representatives, have the greatest prestige, general standing, and the highest reputations or "evaluative status" in the community. As compared with the three other sociometric questions in the Springdale survey schedule, these items have the highest degree of concentration of choices received in the population, and the lowest rates of reciprocal choice. These facts and others[3] tend to provide some internal basis for the interpretation of the sociometric score as a measure of overall community prestige, irrespective of any shift in the interpretation of the questions from subject to subject, and such influences as varying interview situations.

An *external* test of the validity of this prestige index, as well as of the validity of the anthropologist's ratings, is the degree of correspondence between the two. Table 1 shows the correspondence between prestige, as measured by each of the two methods.

If we had found no correspondence in Table 1 between the two methods (or a small correspondence just exceeding chance expectancy), we would have no basis for choosing one method as more "valid" than the other. However, remarkably strong correspondence between the two methods is shown. The correspondence does not "prove" the validity of either method, but it does reinforce willingness on our part to accept both methods of measuring prestige. Since this mutual validation is so strong, we should be willing to accept the survey results for ranking the 207 cases not known by the participant observer.

Aside from the correspondence of the methods, the data of Table 1 show that only 12 per cent of those not known by the observer received at least one choice while 36 per cent of those who were known received one or more. This

---

3.   A more complete analysis of the validity of the sociometric measure of prestige, which cannot be provided here, will be found in Shapiro, *op. cit.*

TABLE 2   Percentage of Various Sub-Groups of the
Springdale Sample Which Were Known Well Enough to Be Rated

GROUP	PER CENT KNOWN	TOTAL NUMBER IN GROUP	GROUP	PER CENT KNOWN	TOTAL NUMBER IN GROUP
Entire sample	62	547	Education (*cont.*)		
Sex			Some college	87*	23
Males	70*	265	College graduate	84*	49
Females	55*	282	Employment status		
Age			Retired	56*	36
20–29	65	81	Not in labor force	55*	205
30–39	64	123	Self-employed	69*	125
40–49	58	106	Employed by others	66	178
50–59	66	83	Occupation		
60–69	61	90	Manager, proprietors	88*	41
70–79	56*	64	Professionals, semi-		
Education			prof.	80*	30
Some grade school	48*	93	Clerical and sales	76*	25
Grade school graduate	58	98	Industrial workers	63	134
Some high school	58	124	Farmers and farm		
High school graduate	66	147	laborers	59	90
			Housewives	56*	210

* Starred percentages differ from the per cent known of the entire sample beyond the 1 per cent level of significance.

clearly indicates that the unknown group contains a disproportionate number of those with low prestige. Thus, even though the observer had made deliberate efforts to establish contact with lower prestige groups, his knowledge of community members was biased in favor of individuals with higher prestige. Table 1 indicates that the observer's efforts to meet and learn about all segments of the community were largely successful—almost two-thirds of the sample was known well enough to be rated. A large number of even the low prestige community members was known. Yet, despite all efforts to counteract the tendency, definite selectivity is indicated, and it would be surprising if this selective association of the observer with the community did not somehow influence his understanding of the local culture. Without the survey data, the observer could only make reasonable guesses about his areas of ignorance in the effort to reduce bias. The survey data give him more exact information regarding the degree and kind of selectivity operating, and thereby allow him to make better compensatory allowances in planning his observational activities.

Table 2 provides more information about the selectivity of the anthropological observer's contacts.

As might be expected in a society which segregates the activities of the sexes in so many contexts, a disproportionate number of those known by the male observer were males. Age groups, however, were all fairly equally represented. A clear, consistent relationship is found between educational level and the probability that a person is known by the observer. This relationship may be interpreted as a consequence of educational attainment as such, or of the relationship between educational level and socio-economic status. Those in the labor force, whether self-employed or not, are more likely to be interviewed by the observer than are housewives, retired people, and the like. Finally, the probability of being known by the observer increases with the prestige of the individual's occupation as customarily ranked in American society. In short, the observer's status in the community as an employed male, middle class professional, is reflected in the types of people with whom he is likely to make contact. This fact is consistent with the findings of Table 1, where we found that the unknowns contained a disproportionate number of those who, by survey criteria, had low prestige.

Finally, we consider the bias introduced by selectivity of respondents in the survey. We compare the background characteristics of those in the achieved sample described above with those of the entire adult population of the survey area. Data on the whole population were collected prior to the survey on a typical census basis; every effort was made to get as complete a report as possible on every adult in every household. Occasionally, when members of the household were unavailable, information was collected from neighbors, provided by the participant observer, or pieced together from the sources. For this reason, and because the census schedule was shorter and less personal in content, the census had fewer incomplete schedules and a far lower refusal rate; altogether only 24 out of 765 were not completed. Another reason for the greater completeness of the census data is the fact that any member of the household could give the information required, while the sample survey interview had to be conducted with the household member whose name arose in the random choice. For these reasons we consider the census frequencies to be close approximations of the actual parameters of the population. We can, therefore, measure the bias introduced by the selective failure to interview people whose names arose in the random sample by comparing frequencies in the achieved sample with those in the population. Table 3 compares the sample and population frequencies on the same characteristics used in Table 2 to find the characteristics of the anthropologist's contacts.

None of the differences between sample and population frequencies shown in Table 3 are significant at the 5 per cent level. As contrasted with the findings of Table 2, the survey techniques seem to reach the various segments of the population more evenly than the contacts of the anthropological observer. Whatever its comparative defects on other grounds, selectivity of respondents as a source of bias in the collection of data is not present in the achieved random sample to the extent that it is found in our analysis of the observer's contacts.

The selectivity of respondents is only one of a host of potential sources of bias in social research. What the survey method gains in representative coverage of a population is probably of no greater methodological significance than the increased *depth* of understanding and interpretation possible with partici-

TABLE 3   Frequencies of Selected Background
Characteristics in the Achieved Sample and in the
Population as Estimated by Census Interview

	PER CENT OF SAMPLE	PER CENT OF POPULATION		PER CENT OF SAMPLE	PER CENT OF POPULATION
Sex			Employment status		
Male	48	48	Not in labor force	37	37
Female	52	52	Retired	6	6
Age			Unemployed	1	1
20–29	15	18	Self-employed	24	21
30–39	23	22	Employed by others	32	35
40–49	19	18	Occupation		
50–59	15	16	Housewife	39	38
60–69	16	16	Managerial, proprietor	7	6
70–79	12	9	Professional, semi-prof.	5	5
Education			Clerical	3	3
None	0	1	Sales	2	2
Some grade school	17	16	Farmer	15	14
Grade school graduate	18	19	Farm laborer	2	3
Some high school	23	26	Industrial		
High school graduate	27	24	Skilled and semi-skilled	18	21
Some college	4	3	Manual	6	6
College graduate	9	7			

pant observation techniques. This is evident when we contrast the position of a survey analyst and a participant observer when both face the problem of interpreting the *meaning* of a question. The desk chair analyst can give at best an intelligent guess based upon sketchy pretest and tabular data. The observer, in contrast, can call upon the wealth of his experience with the linguistic habits, the attitudes, values and beliefs of the group and provide a much richer, and probably sounder interpretation. This is indicated in the present study by the descriptions of the prestige rating categories as compared with the sociometric scores. The latter are mere numbers symbolizing, at best, indices of an abstract variable expressed in a single word—prestige. The prestige rating categories, however, are groups of people with a wealth of specified characteristics which are, for one reason or another, sources of respect in the community. We have an immediate idea from the prestige group descriptions of the important criteria of assigning prestige in Springdale, as well as other clues to the stratification system. These descriptions of the prestige system can be frequently tested with the survey data. This point indicates that the techniques of participant observation and the sample survey are not competitive, but, in the well conducted community study, will be complementary. The survey provides representative information which is given meaning by the anthropological observer. Frequently, but not always, survey methods may be used to test hypotheses developed out of the less formal experience of the observer, particularly in those areas where information is admissible at a public level and where replication is both possible and meaningful.

Vidich and Shapiro raise the important point that in comparing two procedures, the validation may be considered symmetrical. That is, one may study the results not only to evaluate the validity of participant observation on the basis of, say, survey research, but also to evaluate the validity of survey research, *if* we have confidence in the results of participant observation.

A number of comparative papers have been written with just this intent: seeking to *evaluate*—or at the least to illuminate—*other research procedures* in terms of participant observation. The following selection by Ivan Mensh and Jules Henry, for example, critically examines the use of psychological tests in light of participant observation.

DIRECT OBSERVATION AND PSYCHOLOGICAL TESTS IN ANTHROPOLOGICAL FIELD WORK

IVAN N. MENSH AND JULES HENRY

I

It seems to the writers that in order to make general observations about the use of projective psychological tests in anthropological field work we first need to make some statement about the goals of cultural anthropology. Such a statement would appear to be indispensable, since psychological investigation in anthropology ought to be considered, like physical anthropology, archeology, and linguistics, one of the roads that leads ultimately to the common goal—the global understanding of man.

Anthropology aims at the understanding of man, through elucidation of biological, psychological, historical, and social processes. In "biological" we include physiological function as well as physical differentiation (racial differentiation and evolution). By "historical" we understand the dynamics of interlocking event-sequences involved in cultural changes. By "social" we understand social structure and the dynamics of social process. By "psychological" we mean the processes of concept-formation, learning, personality development, perception, etc.; in short, all the events that take place inside individuals' minds as functions of outer events impinging on a neural network. It is clear that this aim is comprehensive and complex, and is not exclusively anthropology's. Other disciplines are concerned with the same things, and, like anthropology, are confronted with the same problem, of a constantly expanding universe of research, and increasingly unmanageable data. However, the reality is clear: anthropology, like all the sciences of human behavior, has the problem of vanishing disciplinary boundaries, and the interests of anthropologists increasingly embrace the areas of research just outlined.

Reproduced by permission of the authors and the American Anthropological Association from the *American Anthropologist,* Vol. 55, pp. 461–80 (Oct., 1953).

Where do psychological tests fit into the aim of global understanding? Let us look at the following model:

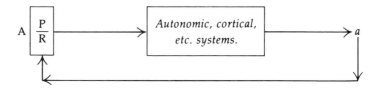

Here the model sets forth the argument that in the presence of stimulus configuration A, which we call, *for the moment,* and as an illustration only, a certain constant ratio between reward and punishment, operating in a relatively homogeneous cultural environment, the autonomic, cortical and other mediating systems of the individuals·in the culture will be relatively permanently conditioned to response "set" *a*. It will readily be seen that the model brings together, in an ideal, but in a relatively plausible way, three of the important dimensions of research we have been concerned with in anthropology: the biological, the cultural and the psychological, for culture and the structure of society determine the character of the ratio P/R; and its effect on the autonomic nervous system is clearly a matter to be understood in terms of the biology of man and the structure of his nervous and other organic systems. There is implied, however, in the model, another biological consideration: the process of the evolution of man; for since culture, acting on the organism, brings about certain characteristic psychosomatic sets—like the tendency to dominate, to submit, or to develop hypertension, asthma, or gastro-intestinal, or other psychosomatic disorders—it is clear that culture, through its instability, plays an important role in the bodily changes that take place in man over time. [Thompson (1951: 252) used the expression "psychosomatic sets" for the action of core values on the organism.]

Thus the role of psychological investigation in anthropology is an important one, for it not only enables us to understand what happens when certain environmental phenomena impinge on the psycho-physiological processes of human beings, but it also helps toward an understanding of the role culture has played in physical evolution.

The Role of Direct Observation. The immediate issue for the anthropologist is to arrive at the best possible understanding of A in Figure 1. In other words, the first step is to understand the stimuli that impinge on the organism. If, for example, there exists in any society a relatively constant ratio of rewards to punishments, then what are the rewards and punishments and precisely what are the quantitative relations between the two? Obviously there is one good way we can learn the answers to the questions: we must watch reward and punishment being administered. This brings us to the crux of the matter as far as psychological tests are concerned: tests tend to measure *a*—the *end results* of the conditioning process—rather than the *conditioning events*. On the other hand, even when they do, as in the TAT, for example, pick up something of the conditioning process, the data are drastically condensed: the whole punishment process, for example, may be summed up in a response like "he was punished," and the crucial details are left out. Furthermore, the time dimension is not stated. That is to say, we learn little about frequency of punishment or the lag between act and the punishment for it. Thus if we have *only* psychological tests on our subjects we frequently have to guess how the subjects came to be the way they are. Thus tests often tell us little or nothing about many of the crucial details of the way in which the autonomic and other organic systems of the population are impinged upon by the socio-cultural process.

There are only two ways in which a human being can observe a phenomenon: he can watch it with the naked eye, or with an instrument. In each case interpretation of what is observed must take place in order to make the observed phenomenon have meaning to the observer. However, in the second case the accuracy of the instrument is always in question. Hence it can be argued that at the present time in the sciences of human behavior direct observation is at least as accurate as trans-instrument observation until it can be shown that instruments are more precise and more comprehensive than the scope of direct observation. The instruments presently in use are imprecise, as proved by the revision that is constantly going on; and it would be a rare clinical psychologist who would argue that personality evaluations derived from tests are more valid than those based on extensive interviewing and observation of the subject. An instrument like the TAT has often been used in anthropological field studies without objective devices for interpreting the responses to it, and thus may be entirely dependent on individual variations among examiners. It ought to be pointed out, meanwhile, that while he who observes directly has only his own past experiences to deal with in interpreting his data, whoever uses an instrument must employ not only his own past experiences, but also the past experiences of the instrument.

Interpretation of personality on the basis of direct observation of the human organism functioning in its native habitat has sometimes been called "impressionism." In the first place it seems necessary to indicate that these interpretations have never been proved to be false. In the second place the recent paper by Henry and Spiro (1953) has shown that there is a close correspondence between anthropologists' direct observations and psychological test data.

An objection to direct observation has been that the observer, by his mere presence, biases the situation he is observing, hence what he sees is not "reality" as it actually occurs in nature, but a reality distorted by the presence of the observer. We believe that in anthropology we must accept this as a constant possibility, but we cannot for this reason stop observing; nor can we surround our cultures with one way screens. What can be done in anthropology to reduce distortion, is to remain with the groups studied long enough to repeat observations many times and in different contexts. This also permits the observer to become more of a participant observer, and less of an external factor introducing uncontrolled variation.

If we wish to determine whether a given child is anxious or not, we can: (a) watch him with his parents; (b) watch him with other children; (c) watch him in general gatherings; (d) talk to the child; (e) have the child observed by more than one anthropologist; (f) ask the people around the child whether he is upset; (g) give the child a projective test. We can watch the child getting up in the morning, eating, bathing, and even watch him while he sleeps, in order to see whether he has night-terrors or other symptoms of anxiety. It is common knowledge nowadays that error can be reduced through multiplying observers and by multiplying the number of points of view from which the phenomenon is observed. It should be borne in mind that the critics from outside anthropology who feel that anthropologists' reports on personality are like those of a tourist, do not fully appreciate the increase in reliability gained through the opportunity to observe systematically subjects in a great variety of life situations. The anthropologist who spends a year in the field in "participant-observer" field work can have some of his subjects under observation over relatively long periods of time, come to see them functioning in relation to a complex milieu; and in addition may also obtain from his subjects accounts of how they view their own life's experiences. Thus it seems to us that some of the misunderstanding about anthropologists' evaluations of personality may stem from lack of appreciation of this variety in the sources the anthropologist may tap during the course of participant-observer field work.

The anthropologist who spends a year in the field has at least some of his subjects under constant observation, can study the entire milieu, and can *also* obtain the subject's account of his experiences.

When we come to the clinical psychologist we see that in a good clinical psychological work-up the psychologist spends only a few hours with the subject and generally sees him but once or twice. To be sure, he attempts to compensate for the difficulties by varying the stimuli throughout a range, thus increasing the number of positions he takes as observer, and the number and range of the reactions the subject must make, but nevertheless he still lacks the advantages the anthropologist has in having subjects under long-time observation.

In all of this, of course, there is implied no derogation of the methods of clinical psychology which is adapted to the purposes for which it is needed in the clinical situation in our culture. All we intend to point out is that anthropological observation is not as vague as has been thought, but on the contrary, has features to commend it to those who rightly insist that good observations are the first requisite for a respectable science.

One of the obvious results of the use of instruments for the study of the universe is that we perceive only what the inherent design of the instrument permits it to transmit. A pair of eight-power binoculars permits us to see objects at a certain distance, but a pair of sixteen-power binoculars will permit us to see objects much farther away. It is also true that with binoculars objects close to us will be blurred. An instrument is always a mixed blessing. When we come to the use of psychological tests, however, we deal with phenomena of much greater complexity than binoculars. Binoculars do not have to reduce the universe to specific theoretical categories. All they are "asked" to do is to transmit light rays, and no one asks them to do it in terms of the wave or the corpuscular theory of light. But a projective test like the Rorschach has an interpretive system, structured in definite categories, in terms of which personality *must* be perceived. It is as if looking through a pair of binoculars one *had* to see the universe in terms of either the wave or the corpuscular theory of light. Now, since the Rorschach categories are organized in a special way, it means that as long as we use the test we will perceive people in terms of Rorschach theory. Thus the instrument we use to look at the universe determines what we shall see. As long as we use the same instrument we will see only what it transmits to us. In this way we build for our minds a prison out of the very instruments that were designed to set them free. This, of course, has been the fate of theories and scientific apparatus throughout the history of science.

In this situation direct observation enables us to discover relationships among phenomena that the projective test used alone might not permit us to do. It is true that the eye itself is not untrammeled by theory and by preconceived categories, for we bring to any situation biases determined by previous experience. But at least, so it seems to us, when we use direct observation we have not double-locked the door of science by using a "standardized" eye that will look in only one direction (Luchins 1952).

It is important to note that the above discussion applies to the use of psychological tests in anthropological field work, and specifically to studies in which no direct observations on the subjects accompany the projective test data, for obviously the criticism that the instrument limits what shall be seen does not apply strictly where direct observation enters into the study.

The quantitative problem. The issues here are: (a) the quantification of direct observations; (b) the obtaining of enough cases to lend credibility to the data on personality.

a) It will possibly remain forever a matter of taste whether in describing human behavior one wishes to use numbers or not. In the present discussion, however, the authors accept the orthodox scientific position that understanding the universe is closely related to our capacities to describe it in quantitative terms. We also assume that since human life is made up of experiences and events, the frequency of the occurrence of these experiences and events can be counted. The question arises, can one reduce to quantifiable terms the enormous variety of human experience? The answer to this question is as follows: most of the things the anthropologist sees can be described. What we see, however, and the power of accurate description are functions of the developmental stage of science at the moment. Hence we can always observe and describe within the limits of our scientific achievements. The next step depends on the selection of units for quantification. If we cannot find units it means that we have not reached the stage in science where we are ready for quantification. But it is also a shrewd guess that if we cannot find units we cannot give a description of the phenomena we see.

The quantification of direct observations depends therefore on the state of the human sciences at the moment and our capacity to discover units. The task of the field anthropologist becomes, therefore, the selection of units of observation. We give below two examples, one from our culture and one from the Pilaga (Henry and Boggs 1952: 266–268), of types of units that may be selected for the study of psychological characteristics, on the basis of direct observation:

TABLE I* Nutritional Behavior of Four Pilaga Indian Children

	YORODAIKOLIK (4 YEARS)	TAPANI (8–9 YEARS)	NAICHO (6 YEARS)	DENIKI (15 MONTHS)
1. Given food	9	7	27	42
2. Deprived of food	7	0	2	4
3. Deprivation followed by restitution	1	0	1	2
4. Attempt made to deprive of food	2	1	1	4
5. Gives food	8	7	1	3
6. Withholds food	6	5	2	3
7. Deprives others of food	2	6	1	0
8. Attempts to deprive others of food	1	5	0	1
9. Receives part of a whole	0	1	0	4
10. Punished while eating	0	0	0	3

* The total number of observations, including nutritional behavior, for each of these children is as follows: Yorodaikolik, 190; Tapani, 207; Naicho, 238; Deniki, 208.

SUMMARY OF TABLE I

	YORODAIKOLIK	TAPANI	NAICHO	DENIKI
Subject Given Food	9	7	27	42
Other Nutritional Behavior	27	25	8	24
Total Nutritional Observations	36	32	35	66

Table I is constructed from nearly a thousand observations, of which the following are but two examples:

► The three children of Diwa'i are feeding peacefully together. Deniki, the baby, waves his hand for food and mother gives him a small piece of palm dipped in fat. After eating a second piece he is given the breast.

Deniki, Naicho and Soroi are together. Deniki is holding a dish with a very small quantity of cooked fruit in it. Soroi says, "Share it with me," and takes one fruit out of the dish.   Naicho immediately snatches another one away violently, but not before Deniki has already taken one out, which he then offers to Naicho, appearing not to comprehend her action.   (Henry and Boggs 1952: 265) ◀

It will be seen that the units "given food" and "deprived of food" are clearly discernible in these matter-of-fact descriptions of what transpired before the eyes of the anthropologist, planted near the situation with his open notebook.   Obviously, however, other gross units can be discerned also.   For example, in the first observation the following additional units can be separated out: (1) relatively conflict free feeding situation; (2) in the presence of all the children, mother feeds only baby with delicacy; (3) baby asks for solid food of mother and is given it; (4) solid food alternated with breast.

In the second observation the following additional units can be isolated from the total matrix: (1) use of the expression "Share it with me" accompanied by forcible deprivation of infant of food; (2) enforcement by peer-group (i.e. other children) of cultural imperatives; (3) mass attack on food by other children, i.e. three against one; (4) apparent effort of infant to proffer food "voluntarily."

TABLE II   Frequency of Utterances of Mothers to Their Babies, Expressed as Percentages of Total Number of Utterances Counted (N = 472)*

UTTERANCE	PERCENTAGE
1. Utterances containing the expression "Come on"	32
2. "Wake up" or some related phrase	27
3. Utterances pertaining to quantity or speed	22
4. Utterances in which the adult's wishes are opposed to the baby's wishes	15
5. Utterances pertaining to achievement, work, failure, or success of the baby or the mother	11
6. Miscellaneous	13

* Not all utterances were counted because some of them had to do with matters not immediately relevant to this study.   It is to be noted that since many utterances were coded under more than one category, the percentages add up to more than 100.   Not all categories are listed in the table.   Categories not listed have very low frequencies.

Table II is constructed from fourteen 600-word protocols of observations of the 45-minute feeding periods of neo-nates with their mothers in a maternity hospital.   The following is an abstract from one such protocol:

▶ The mother was lying on her back in a slightly raised position when the nurse carried the baby in and laid it on the bed beside the mother. The mother took the bottle and put the nipple in the baby's mouth at 0-00.   "Every time he comes in here he's asleep."   Baby moved arm.   Mother took nipple out at 0-05.

After two attempts the nipple was successfully inserted at 0-47.   "He's not doing anything.   Can they when they're asleep?"   Observer replied, "Not very well."   As baby started sucking mother said: "There he goes."   Baby sucked from 1-23 to 1-27. Mother jiggled nipple and patted baby's buttocks. Baby moved arms. "They have a hard time opening their eyes." Mother jiggled baby's arms. "Oh, sleepyhead." Mother jiggled nipple and baby moved arms. "Come on." Mother laughed. Mother patted baby's back and pulled baby's arm away from his face. Mother patted baby's hair, said, "Come on," and shook baby. "He just doesn't want to wake up." (Henry and Boggs 1952: 268) ◄

It will be seen at once that several of the types of verbalization presented in the table appear in the protocol. Other units that might be isolated with relative ease for purposes of analysis are: (1) Role of the nurse in the feeding situation; (2) average length of sucking time; (3) motility patterns of mother, e.g., patting, rolling, pinching, holding, controlling baby; (4) motility patterns of baby, e.g., relative vigor of sucking, position of hands.

b) One of the major contributions of the use of psychological tests in field studies lies in the opportunity to increase the range of sampling with systematic, standardized observations requiring relatively brief periods of administration. However, in statistical treatment of data from projective tests it should be recalled that these tests were designed for study of the individual case, and only later adapted for group use. The problem therefore arises (Mensh 1950) that the distribution of scores and of scoring categories of the projective tests frequently are not consistent with the assumptions of statistical analysis designed for the usual group data of the so-called psychometric techniques, i.e., the traditional-type psychological measures. For example, normal distributions of test scores are assumed in the usual statistical method of analysis, yet projective test data, as from the Rorschach, seldom meet this criterion, e.g., the range of M responses is 0–20+, mean of 3.50, standard deviation of 3.24, skewed with "the vast majority . . . massed in the 0–2 range." (Beck *et al.*)

The projective test as a check on direct observation. The argument for the use of the projective test as a check on the observations of the anthropologist has been advanced on a number of grounds. The most usual argument is that observations tend to be biased because of the anthropologist's own past experience, while psychological tests are not biased. Thus the test is conceived to be a kind of mechanism without heart and without past experience. Some discussion of this has already been given. We may now consider other aspects of the problem. In the first place, the fact that Henry and Spiro (1953) found that generally the test results support the anthropologist's findings based on direct observation might readily be taken to prove not that the anthropologist was correct in the first place, but that contamination phenomena are present in the observer-test experiment. That is to say that the anthropologist biased the test results in favor of his own findings. This danger is obvious when the anthropologist does his own interpretation of the tests, but it is equally present when someone else interprets the results for the anthropologist.

This is because the anthropologist has always consulted with his interpreting psychologist, and there are very few cases in which the anthropologist did not tell the psychologist much about the culture before, during and after the process of interpretation of the test results. It has seemed obvious that this must be done in order that meaningless interpretations of the Rorschach test, for example, might be avoided. In this way, however, we come face to face with the principle of *indeterminateness* in the observation-test problem; for in order to make the "objective" instrument work in the situation and produce meaningful results, we rob it of its objectivity.

Another factor that enters the picture at this point is the cultural bias of the instrument *and* the observer together. One of the most striking findings of projective testing of primitive people, and in general of people from cultures other than our own, is that they regularly turn out to show signs of deep-going psychopathology; and the anthropological works on projective tests are full of the language of psychopathology. It is difficult to understand why this should be so, unless we take the position that everybody is sick but the observer. Our impression is that not only do such interpretations stem from preconceived notions of what is "normal," but that something inherent in the instrument's past history in our culture compels us to see the responses of peoples from other cultures as psychopathological. What this something is, is clearest in the Rorschach test, where preponderance of small detail (Dd) responses, poorly assembled wholes, certain proportions of human movement (M) to color (C) responses and so on, are considered evidences of psychopathology. The traditional anthropological position in these matters still seems to us a good one: psychic characteristics are to be thought of in terms of the individual who has them and in terms of the response of the environment to those characteristics. A person may have what we might call "psychotic" or "neurotic" characteristics, but if the environment does not become punitive or does not withdraw, the individual may go on functioning without serious difficulty. The crux of the matter is the response of the environment to the psychic traits of the individual. (This matter has been brought home to J. Henry and made particularly vivid through his discussion of the problem with Dr. Humphry Osmund, Director of the Psychiatric Hospital, Weyburn, Saskatchewan.) It seems to us impossible, therefore, to engage in cross-cultural diagnosis via projective tests, or in any other way, unless the response of the environment to the individual's psychic characteristics is known. After all, this turns out to be just good clinical psychology, for clinical psychology developed as a diagnostic device for the purpose of special study of people rejected by or unable to get along in their human environment.

To summarize this section, psychological studies in anthropology make their contribution, side by side with the more traditional branches of anthropology, to a global understanding of man and his evolution. Direct observation of the human organism functioning in its native habitat is an important device for reaching this understanding, when it is carried out systematically over periods of considerable duration, and manipulated quantitatively. It then provides data on the conditioning and learning process which generally is not provided by the cross-sectional psychological tests. It may also pick up leads to the understanding of behavior characteristics which might have been missed had the whole observational situation been confined to tests alone.

Meanwhile it is important to note that psychological tests in anthropological field studies may not at present be considered to be more precise or comprehensive than direct observation. Furthermore, because of the principle of indeterminateness, psychological tests may not be considered as a check on direct observation, yet they have value in field studies by expanding the scope through increasing the range of sampling, and through turning up facts and giving insights that direct observation alone might not reveal. All of this, however, is contingent on observing certain precautions to be discussed in the next section.

II

Henry and Spiro (1953) have pointed out the shift of orientation from anthropological field studies concerned with groups to the study of the individual. They suggested that interest of anthropologists in cultural dynamics and cultural integration was significant in this shift of emphasis, particularly in personality and culture studies—the "cultural anthropology" of American and "social anthropology" of Britain. Paralleling this shift in anthropological field studies is a similar reorientation in clinical psychology, extending presently not only to gathering data on human behavior but also including statistical treatment of "individual-centered" psychodiagnostic studies. This latter trend has been reviewed by Mensh (1950) in a survey of statistical techniques in present-day psychodiagnostics. It would seem then that there has occurred the psychological threshold in at least cultural anthropology and clinical psychology, marking a new awareness of the importance of the individual in studies of human behavior.

The use of tests grew out of study of individual differences (Boring 1929; Freeman 1939), originating with Galton in England, but influenced principally in the early developmental years by Binet in France. Just as "the study of personality and culture, with notably few exceptions, has been exclusively an American concern," so the movement in psychological testing also has been essentially American (Boring 1929; Henry and Spiro 1953), though this is not to say that European contributions to the development of testing have not been important. Boring described Galton as "a genius . . . ."

▶ His scientific contributions, beside his early ventures in exploration, include investigations in simple mechanics and the invention of apparatus, his persistent interest in meteorology, his continued study of inheritance and his foundation of the art of eugenics, his development of Quetelet's methods of statistics and their application to anthropological and psychological problems, his numerous researches in anthropometry, and his initiation of the experimental psychology of tests in England. (p. 454)

... To measure the capacities of a large number of persons, and thus to sample the populations, requires as a practical matter the development of apparatus and methods by which the measurements of a single individual can be easily and quickly made .... For this purpose Galton invented the 'test,' and in particular the 'mental test,' an experimental method of measurement which is characterized by its brevity. ... (p. 474) ◄

Historically, it was J. Mck. Cattell in America who first used the term "mental tests" in 1890, and influenced the American tradition of individual psychology and mental tests. Galton's *Inquiries into Human Faculty and its Development* (1883) was followed by Kraepelin's and Oehrn's development of tests for research in psychopathology in the 1890's, Ebbinghaus' invention of tests in Germany in the same decade and Cattell's introduction of the term mental tests (1890: 15, 373–380), and the research in France of Binet and Henri. By the turn of the century the test movement included Boring (1929) in addition to Cattell, such early psychologists in America as Jastrow, Boas, Münsterberg, Gilbert, Farrand, Sharp (a student of Titchener), Thorndike, Woodworth, and Helen Thompson, and the anthropologist Wissler.

The major shift from individual to group tests came with World War I and in the United States over 1,700,000 men were given the Army Alpha Test. During the 1920's the awareness of the value of tests in education greatly increased their use. For example, a single test-publishing firm distributed $2\frac{1}{2}$ million copies of intelligence tests in 1922–23 (Freeman 1939), and this increased use of tests has continued in educational systems at all levels of schooling. World War II produced another great demand for psychological measures, and during the war period some 16 million individuals had responded to some form of psychological test. Since the recent war, however, increased attention has been paid to individual studies rather than to group studies, and the controversy of nomothetic versus idiographic orientation (Mensh 1950) has become prominent again, in part a function of the increased emphasis on projective techniques as psychological test methods. The use of such techniques recently was reviewed by Henry and Spiro (1953) at the Wenner-Gren Foundation International Symposium on Anthropology.

The use of psychological tests, whether projective devices or more structured techniques, demands that certain criteria be observed. It is just here that the crucial problem of psychological tests in anthropological field studies lies. Uncritical use of tests introduces many uncontrolled biases and errors in the collection and analysis of data. Fortunately, anthropologists have recognized the limitations placed on psychological test data when criterion conditions are not met. Thus, more than a decade ago Hallowell (1940, 1941) cautioned that adequate sampling was necessary in the study of nonliterate societies, and that data must be collected for local group norms. Du Bois (1944) also reported "two cautions"—the lack of quantification and the great range of experiences sampled. And Henry (1941) reviewed "common experiences in Western culture" which are not common to other societies, including the "test-taking attitude," familiarity with pictorial representations of objects, and language and other symbolism differing from that of Western culture experience.

The "common experiences" noted by Henry form the basis of the rationale of Cattell's test (1940; Cattell *et al.* 1941), and Cattell concluded that "suitable tests could be built on a properly investigated 'greatest common knowledge.'" These common experiences were seen as the human body in its various parts, processes, and systems; and natural, environmental elements as smoke, fire and water. Cattell has utilized spatial perception as a more universally common experience than verbal, symbolic, or mechanical skills. He emphasized, as has Klineberg (1927), the significance of motivation, and "habits of attention and normal speeds of working" in cross-cultural studies. Abel and Calabresi vividly portray the problem of motivation:

▶ The children did not enjoy being the center of attention in the testing situation. They were shy, ill at ease, and unaccustomed to taking tests involving much talking, and they soon became weary with the effort of expressing themselves. There is a general feeling in the village that it is not good for a person to study or think too much, and the questions were *molestia* (a bother). One mother objected to the continuation of a test on the grounds that . . . the child's head would get too hot from thinking so much! (Lewis 1951: 307–308) ◀

Such cultural attitudes as these stimulate the question of how representative of the children's behavior are the data thus obtained. They may represent accurately inter-culture interaction of observer and cultural representative, but what do they tell us about intra-cultural behavior? Further, several anthropological field studies have gathered psychological test data at one period and brought them to the psychologist for scoring and interpretation at a later time, as long as six years in some studies. The extent of observation at time of administration of the tests may significantly affect the meaning of the test scoring and interpretation, because the contextual data of the subject's behavior in the test situation are extremely important in a clinical study. This is the well-known problem in the comparison of psychometrician, test-bound to the cook-book method, and clinical psychologist who utilizes the total behavior of the subject in the test situation to understand personality, and not merely the test scores.

What then are the criteria which the psychologist insists upon if psychological tests are used in anthropological field studies? The major contribution of the test is its objectivity and standardized procedure in administration, scoring, and interpretation. This objectivity and standardization is a function of several factors; and criteria for the selection of a mental test for anthropological field study are neither less important nor different from the criteria observed in other investigations of human behavior whether by psychologist, psychiatrist, sociologist, or other social scientist.   Some of the significant factors (Freeman 1939; Watson 1951) in choice of a psychological test for a specific research design are: economy of subject and examiner time in administration, and examiner time in scoring and interpretation; cost; completeness and convenience of material; fullness, simplicity and clearness of directions; adaptability to subjects under investigation; appeal value; length of test ["... chance errors are diminished by an increase in the number of responses.... (but) What is the point at which we begin to have rapidly diminishing returns from an increase in the length of the test?" (Freeman 1939)]; ease and simplicity of administration and scoring, and of the response required of the subject; availability of suitable norms and their reliability and validity for the specific research; and relevance of test data to the problem under investigation.   Finally, there are the significant conclusions of Henry (1947) which should be considered.

▶ The single most outstanding limitation of a study of this sort is the unfortunate fact that the method of analysis for individual and for group use is so extremely difficult to document and delineate for other investigators. This fact is partly due to the newness of the techniques and the scarcity of research reports on the method of analysis. It is to a very large extent due, however, to the fact that much of the methods and principles of analysis must lie within the training and experience of the analyst in general psychological theory and practice rather than within his mere acquaintance with the material of the TAT alone. (p. 127) ◀

These then are criteria formulated by the psychologist, but there also are certain conditions presented by the anthropologist. Henry and Spiro (1953) list four requirements: measurement of the personality "as a whole" rather than by limited techniques, material which is not "culture-bound," tests permitting sampling of large numbers of subjects, and brief tests capable of rapid and easy administration, the analysis of which may be done by other than the investigating anthropologist to permit "the checking of the data by independent analysts and by persons whose judgment was not biased by previous knowledge of the people."

In cooperative enterprise both the anthropologist and the psychologist can meet the criteria which each desires of psychological measurement. Not every requirement can be met, however, and the investigator must attempt a balance between flexibility and objectivity which does not sacrifice one or the other quality. For example, although Cattell (1940; Cattell et al. 1941) has designed what he terms a "culture-free" test, Vernon (1951) has written that it is "... virtually impossible to find a culturally neutral test for the purpose of making interracial comparisons," and De Groot (1951) has made a similar statement on the basis of his experience. Further, in a recent review by Auld (1952) of the influence of social class on personality test responses the conclusion was drawn that error is introduced unless the investigator "consciously take(s) social-class differences into account." If one extrapolates from the differences between middle- and lower-class responses in our culture to the differences between our culture and others, the influence of cultural differences raises a significant problem in the use of normative data obtained in our society but used as reference in other cultures.

Other sampling and normative difficulties are reflected in such studies as that of MacGregor (1946) in which Indians of mixed heritage were studied, raising the question of appropriateness of norms—whether to use data from Indian or from white samples as norms. Also, how responses are affected by change in the stimuli demands an entire study in itself. In MacGregor's study, the TAT stimulus cards were "redrawn to present Indian characteristics," yet analysis and interpretation of the data were carried on in terms of norms derived from a different set of stimulus cards presented to a sample culturally different from the experimental group under study. Similarly, in Vogt's study of Navaho veterans (1951), a set of stimulus cards was devised which pictured the veteran in "both white and Navaho social situations." However, the standard series of TAT also were used, and in such a research design where both the standard set and an experimental set are used, there are then available referent data from the responses to the standard cards. Lantz's review (1948) of the studies of Cook, Hallowell, and DuBois also stresses the normative problem:

► The procedure of using Western norms when they corroborate the ethnographers' results, and of using explanations from the immediate culture when Western norms fail, seems highly unreliable and invalid. . . . In general it appears that the findings of Rorschach studies of pre-literate societies tend primarily to be highly general and somewhat vague . . . in part due to the inexperience of those using Rorschach as a test for cross-cultural personality investigation. Rorschach . . . devised . . . to describe the dynamic intellectual-emotional configuration among persons in Western society. Using it otherwise results in much speculation without any real scientific basis. (p. 291)[1] ◄

Other sources of error may arise in the interpretation of test data, even though administration of the psychological test was conducted with standard material. An example of this sort is seen in Mead's report (1949) on the Mountain Arapesh where Dr. Mead describes the several ways in which Unabelin's Rorschach data were analyzed four times by five clinical psychologists. Two of the four analyses are based on the protocol and localization chart; the other two also used the scoring, done by a sixth person. Dr. Klopfer discussed his interpretation with Dr. Mead, "occasionally asking . . . corroborative questions about the culture." Drs. Harrower and Miale discussed the protocol and chart, and "summarized the discussion . . . followed by a long interpreta-

---

1.   From "Rorschach Testing in Preliterate Cultures," by Herman Lantz, *American Journal of Orthopsychiatry*, Vol. 18, No. 2, April 1948. Copyright, the American Orthopsychiatric Association, Inc. Reproduced by permission.

tive discussion among the three of us (including Dr. Mead), from which special points have been selected for publication." Dr. Wolfenstein "made a very rapid assessment . . . and Dr. Abel . . . wrote an analysis emphasizing the cultural relevance of the material." It seems apparent that the same critieria were not applied in the four analyses, nor was the same amount of data used. Further, independent interpretations were made in some instances and not in others, and knowledge of cultural factors was available to some of the psychologists and not to others. This variation in task and material and independence of report does not suggest a rigorous test of the use of the Rorschach technique in studying personality. Dr. Mead mentions "the variety of types of interpretation that have been used on this single (Unabelin's) Rorschach record," and there is indeed a variety, but then there is such a variety of conditions under which the five psychologists worked. Mead also reports "a high degree of agreement," but this does not seem to be supported by the objective evidence of the emphasis by one interpreter on the psychotic elements, because of unawareness of cultural factors; in another case, emphasis on timidity, fear, and caution; intellectual aspects emphasized in a third interpretation; and concentration on specific cultural factors as aids to interpretation in a fourth analysis. Whether these differences are a function of the interpreter, the Rorschach method, the amount of data, or the task assigned each psychologist, cannot be said in light of the varying conditions obtaining in at least the latter two factors.

Sampling variation and its effect on representativeness of sampling has been carefully considered by Du Bois in connection with autobiographical material, and her concern applies equally well to sampling when psychological tests are used.

▶ The persons from whom autobiographies were secured do not represent the ideal or "type" person. . . . The most successful men said they were too busy. . . . The "ideal" women . . . were either too unassertive or too engrossed in work. I am under the impression that inability to secure autobiographical material from the successful type individuals of a culture is an experience many ethnographers have had in functioning societies. (Du Bois 1944: 191)[2] ◀

In the same study, Kardiner pointed to other factors capable of biasing data. First, there is the subjects' reaction to the ethnographer, seen for example in their seeking rewards for responding and in the seeking out of the ethnographer by some subjects who wanted the opportunity of being interviewed. Second, the presence of an interpreter has an effect which has not been controlled experimentally, although anthropologists frequently have discussed interpreter influence in studies. Further, the criteria of standard administration of psychological tests were not met, as seen in Porteus' comments on use of the Porteus maze test.

---

2.   From Cora Du Bois, *The People of Alor*, University of Minnesota Press, Minneapolis © Copyright 1944, University of Minnesota.

▶ ... at a great disadvantage in not being able to observe the test responses ... whether the mistakes were due to impulsiveness or to mental confusion and anxiety. ... There were quite a number of cases in which there was evident misunderstanding of the nature of the test ... native peoples ... are less willing to attempt the test and seem to think that it represents a task that is outside the feminine province ... your (Du Bois') results are not perhaps strictly comparable to mine, as the conditions of testing were somewhat different. Your subjects had the advantage of an interpreter and you also modified the procedure by marking the point of exit in each test. (Du Bois 1944: 533–554) ◀

One more comment seems in order. It has been noted that "modal" or "basic" personalities have been constructed out of the statistics derived from psychological test data. This is seen, for example, in the description of the Alorese (Du Bois 1944). Statistics are short-hand methods for communicating certain information about characteristics of the distribution of data, and therefore valuable in scientific studies. However, a mode or mean statistic of central tendency tells nothing of the extent of variability of the data from which the central tendency is extracted. The standard deviation and form of distribution, whether normal, J-curve, or bi- or multi-modal also must be considered in reporting data. And it is the rule rather than the exception that field studies using psychological tests have revealed extreme variability among the samples studied, so that a mean or modal value reported for a culture often is misleading in that it neglects to record the more significant factor of wide variation. Thus, to say of a sample of a culture that the mean number of Dd responses is 9 has significantly different meaning with a standard deviation of 10 than in a more homogeneous sample with much less variability (Du Bois 1944).

These several samples of possible biases in the administration, scoring and interpretation of psychological tests in anthropological field studies are not intended as condemnations of the studies or techniques. Rather, they warn of the care necessary in the use of tests, and also illustrate the awareness of anthropologists and psychologists of the problems of psychological measurement. Henry and Spiro (1953), Cook (1942), Hallowell (1940; 1941), Du Bois (1944), Henry (1941), Joseph and Murray (1951), have recorded the errors in sampling, normative data, and test technique which limit the results of their studies. Psychologists also have been concerned with the uncritical use of psychological tests, reflected, for example, in the reviews of Lantz (1948), McNemar (1952), Auld (1952), and Heathers (1952). The solution to the problem of adjusting the test criteria of the psychologist to the field study criteria of the anthropologist does not lie in the abandonment of tests, but rather it seems to be in the more critical use of tests and test data. The difficulties raised in the field by use of interpreters, modifications of test material and procedure, cultural attitudes, sampling variation and lack of adequate norms; and the difficulties in the psychological laboratory to which field test data are brought, because of the necessity for "blind analysis," are factors which limit the generalizations from field studies but do not demand that the data be discarded as useless. Instead, both the anthropologist and psychologist must see to it that their criteria of test selection and procedure are observed and limiting factors clearly stated. Further, there is to be considered the degree of "blindness" of the psychologist in blind analysis—how much information about the subjects and their culture can be revealed without biasing the data interpretation. For example, Watson (1951) has summarized his philosophy of the clinical method in the following manner:

► Regardless of the nature of the clinical problem, it is unlikely that any one battery of tests will permit the derivation of a complete diagnostic appraisal . . . valid interpretation . . . demands complementation from . . . developmental and school history, mental status examination, . . . entire case study . . .(these) are needed for adequate interpretation. ◄

In summary, psychological measurement had its beginning in part in anthropological studies; it has moved from individual- to group- and now back again to individual-oriented emphasis in both anthropology and psychology; and it has been valuable to both fields in quantifying information gathered under objective and standardized conditions. There are criteria of test selection and procedure which must be satisfied, and other criteria of the cultural anthropologist which can be met in application of tests in field studies. Limiting factors in terms of tests or field conditions do not demand abandonment of the techniques but do require scientific caution in the generalizations drawn from the data. Anthropologists fortunately are aware of the limiting conditions of language barriers, differing cultural attitudes and experiences, and inadequate normative data, but often there is too much emphasis upon psychological tests and other observational data without the reminder that different test conditions, from administration through the normative comparison stage, introduce distortion and bias which is uncontrolled so that evaluation of the data is difficult.

Although both anthropologists and psychologists have formulated criteria for psychological measurement in anthropological field studies, there remain several problems on which both anthropologists and psychologists can work collaboratively. The accumulation of adequate norms and discussion of "culture-free" qualities of psychological tests, and the limits of "blind analysis" of field data in the laboratory represent major areas where community of interests and experiences may be productive.

In applying psychological measures to the data of anthropological field study, the criteria of selection and administration of the techniques, and scoring and interpretation of the responses, constitute the scientific basis for the utility of the measures. Validity; reliability of the test situation and of the responses to it; ease and economy of administration, scoring and interpreting;

applicability and relevance to the goals of the specific study—all these characteristics are as significant to anthropology's use of psychological techniques as to other applications. Multidimensional research has many advantages, but uncritical use of techniques from the various cooperating sciences, principally a function of the lack of communication among the disciplines, may seriously reduce the value of the "team approach." The objectivity and standardization of the psychological test are its major strengths, and if these are sacrificed then the test data offer no more than do other avenues for observing human behavior. The psychological test as a scientific experiment is valuable only when it is conducted with scientific control, in its elements of selection and administration, and scoring and interpretation of its data. A survey of the literature on anthropological field studies which have included psychological test measurement suggests that greater attention must be paid to the criteria for adequate psychological evaluation. Psychological measurement has demonstrated its significance in many areas of human behavior study but there are cautions to be observed and the specialized nature of tests requires trained personnel and an appreciation of the limitations of tests as field conditions vary.

BIBLIOGRAPHY

ABEL, T. M. 1948 The Rorschach Test in the Study of Culture. Rorschach Research Exchange and Journal of Projective Techniques 12: 79–93.

ABEL, T. M. AND F. L. K. HSU 1949 Some Aspects of Personality of Chinese as Revealed by the Rorschach test. Rorschach Research Exchange and Journal of Projective Techniques 13: 285–301.

AULD, F., JR. 1952 Influence of Social Class on Personality Test Responses. Psychological Bulletin 49: 318–332.

BECK, S. J., A. I. RABIN, W. G. THIESEN, H. MOLISH AND W. N. THETFORD 1950 The Normal Personality as Projected in the Rorschach Test. Journal of Psychology 30: 241–288.

BORING, E. G. 1929 A History of Experimental Psychology. Appleton-Century, New York.

CARLSON, H. B. AND N. HENDERSON 1950 The Intelligence of American Children of Mexican Parentage. Journal of Abnormal and Social Psychology 45: 544–551.

CATTELL, J. MCK. 1890 Mental Tests and Measurements. Mind 15: 373–380.

CATTELL, R. B. 1940 A Culture-Free Intelligence Test. Journal of Educational Psychology 31: 161–179.

CATTELL, R. B., S. N. FEINGOLD, AND S. B. SARASON 1941 A Culture-free Intelligence Test: II. Evaluation of Cultural Influence on Test Performance. Journal of Educational Psychology 32: 81–100.

COOK, P. H. 1942. The Application of the Rorschach Test to a Samoan Group. Rorschach Research Exchange 6: 52–60.

DE GROOT, A. D. 1951 War and the Intelligence of Youth. Journal of Abnormal and Social Psychology 46: 596–597.

DU BOIS, C. 1944 The People of Alor. University of Minnesota Press, Minneapolis.

FREEMAN, F. N. 1939 Mental Tests: Their History, Principles and Applications. Houghton Mifflin, New York, rev. ed.

HALLOWELL, A. I. 1940 Rorschach as an Aid in the Study of Personalities in Primitive Societies. Rorschach Research Exchange 4: 106.

————, 1941 The Rorschach Test as a Tool for Investigating Culture Variables and Individual Differences in the Study of Personality in Primitive Societies. Rorschach Research Exchange 5: 31–34.

HEATHERS, G. 1952 Review of L. Thompson's Culture in Crisis. Psychological Bulletin 49: 187–189.

HENRY, J. 1941 Rorschach Techniques in Primitive Cultures. American Journal of Orthopsychiatry 11: 230–234.

HENRY, J. AND J. W. BOGGS 1952 Child Rearing, Culture and the Natural World. Psychiatry: Journal of Studies in Interpersonal Processes 15: 261–271.

HENRY, J. AND M. SPIRO 1953 Psychological Tests in Anthropological Field Work in Anthropology Today: An Encyclopedic Inventory, ed. by A. Kroeber. University of Chicago Press, Chicago.

HENRY, W. E. 1947 The Thematic Apperception Technique in the Study of Culture-Personality Relations, Genetic Psychology Monographs 35: 3–135.

JOSEPH, A, AND V. F. MURRAY 1951 Chamorros and Carolinians of Saipan. Harvard University Press, Cambridge.

KLINEBERG, O. 1927 Racial Differences in Speed and Accuracy. Journal of Abnormal and Social Psychology 22: 273–277.

LANTZ, H. 1948 Rorschach Testing in Pre-literate Cultures. American Journal Orthopsychiatry 18: 287–291.

LEWIS, O. 1951 Life in a Mexican Village: Tepotzlan Restudied. University of Illinois Press, Urbana.

LUCHINS, A. S. 1952 Towards an Experimental Clinical Psychology. Journal of Personality 20: 440–456.

MAC GREGOR, G. 1946 Warriors Without Weapons. University of Chicago Press, Chicago.

MC NEMAR, Q. 1952 Review of K. Eels, A. Davis, R. J. Havighurst, V. E. Herrick and R. Tyler's Intelligence and Cultural Differences. Psychological Bulletin 49: 370–371.

MEAD, M. 1949 The Mountain Arapesh: V. The Record of Unabelin with Rorschach Analysis. Anthropological Papers of the American Museum of Natural History 41: 289–390, New York.

MENSH, I. N. 1950 Statistical Techniques in Present-day Psychodiagnostics. Psychological Bulletin 47: 475–492.

PASAMANICK, B. 1951 The Intelligence of American Children of Mexican Parentage: A Discussion of Uncontrolled Variables. Journal of Abnormal and Social Psychology 46: 598–602.

SCHACHTEL, A. H., J. AND Z. HENRY 1942 Rorschach Analysis of Pilaga Indian Children. American Journal of Orthopsychiatry 12: 679–712.

THOMPSON, LAURA 1951 Personality and Government. America Indigena 11, no. 3: 235–269.

VERNON, P. E. 1951 Recent Investigations of Intelligence and its Measurement. Eugenics Review 43: 125–137.

VOGT, E. Z. 1951 Navaho Veterans: A Study of Changing Values. Papers of the Peabody Museum of American Archaeology 41: No. 1. Cambridge.

WATSON, R. I. 1951 The Clinical Method in Psychology. Harper, New York.

Neil Friedman (1967) has argued that psychological experimentation, as well as psychological testing, can be profitably evaluated from the viewpoint of participant observation. The growing literature on experimenter effect reveals a considerable reactive effect of experimenter behavior on subject behavior.[2] Friedman proposes

---

2.   See, for example, Rosenthal (1966); Orne (1962).

modifications of experimental methodology to take full account of the fact that an experiment is a complicated social interaction within a formal organization.

▶ This means that some of the disdain with which psychological researchers customarily treat data obtained by sociologists and anthropologists working in the field is inappropriate. It might be profitably replaced by the study and application of their considerable literature on participant-observation methodology. For, whereas the ideal psychological experimenter is an immaculate perceiver of an objective reality, the real psychological experimenter is, to a far greater extent than has been suspected, very much like his counterparts in the other social studies. He, too, is a *participant-observer*.[3] ◀

Howard Becker and Blanche Geer round out the evaluation of other research procedures by examining interview techniques with relation to participant observation. The commentary aroused by this selection, also reprinted here, has been of considerable importance in placing such evaluative efforts in proper perspective.

PARTICIPANT OBSERVATION AND INTERVIEWING: A COMPARISON

HOWARD S. BECKER AND BLANCHE GEER

The most complete form of the sociological datum, after all, is the form in which the participant observer gathers it: An observation of some social event, the events which precede and follow it, and explanations of its meaning by participants and spectators, before, during, and after its occurrence. Such a datum gives us more information about the event under study than data gathered by any other sociological method. Participant observation can thus provide us with a yardstick against which to measure the completeness of data gathered in other ways, a model which can serve to let us know what orders of information escape us when we use other methods.[1]

By participant observation we mean that method in which the observer participates in the daily life of the people under study, either openly in the role of researcher or covertly in some disguised role, observing things that happen, listening to what is said, and questioning people, over some length of time.[2]

---

3. From *The Social Nature of Psychological Research* by Neil Friedman, Basic Books, Inc., Publishers. New York, 1967, p. 179.

Reprinted from *Human Organization* (1957), **16**, No. 3, 28–32, by permission of the authors and the publisher.

1. We wish to thank R. Richard Wohl and Thomas S. McPartland for their critical reading of an earlier version of this paper.

2. Cf. Florence R. Kluckhohn, "The Participant Observer Technique in Small Communities," *American Journal of Sociology*, 45 (Nov., 1940), 331–43; Arthur Vidich, "Participant Observation and the Collection and Interpretation of Data," *ibid.*, 60 (Jan., 1955), 354–60; William Foote Whyte, "Observational Field-Work Methods," in Marie Jahoda, Morton Deutsch, and Stuart W. Cook (eds.), *Research Methods in the Social Sciences* (New York: Dryden Press, 1951), II, 393–514, and *Street Corner Society* (Enlarged Edition) (Chicago: University of Chicago Press, 1955), 279–358.

We want, in this paper, to compare the results of such intensive field work with what might be regarded as the first step in the other direction along this continuum: the detailed and conversational interview (often referred to as the unstructured or undirected interview).[3] In this kind of interview, the interviewer explores many facets of his interviewee's concerns, treating subjects as they come up in conversation, pursuing interesting leads, allowing his imagination and ingenuity full rein as he tries to develop new hypotheses and test them in the course of the interview.

In the course of our current participant observation among medical students,[4] we have thought a good deal about the kinds of things we were discovering which might ordinarily be missed or misunderstood in such an interview. We have no intention of denigrating the interview or even such less precise modes of data gathering as the questionnaire, for there can always be good reasons of practicality, economy, or research design for their use. We simply wish to make explicit the difference in data gathered by one or the other method and to suggest the differing uses to which they can legitimately be put. In general, the shortcomings we attribute to the interview exist when it is used as a source of information about events that have occurred elsewhere and are described to us by informants. Our criticisms are not relevant when analysis is restricted to interpretation of the interviewee's conduct *during the interview,* in which case the researcher has in fact observed the behavior he is talking about.[5]

The differences we consider between the two methods involve two interacting factors: the kinds of words and acts of the people under study that the researcher has access to, and the kind of sensitivity to problems and data produced in him. Our comparison may prove useful by suggestive areas in which interviewing (the more widely used method at present and likely to continue so) can improve its accuracy by taking account of suggestions made from the perspective of the participant observer. We begin by considering some concrete problems: learning the native language, or the problem of the degree to which the interviewer really understands what is said to him; matters interviewees are unable or unwilling to talk about; and getting information on matters people see through distorting lenses. We then consider some more general differences between the two methods.

---

3.   Two provisos are in order. In the first place, we assume in our comparison that the hypothetical interviewer and participant observer we discuss are equally skilled and sensitive. We assume further that both began their research with equally well formulated problems, so that they are indeed looking for equivalent kinds of data.

4.   This study is sponsored by Community Studies, Inc., of Kansas City, Missouri, and is being carried out at the University of Kansas Medical Center, to whose dean and staff we are indebted for their wholehearted cooperation. Professor Everett C. Hughes of the University of Chicago is director of the project.

5.   For discussion of this point, see Thomas S. McPartland, *Formal Education and the Process of Professionalization: A Study of Student Nurses* (Kansas City, Missouri: Community Studies, Inc., 1957), 2–3.

LEARNING THE NATIVE LANGUAGE

Any social group, to the extent that it is a distinctive unit, will have to some degree a culture differing from that of other groups, a somewhat different set of common understandings around which action is organized, and these differences will find expression in a language whose nuances are peculiar to that group and fully understood only by its members. Members of churches speak differently from members of informal tavern groups; more importantly, members of any particular church or tavern group have cultures, and languages in which they are expressed, which differ somewhat from those of other groups of the same general type. So, although we speak one language and share in many ways in one culture, we cannot assume that we understand precisely what another person, speaking as a member of such a group, means by any particular word. In interviewing members of groups other than our own, then, we are in somewhat the same position as the anthropologist who must learn a primitive language,[6] with the important difference that, as Icheiser has put it, we often do not understand that we do not understand and are thus likely to make errors in interpreting what is said to us. In the case of gross misunderstandings the give and take of conversation may quickly reveal our mistakes, so that the interviewee can correct us; this presumably is one of the chief mechanisms through which the anthropologist acquires a new tongue. But in speaking American English with an interviewee who is, after all, much like us, we may mistakenly assume that we have understood him and the error be small enough that it will not disrupt communication to the point where a correction will be in order.

The interview provides little opportunity of rectifying errors of this kind where they go unrecognized. In contrast, participant observation provides a situation in which the meanings of words can be learned with great precision through study of their use in context, exploration through continuous interviewing of their implications and nuances, and the use of them oneself under the scrutiny of capable speakers of the language. Beyond simply clarifying matters so that the researcher may understand better what people say to each other and to him, such a linguistic exercise may provide research hypotheses of great usefulness. The way in which one of us learned the meaning of the word "crock," as medical students use it, illustrates these points.

▶ I first heard the word "crock" applied to a patient shortly after I began my field work. The patient in question, a fat, middle-aged woman, complained bitterly of pains in a number of widely separated locations. When I asked the student who had so described her what the word meant, he said that it was used to refer to any patient who had psychosomatic complaints. I asked if that meant that Mr. X———, a young man on the ward whose stomach ulcer had

---

6. See the discussion in Bronislaw Malinowski, *Magic, Science, and Religion and Other Essays* (Glencoe: The Free Press, 1948), 232–8.

been discussed by a staff physician as typically psychosomatic, was a crock. The student said that that would not be correct usage, but was not able to say why.

Over a period of several weeks, through discussion of many cases seen during morning rounds with the students, I finally arrived at an understanding of the term, realizing that it referred to a patient who complained of many symptoms but had no discoverable organic pathology. I had noticed from the beginning that the term was used in a derogatory way and had also been inquiring into this, asking students why they disliked having crocks assigned to them for examination and diagnosis. At first students denied the derogatory connotations, but repeated observations of their disgust with such assignments soon made such denials unrealistic. Several students eventually explained their dislike in ways of which the following example is typical: "The true crock is a person who you do a great big workup for and who has all of these vague symptoms, and *you really can't find anything the matter with them.*"

Further discussion made it clear that the students regarded patients primarily as objects from which they could learn those aspects of clinical medicine not easily acquired from textbooks and lectures; the crock took a great deal of their time, of which they felt they had little enough, and did not exhibit any interesting disease state from which something might be learned, so that the time invested was wasted. This discovery in turn suggested that I might profitably investigate the general perspective toward medical school which led to such a basis for judgment of patients, and also suggested hypotheses regarding the value system of the hospital hierarchy at whose bottom the student stood. ◄

At the risk of being repetitious, let us point out in this example both the errors avoided and the advantages gained because of the use of participant observation. The term might never have been used by students in an ordinary interview; if it had, the interviewer might easily have assumed that the scatological term from which it in fact is descended provided a complete definition. Because the observer saw students on their daily rounds and heard them discussing everyday problems, he heard the word and was able to pursue it until he arrived at a meaningful definition. Moreover, the knowledge so gained led to further and more general discoveries about the group under study.

This is not to say that all of these things might not be discovered by a program of skillful interviewing, for this might well be possible. But we do suggest that an interviewer may misunderstand common English words when interviewees use them in some more or less esoteric way and not know that he is misunderstanding them, because there will be little chance to check his understanding against further examples of their use in conversation or instances of the object to which they are applied. This leaves him open to errors of misinterpretation and errors of failing to see connections between items of information he has available, and may prevent him from seeing and exploring important research leads. In dealing with interview data, then, experience with participant observation indicates that both care and imagination must be used in making sure of meanings, for the cultural esoterica of a group may hide behind ordinary language used in special ways.

MATTERS INTERVIEWEES ARE
UNABLE OR UNWILLING TO TALK ABOUT

Frequently, people do not tell an interviewer all the things he might want to know. This may be because they do not want to, feeling that to speak of some particular subject would be impolitic, impolite, or insensitive, because they do not think to and because the interviewer does not have enough information to inquire into the matter, or because they are not able to. The first case—the problem of "resistance"—is well known and a considerable lore has developed about how to cope with it.[7] It is more difficult to deal with the last two possibilities for the interviewee is not likely to reveal, or the interviewer to become aware, that significant omissions are being made. Many events occur in the life of a social group and the experience of an individual so regularly and uninterruptedly, or so quietly and unnoticed, that people are hardly aware of them, and do not think to comment on them to an interviewer; or they may never have become aware of them at all and be unable to answer even direct questions. Other events may be so unfamiliar that people find it difficult to put into words their vague feelings about what has happened. If an interviewee, for any of these reasons, cannot or will not discuss a certain topic, the researcher will find gaps in his information on matters about which he wants to know and will perhaps fail to become aware of other problems and areas of interest that such discussion might have opened up for him.

This is much less likely to happen when the researcher spends much time with the people he studies as they go about their daily activities, for he can see the very things which might not be reported in an interview. Further, should he desire to question people about matters they cannot or prefer not to talk about, he is able to point to specific incidents which either force them to face the issue (in the case of resistance) or make clear what he means (in the case of unfamiliarity). Finally, he can become aware of the full meaning of such hints as are given on subjects people are unwilling to speak openly about and of such inarticulate statements as people are able to make about subjects they cannot clearly formulate, because he frequently knows of these things through his observation and can connect his knowledge with these half-communications.

Researchers working with interview materials, while they are often conscious of these problems, cannot cope with them so well. If they are to deal with matters of this kind it must be by inference. They can only make an educated guess about the things which go unspoken in the interview; it may be a very good guess, but it must be a guess. They can employ various tactics to explore for material they feel is there but unspoken, but even when these are fruitful

---

7.   See, for example, Arnold M. Rose, "A Research Note on Interviewing," *American Journal of Sociology,* 51 (Sept., 1945), 143–4; and Howard S. Becker, "A Note on Interviewing Tactics," *Human Organization,* 12:4 (Winter, 1954), 31–2.

they do not create sensitivity to those problems of which even the interviewer is not aware. The following example indicates how participant observation aids the researcher in getting material, and making the most of the little he gets, on topics lying within this range of restricted communication.

▶ A few months after the beginning of school, I went to dinner at one of the freshman medical fraternities. It was the night non-resident members came, married ones with their wives. An unmarried student who lived in the house looked around at the visitors and said to me, "We are so much in transition. I have never been in this situation before of meeting fellows and their wives."

This was just the sort of thing we were looking for—change in student relationships arising from group interaction—but I failed in every attempt to make the student describe the "transition" more clearly.

From previous observation, though, I knew there were differences (other than marriage) between the nonresidents and their hosts. The former had all been elected to the fraternity recently, after house officers had gotten to know them through working together (usually on the same cadaver in anatomy lab). They were older than the average original member; instead of coming directly from college, several had had jobs or Army experience before medical school. As a group they were somewhat lower in social position.

These points indicated that the fraternity was bringing together in relative intimacy students different from each other in background and experience. They suggested a search for other instances in which dissimilar groups of students were joining forces, and pointed to a need for hypotheses as to what was behind this process of drawing together on the part of the freshman and its significance for their medical education. ◀

An interviewer, hearing this statement about "transition," would know that the interviewee felt himself in the midst of some kind of change but might not be able to discover anything further about the nature of that change. The participant observer cannot find out, any more than the interviewer can, what the student had in mind, presumably because the student had nothing more in mind than this vague feeling of change. (Interviewees are not sociologists and we ought not to assume that their fumbling statements are attempts, crippled by their lack of technical vocabulary, to express what a sociologist might put in more formal analytic terms.) But he can search for those things in the interviewee's situation which might lead to such a feeling of transition.

While the participant observer can make immediate use of such vague statements as clues to an objective situation, the interviewer is often bothered by the question of whether an interviewee is not simply referring to quite private experiences. As a result, the interviewer will place less reliance on whatever inferences about the facts of the situation he makes, and is less likely to be sure enough of his ground to use them as a basis for further hypotheses. Immediate observation of the scene itself and data from previous observation enable the participant observer to make direct use of whatever hints the informant supplies.

THINGS PEOPLE SEE THROUGH DISTORTING LENSES

In many of the social relationships we observe, the parties to the relation will have differing ideas as to what ought to go on in it, and frequently as to what does in fact go on in it. These differences in perception will naturally affect what they report in an interview. A man in a subordinate position in an organization in which subordinates believe that their superiors are "out to get them" will interpret many incidents in this light though the incidents themselves may not seem, either to the other party in the interaction or to the observer, to indicate such malevolence. Any such mythology will distort people's view of events to such a degree that they will report as fact things which have not occurred, but which seem to them to have occurred. Students, for example, frequently invent sets of rules to govern their relations with teachers, and, although the teacher may never have heard of such rules, regard the teachers as malicious when they "disobey" them. The point is that things may be reported in an interview through such a distorting lens, and the interviewer may have no way of knowing what is fact and what is distortion of this kind; participant observation makes it possible to check such points. The following is a particularly clear example.

▶ Much of the daily teaching was done, and practical work of medical students supervised, in a particular department of the hospital, by the house residents. A great deal of animosity had grown up between the particular group of students I was with at the time and these residents, the students believing that the residents would, for various malicious reasons, subordinate and embarrass them at every opportunity. Before I joined the group, several of the students told me that the residents were "mean," "nasty," "bitchy," and so on, and had backed these characterizations up with evidence of particular actions.
   After I began participating daily with the students on this service, a number of incidents made it clear that the situation was not quite like this. Finally, the matter came completely into the open. I was present when one of the residents suggested a technique that might have prevented a minor relapse in a patient assigned to one of the students; he made it clear that he did not think the relapse in any way the student's fault, but rather that he was simply passing on what he felt to be a good tip. Shortly afterward, this student reported to several other students that the resident had "chewed him out" for failing to use this technique: "What the hell business has he got chewing me out about that for? No one ever told me I was supposed to do it that way." I interrupted to say, "He didn't really chew you out. I thought he was pretty decent about it." Another student said, "Any time they say anything at all to us I consider it a chewing out. Any time they say anything about how we did things, they are chewing us out, no matter how God damn nice they are about it." ◀

In short, participant observation makes it possible to check description against fact and, noting discrepanices, become aware of systematic distortions made by the person under study; such distortions are less likely to be discovered by interviewing alone. This point, let us repeat, is only relevant when the interview is used as a source of information about situations and events the researcher himself has not seen. It is not relevant when it is the person's behavior in the interview itself that is under analysis.

INFERENCE, PROCESS AND CONTEXT

We have seen, in the previous sections of this paper, some of the ways in which even very good interviews may go astray, at least from the perspective of the field observer. We turn now to a consideration of the more general areas of difference between the two methods, suggesting basic ways in which the gathering and handling of data in each differ.

Since we tend to talk in our analyses about much the same order of thing whether we work from interviews or from particpant-observational materials, and to draw conclusions about social relations and the interaction that goes on within them whether we have actually seen these things or only been told about them, it should be clear that in working with interviews we must necessarily infer a great many things we could have observed had we only been in a position to do so. The kinds of errors we have discussed above are primarily errors of inference, errors which arise from the necessity of making assumptions about the relation of interview statements to actual events which may or may not be true; for what we have solid observable evidence on in the first case we have only secondhand reports and indices of in the second, and the gap must be bridged by inference. We must assume, when faced with an account or transcription of an interview, that we understand the meaning of the everyday words used, that the interviewee is able to talk about the things we are interested in, and that his account will be more or less accurate. The examples detailed above suggest that these assumptions do not always hold and that the process of inference involved in interpreting interviews should always be made explicit and checked, where possible, against what can be discovered through observation. Where, as is often the case, this is not possible, conclusions should be limited to those matters the data directly describe.

Let us be quite specific, and return to the earlier example of resident-student hostility. In describing this relationship from interviews with the students alone we might have assumed their description to be accurate and made the inference that the residents were in fact "mean." Observation proved that this inference would have been incorrect, but this does not destroy the analytic usefulness of the original statements made to the fieldworker in an informal interview. It does shift the area in which we can make deductions from this datum, however, for we can see that such statements, while incorrect factually, are perfectly good statements of the perspective from which these students interpreted the events in which they were involved. We could not know without observation whether their descriptions were true or false; with the aid of observation we know that the facts of the matter are sometimes quite different, and that the students' perspective is strong enough to override such variant facts. But from the interview alone we could know, not what actually happened in such cases, but what the students thought happened and how they felt about it, and this is the kind of inference we should make. We add to the accuracy of our data when we substitute observable fact for inference. More important, we open the way for the discovery of new hypotheses for the fact we observe may not be the fact we expected to observe. When this happens we face a new problem requiring new hypothetical explanations which can then be further tested in the field.

Substitution of an inference about something for an observation of that thing occurs most frequently in discussions of social process and change, an area in which the advantages of observation over an extended period of time are particularly great. Much sociological writing is concerned, openly or otherwise, with problems of process: The analysis of shifts in group structure, individual self-conception and similar matters. But studies of such phenomena in natural social contexts are typically based on data that tell only part of the story. The analysis may be made from a person's retrospective account, in a single interview, of changes that have taken place; or, more rarely, it is based on a series of interviews, the differences between successive interviews providing the bench marks of change. In either case, many crucial steps in the process and important mechanisms of change must be arrived at through inferences which can be no more than educated guesses.

The difficulties in analyzing change and process on the basis of interview material are particularly important because it is precisely in discussing changes in themselves and their surroundings that interviewees are least likely or able to give an accurate account of events. Changes in the social environment and in the self inevitably produce transformations of perspective, and it is characteristic of such transformations that the person finds it difficult or impossible to remember his former actions, outlook, or feelings. Reinterpreting things from his new perspective, he cannot give an accurate account of the past, for the concepts in which he thinks about it have changed and with them his perceptions and memories.[8] Similarly, a person in the midst of such change may find it difficult to describe what is happening, for he has not developed a perspective or concepts which would allow him to think and talk about these things coherently; the earlier discussion of changes in medical school fraternity life is a case in point.

Participant observation does not have so many difficulties of this sort. One can observe actual changes in behavior over a period of time and note the events which precede and follow them. Similarly, one can carry on a conversation running over weeks and months with the people he is studying and thus become aware of shifts in perspective as they occur. In short, attention can be focused both on what has happened and on what the person says about what

8.   Anselm L. Strauss, "The Development and Transformation of Monetary Meanings in the Child," *American Sociological Review,* 17 (June, 1952), 275–86, and *An Essay on Identity* (unpublished manuscript), *passim.*

has happened. Some inference as to actual steps in the process or mechanisms involved is still required, but the amount of inference necessary is considerably reduced. Again, accuracy is increased and the possibility of new discoveries being made is likewise increased, as the observer becomes aware of more phenomena requiring explanation.

The participant observer is both more aware of these problems of inference and more equipped to deal with them because he operates, when gathering data, in a social context rich in cues and information of all kinds. Because he sees and hears the people he studies in many situations of the kind that normally occur for them, rather than just in an isolated and formal interview, he builds an evergrowing fund of impressions, many of them at the subliminal level, which give him an extensive base for the interpretation and analytic use of any particular datum. This wealth of information and impression sensitizes him to subtleties which might pass unnoticed in an interview and forces him to raise continually new and different questions, which he brings to and tries to answer in succeeding observations.

The biggest difference in the two methods, then, may be not so much that participant observation provides the opportunity for avoiding the errors we have discussed, but that it does this by providing a rich experiential context which causes him to become aware of incongruous or unexplained facts, makes him sensitive to their possible implications and connections with other observed facts, and thus pushes him continually to revise and adapt his theoretical orientation and specific problems in the direction of greater relevance to the phenomena under study. Though this kind of context and its attendant benefits cannot be reproduced in interviewing (and the same degree of sensitivity and sense of problem produced in the interviewer), interviewers can profit from an awareness of those limitations of their method suggested by this comparison and perhaps improve their batting average by taking account of them.[9]

---

9.   We are aware that participant observation raises as many technical problems as it solves. (See, for instance, the discussions in Morris S. Schwartz and Charlotte Green Schwartz, "Problems in Participant Observation," *American Journal of Sociology*, 60 (Jan., 1955), 343–53, and in Vidich, *op. cit.*) We feel, however, that there is considerable value in using the strong points of one method to illuminate the shortcomings of another.

COMMENT ON "PARTICIPANT
OBSERVATION AND INTERVIEWING: A COMPARISON"

MARTIN TROW

I

Insofar as the paper by Becker and Geer says: "Participant observation is a very useful way of collecting data, and here are some illustrations to show how useful we found it in one study," I can take no issue with them. On the contrary, I profited from their discussion of the method and their illustrations of its use.

But, unfortunately, Becker and Geer say a good deal more than that. In their first paragraph they assert that participant observation, by virtue of its intrinsic qualities, "gives us more information about the event under study than data gathered by any other sociological method." And since this is true, "it provides us with a yardstick against which to measure the completeness of data gathered in other ways. . . ."

It is with this assertion, that a given method of collecting data—*any* method —has an inherent superiority over others by virtue of its special qualities and divorced from the nature of the problem studied, that I take sharp issue. The alternative view, and I would have thought this the view most widely accepted by social scientists, is that different kinds of information about man and society are gathered most fully and economically in different ways, and that the problem under investigation properly dictates the methods of investigation. If this is so, then we certainly can use other methods of investigation as "yardsticks" against which to measure the adequacy of participant observation for the collection of certain kinds of data. And my impression is that most of the problems social scientists are studying seem to call for data gathered in other ways than through participant observation. Moreover, most of the problems investigated call for data collected in several different ways, whether in fact they are or not. This view seems to me implied in the commonly used metaphor of the social scientist's "kit of tools" to which he turns to find the methods and techniques most useful to the problem at hand. Becker and Geer's argument sounds to me very much like a doctor arguing that the scalpel is a better instrument than the forceps—and since this is so we must measure the forceps' cutting power against that of the scalpel.

Much of the paper by Becker and Geer is devoted to measuring "the interview" against the yardstick of "participant observation." To make the "contest" between interviewing and participant observation a fair one, the authors make the proviso (footnote 3) that they are employed by men who are equally competent, and who start with equally well formulated problems, "so that they

Reprinted from *Human Organization* (1957), **16,** No. 3, 33–35, by permission of the author and publisher.

are indeed looking for equivalent kinds of data." I would assume, on the contrary, that interviewing and participant observation would rarely produce "equivalent" kinds of data, and should not be asked to, but rather produce rather different kinds of data designed to answer quite different kinds of questions about the same general phenomenon. Here again we have Becker and Geer's view of the forceps as a rather poor kind of cutting instrument.

But if I respectfully decline to enter debate on the question of whether the scalpel is a better instrument than the forceps (unless it is rather closely specified "for what")—nevertheless, it may be useful to consider some of the assumptions about the nature of social research out of which such an unreal question can emerge.

II

The first thing that struck me on reading this paper is its oddly parochial view of the range and variety of sociological problems. To state flatly that participant observation "gives us more information about the event under study than . . . any other sociological method" is to assume that all "events" are directly apprehensible by participant observers. But what are some of the "events" that sociologists study? Is a national political campaign such an "event"? Is a long-range shift in interracial attitudes an "event"? Is an important change in medical education and its aggregate of consequences an "event"? Are variations in suicide rates in different social groups and categories an "event"? If we exclude these phenomena from the definition of the term "event" then we exclude most of sociology. If we define "event" broadly enough to include the greater part of what sociologists study, then we find that most of our problems require for their investigation data of kinds that cannot be supplied by the participant observer alone.

But the answer of the participant observation enthusiast, if I read Becker and Geer correctly, would be "that is all very true, but very sad. Many students do require the gathering of data in all kinds of defective and suspect ways, but the closer they approximate to participant observation, and the more frequently they check their findings against those of participant observation, the better." To deal with this, let us for the moment drop the whole question of scalpel *versus* forceps, and consider one or two specific research studies, and the ways their data bear on their questions. This may allow us at least to raise what I feel is a far more fruitful set of questions: What kinds of problems are best studied through what kinds of methods; what kinds of insights and understandings seem to arise out of the analysis of different kinds of data; how can the various methods at our disposal complement one another? I can hardly attempt to contribute to the systematic discussion of these questions in a short "rebuttal" paper, but we can perhaps at least restate the questions in connection with some illustrative evidence.

The central problem of a recent study of the organization and internal politics of a trade union[1] was to explain the development, and especially the persistence, of a two party system within the union's political structure. To this end the research team examined a variety of documents, conducted various kinds of unstructured, focused, and highly structured interviews, examined voting records, and also engaged in participant observation.

Among the problems that we confronted was that of assessing the degree of legitimacy imputed to the party system by various groups and social categories within the union. This, I maintain, we could not have done at all adequately through participant observation. Let us leave aside the question, clearly not within the grasp of the participant observer, of whether the several hundred union officers and "leaders" were more or less inclined to think the party system a good thing in its own right as compared with the ten thousand men in a local or the one hundred thousand men in the international union we were studying. More to the point is the fact that the workings of the party system inhibited direct expressions of hostility to the system. In the ordinary give and take of conversation in the shop, party meeting, club meeting, informal gatherings after hours, such expressions were not likely to be expressed; they violated strongly held norms, and called down various kinds of punishments. It was only when we interviewed leaders individually and intensively that we could get some sense of the reservations that they held about the party system, how widely and strongly those reservations were held, and thus could make some assessment of those sentiments as a potentially disruptive force in the party system. It is true, as Becker and Geer point out, that men will do and say things in their customary activities and relationships that point to factors which might be wholly missed in the course of an interview—and where these things come to the attention of a participant observer he gains insights thereby. But the converse is also true, though perhaps not as widely recognized: Ordinary social life may well inhibit the casual expression of sentiments which are actually or potentially important elements in the explanation of the social phenomena under study. And participant observation is a relatively weak instrument for gathering data on sentiments, behaviors, relationships which are normatively proscribed by the group under observation.

I might note in passing that we gained useful insights into some of the mechanisms operating to sustain this union's political system through our observations at union meetings, party meetings, and during ordinary working days (and nights) spent in the shops. But these insights only took on full meaning in light of much other knowledge about that organization and its social and political structure that had been gained in other ways.

---

1. S. M. Lipset, M. A. Trow, and J. C. Coleman, *Union Democracy*, Glencoe, The Free Press, 1956.

A recent study in the sociology of medicine—the field from which Becker and Geer draw their own illustrations—emphasizes the need for the widest variety of research methods in attacks on comprehensive problems.[2] The index to the volume in which the first reports of this study are published list, under the heading "Methods of social research," the following sources of information used: diaries; documentary records; intensive interviews; observation; panel techniques; questionnaires; sociometry. Most of the papers in this volume deal with problems that could not have been studied solely through direct observation. One paper, for example, deals with the question of the processes by which medical students select their profession.[3] The author finds, among other things, that the occupation of the student's father was an important element in how and when he made that decision. Becker and Geer argue that the interview is not a good source of information "about events that have occurred elsewhere and are described to us by informants." But surely certain important facts about a man's early life experience—and these include what his father did for a living—can be reported quite accurately to an interviewer or on a questionnaire, and give the analyst invaluable data for the analysis of the forces and processes involved in the choice of a profession or occupation. But the bearing of one's father's occupation, or of one's religion, on attitudes and behaviors may never emerge in the ordinary course of events which the participant observer apprehends. Moreover, it is just not true, as Becker and Geer suggest, that the interview is a reliable source of information only regarding the interviewer's conduct *during the interview*. The amount of information people can tell us, quite simply and reliably, about their past experience is very great; and it is only in light of that information, I would maintain, that we can frequently understand their behaviors in the "here and now" that the participant observer is so close to.[4]

True, if we imagine that interviews can deal with past events only through questions of the sort: "Now, why did you choose medicine as a career?" then we may indeed worry about the distortions in reporting information retrospectively. But this effort to make the respondent do the analysis for the sociologist is not the only, and almost certainly not the best, way to assess the bearing of prior events on past or current decisions.

---

2.   R. K. Merton, George Reader, and P. L. Kendall, eds., *The Student-Physician*, Cambridge, Mass., The Harvard University Press, 1957. See especially George Reader, "The Cornell Comprehensive Care and Teaching Program," section on "Methods," pp. 94–101.

3.   Natalie Rogoff, "The Decision to Study Medicine," in Merton, Reader, and Kendall, eds., *op. cit.*, pp. 109–131.

4.   This suggests, more generally, that participant observation *by itself* is most nearly satisfactory in studies of small, isolated, relatively homogeneous populations, such as primitive tribes, where variations in the character of early life experience, and the effects of those variations on present sentiments and behaviors, are not so great. Where variations in experience outside the arena being observed are great, we must, for most problems, turn to other methods of data collection to learn about them.

III

We all profit, as I have from this paper, when social scientists broaden our knowledge of the special strengths of the methods which they have found useful and in the use of which they have acquired expertise. The danger lies in the kind of exclusive preoccupation with one method that leads to a systematic neglect of the potentialities, even the essential characteristics, of another. Becker and Geer seem to display this neglect when they contrast participant observation with "the interview." But with some exceptions, the data gathered by the interviewer are not usually embodied in "the interview" taken one at a time, but in the series of interviews through which a body of comparable data has been gathered. It is all of the comparable interviews, with their analysis, that must be compared with participant observation, and not the interviews taken one at a time. The charge is frequently made, and Becker and Geer repeat it, that the interview (and especially the highly structured survey interview) is a very "crude" instrument for collecting data—its artificiality and directedness ensure that much of the "richness" of social life as it is lived passes through its meshes. I would argue that there is more than one way to gain knowledge of the richness, the subtlety and infinite variety, of social life, and that sufficiently sensitive and intensive analysis of "crude" survey data is one such way. Durkheim, whose data in his study of suicide was even "cruder" and further removed from the "rich experiential context" than that of the survey analyst, nevertheless adds much to our understanding of some of the most subtle and complex aspects of social life. How much a social scientist can add to our understanding of society, I submit, is more a product of the way he defines his problem, the questions he brings to his data, and the adequacy of his data to answer his questions and suggest new ones, than it is of how "close," in a physical sense, he gets to the social life he is studying. And this, I think, is as true for social scientists who gather most of their data through participant observation, as for those who use that method to supplement others, and for those who use it not at all.

It is no disparagement of the legitimate uses of participant observation to suggest that some of the uncritical enthusiasm and unwarranted claims for it show what seems to be a certain romantic fascination with the "subtlety and richness" of social life, and especially with "cultural esoterica," the ways very special to a given group. But it seems to me profoundly mistaken to search for the special essence of a method of data collection, and appraise it in terms of its ability to directly reflect this "subtlety and richness." As social scientists, our business is with describing and explaining social phenomena; our judgment of the usefulness of data is properly made against the criterion: how much does this help us understand the phenomenon we are studying? It may well be that participant observation is more successful than any other method in gathering data on the "cultural esoterica" of a group. But this is not a good in itself; the question remains, is this information useful, and importantly useful, for our purposes? And that of course will depend on our purposes. The correlative question is equally important: could the matters which these esoteric cultural items point to—the matters we are *really* interested in—have been learned in other, and perhaps more economical, ways? I suspect that very often they can. But at the very least the question should be raised more often than it is.

The argument the authors make for the superiority of participant observation comes finally to an expression of a preference for what can be observed "directly" over what we must make inferences about. But the authors' strong commitment to observation leads them, I believe, to an unnecessarily dim, and basically incorrect, view of the process of inference in social science. All interpretations of data, however collected—through observations, interviews, or whatever—involve inferences regarding their meaning and significance. We confuse ourselves if we believe that the people whose behavior we are concerned with, whether we observe them or interview them, can themselves provide an adequate explanation of their own behavior. That is our job, and the participant observer makes inferences from the data he collects just as the survey analyst makes inferences from the data collected for him. The data gathered by participant observers are still data, despite the perhaps misleading circumstance that the participant observer usually both gathers and interprets the data himself, and to a large degree simultaneously.[5] But the data he collects are not a substitute for the interpretive inference. We all forget that at our peril.

The fact that social scientists are constantly making inferences from their data does not especially disturb me, as it does Becker and Geer. Our progress in social science will come not through an effort to get "closer" to the source of data, and thus try to minimize or do away with the process of inference by dissolving it back into data collection and somehow apprehending reality directly. That simply isn't possible. Our progress will come as we are increasingly able to develop systems of theoretically related propositions—propositions which are "checked" at more and more points against data collected through a variety of means. The inferences that we make from data, and the theory from which they derive and to which they contribute, may indeed be nothing more than "educated guesses"—but that is the nature of scientific theory. Our aim is to make them increasingly highly educated guesses. We cannot evade that fate, which is the fate of science, through reliance on a wrongly conceived participant observation which apprehends social reality "directly."

IV

Every cobbler thinks leather is the only thing. Most social scientists, including the present writer, have their favorite research methods with which they are familiar and have some skill in using. And I suspect we mostly choose to

---

5. This involves special strengths and hazards, a matter which has been discussed extensively elsewhere, and also in the paper by Becker and Geer and their references.

investigate problems that seem vulnerable to attack through these methods. But we should at least try to be less parochial than cobblers. Let us be done with the arguments of "participant observation" *versus* interviewing—as we have largely dispensed with the arguments for psychology *versus* sociology—and get on with the business of attacking our problems with the widest array of conceptual and methodological tools that we possess and they demand. This does not preclude discussion and debate regarding the relative usefulness of different methods for the study of specific problems or types of problems. But that is very different from the assertion of the general and inherent superiority of one method over another on the basis of some intrinsic qualities it presumably possesses.

"PARTICIPANT OBSERVATION AND INTERVIEWING": A REJOINDER

HOWARD S. BECKER AND BLANCHE GEER

We read Martin Trow's "Comment"[1] on our "Participant Observation and Interviewing: A Comparison"[2] with interest and profit. An unfortunate ambiguity in key terms led Trow to misinterpret our position radically. We would like to clear up the confusion briefly and also to discuss a few interesting questions raised in this argument.

Trow believes us to have said that participant observation is the best method for gathering data for all sociological problems under all circumstances. We did not say this and, in fact, we fully subscribe to his view "that different kinds of information about man and society are gathered most fully and economically in different ways, and that the problem under investigation properly dictates the methods of investigation." We did say, and now reiterate, that participant observation gives us the most complete information about social events and can thus be used as a yardstick to suggest what kinds of data escape us when we use other methods. This means, simply, that, if we see an event occur, see the events preceding and following it, and talk to various participants about it, we have more information than if we only have the description which one or more persons could give us.

Perhaps Trow accused us of insisting on "the general and inherent superiority" of participant observation, when, in fact, we did not, because he misunderstood the sense in which we meant it to be used as a "yardstick." We did not mean that the *value* of any method used for any purpose must be as-

Reprinted from *Human Organization* (1958), **17**, No. 2, 39–40, by permission of the authors and publisher.

1. *Human Organization*, 16:3 (Fall, 1957), 33–35.

2. *Ibid.*, 28–32.

sessed by such a comparison. Since completeness is obviously not the only criterion one would apply to data gathered by any method—relevance, accuracy, and reproducibility are others that come immediately to mind—a discussion centered on this criterion does not imply any claim for general superiority. But, if comparison with participant observation can make one aware of what kinds of data may be lost by use of another method, it seems to us that a conscientious researcher would want to assess his data by a systematic consideration of the points we raised rather than by an offhand dismissal of the problem.

It is possible Trow thought we were arguing the general superiority of participant observation because he misunderstood our use of the word "event." We intended to refer only to specific and limited events which are observable, not to include in the term such large and complex aggregates of specific events as national political campaigns. Naturally, such events are not "directly apprehensible" by an observer. But to restate our position, the individual events of absorbing information about an election, discussing it with others, and deciding which way to vote are amenable to observation. It is the information that one gets about these events, and then combines in order to arrive at generalizations, which one might want to examine for completeness by the yardstick of participant observation.

We evidently failed to make the flexible nature of participant observation clear enough to prevent Trow from concluding that we are claiming a great deal for a restricted technique. As we and others have used it, it does not preclude private conversations with members of the group under observation as opportunities for such conversation arise. These conversations are in many ways the functional equivalent of an interview and can be used to get the same sort of information. Thus, even though "ordinary social life may well inhibit the casual expression" of deviant attitudes, the participant observer can uncover such attitudes.[3] Again, to avoid misunderstanding, we do not believe all information is accessible to a participant observer.

Finally, Trow misunderstands our view of the role of inference in social science. We do not wish to do away with inference by getting closer to the source of the data. But we would like to distinguish between inferences about things which can only be discovered by observation. Since social systems, for instance, are not directly observable, but can only be characterized by inference from data which are themselves observable, such inferences are not only necessary but inevitable. But the question of whether to rely on inference for information on points which could be settled by observation is a pragmatic one, to be decided by the importance of the inference, the degree of our confidence in

---

3.   An account of our own use of such techniques is found in Howard S. Becker, "Interviewing Medical Students," *American Journal of Sociology*, LXII (Sept., 1956), 199–201. Numerous examples can be found in William Foote Whyte, *Street Corner Society*, The University of Chicago Press, Chicago, enlarged edition, 1955, *passim*.

it, and the difficulty of making the necessary observations. Many circumstances may decide us to infer certain facts rather than find them out directly, but the inference can never be more accurate than the observation and may be less so. Analysts of projective tests are able to infer the sex of a subject from the protocol alone with great accuracy, but there are still better and easier ways to do it.

None of what has been said should obscure the fact that we do not argue that participant observation should be used in all studies, but simply that it is possible to tell by comparison with the data it produces what data is lost by use of another method. Whether the loss is important or not depends on the character of the problem under investigation; whether the loss is unavoidable or too expensive to avoid is a practical, not a logical, problem. Though our paper did not touch on the problem, it may be appropriate for us to state here the kind of problem participant observation is most suited to. Briefly, it is the problem in which one is more interested in understanding some particular group or substantive social problem rather than in testing hypotheses about the relations between variables derived from a general theory. These two aims are naturally not mutually exclusive, but many studies are particularly focused in one or another of these directions. In the study aimed at understanding substantive problems, the greatest difficulties lie in discovering appropriate problems for sociological analysis and in discovering valid indicators for theoretical variables. Participant observation is particularly useful in meeting these difficulties. Also, when one wishes to construct a model of the social systems of an organization, a technique which allows one to see the interrelations of elements of that system in action is especially helpful.

Trow's comment on the Becker and Geer comparison of participant observation and interviewing is based on a narrower concept of participant observation than that which we have employed in this volume or which Becker and Geer employ. As Becker and Geer note in their rejoinder, this difference in conception vitiates much of Trow's commentary which then rests on a misunderstanding. It is *because* many social scientists entertain a quite narrow conception of participant observation that Trow's comment is reproduced here, with the rejoinder by Becker and Geer. The objections of many scientists to evaluating specific methods by referring to participant observation rest in good part on this difference in conception.

Objections to such comparison with participant observation may also stem from the fact that the evaluations often point up relative deficiencies in the more structured, conventional methods. This outcome will be the case only when participant observation is chosen as the "yardstick" against which another method is to be measured. We have already seen that comparison need not be, and often is not, asymmetrical. Vidich and Shapiro, for example, in their selection above, empirically locate certain advantages of survey research results over those of participant observation, and vice versa.

The real point in comparison of research procedures is to discover their relative strengths and weaknesses so that a rational choice among procedures can be made in the context of a particular study. Becker and Geer suggest that, for studying concrete events, participant observation generates more complete data than does interviewing, but that completeness is only one of several criteria which must be balanced out in choosing a research procedure, even for the study of concrete events. Other criteria which we have mentioned include validity, reliability, relevance, feasibility, and economy.

Taking into consideration the various criteria, Zelditch, for example, proposes that to obtain certain types of data certain procedures are generally best.[4] Survey research is typically to be preferred for documenting frequency data, observation techniques for documenting incidents or events, and informant interviewing for documenting institutionalized norms and statuses. In earlier chapters we have further discussed contingencies under which one method, e.g. observation, is to be preferred over other methods, e.g. respondent interviewing, and vice versa. We shall not here repeat these discussions.

Rather, we wish once more to emphasize that participant observation, as we have defined it, is not exactly a research method, commensurable with methods such as scientific interviewing or observation. It is instead a style or strategy of research, a characteristic type of research enterprise which makes use of several methods and techniques organized in a distinctive research design. Participant observation should be compared not to interviewing but to interview *studies* (or observational studies, surveys, experimental studies, and the like). By and large, the selections reprinted in this chapter do in fact lend themselves to this interpretation.

In this book, we have argued that participant observation is especially useful in one particular research context—the study of the dynamics of a social organization or situation. While it *may* be employed in other contexts, such as the study of food-buying preferences, racial attitudes, the location of industrial plants and the like, other types of research will most often prove superior in these areas.

Let us conclude this volume, therefore, by reiterating the statements with which we began: participant observation is a type of research enterprise which has proved most popular and fruitful in the study of the dynamics of all varieties of reasonably compact social organizations, and it is useless to belittle or to romanticize participant observation; we will do better to study it so that we may make better use of it in acquiring scientific information.

---

4.   Zelditch (1962).

BIBLIOGRAPHY

ADAMS, RICHARD N. AND JACK J. PREISS (Eds.) (1960). *Human Organization Research.* Homewood, Ill.: Dorsey Press.

ALLPORT, GORDON W. (1942). *The Use of Personal Documents in Psychological Science.* New York: Social Science Research Council.

ANGELL, ROBERT C. AND RONALD FREEDMAN (1953). "The use of documents, records, census materials, and indices." In Leon Festinger and Daniel Katz (Eds.), *Research Methods in the Behavioral Sciences.* New York: Holt, pp. 300–326.

ANGELL, ROBERT C. AND RALPH H. TURNER (1954). "Comment and reply on discussions of the analytic induction method." *American Sociological Review,* 19:476–478.

ARENSBERG, CONRAD M. (1954). "The community-study method." *American Journal of Sociology,* 60:109–124.

ARGYRIS, CHRIS (1952). "Diagnosing defenses against the outsider." *Journal of Social Issues,* 8(3): 24–34.

ARRINGTON, R. (1943). "Time sampling in studies of social behavior." *Psychological Bulletin,* 40:81–124.

BABCHUCK, NICHOLAS (1962). "The role of the researcher as participant observer and participant-as-observer in the field situation." *Human Organization,* 21(3): 225–228.

BACK, KURT W. (1956). "The well-informed informant." *Human Organization,* 14(4): 30–33.

BADER, CAROLYN (1948). "Standardized field practice." *International Journal of Opinion and Attitude Research,* 2: 243–244.

BAIN, ROBERT K. (1950). "The researcher's role: a case study." *Human Organization,* 9(1): 23–28.

BALDAMUS, W. (1951). "Incentives and work analysis." *University of Birmingham Studies in Economics and Sociology,* No. A1.

BARKER, ROGER G. (Ed.) (1963). *The Stream of Behavior.* New York: Appleton-Century-Crofts.

BARTLETT, F. C. (1937). "Psychological methods and anthropological problems." *Africa,* 10: 401–420.

BARTLETT, F. C., E. J. LINDGREN, MORRIS GINSBERG, AND R. H. THOULESS (Eds.) (1939). *The Study of Society.* London: Kegan Paul.

BARTON, ALLEN H. AND PAUL F. LAZARSFELD (1955). "Some functions of qualitative analysis in social research." *Frankfurter Beiträge zur Soziologie,* 1: 321–361.

BATESON, GREGORY (1941). "Experiments in thinking about observed ethnological materials." *Philosophy of Science,* 8: 53–68.

BEALS, RALPH L. (1957). "Native terms and anthropological methods." *American Anthropologist,* 59: 716–717.

BECKER, HOWARD S. (1954). "A note on interviewing tactics." *Human Organization,* 12(4): 31–32.

BECKER, HOWARD S. (1956). "Interviewing medical students." *American Journal of Sociology,* 62: 199–201.

BECKER, HOWARD S. (1958). "Problems of inference and proof in participant observation." *American Sociological Review,* 23: 652–660.

BECKER, HOWARD S. (1964). "Problems in the publication of field studies." In Arthur J. Vidich, Joseph Bensman, and Maurice R. Stein (Eds.). *Reflections on Community Studies.* New York: Wiley, pp. 267–284.

BECKER, HOWARD S. AND ELLIOT FRIEDSON (1964). "Against the code of ethics." *American Sociological Review,* 29: 409–410.

BECKER, HOWARD S. AND BLANCHE GEER (1957). "Participant observation and interviewing: a comparison." *Human Organization,* 16(3): 28–32.

BECKER, HOWARD S. AND BLANCHE GEER (1958). "'Participant observation and interviewing': a rejoinder." *Human Organization,* 17(2): 39–40.

BECKER, HOWARD S. AND BLANCHE GEER (1960). "Participant observation: the analysis of qualitative field data." In Richard N. Adams and Jack J. Preiss (Eds.). *Human Organization Research.* Homewood, Ill.: Dorsey Press, pp. 267–289.

BECKER, HOWARD S., BLANCHE GEER, EVERETT C. HUGHES, AND ANSELM L. STRAUSS (1961). *Boys in White: Student Culture in Medical School.* Chicago: University of Chicago Press.

BEEZER, ROBERT H. (1956). "Research on methods of interviewing foreign informants." *George Washington University Human Resources Research Office Technical Report,* No. 30.

BENDIX, REINHARD (1963). "Concepts and generalizations in comparative sociological studies." *American Sociological Review,* 28: 532–539.

BENNETT, JOHN W. (1948). "The study of cultures: a survey of technique and methodology in field work." *American Sociological Review,* 13: 672–689.

BENSMAN, JOSEPH AND ARTHUR VIDICH (1960). "Social theory in field research." *American Journal of Sociology,* 65: 577–584.

BERNARD, JESSE (1945). "Observation and generalization in cultural anthropology." *American Journal of Sociology,* 50: 284–291.

BERREMAN, GERALD D. (1962). *Behind Many Masks.* Lexington, Ky.: Society for Applied Anthropology, Monograph No. 4.

BEVIS, JOSEPH C. (1950). "Interviewing with tape recorders." *Public Opinion Quarterly,* 13: 629–634.

BIERSTEDT, ROBERT (1949). "A critique of empiricism in sociology." *American Sociological Review,* 24: 584–592.

BLALOCK, HUBERT M., JR. (1960). *Social Statistics.* New York: McGraw-Hill.

BLAU, PETER M. (1964). *Exchange and Power in Social Life.* New York: Wiley.

BLUM, FRED H. (1952). "Getting individuals to give information to the outsider." *Journal of Social Issues,* 8(3): 35–42.

BLUMER, HERBERT (1939). *An Appraisal of Thomas and Znaniecki's 'The Polish Peasant in Europe and America.'* New York: Social Science Research Council.

BOWERS, R. V. (1954). "Research methodology in sociology: the first half-century." In R. F. Spencer (Ed.). *Method and Perspective in Anthropology.* Minneapolis: University of Minnesota Press, pp. 251–270.

BROOKOVER, LINDA A. AND KURT W. BACK (1966). "Time sampling as a field technique." *Human Organization,* 25: 64–70.

BRUYN, SEVERYN T. (1966). *The Human Perspective in Sociology: the Methodology of Participant Observation.* Englewood Cliffs, N.J.: Prentice-Hall.

BRYMER, RICHARD A. AND BUFORD FARIS (1967). "Ethical and political dilemmas in the investigation of deviance: a study of juvenile delinquency." In Gideon Sjoberg (Ed.). *Ethics, Politics, and Social Research.* Cambridge, Mass.: Schenckman, pp. 297–318.

BURCHARD, WALDO W. (1958). "Lawyers, political scientists, sociologists—and concealed microphones." *American Sociological Review,* 23: 686–691.

BURGESS, ERNEST W. (1945a). "Research methods in sociology." In Georges Gurvitch and Wilbur Moore (Eds.). *Twentieth Century Sociology.* New York: Philosophical Library, pp. 20–41.

BURGESS, ERNEST W. (1945b). "Sociological research methods." *American Journal of Sociology,* 50: 474–482.

CAMPBELL, DONALD T. (1955). "The informant in quantitative research." *American Journal of Sociology,* 60: 339–342.

CAMPBELL, DONALD T. (1957). "Factors relevant to the validity of experiments in social settings." *Psychological Bulletin,* 54: 297–312.

CAMPBELL, DONALD T. (1959). "Systematic error on the part of human links in communication systems." *Information and Control,* 1: 334–369.

CAMPBELL, DONALD T. AND JULIAN C. STANLEY (1966). *Experimental and Quasi-experimental Designs for Research.* Chicago: Rand McNally.

CANNELL, CHARLES F. AND MORRIS AXELROD (1956). "The respondent reports on the interview." *American Journal of Sociology,* 62: 177–181.

CAPLOW, THEODORE (1956). "The dynamics of information interviewing." *American Journal of Sociology,* 62: 165–171.

CAUDILL, WILLIAM (1958). *The Psychiatric Hospital as a Small Society.* Cambridge, Mass.: Harvard University Press.

CHAPIN, F. STUART (1920). *Field Work and Social Research.* New York: Century.

CHEIN, ISIDOR (1959). "An introduction to sampling." In Claire Selltiz, Marie Jahoda, Morton Deutsch, and Stuart W. Cook. *Research Methods in Social Relations* (rev. ed.). New York: Holt, pp. 509–545.

CHESLER, MARK, AND RICHARD SCHMUCK (1963). "Participant observation in a super-patriot discussion group." *Journal of Social Issues,* 19(2): 18–30.

COLEMAN, JAMES S. (1958). "Relational analysis: the study of social organizations with survey methods." *Human Organization,* 17(4): 28–36.

COLLIER, JOHN, JR. (1967). *Visual Anthropology: Photography as a Research Method.* New York: Holt.

COLVARD, RICHARD (1967). "Interaction and identification in reporting field research: a critical reconsideration of protective procedures." In Gideon Sjoberg (Ed.). *Ethics, Politics, and Social Research.* Cambridge, Mass.: Schenkman, pp. 319–358.

COOK, P. H. (1951). "Methods of field research." *Australian Journal of Psychology,* 3(2): 84–98.

COOPER, KENNETH J. (1959). "Rural-urban differences in responses to field techniques." *Human Organization,* 18(3): 135–139.

COSER, LEWIS A., JULIUS A. ROTH, MORTIMER A. SULLIVAN, JR., AND STUART A. QUEEN (1959). "Participant observation and the military: an exchange." *American Sociological Review,* 24: 397–400.

DALTON, MELVILLE (1959). *Men Who Manage.* New York: Wiley.

DALTON, MELVILLE (1964). "Preconceptions and methods in *Men Who Manage.*" In Phillip E. Hammond (Ed.). *Sociologists at Work.* New York: Basic Books, pp. 50–95.

DANIELS, ARLENE KAPLAN (1967). "The low-caste stranger in social research." In Gideon Sjoberg (Ed.). *Ethics, Politics, and Social Research.* Cambridge, Mass.: Schenkman, pp. 267–296.

DAVIS, FRED AND JOHN F. LOFLAND (1961). "Comment and reply to Davis." *Social Problems,* 8: 364–367.

DEAN, JOHN P. (1954). "Participant observation and interviewing." In John T. Doby (Ed.). *An Introduction to Social Research.* Harrisburg, Pa.: Stackpole, pp. 225–252.

DEAN, JOHN P., ROBERT L. EICHHORN, AND LOIS R. DEAN (1967). "Observation and interviewing." In John T. Doby (Ed.). *An Introduction to Social Research* (2nd ed.). New York: Appleton-Century-Crofts, pp. 274–304.

DEAN, JOHN P. AND WILLIAM F. WHYTE (1958). "How do you know if the informant is telling the truth? *Human Organization,* 17 (2): 34–38.

DEAN, LOIS R. (1958). "Interaction, reported and observed: the case of one local union." *Human Organization,* 17 (3): 36–44.

DE LAGUNA, FREDERICA (1957). "Some problems of objectivity in ethnology." *Man,* 57: 179–182.

DEXTER, LEWIS A. (1956). "Role relationships and conceptions of neutrality in interviewing." *American Journal of Sociology,* 62: 153–157.

DEXTER, LEWIS A. (1964). "The good will of important people: more on the jeopardy of the interview." *Public Opinion Quarterly,* 28: 556–563.

DOLLARD, JOHN (1935). *Criteria for the Life History.* New York: Social Science Research Council.

DOLLARD, JOHN (1949). *Caste and Class in a Southern Town* (2nd ed.). New York: Harper.

DRIVER, HAROLD E. (1961). "Introduction to statistics for comparative research." In Frank W. Moore (Ed.). *Readings in Cross-cultural Methodology.* New Haven: Human Area Relations Files, pp. 303–331.

EATON, JOSEPH W. AND R. J. WEIL (1951). "Social processes of professional teamwork." *American Sociological Review,* 16: 707–713.

EGGAN, FRED (1954). "Social anthropology and the method of controlled comparison." *American Anthropologist,* 56: 743–763.

EPSTEIN, A. L. (Ed.) (1967). *The Craft of Social Anthropology.* New York: Barnes & Noble.

ERIKSON, KAI T. (1967). "A comment on disguised observation in sociology." *Social Problems,* 14: 366–373.

FESTINGER, LEON, AND DANIEL KATZ (Eds.) (1953). *Research Methods in the Behavioral Sciences.* New York: Holt.

FESTINGER, LEON, HENRY RIECKEN, AND STANLEY SCHACTER (1956). *When Prophecy Fails.* Minneapolis: University of Minnesota Press.

FICHTER, JOSEPH H. AND WILLIAM L. KOLB (1953). "Ethical limitations on sociological reporting." *American Sociological Review,* 18: 544–550.

FRANCIS, ROY G. (1961). *The Rhetoric of Science.* Minneapolis: University of Minnesota Press.

FRENCH, JOHN R. P., JR. (1953). "Experiments in field settings." In Leon Festinger and Daniel Katz (Eds.). *Research Methods in the Behavioral Sciences.* New York: Holt, pp. 98–135.

FRENCH, KATHRINE S. (1962). "Research interviewers in a medical setting: roles and social systems." *Human Organization,* 21(3): 219–224.

FRIEDMAN, NEIL (1967). *The Social Nature of Psychological Research: the Psychological Experiment as a Social Interaction.* New York: Basic Books.

GALLAHER, ART, JR. (1964). "Plainville: the twice studied town." In Arthur J. Vidich, Joseph Bensman, and Maurice R. Stein (Eds.). *Reflections on Community Studies.* New York: Wiley, pp. 285–303.

GARDNER, BURLEIGH B. AND WILLIAM F. WHYTE (1946). "Methods for the study of human relations in industry." *American Sociological Review,* 11: 506–512.

GEER, BLANCHE (1964). "First days in the field." In Phillip E. Hammond (Ed.). *Sociologists at Work.* New York: Basic Books, pp. 322–344.

GLASER, BARNEY G. (1965). "The constant comparative method of qualitative analysis." *Social Problems,* 12: 436–445.

GLASER, BARNEY G. AND ANSELM STRAUSS (1967). *The Discovery of Grounded Theory.* Chicago: Aldine.

GOLD, DAVID (1959). "Comment on 'A critique of tests of significance.'" *American Sociological Review,* 24: 328–338.

GOLD, RAYMOND L. (1958). "Roles in sociological field observations." *Social Forces,* 36: 217–223.

GOLDNER, FRED H. (1967). "Role emergence and the ethics of ambiguity." In Gideon Sjoberg (Ed.). *Ethics, Politics, and Social Research.* Cambridge, Mass.: Schenkman, pp. 245–266.

GOOD, I. J. (1965). *The Estimation of Probabilities: an Essay on Modern Bayesian Methods.* Cambridge, Mass.: M.I.T. Press.

GOODE, WILLIAM J. AND PAUL K. HATT (1952). *Methods in Social Research.* New York: McGraw-Hill.

GORDEN, RAYMOND L. (1956). "Dimensions of the depth interview." *American Journal of Sociology,* 62: 158–164.

GOTTSCHALK, LOUIS, CLYDE KLUCKHOHN, AND ROBERT C. ANGELL (1945). *The Use of Personal Documents in History, Anthropology, and Sociology.* New York: Social Science Research Council.

GULLAHORN, JOHN AND GEORGE STRAUSS (1954). "The field worker in union research." *Human Organization,* 13(3): 28–32.

GUSFIELD, JOSEPH G. (1955). "Field work reciprocities in studying a social movement." *Human Organization,* 14(3): 29–34.

HADER, J. J. AND EDUARD C. LINDEMAN (1933). *Dynamic Social Research.* London: Kegan Paul.

HAMMOND, PHILLIP E. (Ed.) (1964). *Sociologist at Work: the Craft of Social Reseach.* New York: Basic Books.

HARING, DOUGLAS G. (1954). "Comment on field techniques in ethnography, illustrated by a survey in the Ryuku islands." *Southwestern Journal of Anthropology,* 10: 255–267.

HENRY, JULES AND MELVIN SPIRO (1953). "Psychological techniques: projective tests in field work." In Alfred Kroeber (Ed.). *Anthropology Today.* Chicago: University of Chicago Press, pp. 417–429.

HERSKOVITS, MELVILLE J. (1948). *Man and His Works.* New York: Knopf.

HERSKOVITS, MELVILLE J. (1950). "The hypothetical situation: a technique of field research." *Southwestern Journal of Anthropology,* 6: 32–40.

HEYNS, ROGER W. AND RONALD LIPPITT (1954). "Systematic observational techniques." In Gardner Lindzey (Ed.). *Handbook of Social Psychology,* Vol. I. Cambridge, Mass.: Addison-Wesley, pp. 370–404.

HINKLE, ROSCOE C., JR. AND GISELA J. HINKLE (1954). *The Development of Modern Sociology.* New York: Random House.

HOMANS, GEORGE C. (1961). *Social Behavior: its Elementary Forms.* New York: Harcourt Brace.

HOMANS, GEORGE C. (1964). "Contemporary theory in sociology." In R. E. L. Faris (Ed.). *Handbook of Modern Sociology.* Chicago: Rand McNally, pp. 951–977.

HYMAN, HERBERT H. (1944). "Do they tell the truth?" *Public Opinion Quarterly,* 8: 557–559.

HYMAN, HERBERT H. (1955). *Survey Design and Analysis.* New York: Free Press.

HYMAN, HERBERT H., WILLIAM J. COBB, JACOB J. FELDMAN, CLYDE W. HART, AND CHARLES H. STEMBER (1954). *Interviewing in Social Research.* Chicago: University of Chicago Press.

JANES, ROBERT W. (1961). "A note on phases of the community role of the participant-observer." *American Sociological Review,* 26: 446–450.

JUNKER, BUFORD H. (1960). *Field Work: an Introduction to the Social Sciences.* Chicago: University of Chicago Press.

KAHN, ROBERT L. AND CHARLES F. CANNELL (1957). *The Dynamics of Interviewing.* New York: Wiley.

KAHN, ROBERT L. AND FLOYD MANN (1952). "Developing research partnerships." *Journal of Social Issues,* 8(3): 4–10.

KATZ, DANIEL (1947). "Psychological barriers to communication." *Annals of the American Academy of Political and Social Science,* 250: 17–25.

KISH, LESLIE (1965). *Survey Sampling.* New York: Wiley.

KLUCKHOHN, CLYDE (1938). "Participation in ceremonials in a Navajo community." *American Anthropologist,* 40: 359–369.

KLUCKHOHN, CLYDE (1939). "Theoretical basis for an empirical method of studying the acquisition of culture by individuals." *Man,* 39: 98–103.

KLUCKHOHN, FLORENCE (1940). "The participant observer technique in small communities." *American Journal of Sociology,* 46: 331–343.

KÖBBEN, A. J. (1952). "New ways of presenting an old idea: the statistical method in social anthropology." *Journal of the Royal Anthropological Institute of Great Britain and Ireland,* 82: 129–146.

KÖBBEN, A. J. (in press). "Participation and quantification: fieldwork among the Bushnegroes of Surinam." In *Anthropologists in the Field.* Assen, Netherlands: van Gorcum.

KOLAJA, JIRI (1956). "Contribution to the theory of participant observation." *Social Forces,* 35: 159–163.

KROEBER, ALFRED L. (Ed.) (1953). *Anthropology Today.* Chicago: University of Chicago Press.

LANG, KURT AND GLADYS ENGEL LANG (1953). "The unique perspective of television and its effect: a pilot study." *American Sociological Review,* 18: 3–12.

LANGNESS, LEWIS L. (1965). *Life History in Anthropological Science.* New York: Holt.

LASSWELL, HAROLD D. (1939). "The contributions of Freud's insight interview to the social sciences." *American Journal of Sociology,* 45: 375–390.

LAZARSFELD, PAUL F. (1935). "The art of asking why." *National Marketing Review,* 1: 26–38.

LAZARSFELD, PAUL F. (1959). "Evidence and inference in social research." In Daniel Lerner (Ed.). *Evidence and Inference.* New York: Free Press, pp. 107–138.

LAZARSFELD, PAUL F. AND W. S. ROBINSON (1940). "The quantification of case studies." *Journal of Applied Psychology,* 24: 817–825.

LAZARSFELD, PAUL F. AND MORRIS ROSENBERG (Eds.) (1955). *The Language of Social Research.* New York: Free Press.

LESSER, ALEXANDER (1939). "Research procedure and laws of culture." *Philosophy of Science,* 6: 345–355.

LEWIS, OSCAR (1953). "Controls and experiments in field work." In A. L. Kroeber (Ed.). *Anthropology Today.* Chicago: University of Chicago Press, pp. 452–475.

LEZNOFF, MAURICE (1956). "Interviewing homosexuals." *American Journal of Sociology,* 62: 202–204.

LINDEMAN, EDUARD C. (1924). *Social Discovery.* New York: Republic.

LINDESMITH, ALFRED R., S. KIRSON WEINBERG, AND W. S. ROBINSON (1952). "Two comments and rejoinder to 'The logical structure of analytic induction.'" *American Sociological Review,* 17: 492–494.

LIPETZ, BEN-AMI (1966). "Information storage and retrieval." *Scientific American,* 215(3): 224–242.

LOFLAND, JOHN A. AND ROBERT A. LEJEUNE (1960). "Initial interaction of newcomers in Alcoholics Anonymous: a field experiment in class symbols and socialization." *Social Problems,* 8: 102–111.

LOHMAN, JOSEPH D. (1937). "The participant observer in community studies." *American Sociological Review,* 2: 890–897.

LOMBARD, G. F. F. (1950). "Self-awareness and scientific method." *Science,* 112: 289–293.

MCCALL, GEORGE J. (1963). "Symbiosis: the case of hoodoo and the numbers racket." *Social Problems,* 10: 361–371.

MCCALL, GEORGE J. AND J. L. SIMMONS (1966). *Identities and Interactions.* New York: Free Press.

MCEWEN, WILLIAM J. (1963). "Forms and problems of validation in social anthropology." *Current Anthropology,* 4: 155–169.

MCGINNIS, ROBERT (1957). "Randomization and inference in sociological research." *American Sociological Review,* 22: 408–414.

MADGE, JOHN (1953). *The Tools of Social Science.* London: Longmans, Green.

MALINOWSKI, BRONISLAW (1932). *Argonauts of the Western Pacific.* London: Routledge.

MANN, FLOYD C. (1951). "Human relations skills in social research." *Human Relations,* 4: 341–354.

MARTEL, MARTIN U. AND GEORGE J. MCCALL (1964). "Reality-orientation and the pleasure principle: a study of American mass-periodical fiction (1890–1955)." In Lewis A. Dexter and David M. White (Eds.). *People, Society, and Mass Communications.* New York: Free Press, pp. 283–334.

MASLING, J. (1960). "The influence of situational and interpersonal variables in projective testing." *Psychological Bulletin,* 57: 65–85.

MEAD, MARGARET (1933). "More comprehensive field methods." *American Anthropologist,* 35: 1–15.

MEAD, MARGARET AND RHODA METRAUX (1953). *The Study of Culture at a Distance.* Chicago: University of Chicago Press.

MELBIN, MURRAY (1954) "An interaction recording device for participant observers." *Human Organization,* 13(2): 29–33.

MENSH, IVAN N. AND JULES HENRY (1953). "Direct observation and psychological tests in anthropological field work." *American Anthropologist,* 55: 461–480.

MERTON, ROBERT K. (1947). "Selected problems of field work in the planned community." *American Sociological Review,* 12: 304–312.

MERTON, ROBERT K. (1957). *Social Theory and Social Structure* (rev. ed.). New York: Free Press.

METRAUX, RHODA AND MARGARET MEAD (1954). *Themes in French Culture.* Stanford: Stanford University Press.

MILLER, S. M. (1952). "The participant observer and 'over-rapport.'" *American Sociological Review,* 17: 97–99.

MURDOCK, GEORGE P. (1953). "The processing of anthropological materials." In A. L. Kroeber (Ed.). *Anthropology Today.* Chicago: University of Chicago Press, pp. 476–487.

NADEL, S. F. (1939). "The interview in social anthropology." In F. C. Bartlett *et al.* (Eds.). *The Study of Society.* London: Kegan Paul, pp. 317–327.

NADEL, S. F. (1951). *The Foundations of Social Anthropology.* New York: Free Press.

NADER, LAURA (1964). "Perspectives gained from fieldwork." In Sol Tax (Ed.). *Horizons of Anthropology.* Chicago: Aldine, pp. 148–159.

NAROLL, RAOUL (1962). *Data Quality Control.* New York: Free Press.

NAROLL, RAOUL AND F. NAROLL (1963). "On bias of exotic data." *Man,* 25: 24–26.

NASH, DENNISON (1963). "The ethnologist as stranger: an essay in the sociology of knowledge." *Southwestern Journal of Anthropology,* 19: 149–167.

OESER, O. A. (1937). "Methods and assumptions of field work in social psychology." *British Journal of Psychology,* 27: 343–363.

OESER, O. A. (1939). "The value of team work and functional participation as methods in social investigation." In F. C. Bartlett *et al.* (Eds.). *The Study of Society.* London: Kegan Paul, pp. 402–417.

OLESON, VIRGINIA L. AND ELVI WAIK WHITTAKER (1967). "Role-making in participant observation: processes in the researcher-actor relationship." *Human Organization,* 26: 273–281.

ORLANS, HAROLD (1967). "Ethical problems in the relations of research sponsors and investigators." In Gideon Sjoberg (Ed.). *Ethics, Politics, and Social Research.* Cambridge, Mass.: Schenkman, pp. 3–24.

ORNE, MARTIN T. (1962). "On the social psychology of the psychological experiment." *American Psychologist,* 17: 776–783.

OSGOOD, CORNELIUS (1940). "Informants." In Cornelius Osgood (Ed.). *Ingalik Material Culture. Yale University Publications in Anthropology,* No. 22, 50–55.

PALMER, VIVIEN M. (1928). *Field Studies in Sociology: a Student's Manual.* Chicago: University of Chicago Press.

PARK, ROBERT E. (1930). "Murder and the case study method." *American Journal of Sociology,* 36: 447–454.

PASSIN, HERBERT (1942). "Tarahumara prevarication: a problem in field method." *American Anthropologist,* 44: 235–247.

PAUL, BENJAMIN (1953). "Interview techniques and field relationships." In A. L. Kroeber (Ed.). *Anthropology Today.* Chicago: University of Chicago Press, pp. 430–451.

PAYNE, STANLEY L. (1951). *The Art of Asking Questions.* Princeton: Princeton University Press.

PEARSALL, MARION (1965). "Participant observation as role and method in behavioral research." *Nursing Research,* 14: 37–42.

POLANSKY, NORMAN, W. FREEMAN, M. HOROWITZ, L. IRWIN, N. PAPANIA, D. RAPAPORT, AND F. WHALEY (1949). "Problems of interpersonal relations in research on groups." *Human Relations,* 2: 281–292.

POLYA, GEORGE (1954). *Patterns of Plausible Inference.* Princeton: Princeton University Press.

POWDERMAKER, HORTENSE (1967). *Stranger and Friend: the Way of an Anthropologist.* New York: Norton.

RADIN, PAUL (1933). *The Method and Theory of Ethnology.* New York: McGraw-Hill.

RAINWATER, LEE AND DAVID J. PITTMAN (1967). "Ethical problems in studying a politically sensitive and deviant community." *Social Problems,* 14: 357–366.

RECORD, JANE CASSELS (1967). "The research institute and the pressure group." In Gideon Sjoberg (Ed.). *Ethics, Politics, and Social Research.* Cambridge, Mass.: Schenkman, pp. 25–49.

REDLICH, FREDERICK AND EUGENE B. BRODY (1955). "Emotional problems of interdisciplinary research in psychiatry." *Psychiatry,* 18: 233–240.

REISS, ALBERT J., JR. (1954). "Some logical and methodological problems in community research." *Social Forces,* 33: 52–54.

REISS, ALBERT J., JR. (1959). "The sociological study of communities." *Rural Sociology,* 24: 118–130.

RICE, STUART A. (1929). "Contagious bias in the interview: a methodological note. *American Journal of Sociology,* 35: 420–423.

RICHARDS, AUDREY I. (1939). "The development of field work methods in social anthropology." In F. C. Bartlett *et al.* (Eds.). *The Study of Society.* London: Kegan Paul, pp. 272–316.

RICHARDSON, STEPHEN A. (1952). "Training in field relations skills." Journal of Social *Issues,* 8: 43–50.

RICHARDSON, STEPHEN A. (1953). "A framework for reporting field relations experiences." *Human Organization,* 12(3): 31–37.

RICHARDSON, STEPHEN A. (1960). "A framework for reporting field relations experiences." In Richard N. Adams and Jack J. Preiss (Eds.). *Human Organization Research.* Homewood, Ill.: Dorsey Press, pp. 124–139.

RICHARDSON, STEPHEN A., BARBARA SNELL DOHRENWEND, AND DAVID KLEIN (1965). *Interviewing: Its Forms and Functions.* New York: Basic Books.

RICHTER, C. P. (1953). "Free research versus design research." *Science,* 118: 91–93.

RIECKEN, HENRY W. (1956). "The unidentified interviewer." *American Journal of Sociology*, 62: 210–212.

RIESMAN, DAVID AND MARK BENNEY (1956). "The sociology of the interview." *Midwest Sociologist*, 18: 3–15.

ROBINSON, W. S. (1951). "The logical structure of analytic induction." *American Sociological Review*, 16: 812–818.

ROGERS, CARL R. (1945). "The non-directive method as a technique for social research." *American Journal of Sociology*, 50: 279–283.

ROGERS, CARL R. AND F. J. ROETHLISBERGER (1952). "Barriers and gateways to communication." *Harvard Business Review*, 30(4): 46–52.

ROSE, ARNOLD M. (1945). "A research note on interviewing." *American Journal of Sociology*, 51: 143–144.

ROSENTHAL, ROBERT (1966). *Experimenter Effects in Behavioral Research*. New York: Appleton-Century-Crofts.

ROTH, JULIUS A. (1962). "Comments on secret observation." *Social Problems*, 9: 283–284.

ROY, DONALD F. (1953). "Work satisfaction and social reward in quota achievement: an analysis of piecework incentives." *American Sociological Review*, 18: 507–514.

ROY, DONALD F. (1965). "The role of the researcher in the study of social conflict: a theory of protective distortion of response." *Human Organization*, 24: 262–271.

SCHNEIDER, EUGENE V. (1950). "Limitations on observation in industrial sociology." *Social Forces*, 28: 279–284.

SCHWAB, WILLIAM B. (1965). "Looking backward: an appraisal of two field trips." *Human Organization*, 24: 372–380.

SCHWARTZ, MORRIS S. AND CHARLOTTE G. SCHWARTZ (1955). "Problems in participant observation." *American Journal of Sociology*, 60: 343–354.

SCOTT, W. RICHARD (1963). "Field work in a formal organization: some dilemmas in the role of observer." *Human Organization*, 22(2): 162–168.

SEASHORE, STANLEY E. (1964). "Field experiments with formal organizations." *Human Organization*, 23(2): 164–170.

SELLS, SAUL B. AND R. M. W. TRAVERS (1945). "Observational methods of research." *Review of Educational Research*, 40: 394–407.

SELLTIZ, CLAIRE, MARIE JAHODA, MORTON DEUTSCH, AND STUART W. COOK (1959). *Research Methods in Social Relations* (rev. ed.). New York: Holt.

SELVIN, HANAN C. (1957). "A critique of tests of significance in survey research." *American Sociological Review*, 22: 519–527.

SIEGEL, SIDNEY (1956). *Nonparametric Statistics for the Behavioral Sciences*. New York: McGraw-Hill.

SJOBERG, GIDEON (Ed.) (1967). *Ethics, Politics, and Social Research*. Cambridge, Mass.: Schenkman.

SMITH, H. T. (1958). "A comparison of interview and observation methods of studying mother behavior." *Journal of Abnormal and Social Psychology*, 57: 278–282.

SPENDER, R. F. (Ed.) (1954). *Method and Perspective in Anthropology*. Minneapolis: University of Minnesota Press.

SPINDLER, GEORGE AND WALTER GOLDSCHMIDT (1952). "Experimental design in the study of culture change." *Southwestern Journal of Anthropology*, 8: 68–83.

STAVRIANOS, BERTHA K. (1950). "Research methods in cultural anthropology in relation to scientific criteria." *Psychological Review,* 57: 334–344.

STONE, PHILLIP J., ROBERT F. BALES, JAMES Z. NAMENWIRTH, AND D. M. OGILIVIE (1962). "The General Inquirer: a computer system for content analysis and retrieval based on the sentence as a unit of information." *Behavioral Science,* 7: 1–15.

STRAUSS, ANSELM AND LEONARD SCHATZMAN (1955). "Social class and modes of communication." *American Journal of Sociology,* 60: 329–338.

STRAUSS, ANSELM, LEONARD SCHATZMAN, RUE BUCHER, DANUTA EHRLICH, AND MELVIN SABSHIN (1964). *Psychiatric Ideologies and Institutions,* New York: Free Press.

SULLIVAN, HARRY STACK (1937). "A note on implications of psychiatry, the study of interpersonal relations, for investigations in social science." *American Journal of Sociology,* 42: 848–861.

SULLIVAN, MORTIMER A., JR., STUART A. QUEEN, AND RALPH C. PATRICK, JR. (1958). "Participant observation as employed in the study of a military training program." *American Sociological Review,* 23: 660–667.

TAX, SOL (Ed.) (1964). *Horizons of Anthropology.* Chicago: Aldine.

THIBAUT, JOHN W. AND HAROLD H. KELLEY (1959). *The Social Psychology of Groups.* New York: Wiley.

THOMAS, W. I. AND FLORIAN ZNANIECKI (1927). *The Polish Peasant in Europe and America.* New York: Knopf.

THRASHER, FREDERIC M. (1928). "How to study the boys' gang in the open." *Journal of Educational Psychology,* 1: 244–254.

TRICE, H. M. (1956). "Outsider's role in field study." *Sociology and Social Research,* 41: 27–32.

TROW, MARTIN (1957). "Comment on 'Participant observation and interviewing: a comparison.'" *Human Organization,* 16(3): 33–35.

TURNER, RALPH H. (1953). "The quest for universals in sociological research." *American Sociological Review,* 18: 604–611.

VIDICH, ARTHUR J. (1955a). "Methodological problems in the observation of husband-wife interaction." *Marriage and Family Living,* 28: 234–239.

VIDICH, ARTHUR J. (1955b). "Participant observation and the collection and interpretation of data." *American Journal of Sociology,* 60: 354–360.

VIDICH, ARTHUR AND JOSEPH BENSMAN (1954). "The validity of field data." *Human Organization,* 13(1): 20–27.

VIDICH, ARTHUR, JOSEPH BENSMAN, AND MAURICE R. STEIN (1964). *Reflections on Community Studies.* New York: Wiley.

VIDICH, ARTHUR AND GILBERT SHAPIRO (1955). "A comparison of participant observation and survey data." *American Sociological Review,* 20: 28–33.

WALD, ABRAHAM (1947). *Sequential Analysis.* New York: Wiley.

WAX, MURRAY AND LEOPOLD J. SHAPIRO (1956). "Repeated interviewing." *American Journal of Sociology,* 62: 215–217.

WAX, ROSALIE HANKEY (1952). "Reciprocity as a field technique." *Human Organization,* 11(3): 34–37.

WAX, ROSALIE HANKEY (1957). "Twelve years later: an analysis of field experience." *American Journal of Sociology,* 63: 133–142.

WEBB, EUGENE J., DONALD T. CAMPBELL, RICHARD D. SCHWARTZ, AND LEE SECHREST (1966). *Unobtrusive Measures: Nonreactive Research in the Social Sciences.* Chicago: Rand McNally.

WEISS, ROBERT S. (1966). "Alternative approaches in the study of complex situations." *Human Organization,* 25: 198–206.

WHYTE, WILLIAM F. (1951). "Observational field methods." In Marie Jahoda, Morton Deutsch, and Stuart W. Cook (Eds.). *Research Methods in Social Relations* (1st ed.). Vol. II. New York: Holt, pp. 493–513.

WHYTE, WILLIAM F. (1953). "Interviewing for organizational research." *Human Organization,* 12(2): 15–22.

WHYTE, WILLIAM F. (1955). *Street Corner Society.* Chicago: University of Chicago Press.

WHYTE, WILLIAM F. (1957). "On asking indirect questions." *Human Organization,* 15(4): 21–23.

WHYTE, WILLIAM F. (1960). "Interviewing in field research." In Richard N. Adams and Jack J. Preiss (Eds.). *Human Organization Research.* Homewood, Ill.: Dorsey Press, pp. 352–374.

WILLIAMS, THOMAS R. (1967). *Field Methods in the Study of Culture.* New York: Holt.

WILSON, JOHN (1962). "Interaction analysis: a supplementary fieldwork technique used in the study of leadership in a 'new-style' Australian aboriginal community." *Human Organization,* 21(4): 290–294.

WOHL, J. (1963). "Traditional and contemporary views of psychological testing." *Journal of Projective Techniques,* 27: 359–365.

WOLFF, KURT H. (1945). "A methodological note on the empirical establishment of cultural patterns." *American Sociological Review,* 10: 176–184.

YOUNG, FRANK W. AND RUTH C. YOUNG (1961). "Key informant reliability in rural Mexican villages." *Human Organization,* 20(3): 141–148.

ZELDITCH, MORRIS, JR. (1962). "Some methodological problems of field studies." *American Journal of Sociology,* 67: 566–576.

ZETTERBERG, HANS L. (1963). *On Theory and Verification in Sociology* (rev. ed.). Totowa, N.J.: Bedminster Press.